MW00713716

EARLY NEAR EASTERN SEALS

IN THE YALE BABYLONIAN COLLECTION

EARLY NEAR EASTERN SEALS

IN THE

YALE BABYLONIAN

COLLECTION

BRIGGS BUCHANAN

Introduction and Seal Inscriptions by William W. Hallo

Ulla Kasten, editor

New Haven and London, Yale University Press

Published with assistance from Barbara Clay Debevoise and the Clay Fund.

Copyright © 1981 by Yale University.
All rights reserved. This book may not be
reproduced, in whole or in part, in any form
(beyond that copying permitted by Sections 107
and 108 of the U.S. Copyright Law and except by
reviewers for the public press), without written
permission from the publishers.

Designed by John O. C. McCrillis
and set in Baskerville type.
Photographs by David Richards
and staff, Yale Audio Visual Center.
Drawings by Dale Osterle.
Printed in the United States of America by
The Murray Printing Co., Westford, Massachusetts.

Published in Great Britain, Europe, Africa, and
Asia (except Japan) by Yale University Press,
Ltd., London. Distributed in Australia and
New Zealand by Book & Film Services, Artarmon,
N.S.W., Australia; and in Japan by Harper & Row,
Publishers, Tokyo Office.

Library of Congress Cataloging in Publication Data

Buchanan, Briggs.
  Early Near Eastern seals in the Yale
Babylonian Collection.

  Bibliography: p.
  1. Seals (Numismatics) — Near East — Catalogs.
2. Yale University. Babylonian Collection —
Catalogs. I. Hallo, William W. II. Kasten,
Ulla. III. Yale University. Babylonian
Collection. IV. Title.
CD5344.B82   737'.6'0939407401467   75-43309
ISBN 0-300-01852-5

CONTENTS

ACKNOWLEDGMENTS

The appearance of this book owes much to the generosity of Barbara Clay Debevoise who, in the spirit of the late Albert T. Clay, her father, lent personal and material encouragement to the enterprise over many years. Additional support was provided by the author himself before his untimely death.

Editorial assistance, all the more crucial in a posthumous publication, was rendered with unfailing devotion by Ulla Kasten on behalf of the Babylonian Collection and by Jane Isay on behalf of the Yale University Press. Edith Porada read the manuscript in 1974, and her detailed comments were carefully considered and frequently incorporated by the author. She also supplied the description of No. 455. This fine piece (YBC 16396) was donated to the Collection by Mrs. Alden K. Sibley (New York) after the manuscript's completion. Special thanks are due to David Richards for the photographs, to Dale Osterle for the drawings, and to Brian Lewis for the indices.

INTRODUCTION

The seals of the ancient Near East are a precious resource for the historian of art. No other medium affords so continuous or so abundant a record of the graphic response to the world as observed and imagined by the ancients. But this record is not an open book; it requires decipherment and explication as surely as the most inscrutable of texts. The present work is offered as a contribution to such an explanation. The first of two projected volumes, it catalogues one of the world's major collections of ancient Near Eastern seals, from prehistoric times to c. 1600 B.C. The second volume will deal with the items of the Late Bronze Age and subsequent periods.

The Yale Babylonian Collection comprises not only the items listed in its own name (YBC) but also a number of other collections, including those which were bequeathed or endowed by James B. Nies (NBC), J. P. Morgan (MLC), and Edward T. Newell (NCBS and NCBT). The last in particular includes a very rich collection of seals, some of them previously catalogued by von der Osten in 1934 (*OIP* 22), but others acquired since then; almost all of them are included in the present work.

Seals played a number of different roles in their ancient Near Eastern setting. They were by nature legal instruments; they also fulfilled a ritual function as amulets;[1] or, as "an artistic replica of an object used in daily life in the domestic, commercial, or military sphere," they could serve as votive objects.[2] But above all they were *objets d'art* and it is this aspect to which the catalogue that follows is primarily devoted. As such they were of considerable intrinsic value to their ancient owners. They could at all periods be cut from shell, bone (cf. No. 208), or local limestone, but the more prized examples were carved in semiprecious stones which, in Mesopotamia at least, constituted imported luxuries, subject to changes in availability or taste. Thus marble was most characteristic of the earliest periods, calcite of the Early Dynastic period, serpentine of the Akkadian and Ur III periods, and hematite of the Old Babylonian period. At all periods a few examples in lapis lazuli, obsidian, alabaster, jasper, and other, rarer stones occur.

---

1. B. L. Goff, "Cylinder seals as amulets," in *Symbols of Prehistoric Mesopotamia* (1963), pp. 195–210, reprinted (with revisions) from *Journal of the Warburg and Courtauld Institutes* 19 (1956), pp. 23–38.
2. W. W. Hallo, "The royal inscriptions of Ur: a typology," *HUCA* 33 (1962), pp. 12f. and n. 107.

The earliest cylinder seals were up to 60 mm in height (cf. No. 138), and often their diameter equalled or even exceeded their height. But by Early Dynastic times their average height was closer to 20 mm, and this remained the rule in later periods (except under the Kassites) but for costly votive seals like "Šulgi 48" (40 mm).[3] The small size of the typical (nonvotive) seal may have served to keep down the expense of what became a relatively popular form of artistic expression. Or it may have been dictated by the practical (legal) functions of the seal, whether as a mark of ownership on a vessel or on a small bulla attached to a shipment, or as a mark of origin, authority, acknowledgment, or obligation on a letter or document. In any event, the loss of a prized seal was a noteworthy event which entailed not only legal consequences but also ominous implications calling for ritual measures.[4]

More often, high value and small size conspired to extend the "life span" and the habitat of many a seal far beyond the place and time of its original maker or owner. To illustrate this observation, one need only point to numerous Near Eastern cylinder seals which made their way to the Aegean basin,[5] including those of Middle Babylonian (Kassite) date found as far away as Thebes in Greece,[6] or to the vassal-treaties of Esarhaddon, sealed with three dynastic seals, one dated to his Neo-Assyrian father Sennaherib, one to Middle Assyrian, and one back to Old Assyrian times.[7]

Given this tendency of seals to survive over many centuries and to travel far from their place of origin, it is difficult to assess the date and provenience even of those found *in situ* in a scientific excavation with clearly defined stratigraphy. The difficulty is compounded when the seals are acquired by gift or purchase and no appeal to excavation records is possible. Such is the case with the vast majority of the seals at Yale. Yet the seal cutter's art cannot be appreciated, even on a purely esthetic level, without some sense of time and place. Where does a given piece fit into the long evolution of the glyptic technique? And how close is it to the great centers of seal designing, or how far removed to the periphery or the provinces? Fortunately, the scholarly study of the genre has advanced to the point where these questions can be answered with some assurance on internal grounds. Such indications as material, size, shape, techniques of workmanship, choice and treatment of motifs — all duly noted in the descriptive entries of the

---

3. *HUCA* 33, p. 33 (= *Louvre T*, 111).

4. Hallo, "Seals lost and found" in M. Gibson and R. D. Biggs, eds., *Seals and Sealing in the Ancient Near East* (= Bibliotheca Mesopotamica 6, 1977), pp. 55–60.

5. For a complete list of these see H. -G. Buchholz in G. F. Bass et al., *Cape Gelidonya: A Bronze Age Shipwreck* (= TAPhS 57, 1967), ch. xii.

6. H. Limet. *Les légendes des sceaux cassites* (1971), pp. 12f. with literature; for an illustration, cf. simply Hallo and Simpson, *The Ancient Near East: a History* (1971), p. 109 (fig. 21).

7. D. J. Wiseman, "The Vassal Treaties of Esarhaddon," *Iraq* 20 (1958), esp. pp. 14–22. Cf. also 978x below.

catalogue — come to the aid of the glyptic specialist. In addition, he can avail himself of the help of the textual expert.

This seal catalogue, perhaps more than some of its predecessors, reflects a continuing collaboration between archaeologist and philologist. That is as it should be, for the art of the seal cutter and the skill of the scribe developed in tandem. Recent discoveries have only served to underline the antiquity and persistence of this parallel evolution. The earliest writing now known, such as that at Godin Tepe in Central Western Iran, consists entirely of impressions of number signs and impressions of seals side by side on the same tablet.[8] In India to the east, the so-called Indus Valley script combined these two techniques to produce a kind of writing by means of impressing stamp seals singly or in groups, or so at least according to recent attempts at decipherment.[9] In Sumer to the west, where both seals and writing evolved to their maximum potential, they did so separately but at the same time conjointly, for the typical seal came to include an inscription, while for its part the typical cuneiform tablet (at least in certain categories of texts) came to include a seal impression.

The Yale Babylonian Collection is particularly rich in tablets bearing the impressions of such a seal or seals. Although these tablets most often entered the collection by gift or purchase, their date and provenience can frequently be fixed by the explicit testimony of their contents, or implicitly by other internal evidence. A particularly significant example is represented by No. 1090. This stamp seal, impressed on a tablet dated to the tenth year of King Gungunum of Larsa (1923 B.C. in the "middle chronology") has helped to date the entire family of so-called "Persian Gulf" seals and, in turn, the end of the Indus Valley (Harappa) culture, an event which had fluctuated previously between estimates as far apart as 2500 B.C. and 1500 B.C.[10] Thus tablets inscribed with cuneiform texts can provide valuable clues to the chronological and geographical variations in the style of the seals impressed on them — and of actual examples of preserved seals in comparable styles. While it was not possible to incorporate all such sealed tablets in the catalogue, a special effort has been made to include a large and representative sample.

The systematic use of the seal impressions has involved greater attention than sometimes customary to the tablets on which they were impressed. It is

---

8. See for now H. Weiss and T. Cuyler Young, Jr., "The Merchants of Susa," *Iran* 13 (1975), pp. 1–17.

9. Cf. J. V. Kinnier Wilson, *Indo-Sumerian* (1974). For a dissenting view see E. Sollberger, *BSOAS* 39 (1976), pp. 183f.

10. For some of the chronological implications of this finding, see the literature cited ad loc. below and Edith Porada, "Remarks on seals found in the Gulf States," *Artibus Asiae* 33 (1971), pp. 331–37. Cf. also G. Bibby, *Looking for Dilmun* (1969), p. 362.

therefore fortunate that large and coherent bodies of texts were being edited for publication while work on the seal catalogue was in progress. Such volumes as Simmons's *Early Old Babylonian Documents* (*YOS* 14), Feigin's *Legal and Administrative Texts of the Reign of Samsu-iluna* (*YOS* 12), and Finkelstein's *Late Old Babylonian Documents and Letters* (*YOS* 13) — to mention only the examples of Old Babylonian date — were reviewed in the light of the seal evidence to the mutual benefit both of those volumes and the present one.

Thus the evidence of seals and seal impressions is complementary. The ancient impressions resemble the impressions made on modern clay from the ancient seals and thus help to date and place the latter. But they are never identical; despite all the collaboration between glyptic and textual specialists, no actual impression of a seal on an ancient tablet (or vessel) has yet been successfully identified with an extant ancient seal. This principle was first stated for the Neo-Sumerian period ("there is, to my knowledge, not a single example of an original seal of this period also known from its impression"[11]) and then more generally ("the chances of discovery have so far yielded only one ancient impression that could have been made by a re-covered seal"[12]). It has been reiterated periodically ("It is curious that, though thousands of cylinder seals and impressions are known, only one seal has been found the design of which unquestionably matches that in an impression"[13]) and bears repeating here. The one instance alluded to here involves the Old Babylonian seal of Ana-Sin-taklaku, known from numerous impressions at Mari,[14] and apparently re-inscribed by one Adad-šarrum before turning up in Iran.[15] For Middle Assyrian glyptic, a case has since been documented which may involve a change of inscription without a change of seal owner.[16]

The essential feature of any seal is a negative design, i.e., an intaglio engraving which, when impressed or rolled over wet clay, leaves a positive impression in relief. A secondary feature of the seal is the esthetic appeal of the seal stone itself. On the early stamp seals, this appeal may rest on the elaborate carving of the stone in the round to yield a miniature sculpture, in naturalistic or geometric form, which is itself a work of art. This is especially true in Iran, Assyria, and Anatolia, where the prehistoric stamp seals are best at-

11. Hallo, *HUCA* 33 (1962), p. 14.
12. Buchanan, "A dated 'Persian Gulf' seal and its implications," *Studies . . . Landsberger* (= *AS* 16, 1965), p. 204 n. 4. The one *possible* instance alluded to is an Indus Valley example.
13. Buchanan, *Yale University Library Gazette* 45 (1970), p. 53.
14. A. Parrot, *MAM 2: Le palais* [3] *Documents et Monuments* (1959), pp. 169–85.
15. Parrot, *Syria* 43 (1966), pp. 333–35.
16. Hallo, "The seals of Aššur-remanni," *Symbolae . . . Böhl* (1973), pp. 180–84, esp. p. 184.

tested, and where they continued to flourish in the third millennium.[17] In Babylonia, the frequent employment of early seals on the strip of wet clay which covered and sealed the juncture between a vessel and its cover led earlier to the abandonment of the stamp seal and the emergence of the cylinder seal.[18] The latter lent itself ideally to the purpose; it could be rolled around the juncture in one continuous motion, providing an unbroken frieze which must have discouraged attempts to tamper with the contents. The development seems to be attested first in the south of Mesopotamia, and quickly became a hallmark of Mesopotamian influence wherever that influence spread.

The earliest Mesopotamian cylinder seals, those of the Uruk IV and Jamdat Nasr periods, experimented with a wide range of shapes and sizes, all variations of the basic cylinder form. They sometimes added elaborate carvings on top of the cylinder — a mark, perhaps, of some reluctance to abandon entirely the sculptural aspects of the stamp seals. These periods also witnessed considerable latitude in the choice of materials. Thus, for example, the only instances of metal seals now known all date to the Jamdat Nasr period. Two of these are in the private collection of Dr. Leonard Gorelick (New York), a third is *Newell* 33 (not republished below). All three were analyzed by X-ray fluorescence spectrometry and found to contain high percentages of copper and smaller portions of lead and other metals.[19]

By Early Dynastic times, most of these elaborations and variations were abandoned again, and there emerged what may be described as the standard cylinder seal. It was typically carved from stone[20] or shell, and its size and shape tended to vary within narrower limits, the height of the cylinder being typically just under two times its diameter. As if to make up for the reduction in variety, some of the later seals were carved on stones selected for their inherent appeal — on the basis of coloration, variegation, or rarity — and new techniques were devised for ever more refined carving of the surface. Such technical refinements culminated in a veritable "revolution" in glyptic art at the end of the period covered by this volume.[21]

The increasing emphasis on the decoration of the cylinder seal may also account for another "secondary" aspect — the seal inscription. One function

17. Buchanan, "The prehistoric stamp seal: a reconsideration of some old excavations," *JAOS* 87 (1967), pp. 265–79, 525–40.
18. *Frankfort*, pp. 1–4. Other explanations of the origin of the cylinder seal are offered by E. Porada in Gibson and Biggs, *Seals and Sealing*, p. 7, and by P. Steinkeller, ibid., p. 43 and no. 25.
19. Analysis performed by the Metropolitan Museum of Art and reported by letter of 29 December 1978 from Pieter Meyers to the Yale Babylonian Collection.
20. See above for some of the varieties of stone employed; for details see the catalogue. For an Early Dynastic III seal of bitumen covered with silver see Buchanan, *Ash C*, 183.
21. Buchanan, "Cylinder seal impressions in the Yale Babylonian Collection illustrating a revolution in art circa 1700 B.C.," *Yale University Library Gazette* 45 (1970), pp. 53–65.

of the seal was no doubt to serve as a mark of ownership, but that function was adequately fulfilled by the design, which was more or less different for each seal. The addition of the inscription — initially simply the owner's name — must therefore be regarded as an optional reinforcement of this function, and through Early Dynastic times it is only sporadically attested. Beginning with the Sargonic period, however, it became more and more common and, inevitably, more elaborate. Full transliterations and translations of the seal inscriptions are therefore appended to the catalogue, together with an analysis of some of the more significant or problematical specimens, and a synthesis of the entire inscriptional genre.

Study of the seal inscriptions provides further grounds for collaboration between archaeologist and Assyriologist, and the present work aspires to meet this desideratum. First to be determined is whether design and inscription are of the same date, for in a surprisingly large number of cases they are not. Seal stones were sufficiently valuable so that a new owner might wish to change the inscription on an old seal acquired by inheritance or other means (cf. notes 14–16); more rarely, changing tastes might dictate a new design, or additions to an existing design, without a corresponding change in the inscription.

Having demonstrated that design and inscription were executed together, it is next appropriate to see whether one bears on the other. Here recent studies in iconography are helpful. The appearance of the "shepherd's crook," for instance, and certain other motifs, helps identify some Old Babylonian seals as dedicated to the god Amurru, and in doubtful cases like No. 1043 even to confirm the reading of the inscription. In other cases, a well-preserved inscription may prove the clue to interpreting the traces of the design. A particularly dramatic example is provided by the group of seal inscriptions associated with the "House of Ur-Meme" and the designs reconstructed, in part from numerous fragmentary exemplars, with their help.[22]

Finally, one may hope to gain some thematic correlations from the confrontation of designs and inscriptions in coherent groups. For example, a relatively small group of Neo-Sumerian seals (late Ur III and Early Old Babylonian) regularly departs from the standard formulations of the royal retainer's seal inscription to proclaim the presentation of the seal by the king to the owner (Nos. 653–654). This inscriptional group typically occurs in the company of a distinctive design which includes the portrait of the king in a ceremony that has been interpreted as a cultic lustration.[23]

22. Below, 425, 609, and 681. See the detailed discussions by Hallo, "The House of Ur-Meme," *JNES* 31 (1972). pp. 87–95; Buchanan, "An extraordinary seal impression of the Third Dynasty of Ur," *JNES* 31, pp. 96–101.
23. Cf. J. Börker-Klähn, "Šulgi badet," *ZA* 64 (1975), pp. 235–40. For another interpretation see M. Lambert, "Investiture de fonctionnaires en Élam," *Journal Asiatique* 259 (1971), pp. 217–21.

There is, indeed, some temptation to go further: to interpret the designs of seals, not from the inscriptions (if any) of the seals themselves, but with the evidence of other texts. In particular, the epic and mythical texts preserved in cuneiform have in the past been invoked to interpret complex scenes of ostensibly narrative content. This approach, however, requires great caution. It has been used very sparingly in the present work. Though it may be conceivable that figures of myth such as Etana or of epic such as Gilgamesh are represented on Early Dynastic and especially on Sargonic seals, the identification is never explicit, i.e. there are no captions to this effect, and no unambiguous iconographic hallmarks. In other instances, the identifications are even more speculative. In most cases, the literary evidence is so much later than the glyptic evidence that it is best not to attempt to correlate the two.

A personal note may serve to conclude this brief introduction. Briggs Buchanan devoted the last decades of his life to the seals and seal impressions of the Yale Babylonian Collection, first as a dedicated volunteer and later in more formal capacities. He enlarged the collection by judicious advice on acquisitions, arranged it, conserved it, and catalogued it. His long labors were interrupted only by summers spent at the Ashmolean Museum in Oxford where he rendered comparable service.[24] At his death on December 10, 1976, he had completed all but the introduction of the present volume. What he might have wanted to say there must now be left to the imagination, though the introduction to the Ashmolean volume may be consulted for helpful clues to the organization of the present catalogue.[25] But my association with him since 1962 made me familiar with his basic views; what is said here is, it is hoped, in their spirit.[26]

New Haven, Connecticut   WILLIAM W. HALLO
June 1977

---

24. Buchanan, *Catalogue of Ancient Near-Eastern Seals in the Ashmolean Museum I: Cylinder Seals* (1966). A second volume, to deal with stamp seals, will be published from Buchanan's manuscript by P. R. S. Moorey.
25. *Ash C*, pp. xix-xxv.
26. In connection with the presumed Mesopotamian origin of the cylinder seal (above, at note 18), note that the technical term for "the clay used to close the neck of a storage jar (frequently sealed)" has been identified in Sumerian (IM.ŠÚ) and Akkadian (*imšukku*) by Thorkild Jacobsen *apud* Stephen J. Lieberman, *AJA* 84 (1980), p. 352, note 87.

ABBREVIATIONS

AAA	*Annals of Archaeology and Anthropology.* University of Liverpool.
AASOR	*Annual of the American Schools of Oriental Research.*
AfO	*Archiv für Orientforschung.*
AJA	*American Journal of Archaeology.*
AJSL	*American Journal of Semitic Languages and Literatures.*
Altassyrische Texte	B. Kienast, *Die altassyrischen Texte des orientalischen Seminars der Universität Heidelberg und der Sammlung Erlenmeyer, Basel.* Berlin, 1960.
AMI	*Archäologische Mitteilungen aus Iran.*
Amiet	P. Amiet, *La glyptique mésopotamienne archaïque.* Paris, 1961.
Amurru	J.-R. Kupper, *L'Iconographie du Dieu Amurru dans la glyptique de la 1ᵉ dynastie babylonienne.* Brussels, 1961.
Anadolu	*Anadolu Arastirmalari* (= Jahrbuch für kleinasiatische Forschung).
Anatolia	*Anatolia,* Revue annuelle de l'Institut d'Archéologie de l'Université d'Ankara.
Ancient Iran	E. Porada, *The Art of Ancient Iran.* New York, 1965.
An.Or.	*Analecta Orientalia.*
AOS	*American Oriental Series.*
Ar.Or.	*Archiv Orientální.*
AS	*Assyriological Studies.*
Ash C	B. Buchanan, *Catalogue of Ancient Near Eastern Seals in the Ashmolean Museum, Cylinder Seals.* Oxford, 1966.
Aulock	H. H. von der Osten, *Altorientalische Siegelsteine der Sammlung Hans Silvius von Aulock.* Uppsala, 1957.
Basmadschi	F. Basmadschi, *Landschaftliche Elemente in der mesopotamischen Kunst des IV. und III. Jahrtausends* (Ph.D. Thesis). Basel, 1943.

BASOR	*Bulletin of the American Schools of Oriental Research.*
BBV 10	W. Nagel, *Der mesopotamische Streitwagen und seine Entwicklung im ostmediterranen Bereich* (= Berliner Beiträge zur Vor- und Frühgeschichte 10). Berlin, 1966.
BE	*Babylonian Expedition of the University of Pennsylvania,* Series A: Cuneiform Texts.
Beginn	R. Unger, *Der Beginn der altmesopotamischen Siegelbildforschung.* Vienna, 1966.
Berlin	A. Moortgat, *Vorderasiatische Rollsiegel.* Berlin, 1940.
BIN	*Babylonian Inscriptions in the Collection of James B. Nies.* New Haven.
Bi.Or.	*Bibliotheca Orientalis.*
BJRL	*Bulletin of the John Rylands Library.*
BJV	*Berliner Jahrbuch für Vorgeschichte.*
Bismaya	E. J. Banks, *Bismaya.* New York and London, 1912.
BM	*British Museum.*
BMQ	*British Museum Quarterly.*
BN	L. Delaporte, *Catalogue des cylindres orienteaux de la Bibliothèque Nationale.* Paris, 1919.
Boehmer	R. M. Boehmer, *Die Entwicklung der Glyptik während der Akkad-Zeit.* Berlin, 1965.
Brett	H. H. von der Osten, *Ancient Oriental Seals in the Collection of Mrs. Agnes Baldwin Brett* (= OIP 37). Chicago, 1936.
BRM	*Babylonian Records in the Library of J. Pierpont Morgan.* New Haven, 1912–.
Brussels	L. Speleers, *Catalogue des intailles et empreintes orientales des Musées Royaux du Cinquantenaire.* Brussels, 1917.
Brussels Suppl.	L. Speleers, *Catalogue des intailles et empreintes orientales des Musées Royaux d'Art et d'Histoire, Supplément.* Brussels, 1943.
BSOAS	*Bulletin of the School of Oriental and African Studies.* London.
CAD	*Chicago Assyrian Dictionary.*
CANES	*Corpus of the Ancient Near Eastern Seals in North American Collections* 1, E. Porada, *The Collection of the Pierpont Morgan Library.* New York, 1948.

Carchemish 2	C. L. Woolley, *Carchemish. Report on the Excavations at Jerablus on behalf of the British Museum 2.* London, 1921.
CHEU	G. Conteneau, *Contribution à l'histoire économique d'Umma.* Paris, 1915.
Clay Figurines	E. D. van Buren, *Clay Figurines of Babylonia and Assyria* (= YOR 16). New Haven, 1930.
Copenhagen	O. E. Ravn, *A Catalogue of Oriental Cylinder Seals and Seal Impressions in the Danish National Museum.* Copenhagen, 1960.
Corpus	E. Sollberger, *Corpus des inscriptions "royales" presargoniques de Lagaš.* Geneva, 1956.
CST	T. Fish, *Catalogue of Sumerian Tablets in the John Rylands Library.* Manchester, 1932.
CT	*Cuneiform Texts from Babylonian Tablets . . . in the British Museum.* London, 1896 –.
CTC	T. Jacobsen, *Cuneiform Texts in the National Museum, Copenhagen.* Copenhagen, 1939.
DAFI	*Cahiers de la délégation archéoloque française en Iran.*
De Clercq	L. de Clercq, *Collection de Clercq 1, Cylindres orienteaux.* Paris, 1888.
Eames	A. L. Oppenheim, *Catalogue of the Cuneiform Tablets of the Wilberforce Eames Babylonian Collection in the New York Public Library* (= AOS 32). New Haven, 1948.
Edzard, *SR*	D. O. Edzard, *Sumerische Rechtsurkunden des III. Jahrtausends aus der Zeit vor der III. Dynastie von Ur.* Munich, 1968.
Ehrich	R. W. Ehrich, ed., *Chronologies in Old World Archaeology.* Chicago, 1965.
Elam	P. Amiet, *Elam.* Auvers-sur-Oise, 1966.
Fara	E. Heinrich, *Fara.* Berlin, 1931.
Fauna	E. D. van Buren, *The Fauna of Ancient Mesopotamia* (= An.Or. 18). Rome, 1939.
Figulla	H. H. Figulla, *Catalogue of the Babylonian Tablets in the British Museum.* London, 1961.
Fouilles de Byblos	M. Dunand, *Fouilles de Byblos* 1 and 2. Paris, 1937 and 1950.
Frankfort	H. Frankfort, *Cylinder Seals.* London, 1939.
Gawra 1	E. A. Speiser, *Excavations at Tepe Gawra 1.* Philadelphia, 1935.

Gawra 2	A. J. Tobler, *Excavations at Tepe Gawra* 2. Philadelphia, 1950.
Genève	*Bulletin du Musée d'Art et d'Histoire de Genève.*
GGA	*Göttingen gelehrte Anzeigen.*
Giyan	G. Conteneau and R. Ghirshman, *Fouilles du Tépé Giyan . . . 1931, 1932.* Paris, 1935.
Goucher	Goucher College Collection.
Hallo, *Titles*	W. W. Hallo, *Early Mesopotamian Royal Titles* (= AOS 43) New Haven, 1957.
Hogarth	D. Hogarth, *Hittite Seals.* Oxford, 1920.
HSS	M. I. Hussey, *Sumerian Tablets in the Harvard Semitic Museum* 1 & 2 (= Harvard Semitic Series 3 & 4). Cambridge, Mass., 1912 and 1915.
HUCA	*Hebrew Union College Annual.*
ILN	*Illustrated London News.*
Inscriptions Kultépé	B. Hrozny, *Inscriptions cunéiformes du Kultépé* 1–2. Praha, 1952 and 1962.
IRSA	E. Sollberger and J.-R. Kupper, *Inscriptions royales sumériennes et akkadiennes.* Paris, 1971.
ITT	*Inventaire des tablettes de Tello conservées au Musée Impérial Ottoman.* Paris.
JAOS	*Journal of the American Oriental Society.*
JCS	*Journal of Cuneiform Studies.*
JNES	*Journal of Near Eastern Studies.*
JRAS	*Journal of the Royal Asiatic Society.*
JSOR	*Journal of the Society for Oriental Research.*
KAV	*Keilschrifttexte aus Assur verschiedener Inhalts.* Leipzig, 1920.
Kültepe 1949	T. Özgüç and N. Özgüç, *Kültepe Kazizi Raporu 1949.* Ankara, 1953.
Louvre	L. J. Delaporte, *Catalogue des cylindres, cachets et pierres gravées de style oriental, Musée du Louvre* 1: *Fouilles et missions* (*T.* = Tello, *S.* = Susa, *D.* = Dieulafoi, *K.* = Khorsabad). Paris, 1920; 2: *Acquisitions* (= *A.*). Paris, 1923.
Mackay	E. Mackay, *A Sumerian Palace and the "A" Cemetery at Kish.* Chicago, 1929.
MAD	I. J. Gelb, *Materials for the Assyrian Dictionary.* Chicago, 1952–.
La magie	G. Conteneau, *La magie chez les assyriens et les babyloniens.* Paris, 1947.

MAM 1	A. Parrot, *Mission archéologique de Mari 1, Le temple d'Ishtar.* Paris, 1956.
MAM 2	A. Parrot, *Mission archéologique de Mari 2, Le palais.* Paris, 1958–59.
Mari	A. Parrot, *Mari. Documentation photographique de la Mission archéologique de Mari.* Paris, 1953.
MDAI	*Mitteilungen des deutschen archäologischen Instituts* (Athen und Kairo).
MLC	J. Pierpont Morgan Library Collection.
MMAI	*Mémoires de la Mission archéologique en Iran.* Paris, 1900–.
Mohenjo Daro	Sir J. H. Marshall, ed., *Mohenjo Daro and the Indus Valley Civilization . . .* London 1931.
Moore	G. Eisen, *Ancient Oriental Cylinder and other Seals. Collection of Mrs. William H. Moore* (= OIP 47). Chicago, 1940.
Moortgat Festschrift	K. Bittel et al., eds., *Moortgat Festschrift.* Berlin, 1964.
MSL	B. Landsberger et al., *Materialen zum sumerischen Lexikon.* Rome, 1937–.
Museum Journal	*The Museum Journal.* University of Pennsylvania.
NBC	Nies Babylonian Collection.
NCBS	Newell Collection of Babylonian Seals.
NCBT	Newell Collection of Babylonian Tablets.
Newell	H. H. von der Osten, *Ancient Oriental Seals in the Collection of Mrs. Edward T. Newell* (= OIP 22). Chicago, 1934.
Nikolski, *Dokymenti*	M. V. Nikolski, *Dokymenti khozjaistvennoj otcetnosti Drevnejsej epokhi khaldej iz.* Petrograd, 1908.
NT	Nippur Texts.
Nuzi	E. Porada, "Seal impressions of Nuzi," *AASOR* 24, 1947.
Özgüç, *Anatolian*	N. Özgüç, *The Anatolian Group of Cylinder Seal Impressions from Kültepe.* Ankara, 1965.
Özgüç, *Seals*	N. Özgüç, *Seals and Seal Impressions of level Ib from Karum Kanish.* Ankara, 1968.
OIP	*Oriental Institute Publications.*
OIP 28	*Researches in Anatolia 7,* H. H. von der Osten, *The Alishar Hüyük, Seasons of 1930–32* 1. Chicago, 1937.

SACT	*Sumerian and Akkadian Cuneiform Texts in the Collection of the World Heritage Museum of the University of Illinois* 1, S. T. Kang, *Sumerian Economic Texts from the Drehem Archive.* Urbana, 1972.
Southesk	Lady H. M. Carnegie, ed., *Catalogue of the Collection of Antique Gems Formed by James, Ninth Earl of Southesk, K. T.* London, 1908.
Studies Landsberger	H. G. Güterbock and T. Jacobsen, eds., *Studies in Honor of Professor Benno Landsberger on his Seventy-Fifth Birthday.* Chicago, 1965.
Syria	*Syria,* Revue d'art oriental et d'archéologie.
TAD	S. H. Langdon, *Tablets from the Archives of Drehem.* Paris, 1911.
TAPhS	*Transactions of the American Philosophical Society.*
Tarsus 2	H. Goldman, *Excavations at Gözlü Küle, Tarsus 2.* Princeton, 1956.
TCL	*Textes cunéiformes,* Musée du Louvre.
TCS	A. L. Oppenheim, ed., *Texts from Cuneiform Sources.* Locust Valley, N.Y., n.d.
Telloh	H. de Genouillac, *Fouilles de Telloh* 1–2. Paris, 1934, 1936.
TG	Tepe Giyan.
TIM	*Texts in the Iraq Museum.*
TMH 1	*Texte und Materialen der Frau Professor Hilprecht . . . ,* J. Lewy, ed., *Die Keilschrifttexte aus Kleinasien.* Leipzig, 1932.
TRU	L. Legrain, *Le temps des rois d'Ur.* Paris, 1912.
UCP	*University of California Publications in Semitic Philology.*
UDT	J. B. Nies, *Ur Dynasty Tablets.* Leipzig, 1920.
UDU	G. Contenau, *Umma sous la dynastie d'Ur.* Paris, 1916.
UE	*Ur Excavations* 1–. Oxford, 1927–.
UET	*Ur Excavation Texts* (The British Museum).
Urartu	B. Piotrovskii, *The Kingdom of Urartu.* London, 1967.
UVB	*Vorläufiger Bericht über . . . Uruk-Warka.* Berlin, 1930–.
Ward	W. H. Ward, *The Seal Cylinders of Western Asia.* Washington, D.C., 1910.
Weber	O. Weber, *Altorientalische Siegelbilder.* Leipzig, 1920.

Wiseman	D. J. Wiseman, *Cylinder Seals of Western Asia.* London, n.d.
WVDOG	*Wissenschaftliche Veröffentlichung der deutschen Orient-Gesellschaft.*
YBC	Yale Babylonian Collection.
YNER	*Yale Near Eastern Researches.*
YOR	*Yale Oriental Researches.*
YOS	*Yale Oriental Series.* Babylonian Texts.
ZA	*Zeitschrift für Assyriologie.*
Zylinder- und Stempelsiegel	S. Alp, *Zylinder- und Stempelsiegel aus Karahüyük bei Konya.* Ankara, 1968.
ZZw	D. O. Edzard, *Die "zweite Zwischenzeit" Babyloniens.* Wiesbaden, 1957.

CATALOGUE

A Note on Arrangement

The entries in the catalogue are treated chronologically and within each period stylistically. Peripheral seals are treated separately, but in the chronological phase to which they belong. The Newell Collection has been reclassified and, when desirable, photographs of new impressions have been included; in cases where Newell seals are not illustrated see von der Osten, *OIP* 22. Seals and impressions from the other Collections are fully illustrated with photographs and, where impressions are faint or broken, also with drawings of design.

The individual entries in the catalogue are arranged in the following way:

1. Number in catalogue
2. Shape of seal (if not cylindrical) or, in case of impressions on clay objects, description of object, e.g. envelope, bulla.
3. Color and material
4. Dimension (in mm). For cylinders, height × diameter, e.g. 20×14.

   If shape is basically but not quite cylindrical, deviations are noted with an explanation in parenthesis, e.g. 20×14/16 (convex).

   For other shapes, length × width, diameter, e.g. diameter 16.

   If the height of the engraved area is less than the height of the actual seal, the height of the seal will be in parenthesis, e.g. 20×14(16).

   For impressions on clay objects, the height is given, e.g. seal c. 16.

   Ext. (= extant) in parenthesis indicates a broken seal or an incomplete impression.
5. Condition, e.g. worn.
6. Explanation of illustrations, e.g. (a) Reverse, (b) Drawing.
7. Museum number, e.g. Newell 89, YBC 9999.
8. Date (if known), e.g. Amar-Sin 3.
9. Bibliographical data, e.g. *Yale Library Gazette* 45 (1970–71), p. 61, no. 16.
10. Description of design, usually from left to right of illustration.
11. Comment: often comparisons with similar impressions published elsewhere, or unpublished at Yale, e.g. 807x.
12. Photograph(s), enlarged 1½ times, on facing page.

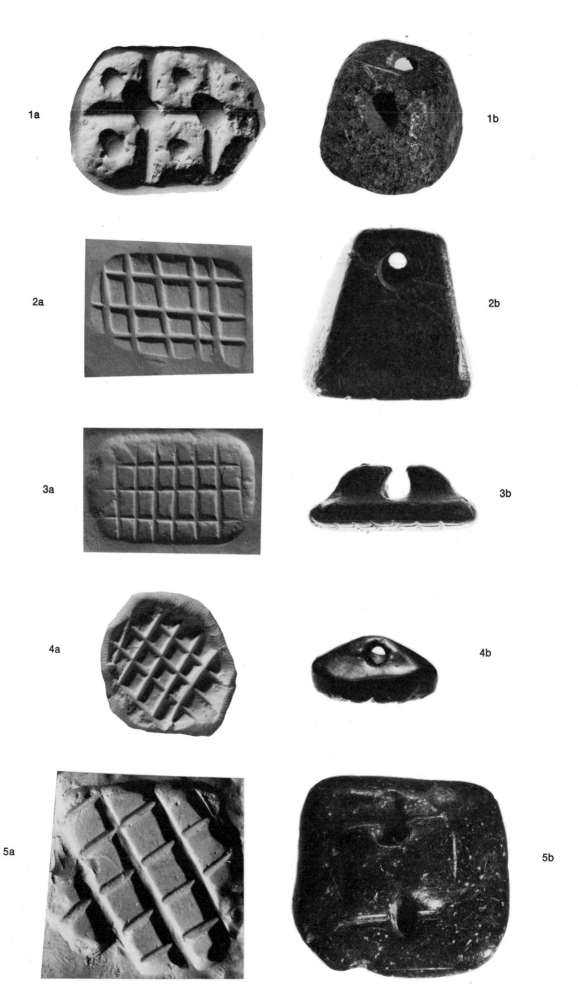

1a   1b

2a   2b

3a   3b

4a   4b

5a   5b

PREHISTORIC
STAMP SEALS

Prehistoric stamp seals have been discussed as follows: Porada, in R. W. Ehrich (ed.), *Chronologies in Old World Archeology,* Chicago, 1965; Buchanan, *Journal of the American Oriental Society* 87 (1967), pp. 265–79, 525–40; Buchanan, *Catalogue of Ancient Near Eastern Seals in the Ashmolean Museum,* vol. 2, Stamp Seals (in press).

Geometric

Very few stamp seal-like objects can be attributed to prepottery levels, c. seventh millennium B.C., and only No. 1 in this collection might conceivably be as early. The stamp seals of the early ceramic phase, c. 5000 B.C., are much more numerous, particularly seals associated with the Amuq Valley of North Syria, 2–10. Later in the Halaf period, c. 4000 B.C., and in the Ubaid phase, c. 3500 B.C., stamp seal types show greater diversity, presenting multi-divided patterns and handled backs, 11–16. Similar designs but with more varied backs came from Western Iran, some small, 17–21, others much larger, 22–26, a few with Ubaid-type hemispheroid shapes, 27–29. From various sources, Ubaid or later, the great majority were basically hemispheroid, 30–39, some with spiral or snakelike designs, 40–42, the last with a whorl-type central bore. A whorl with dotted decor could not be securely dated, 43.

1. Truncated "pyramid." Additional bore through top (accidental?). "Steatite." 30×22×19. Ordinary bore 3½. Crude. (a) Impression, (b) Oblique. NBC 12067.

Crossed lines, two deep drillings at crossings, four more inside "squares."

2. Tall truncated pyramid; shallow irregular groove on one long side by perforation and on two short sides. Dark gray brown schist. 29×21/18(irregular)×30. Bore 7/3 (inside). (a) Impression, (b) Shape. NBC 9376.

Crossed lines.

Compare the crude truncated pyramidal "pebbles" and a tall seal with tapering handle from Amuq A, *OIP* 61, fig. 37. 2, 6, 4 (p. 63).

3. Ridge handle with rounded ends (perforation broken) on oblong base. Speckled dark gray "steatite." 30×18×12. (a) Impression, (b) Shape. NBC 9377.

Crossed lines.

Compare the irregular shapes of ridged seals from Amuq A, *OIP* 61, fig. 37. 1, 3, 5 (p. 63).

4. Low pyramidal ridge on thick irregular base. Dark gray serpentine. 23/20 (irregular)×10. (a) Impression, (b) Shape. NBC 12027.

Crossed lines.

5. Low squarish boss, deeply perforated, on quite thick base. Red serpentine. 35×33×11½ (boss: 17×15×4). Chipped. (a) Impression, (b) Shape from above. NCBS 873.

Crossed lines.

6. Irregular ridge handle on triangular base. Dark gray schist, brown stained. Sides c. 37; height 15. (a) Impression, (b) Shape. YBC 9722.

Crossed lines.

7. Thin loop on sloping, roughly triangular, oval base. "Steatite." 50×36×20. (a) Impression, (b) Shape from above. NBC 12023.

Crossed lines.

8. Thin loop on sloping base. Baked clay. 39(irregular)×17/21(convex). (a) Impression, (b) Shape from above. NBC 12024.

Crossed lines.

6a

6b

7a

7b

8a

8b

9a

9b

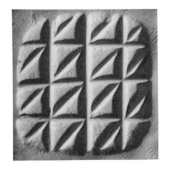

11a

12a

13a

11b

12b

13b

14a

15a

16a

14b

15b

16b

9. Rounded ridge on thick base (broken). Brown limestone (baked?). 56×(ext)31×25. Bore 7/4. (a) Impression, (b) Shape from above. NBC 12047.

Lined rectangle, hatched edge.

Compare *OIP* 61, fig. 379.5 (p. 484), ridge-handled, from Dhahab, probably of Amuq A.

10. Low rounded boss (trace) on thick base. Clawlike contour. Remains of design indicate reshaping. No extant perforation. Dark gray serpentine. 25×17½×10. *Newell* 370. Not shown.

Horizontal and vertical lines, some joined.

11. Loop (broken) on square base. "Steatite." 24 sq.×(ext) 8. (a) Impression, (b) Shape. YBC 13054. Gift Professor Albrecht Goetze.

Squares bisected by diagonal parallel lines.

Compare the more complex design in a rectangular handled seal from Arpachiyah, *Iraq* 2 (1935), fig. 50.14; for square and circular seals with similar designs see ibid. pl. VII (a), also the earlier circular seal with a sloping ridge handle from Amuq B, *OIP* 61, fig. 68.2 (p. 95).

12. Oblong stalk (perforation broken) on sloping base. Dark gray serpentine. 26×20×(ext) 14½/16(convex). (a) Impression, (b) Shape. NBC 12017.

Three drillings in middle of crossed lines, linear fill at ends.

13. Loop on thin base pierced by four holes. Dark gray serpentine. 26×24×9. (a) Impression, (b) Shape. NBC 11019.

Curving lines about four holes; linear fill.

Since only half of the hole under the loop goes through, leaving the loop intact, it would seem that the holes were part of the original design. Compare *OIP* 61, fig. 167.3 (p. 221) of Amuq E (Ubaid), which has four holes through the base near the corners. In the more elaborate design of *Hogarth*, 218 the holes are not pierced through.

14. Sloping ridge on thin base. Dark gray serpentine. 23×11. (a) Impression, (b) Shape. NBC 12042.

Angled cross lines beside dots and linear fill.

15. Boss on high sloping oval base. "Steatite." 27×(ext)19½×12. (a) Impression, (b) Shape. NBC 12045.

Parallel zigzags.

16. Rounded oblong pyramid. Dark gray serpentine. 16×11×10. (a) Impression, (b) Shape. NBC 12059.

Parallel zigzags.

Compare *OIP* 61, fig. 191.1 (p. 254), low "stalk" handled; less so, 191.2, oblong with broken loop, both Amuq F (Uruk).

17. Pyramidal "pebble" with sharply ridged top; rounded triangular base; convex face. Gray brown "steatite." 15×10×10½. (a) Impression, (b) Shape. NBC 10976. Said to be from Tepe Giyan.

Swastikalike design with divider and four drillings.

Compare *AMI* 5, fig. 13, TG (= Tepe Giyan) 2391, without drillings.

18. Elliptical "pebble" with ridged back; convex face. "Steatite." 17½×8½×8. (a) Impression, (b) Shape. NBC 10977. Said to be from Tepe Giyan.

Two diagonal dividers; offset parallel lines as fill.

Compare the lapis lazuli seal, *Giyan,* pl. 38.42 from 14m.; also *AMI* 5, fig. 13, TG 2399, 2400.

19. Pyramidal "pebble" with bluntly pointed top; irregular triangular base; convex face. "Steatite." 17×15×8½. (a) Impression, (b) Shape. NBC 10978. Said to be from Tepe Giyan.

Divider between sloping parallel lines.

For a more regular triangular contour see *AMI* 5, fig. 13, TG 2392, 2655; also the impressions, *OIP* 59, pl. 82.5–7 (first two from A, level III). A similar contour but with a centrally drilled linear design occurs in a low looped seal from a very early mixed range in the Amuq, *OIP* 61, fig. 101.5 (p. 130).

20. Tabloid with rounded corners. "Steatite." 17×11×7/6½ (irregularly flat). (a–b) Impressions, (c) Shape. NBC 10972. Said to be from Tepe Giyan.

(a) Crossed lines. (b) Deeply gouged holes of various sizes.

The plaques from regular excavation at Tepe Giyan are all rounded: *Giyan,* pl. 38.23, 35, 43–44, from 10m.40 to 14m.; but see *AMI* 5, fig. 25, most of which were tabloids, presumably from Tepe Giyan.

21. Elongated oval; convex faces. "Steatite," limestone deposit in part of designs. 17(ext)×12×8. Worn and broken. (a–b) Impressions, (c) Shape. NBC 10979. Said to be from Tepe Giyan.

Offset groups of parallel lines on both faces.

Compare *AMI* 5, fig. 12, TG 2401.

22. Thick lentoid (perhaps had collars at perforation); slightly convex face. Dark gray serpentine. 22×20×9½. Worn. (a) Impression, (b) Shape. NBC 10968. Said to be from Tepe Giyan.

Irregular lines through middle, offset parallel lines on either side, shallow central hole.

23. Lentoid with cutout edges. Mottled light brown marble. 22(20)×7½. (a) Impression, (b) Oblique direct. NBC 10973. Said to be from Tepe Giyan.

Central "circle" (in low relief) with divider through parallel lines; horizontal parallel lines in each notch at edge.

For a cutout edge see *Giyan,* pl. 35.8 (= pl. VI, 4) from 13m.10; *OIP* 59, pl. 8.6 (= 81.31) 8.7 (= 81.22) from A, level III, both handled; for the design, *OIP* 59, pl. 81.20, impression from A, III.

24. "Button" with very convex face and almost flat back into which three connected bores (now broken) were sunk. Mottled light brown marble. 19×10 (face only 8½). (a) Impression, (b) Direct, (c) Back. NBC 10974. Said to be from Tepe Giyan.

Cross with central hole; thick strokes near edge; linear fill.

Compare the "button" with three small connected holes in the base and swastika designs on top, *Giyan,* pl. 38.31 from 11m.60.

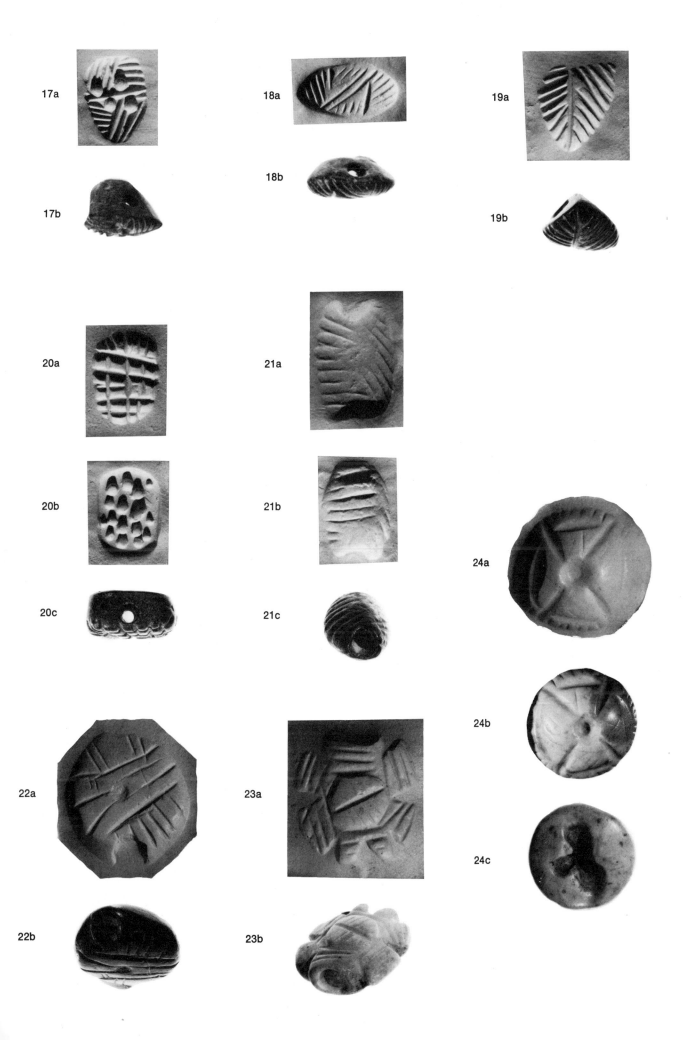

17a

17b

18a

18b

19a

19b

20a

20b

20c

21a

21b

21c

22a

22b

23a

23b

24a

24b

24c

25a

25b

26a

27a

28a

29a

26b

27b

28b

29b

30a

30b

30c

25. "Button" with convex face and almost flat back, with broken boss. Mottled light brown marble. 35/33(irregular)×(ext)14 (face only 7½). Very worn. (a) Impression, (b) Back. NBC 10966. Said to be from Tepe Giyan.

Crossed lines.

Compare the more elaborate deeply cut design in *OIP* 59, pl. 8.12 from A, level III; see also *AMI* 5, fig. 14, TG.

26. Disk with high sides cut into flat base, convex face. Dark gray serpentine. 28×13 (face only 4). (a) Impression, (b) Shape. NBC 10971. Said to be from Tepe Giyan.

Six-part cross, dot filled.

A similarly shaped seal, *AMI* 5, fig. 15, Nih. (top row) shows offset parallel lines.

27. Hemispheroid. Mottled pale brown marble. 21×10½. One end of perforation broken. (a) Impression, (b) Direct. NBC 10970. Said to be from Tepe Giyan.

Central drilling; notched at edge.

28. Hemispheroid; flat at ends of perforation. Speckled reddish brown limestone. 15/14(irregular)×9. (a) Impression, (b) Shape oblique. NBC 10975. Said to be from Tepe Giyan.

Design like 27, but notched more irregularly.

Compare *AMI* 5, fig. 13, TG 2406.

29. Low oval hemispheroid. Dark gray serpentine. 17×15½×6½. (a) Impression, (b) Shape. NBC 10969. Said to be from Tepe Giyan.

Diagonal lines on either side of divider.

Hemispheroid but irregular, *Giyan*, pl. 38.33 (11m.50).

30. Oval with blunt ends. Linear marks on back. "Steatite." 26×23×6. Hole probably not worn in face. (a) Impression, (b) Direct, (c) Back. NBC 12034.

Diagonal cross; crossed lines on one side, angles on other.

FIGS. 25–30

31. Flattened hemispheroid. "Steatite." 23½×12/13(convex). NBC 12030.

Big drillings amidst irregular crossed lines.

31x, NBC 12025, hemispheroid, similar simpler worn design, "steatite," 18×9/10(convex).

32. Gable hemispheroid. "Steatite." 37/36×8. (a) Impression, (b) Shape. NBC 12019.

Cross through hatched concentric squares.

33. Slightly carinated oval hemispheroid; irregular flat face. "Steatite." 25×20×9. Worn. NBC 9338.

Cross; irregular line-filled.

Compare the hemispheroid, *Gawra* 2, 14 of level XII.

34. High hemispheroid; slight in-curve to face. Mottled brown "steatite." 22×14. (a) Impression, (b) Shape. NBC 11009.

Angle-filled cross.

35. Gable hemispheroid. "Steatite." 24×5½. (a) Impression, (b) Direct. NBC 12031.

Like 34.

36. Peaked hemispheroid (conoid?). "Steatite." 13/12½×8. NBC 12052.

Like 34.

37. Hemispheroid. Dark gray serpentine. 16½×10. NBC 12056.

Four-petalled rosette, floral (?) fill.

38. Hemispheroid. Mica-schist. 28×13. (a) Impression, (b) Direct. NBC 12039.

View direct: parallel zigzags.

31

32a

33

34a

32b

36

34b

35a

35b

37

38a

38b

39a

39b

40

41a

41b

42a

42b

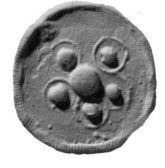

43a

43b

43c

39. Carinatcd hemispheroid; blunt ends at perforation. "Steatite." 34×13. (a) Impression, (b) Direct. NBC 10964. Said to be from Tepe Giyan.

Hatched strip through middle; linear-enclosed hatched segment on either side.

Compare the hemispheroid, *Gawra* 2, 56 of level XI; also *AMI* 5, fig. 18, Nih. For various designs to be viewed direct as is the case here, see *AMI* 5, figs. 14, TG 2656; 16, TG 2405; 17, TG 2355; 19, *Louvre T.* 13; 24, TG s.n.; also the top designs in bottom row, *AMI* 5, fig. 15, Nih., Zakh ii.

40. Hemispheroid. Dark reddish brown marble, lighter mottling. C. 32×13. Broken. NBC 10965. Said to be from Tepe Giyan.

Possibly entwined snakes.

Compare the snake (?) swirl in a convex handled seal, *Giyan*, pl. 38.39 from 13m.

41. Low oval hemispheroid. "Steatite." 23½× 22×9½. (a) Impression, (b) Direct. NBC 11023.

Probably in relief: spiral (snake?).

Compare *Hogarth,* 136. On very early spiral decor in Western Asia, see *JAOS* 87 (1967), p. 266. For the later use of simple spiral designs for stamping, see the clay weights of Early Bronze II, *Tarsus* 2, p. 236, fig. 395.5.

42. Hemispheroid. Central bore added (?) (for use as whorl). Dark gray serpentine. 26×10. (a) Impression, (b) Direct. NBC 12016.

Spiral (snake?).

43. Whorl. Dark gray serpentine, 21×10. (a) Impression, (b) Direct, (c) Shape. NBC 12015.

Five encircled drillings about central hole.

The direct view indicates that the object was not intended for impression and therefore is not a seal.

Compare the stone "whorls" of the "Phrygian" period at Alishar, in general roughly hemispherical in shape with encircled drillings on their flat base, *OIP* 29, fig. 484 (p. 429), p. 427; but see also those much earlier, from Protoliterate Susa, *DAFI* 1 (1971), fig. 54.6–7, p. 182.

ANIMAL DESIGNS

During the first half of the fourth millennium the earlier favored geometric patterns were almost entirely replaced by animal designs. In this period in North Syria a gable shaped back was particularly popular, featuring mammals as in 44–60, but also showing a man and a goat, 61, a bird, 62, and animal heads, 64–66. Preceding the latter came a hemispheroid gable which especially featured a quadruped and animal heads, 63. Similar heads were also centered in a few hemispheroid gables, 67–69.

At about the same time in Western Iran appeared a hemispheroid with an ibex headed demon dominant, 70. Much more rudimentary and not readily located were the figures in 71–72. In contrast, the sexual couple in 73 and the lizard in 74 present quite sophisticated subjects. Animals, especially from Northern Mesopotamia, characterize the hemispheroids of 75–84, the latter two probably in relief. The reel shaped objects, 85–86, have unusual characteristics, even more so a triangular tabloid, 87, and a base with loop on top, 88.

44. Low gable. Gray mica-schist. 77×46×10. One corner chipped. (a) Impression, (b) Shape. NBC 6630.

Three antelopes; two V-shapes and three pellets in field.

Compare the impression *Gawra* 2, 155 of level XIA; see also *Hogarth*, 93.

45. Gable; back rounded perhaps from wear. "Steatite." 31×20½×8. NBC 10999.

Two stags; first three-legged, second five-legged (?), with stroke under jaw.

On the stroke under the jaw of an animal in 45 and 47, see also 49.

46. Gable with rounded back; face slightly rounded at perforation. Speckled gray mica-schist. 31×23×8½. (a) Impression, (b) Shape. NBC 10997.

Two schematic animals.

For the shape compare *Hogarth*, 59, p. 29.

47. Gable with rounded back. "Steatite." 22½×21×8½. NBC 11001.

Ibex (?) with stroke under jaw, curve on back; notched border.

For the notched border compare especially the gable, *Genève* 1, pl. 48.4–6, p. 95, no. 118 (dated much too late); see also *Anadolu* 2 (1965), pl. 37.1, from south-central Anatolia; the tabloids, *Gawra* 1, 29–30 of levels VIII, VII; and the impression, *Gawra* 1, 28 of level VIII.

48. High gable. Red serpentine. 34(ext)×26½×15. Broken and worn. NBC 10996.

Ibex; indeterminate shapes in field.

49. Gable; rounded top perhaps from wear. Gray black serpentine; limestone deposit in design. 22½/22(irregular)×17×6. NBC 9378.

Stag, horns project from top of neck to rear and (?) down in front.

Compare the even cruder design in *Hogarth*, 115; there, however, the stroke before the animal may be accidentally joined to its head; see also the possible leash in *Hogarth*, 69.

50. Gable. Speckled dark gray serpentine. 24×20×9. *Newell* 367. Not shown.

Antelope, in front U-shape over oblique stroke.

44a

44b

45

46a

46b

47

48

49

51

52

53

54

55a

55b

56

57

58

59

60

51. Gable, edge of short sides thick. Dark gray schist. 39×21½×12. NBC 10998.

Antelope, arrow (?) over back, plant (?) at rear below.

Compare *OIP* 61, fig. 253.9 (p. 330), three legs shown, from Amuq G (mostly Jamdat Nasr).

52. Gable. Red brown serpentine. 22×17×7½. Worn. NBC 12033.

Antelope.

52x, NBC 12055, very worn gable, similar design, same material, 18(ext)×18×7.

53. Gable. Material like 52. 18×14×7. Broken. NBC 12020.

Antelope.

54. Gable. Speckled gray mica-schist. 22½× 21×7. NBC 11003.

Squatting (?) goat, two legs shown; stroke above, T-shape below, angle in front.

Compare *OIP* 61, fig. 253.8 (p. 330) from Amuq G (mostly Jamdat Nasr); see also the broadly cut animal in *Hogarth*, 59.

55. High gable. Dark gray serpentine. 21×17½×11. (a) Impression, (b) Shape. NBC 9379.

Goat with bent legs, three shown; head turned back, stroke before it.

The posture of the animal, with only three legs shown, is quite common; see *Hogarth*, 96–97, 112; for its head turned back compare the two-headed creature in *Hogarth*, 101.

56. Low gable. Light "steatite." 37×27½×7½. Worn. NBC 12044.

Goat with bent legs, three shown; two strokes and horned head in field.

57. Gable. Dark gray brown "steatite." 38×27×9. Chipped. YBC 9977.

Lying goat, snake (?) before it.

58. Gable, corners rounded, perhaps only in part from wear. "Steatite." 39×22×11. NBC 11020.

Lying lion, zigzag serpent above.

Compare the more elaborate design with a notched line over the lion in *BMQ* 13 (1939), pl. XIII (a), from Brak.

59. Low gable. Dark brown serpentine. 22 (irregular square)×4½. Very worn. NBC 12029.

Bull (?) over goat (?), both lying with two legs shown.

60. Gable. Black serpentine. 27×25×6. NBC 12063.

Cow feeding kid above bull, blobs in field. Strange style, perhaps not genuine.

FIGS. 51–60

61. Gable. Light brown marble, red and black specks. 55×43×12. Broken at corners. YBC 13051.

Goat, human figure; four drillings and crescent in field.

Compare the more crudely cut gable, *Aulock,* 53.

62. Gable. Black serpentine. 20×16½×6½. NBC 12068.

Bird, blobs in field.

63. Oval gable hemispheroid. "Steatite." 58× 48×10. New impression. *Newell* 366.

Quadruped, animal head above, before it: snake, objects as in 64.

The objects to the right could be the same as those in 64, but in a different order, the ibex head facing downward, the crude "cross" above reversed.

64. Low gable; edge of short sides quite thick. Dark speckled gray mica-schist. 35×20½ ×7½. (a) Impression, (b) Shape. NBC 11000.

Animal head; stroke and crude "cross" with blunt top (manger?) in field.

Compare *Hogarth,* 105.

65. Gable. Dark gray schist. 29×22×8. NBC 11002.

Ibex head; curve and pronged stroke in field.

66. Gable. Dark gray serpentine. 21×20×6½. NBC 11021.

Two diagonal mouflon heads; three curved devices in field.

67. Oval gable hemispheroid; edge of short sides thick. Speckled gray mica-schist. 28×23½×8. (a) Impression, (b) Shape. NBC 11004.

Two reversed mouflon horns, four pellets in field.

61

64a

64b

63

67a

67b

62

65

66

68

70a

70b

69

71

72a

72b

73

74

75

76

77

68. Gable hemispheroid. Dark gray serpentine. 27×8. Chipped. NBC 12037.

Two reversed mouflon horns.

69. Low carinated hemispheroid, face irregularly flat. "Steatite." 19/18½(irregular)×6½. NBC 11022.

Two mouflon heads; two strokes in field.

Compare the confronted mouflon heads in *Gawra* 2, 168, an impression from level XI.

70. Carinated oval hemispheroid; blunt ends at perforation; slightly convex face. Speckled greenish black serpentine. 39×35×16. (a) Impression, (b) Shape. YBC 12758.

Ibex headed demon; to left, above: spread winged bird; below: linear-outlined beast; to right, above: horned animal head (?); below: two snakes (?).

Compare for linear human figures, but with a triangular chest, *Gawra* 2, 76–77 (hemispheroids of levels XII-XIA); for the shoulders, *Gawra* 2, 84 (oval of XIA); for prongs as fingers, *Gawra* 2, 96 (lentoid of X); see also the tabloids, *AMI* 5, fig. 25, TG 2506, 2373, presumably from Tepe Giyan; the tabloid and the later, more naturalistic, hemispheroid, both said to be from Luristan, Porada, *Ancient Iran,* p. 32, pl. 5.

71. Oval hemispheroid, irregularly flat face. "Steatite." 19½×18×7. Worn. NBC 10967. Said to be from Tepe Giyan.

Possibly schematic human figure with bent legs, snake (?) before it, tree behind.

72. Oval hemispheroid. "Steatite," light brown mottling. 29×27×11. Chipped. (a) Impression, (b) Direct. NBC 11007.

In relief: (perhaps) male figure with T-shape and vertical below, right arm extended over oval shape, blob above, blob between two strokes below; animal head (?) above left arm, blob below.

73. Low oval carinated hemispheroid. Dark gray serpentine. 21×19×5. Worn. NBC 12058.

Two creatures (human?), presumably standing, in copulation.

Compare the more humanly depicted figures, apparently likewise engaged, in the gable, *Hogarth,* 77. On the erotic subject see 515 below.

74. Ovoid, slightly flattened at perforation which is parallel to short sides. Speckled dark gray serpentine. 25×18×12. YBC 13034. Perhaps from Iran.

Lizardlike creature with head at top, circle at bottom.

75. Hemispheroid, top flattened (wear?). "Steatite." 22½/22(irregular)×10½. NBC 11005.

Lion over snake; pellet in field.

Compare the simplified style in *Gawra* 2, 139 of level XII, which may be explained by the material, obsidian.

76. Hemispheroid. Reddish brown limestone. 23×(ext)10. Badly broken. YBC 12661.

Animal above goat with head turned back.

For the animal above compare perhaps *Gawra* 1, 23; for the one below, *Gawra* 1, 15, both impressions of level VIII.

77. Hemispheroid. "Steatite." 25×(ext)15. Chipped. NBC 11006.

Leaping stag above snake.

FIGS. 68–77

78. High hemispheroid. "Steatite." 30×15. NBC 12021.

Reversed animal over goat.

The design somewhat resembles the multi-animal impression, *Gawra* 1, 22, level VIII.

79. Hemispheroid. "Steatite." 17×9½. NBC 12048.

One schematic animal over another.

80. Hemispheroid. Brown and black mottled serpentine. 21×10. NBC 12046.

Goat.

81. Hemispheroid. Light "steatite." 17½×9. NBC 12051.

Antelope (three legs shown).

Compare the apparently cruder design in the impression, *Gawra* 1, 9, level VIII.

82. Hemispheroid. "Steatite." 20/19(irregular)×10. YBC 13055. Gift Professor Albrecht Goetze.

Antelope.

83. Hemispheroid. "Steatite." 23½×12. (a) Impression, (b) Direct. NBC 11008.

In relief: schematic horned animal, blob before it.

Compare the design in relief, *Louvre T.*, 13.

84. Oval hemispheroid. Black serpentine. 27½×25×(ext)5, top worn. (a) Impression, (b) Direct (design filled with plasticine). YBC 9995. Bought Baghdad.

Possibly in relief: horned animal head beside horned animal head, amidst blobs.

85. Reel shaped with convex top, flat bottom. No perforation. Brown black "steatite." 22½/20½(bottom)/18(inside)×12. (a-b) Impressions, (c) Shape. NBC 12064.

(a) Two thick uprights in middle separated by two smaller triangles, schematic animal (?) on either side. (b) Cross.

Unlike 86, the high convex top here bears the principal decoration. Amiet, *MDAI* 43, 259, three groups of curved chevrons, perforated between thick edges, convex top.

78

79

80

81

82

83a

84a

83b

84b

85a

85b

85c

86a

86b

87a

87b

88a

88b

86. Reel shaped with high convex top (undecorated). No perforation. Mica-schist. 25 (top) 23(face) 21(inside)×17. Chipped. (a) Impression, (b) Shape. NCBS 874.

Antelope (?).

For the shape compare the "studs" with no decor or with holes for inlay (?) on top, from Judaidah, *OIP* 61, p. 253, fig. 192, Amuq F (Uruk), p. 333, fig. 255.2, Amuq G (mostly Jamdat Nasr), pl. 71.18–20; also the stone "knob" from "Chalcolithic" Alishar, *OIP* 28, fig. 91 (p. 86), C 1588, p. 102.

87. Triangular tabloid. Perforated twice through face. "Steatite." 31×26×7. (a-b) Impressions. NBC 12041.

(a) Snake above goat. (b) Lying mouflon (?), forked line before it.

The perforations cut awkwardly into parts of both designs are probably of later origin, perhaps not prehistoric at all but rather as late as 8th century Urartian.

A stone pendant from Karmir Blur somewhat resembles 87, B. Piotrovskii, *Urartu*, p. 71, fig. 51 (drawn), but it is round and has a frontally pierced handle at top. On one side a male figure stands with raised arms, the other side shows a goat in a style rather like that of (b) here.

88. Loop on thick oval base. "Steatite." 26-½×13(base 7). (a) Impression, (b) Shape. NBC 12060.

Two antelopes with forelegs, reversed on common midsection; filling motifs between heads and legs.

Seals of this shape are rare: *OIP* 61, fig. 253.10 (p. 330), from Amuq G (mostly Jamdat Nasr), a crude linear animal; Amiet, *MDAI* 43, 257–58, linear patterns, Proto-urban; *JAOS* 87 (1967), Tello, fig. 3 (p. 529), p. 533, seal 12, pl. I.7, gouged swirl of animals (?) and horns, late Prehistoric; *Museum Journal* 23 (1933), pl. 107A, H320, p. 381, linear cross design, period II, c. 3000 B.C., among early copper seals from Hissar, Iran.

FIGS. 89–97

In the first half of the fourth millennium Southern Mesopotamia and Susiana featured a number of mostly local types. Among the earliest, though not exclusively so, were the collared ovoids and hemispheroids; of these 89–90 present intricate cross designs; 91–92 show simple horned animals; and 93–95 crude animal (?) variations. Ordinary hemispheroids include an angled design, 96; animal patterns, not very complex, 97–99; a contest scene, 100; varied animals based on drilled designs, 101–04; and a hemispheroid mace head offers a ring of drilled creatures, 105.

A half cylinder presents drilled animals, 106; the same subject in an ordinary tabloid, 107. Other tabloids show a single animal, 108; a schematic insect, 109; crude animals, both sides engraved, 110; an antelope, simply marked on the other side, 111; an animal contest, its reverse bearing a late inscription, 112; finally an oblong tabloid showing four creatures in 113.

An important series offers usually well-executed animal shapes, the flat faces of which, however, were in general crudely executed. Thus the vulture in 114 shows crude animal figures on its base, and the man in 115 presents sketchy males below. Bulls (?), though done with some care, still offer poor animals, 116–21, 124, or dotted patterns, 122–23. Two beautifully rendered foxes show quite well executed dotted animals, 125–26; but a very sketchy ram (?) goes with coarse creatures, 127; a lion in profile is accompanied by crude drilled patterns, 128; and a pig (?) in the round even more so, 129. A simplified lion's head has coarse animals on its face, 130. Less so are the animals in 131 which accompany a magnificent lion's head. A similarly superb head finds its counterpart in a seated horned monkey on its face, 132.

89. Oval hemispheroid with ill-defined collars. Diorite. 24×23×9½. (a) Impression, (b) Shape. NBC 11024.

Irregular swirling cross design.

Compare the better organized design in *Mackay* 2, pl. 42, 2145, a survivor from Early Dynastic rubbish; see also the collared ovoid, *Amiet*, 157, found quite near, at Telloh.

90. Collared hemispheroid. Brown limestone. (a) Impression, (b) Direct. New impression. *Newell* 9.

Cross, its four arms ending with three prongs; animal(?)-shaped fill.

Somewhat like the impressions cited in *JAOS* 87 (1967), p. 267 and n. 11.

91. Oval hemispheroid, slightly collared (worn). Black and white mottled marble, brown tinged. 31(ext)×25×10. NBC 9337.

Two antelopes, dots in field.

92. Oval hemispheroid with faint collars. Dark brown limestone, creamy veined. 43×30 ×13/14(convex). New impression. *Newell* 8 (direct in original).

Spiral of animals, blobs in field.

Compare *Louvre S.*, 233; *UE* 10, II.

93. Collared hemispheroid. Brown limestone, red tinged. 38×33×15. *Newell* 1 (direct in original, also one of back). Not shown.

Six drillings with extended radiations.

94. Collared hemispheroid (one collar lost); slightly convex. Pink-brown limestone. 36(ext)×37×18. YBC 13066. Nippur 4N 132, from surface.

Ibex; three horned heads (?) and two drillings with appendages in field.

95. Collared hemispheroid (one collar lost). Reddish brown marble, lighter mottling. 38(ext)×35×15. Bore 5½/2½. Chipped. (a) Impression, (b) Shape. YBC 8423. Bought Iraq (R. P. Dougherty).

Two schematic animals; indeterminate fill.

Compare *Amiet*, 112 (=*MDAI* 43, 127), *Louvre S.*, 231–32, hemispheroids probably from Susa A.

96. Hemispheroid. Pale brown marble. 46×42 ×21. *Newell* 6. Not shown.

Two dividers with angled lines between them, attached at sides.

Compare *Amiet*, 105 (=*MDAI* 43, 135), probably of Susa A; see also *DAFI* 1 (1971), pl. XXII.10, fig. 357, a collared hemispheroid from medium depth at Susa, level 23, p. 170.

97. Hemispheroid. Brown limestone, gray banded. 46×23. *Newell* 5. Not shown.

Two horned animals back to back, animal and other linear motifs above.

89a   89b

90a   90b   91

92   94

95a   95b

98

99

100

101a

102a

101b

102b

98. Hemispheroid. Curves in to face. Material like 97. 49×48(face 47×46)×26. New impression. *Newell* 4.

Ibex with head turned back in middle, three ibexes at sides, eagle above two zigzag lines.

99. Hemispheroid. Amygdaloidal basalt (dark brown with white spots). 36×14½. Corroded. New impression. *Newell* 2 (direct in original).

Ibex between two angled snakes; snake (?) divider; below reversed: two confronted ibexes, snake under one.

Compare *Amiet*, 109 (=*MDAI* 43, 142), perhaps from Susa A.

100. Hemispheroid. Brown limestone, pink and cream incrustations. 40×17. New impression. *Newell* 7. Cf. *JAOS* 87 (1967), p. 530, n. 24.

Two lions tête-bêche, each consuming animal.

101. Hemispheroid. Greenish gray marble, streaked cream and brown. 43×17. (a) Impression, (b) Shape. NBC 5985.

Antelope head and foreleg, gazelle head and foreleg, reversed and opposed, on common body.

102. Hemispheroid. Light brown limestone. 45×17. (a) Impression, (b) Shape. YBC 9715.

Two ibexes, reversed and opposed; drilling between them.

103. Hemispheroid. Pale brown marble. 42×19. *Newell* 3. Not shown.

Two horned animals tête-bêche.

FIGS. 98–103

104. Hemispheroid. White marble, brown streaked. 23×11½. NBC 9380.

Stag; line of drillings above it.

105. Oval hemispherical mace head; curves in to face. "Steatite." 49×46(face 47×45)×30. Hole of mace head 13. Chipped. (a) Impression, (b) Shape. NBC 5984.

Stag (heading down); deer (?), with insect (?) below, facing bird and two ibexes, indeterminate shape above last; drillings in field.

The careful placing of the design around the hole of the mace head suggests that both the former and the latter were secondary.

106. Half cylinder. Red brown marble. 31×25½×14. (a) Impression, (b) Shape. New impression. *Newell* 11. *Amiet* 169

Two animals tête-bêche.

Compare *Louvre D.*, 2; also, but simpler and of uncertain date, *AMI* 5, fig. 21, Saktsh. 6.

107. Tabloid. Red brown marble. 34×32½ (31½)×11. *Newell* 10. Not shown.

Two animals tête-bêche.

Compare *Louvre S.*, 207, 211.

108. Tabloid. Olive limestone. 15×14×6½. *Newell* 371. Not shown.

Animal.

109. Tabloid. Crudely scratched cross on other face. "Steatite." 31×19×6½. NBC 12061.

Schematic insect.

110. Tabloid. "Steatite." 24½×15½×8½. Scratchy. NBC 12032.

Facing in opposite direction: schematic animal, line (snake?) above.

A gable in *Hogarth,* 115 shows a somewhat less crude design.

111. Tabloid. "Steatite." 20×15½×5½. (a) Impression, (b) Back (linear bands near edge). NBC 12002.

Antelope, linear fill.

Tabloids with simple designs on the back were found in the Brak "Eye Temple"; *Iraq* 9 (1947), pl. 18.2, 4, inset triangles probably for inlay, animals on face 3, p. 122–23; 8, two rows of zigzags in relief, coarse beast on face 9, p. 123; pl. 20.27, "ladders" in two rows, crude horned beast on face 26, p. 131.

104

105a

105b

106a

109

110a

110b

106b

111a

111b

112a

112b

113a

114a

115a

115b

113b

114b

112. Tabloid. White marble, red streaked. 40×35×10. (a) Impression, (b) Shape (oblique). Inscription (later addition, probably forgery) on reverse. YBC 12759.

Lion attacking bull over reversed lion; drillings and drilled shapes in field.

For the design compare the tabloid from the Brak "Eye Temple," showing animals with body markings and other natural detail, *Iraq* 9 (1947), pl. 18.28, p. 125.

113. Oblong tabloid; slightly gabled back; thick sides. Brown alabaster, creamy mottling. 50-×23×10½(side 9). Worn. (a) Impression, (b) Shape. NBC 11018.

Column of four animals; two boars (?) above two horned (?) animals.

For the shape compare Erlenmeyer, *Or* 28 (1959), pl. 37.22, which shows a human head over a lizard, animals on either side, engraved in a flat-cut, linear-outlined style; see also *Philadelphia*, lh of similar shape with a slightly convex back and six holes for inlay, its design a figure and animals in much the same style as 113. For comparable engraving see some tabloids, presumably from Tepe Giyan, with designs on both faces: *AMI* 5, fig. 25, TG 2375–76, 2506–07, 2373; as well as *AMI* 5, pl. III (left), p. 100, a tabloid from the Pusht i Kuh (South Luristan) with a more natural,

careful design on one face only. Compare the even more naturalistic style of the Gawra period, as in *Gawra* 2, 144, a rectangular impression from level XI, or 148, a tabloid from X.

114. Vulture; holes for inlay in eye, on wing, and across lower part. Perforation from back of neck to top of wing. Greenish black serpentine. 67×35×17. Chipped. (a) Impression, (b) Shape. YBC 12757.

Animal (?) shape above reversed antelope; oryx (?) above stag; animal (?) shapes below and to left.

Compare the eagle (?) amulet with hole in eye for inlay and somewhat similar decor, from Brak "Eye Temple" C, *Iraq* 9 (1947), pl. 8, la-c.

115. Squatting man. Brown mottled, creamy marble. 28×19×9. (a) Impression, (b) Shape. New impression. *Newell* 20 (direct in original, also one of back).

Sidewise seated male over two seated males, bent lines under both groups.

Compare the squatting female amulets, *Moore*, 14 and *AMI* 5, fig. 27, FH.; also the seated monkeys: Amiet, *MDAI* 43, 417; *Amiet*, 168 from Brak.

116. Lying bull (?), full face. Greenish gray marble. 48×30×22. (a) Impression, (b) Shape. NBC 5986.

Three animals.

117. Lying bull (?), full face. Pink brown marble, gray mottling. 28×21×16. (a) Impression, (b) Shape. NBC 2550. *BIN* 2, pl. 72c, p. 56 ("pregnant ewe"). *AMI* 5, fig. 30 (Nies Keis. 72c, marked e-f in error).

Three animals (?).

118. Lying bull. 35×25×15. *Newell* 12 (face and back). Not received at Yale. *Fauna*, p. 71, n. 5.

Three animals.

119. Lying bull (?). Pale green calcite. 33×20×17. *Newell* 13 (face and back). Not shown.

Three animals.

120. Lying bull (?). Light brown limestone. 41×26×19. *Newell* 15 (face and back). Not shown.

Two animals.

121. Lying bull (?). Pale green calcite with cream and brown bands. 37×20×20. *Newell* 14 (face and back). Not shown. *Fauna*, p. 71, n. 5.

Animal.

122. Lying bull (?). Light brown limestone. 31×23×15. *Newell* 17 (face and back). Not shown.

Groups of dots (animal heads?).

123. Lying bull (?). Speckled gray serpentine. 40×24×14. Corroded. *Newell* 16 (face and back). Not shown.

Groups of dots.

124. Lying animal, full face. Light brown limestone. 23×20×12. Most of design lost. Shape only shown. NBC 6520.

Two connected drillings with two lines at one end survive.

125. Fox. Light brown limestone. 39×26 (37×26)×18. (a) Impression, (b) Shape. New impression. *Newell* 19 (face and back), "jackal." *Fauna*, p. 19, n. 4, fig. 17.

Three animals (125–26 were probably made at the same time, facing in opposite directions).

126. Like 125. 37×25(face 35×25)×19. *Newell* 18 (face and back). Not shown. *Fauna*, p. 19, n. 4.

Three animals.

127. Ram (?), head back against body. Creamy brown mottled marble. 48×29×12. Worn. (a) Impression, (b) Shape. NCBS 875.

Three animal forms, two drillings, scratches (?).

For the shape compare *Iraq* 9 (1947), pls. 11.3, 12.1, 13.1, 3, 5, from the "Eye Temple" platform, Brak; but with flatter or more linear designs than in 127.

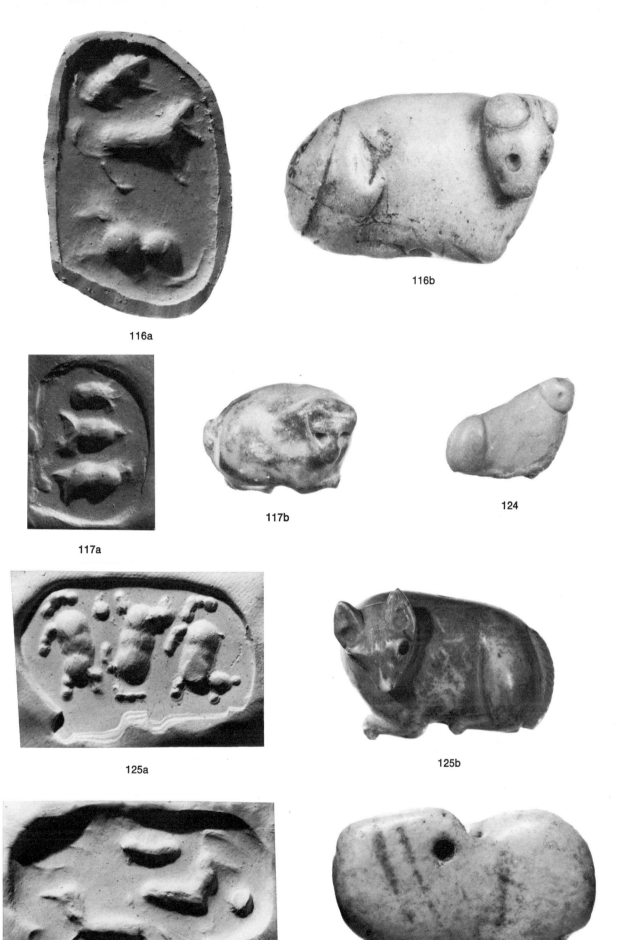

116a

116b

117a

117b

124

125a

125b

127a

127b

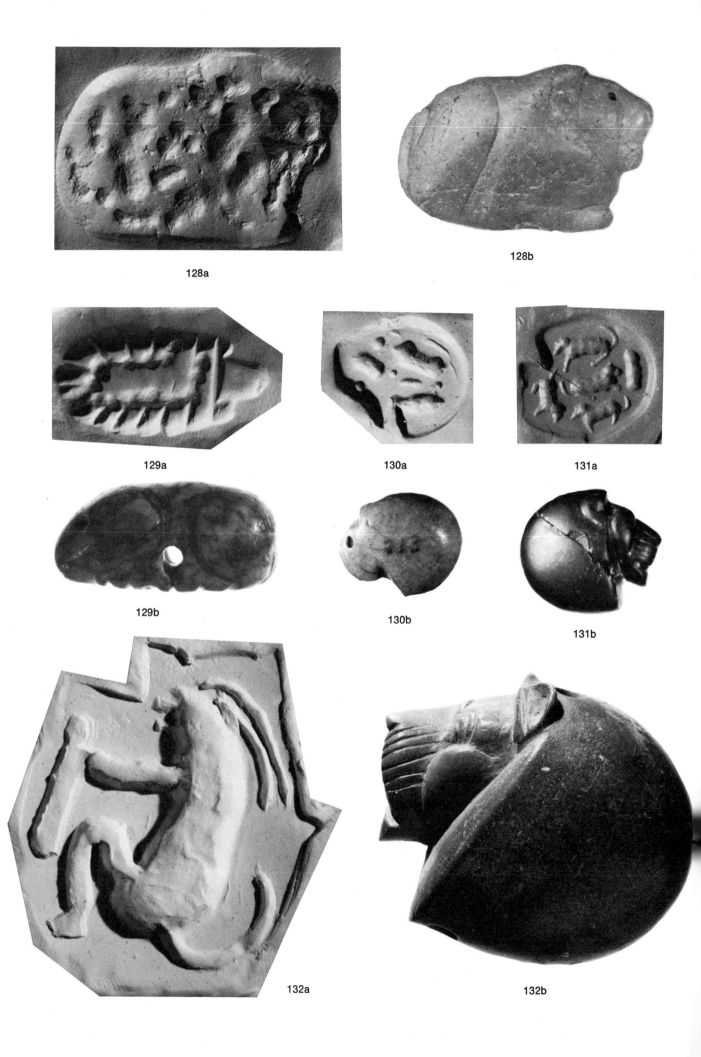

128a

128b

129a

130a

131a

129b

130b

131b

132a

132b

128. Lying lion, head in profile. Engraved face rounded at perforation. Light green calcite, brown streaked. 47×32×18. (a) Impression, (b) Shape. NBC 2547. *BIN* 2, pl. 71i (shape).

Scatter of connected drillings; sidewise animal shape.

Compare the lions in profile: *Louvre T.*, 21 and *S.*, 199.

129. Lying pig (?) in the round. Perforation worn toward engraved face as if carried upside down. Light brown marble, brown and black streaked. 39×16×17½. (a) Impression, (b) Shape. NBC 9360.

Twisted centipedelike creature, line before it.

Compare *AMI* 5, fig. 29; *Louvre S.*, 197 (a two-headed pig from Susa), FH A6; snake decor in both.

130. Simplified lion's head. Gray marble. 22×18×8. (a) Impression, (b) Shape. NBC 9339.

Three amorphous shapes (one lion?); drillings and strokes as fill.

131. Lion's head (split). Hematite. 24×21×8. (a) Impression, (b) Shape. YBC 12598.

Column of three animals; sidewise animals to left and right.

132. Lion's head. Brown limestone. 64×50×19. (a) Impression, (b) Shape. New impression. *Newell* 21 (face and back).

Seated monkey (?) with ibex horns holding mace (?).

Compare the big figures in the hemispheroid, *Louvre S.*, 401, and the rectangular stamp impression, *Amiet*, 232 (= *MDAI* 43, 452), both from Susa; also in the hemispheroid, *Telloh*, pl. 38.2c.

CYLINDER SEALS FROM MESOPOTAMIA

Uruk IV

RITUAL SCENES

The Uruk period, c. 3200 B.C., is perhaps best designated by its most significant phase, associated with Warka IV of Southern Mesopotamia (Porada, *Ehrich,* pp. 154–56). Earlier periods, especially V, can be detected, but the later phase III either continues to show some influence from IV or, more significantly, reflects a degeneration in style, manifest to an even greater extent in the following Brocade phase of Early Dynastic I. The extraordinary succession of styles from the glories presented in Warka IV to the decadence exemplified by Early Dynastic I was first brilliantly demonstrated by *Frankfort,* pp. 14–43. Proto-Sumerian writing appeared in Uruk IV, but in Susa Ca, at Godin Tepe V well north of it (H. Weiss and T. C. Young, Jr., *Iran* 13 [1975], pp. 1–17), and even in Eastern Syria (E. Strommenger, *AfO* 24 [1973], p. 171), all at about the same time; numbers and, a little later, the very different Proto-Elamite script were attested, though the seal impressions of Southern Mesopotamia, Susiana, and related areas are still very similar.

In 133 goats and rosettes, in 134 a leader and his attendant feed cattle, in 135 men present offerings to a temple, 136 show elaborate holy scenes, in 137 a partial view of a pole carrier and a priest appear, in 138 a bull is carrying and followed by standards, in 139 a cow giving birth is attacked by a lion which is speared from above. Possibly from Susa, 140, a complex bored seal, shows an archer followed by dogs. All of these heavily but beautifully sculptured works could be of the time of Uruk IV.

133. Creamy marble, brown mottled. Conoid top (broken) with rosette device (as in main design) in low relief; trace of raised border (probably double) at top of bore; bottom of border separated from top of seal by thin line. 55(ext, seal 40)×38. Bore 12. (a) Impression, (b) Shape. New impression. *Newell* 690, p. 85 (incorrectly "doubtful"). *Frankfort,* p. 6, n. 4. *Amiet,* 619.

Two groups: both showing one above another, pair of sheep each browsing at plant.

134. Creamy brown marble, lighter veined. Loop on top (byre shaped?) with lengthwise perforation. 63(seal 46)×37. Face cracked and broken. (a) Impression, (b) Shape. NBC 2579. Said to be from Warka. *BIN* 2, pl. 76e, pp. 60f. *Frankfort,* pl. 1a, 5d, p. 6. *Amiet,* 640, p. 83.

Attendant carrying branches, bearded male in long transparent skirt offering branches to leaders of two rows of three cattle (cow and two bulls?).

It seems probable that this piece was intended for use as a votive object, rather than as a seal, for the drillwork has such depth that it is virtually impossible to capture all the details of the design in a rolling. For the subject see *Amiet,* 637–39.

The byrelike loop on top resembles those on some early cylinders, except that here it is cut from the seal itself whereas the others were generally made separately to fit into a hole in the top by means of a dowel (*OIP* 72, pp. 13f., fig. 1). Most examples of the latter type are probably of Jamdat Nasr times, so it would seem that there was some overlap from period to period in the use of the two kinds of loops.

133a

133b

134b

134a

135

136a

136b

136c

135. Pale brown marble, white mottling. 35×29. Bore 13. New impression. *Newell* 669, p. 83 (incorrectly "forgery"). *Frankfort,* fig. 2, p. 19. *Amiet,* 642, pp. 87f. *Yale Library Gazette* 43 (1968), p. 93, no. 1.

Attendant holding sacred string and bearded male carrying mutilated feline toward temple, behind them barley and sheep.

136. Multiple impressions, perhaps all of same seal, on tablet. Probable numerals and possible sign on obverse. Seal ext. 19. (a) Obverse (numerals and sign shown reversed), (b) Reverse, (c) Drawing. Goucher 869. B. Goff and Buchanan. *JNES* 15 (1956), pp. 23lff., pls. 18 (fig. 3 should read: Bottom edge) and 19. *Amiet,* pl. 48 bis A (tassels added beside ring on post).

Shrine between two tasseled standards, man carrying embroidered cloth, man (perhaps carrying animal as in 135); (possibly) altar with inset animals back to back on platform (see B in drawing); disk (?) above triangular vessel, ring (?) (two tassels perhaps projecting from it) on post, tasseled standard; byre shaped (?) altar with calf's head projecting from either side, perhaps topped by one or two curved finials; below: ritual objects including tasseled standards and an animal shaped vase.

For the subject matter of 136 compare *Amiet,* 203A–B, 643–44, 656, all probably of Uruk date; see also the degraded version, possibly of early Jamdat Nasr times, in the upper register of *Ash C,* 2. For the ritual objects com-

pare *Ash C,* 9, an impression from Jamdat Nasr; but, like *Ash C,* 3–7, perhaps made by a seal surviving from the Uruk period. On the tasseled standard see *Amiet,* p. 78 (his "hampes bouclées"); though all of the better executed designs cited there should be of Warka IV (of III, 624–25, 627–29, 646, 648, 651). For a byre with animal heads projecting from the sides, like the altar in the top register of 136, compare *UVB* 5, pl. 25d, p. 43 (= *Amiet,* 186), an impression presumably from Warka IV found under the leveling for III. This byre has two curved finials on top, which may also have been true of the altar with projecting heads here.

Other possible changes in the drawing have been suggested in the description of the design. Most important, it is far from certain that the design, as it appears at the top of the reverse and as drawn, was continuous from the leading figure to the triangular vessel. Contrary to the opinion expressed in the article cited above (*JNES* 15 [1956], p. 234), the altar shown as B in the drawing should perhaps be placed before the leading figure; so it is described here.

The tablet on which 136 was impressed has the quite thick, cushion shape probably most typical of Warka IV, in contrast to the thinner shape with rounded corners which was more likely characteristic of the following period. No great number of Warka IV tablets have one or more signs (here one) as well as seal impressions; nevertheless they do occur, see *UVB* 16 (1960), p. 57.

137. Pale green serpentine, brownish mottling. Fragment. 36½×24½. New impression. *Newell* 61. *Frankfort,* p. 15, n. 2. *Amiet,* 673.

Attendant carrying end of pole, handled vessel, priest with sacred vase.

138. Brown flecked, creamy marble. Fragment. 62×(ext)47. New impression. *Newell* 22 (shape and direct in original). *Frankfort,* p. 15, n. 2. *Amiet,* 653.

Temple with tasseled standards on back of bull, two similar standards behind it.

139. Gray green serpentine. 37×20. New impression. *Newell* 695, p. 85 (incorrectly "doubtful"). *Frankfort,* p. 22, n. 1. *Amiet,* 602, p. 76.

Warrior, bull's head behind him, kneeling on back of cow giving birth, attacks lion with spear.

Compare for style and subject: Nagel, *BJV* (1966), pp. 20ff., pl. I., said to have been found near Uruk, showing over a bull a mouflon half swallowed by a large reptile which is being stabbed below by a naked warrior; *MDAI* 43 (1972), 605, also drawn (*Amiet,* 250, Susa), warriors spearing lion from either side, other animals about; *Amiet,* 611, pp. 76f., Uruk stele, at top warrior spearing lion, below second warrior shooting lions with bow.

140. Dark brownish green mottled serpentine. Double perforation: at top loopbore and normal break between the latter and one side of the former. 24×21. (a) Impression, (b) Shape. YBC 12742. *Yale Library Gazette* 35 (1960), p. 24, no. 1 (plate). *Amiet,* 610 bis.

Hunter with bow leading two longeared dogs by leash.

On the loopbore as a peripheral, especially North Syrian, device see *Frankfort,* pp. 6f. and 232 (there and p. 7, n. 2 read: pl. 38 c, g, j), also *Ash C,* p. 127, plus comment under seals. It might be thought that the loopbore in 140 was the original perforation, since so much of it is broken into. However, it is just possible that instead an attempt to add a loopbore was bungled.

The hunter wears high boots with turned up toes. The last feature is often cited as a peripheral, or more specifically an Anatolian, trait; but see the Uruk seal, *Frankfort,* pl. 4h, p. 20, and compare *Frankfort,* pl. 24c or 423 below, both Akkadian seals. A hunter in similar boots appears in a seal of derivative Uruk style from an uncertain context at Nineveh (*AAA* 19 [1932], pl. 63.10, p. 92 = *BM* I, pl. 2b).

For related hunting scenes see *Amiet,* 603–08, the first said to be from Warka, the rest (four impressions and one seal) from Susa; all except perhaps the last should be of the Uruk period. The possible priority in 140 of the loopbore perforation, one example of which comes from Susa (*Louvre S.,* 329, probably of Jamdat Nasr date), and the prevalence of related scenes at Susa suggest that 140 could have originated there.

137

138

139

140a

140b

141a

141b

142a

142b

143a

143b

144

145

A large number of pieces probably mostly of Uruk IV or perhaps slightly earlier, but some a little later, present simplified subjects of varied size in coarse styles. In 141 twenty-eight sheep are regularly but crudely cut, somewhat resembling animal shapes reported from Egypt; in 142 shallow inlay holes surround a spool-shaped group of drillings; in 143 three heavily drilled panels include one female, otherwise pots; in 144–48 females and pots are crudely rendered in simple style, 149–53 presumably show women at looms, 154–55 present crude standing females. A very simplified group, 156–59 presents fish or insect or lozenge shapes for which numerous parallels exist in Susiana (Amiet, *MDAI* 43, 766–824; *DAFI* 1 [1971], fig. 43.10, pl. XXII.4, pp. 165, 209, apparently from the early cylinder stratum 21 at Susa) and Egypt (*Amiet*, pl. 21 bis J–M, O).

FIGS. 141–145

141. Light brown limestone. 22×14. Bore 3/2 (very worn to one side at each end). (a) Impression, (b) Shape. NBC 9143.

Four rows of seven sheep (the columns of sheep cut in seven rounded vertical facets).

Compare *Berlin*, 70 (with dogs?) (= *Fara*, 69b). Similar, but more conspicuously drilled: *Telloh* I, pl. 39.1, p. 41, from not higher than 9 m in the deep pit and therefore, if not a stray, of Warka IV times or earlier; see *JAOS* 87 (1967), pp. 534f. Close in style, but with heavier lionlike figures of blue glaze, comes a cylinder of similar period from Egypt, *JAOS* 87 (1967), p. 535, note 41 = Kantor, *JNES* 11 (1952), fig. 1 E (p. 243), pp. 246–47; *Ehrich*, fig. 8 D (p. 31), p. 10.

142. Dark gray coarse-grained igneous rock. 20×22/17(very concave). Four shallow holes, perhaps for inlay, about perforation at each end (one hole broken away). (a) Impression, (b) Shape. YBC 13060.

Big drillings alternating with smaller ones, each of the latter having two small drillings separated from it above, and two connected with it below (possibly handled vases on stands); dividing line; same pattern reversed.

For the subject compare *Telloh* I, pl. 39, 4d, p. 39, from a shallow context in the deep pit; for the shape see *OIP* 72, 884 = 2r (no inlay holes); for inlay holes see the facetted Susa seal, *Amiet*, 323 (= *MDAI* 43, 727). It is probable that 142 was not intended for use as a seal since no wholly satisfactory impression of it could be obtained.

143. Material like 142. Face divided into three panels. 12×12 (panels 12×8/9). (a) Impression, (b) Shape. NBC 9357.

Panels A–B: one handled vase above another; panel C: squatting pigtailed woman with raised arm.

For the shape and design compare *Amiet*, 322–25, 327. On a possible Uruk date for drilled squatting women with various objects, as in 143–53, see Porada, *Ehrich*, p. 155, fig. VII.1, Inanna 15, Nippur = p. 180, fig. VII.6 = p. 188, fig. VII.5, Inanna temple XVI. A more natural, elaborated version of the theme appears in an impression from Warka IVb (*UVB* 19 [1963], pl. 15d, p. 21); there the squatting figure has one knee raised. For a more complicated figure, see Porada, *Ehrich*, p. 180, fig. VII.5 = p. 188, fig. VII.6, Eanna IVb, Warka. The posture is common in the impressions from Susa presumably of Warka IV times, see *Amiet*, 262–65.

144. Dark gray serpentine, speckled. 18×18. NBC 9100.

One two-handled vase above another before two squatting women, "bench" in middle, curved, two more vases before third woman.

145. Light green calcite. 19×17. Chipped. YBC 12508.

Three squatting pigtailed women, each on "bench" with arms raised toward one spouted pot above another.

146. Red marble. 25×33/26 (very concave). *Newell* 29 (shape and design). Not shown.

Five women on "benches," pots before them, globe with rays also before second.

147. Speckled gray serpentine. 15½×15. NBC 11044.

One spouted pot above another (reversed) before two squatting women, two more pots before third woman.

148. Brown limestone. 22×22. *Newell* 30. Not shown.

Three women before pots on line (lower pots reversed).

149. Material like 142. 15×13. YBC 12504.

Spiderlike device (probably two vases on stand with lower half reversed); three women, one arm raised, all squatting on same "bench."

On the spiderlike device see *Amiet*, p. 103; compare the comment under *Ash C*, 705.

150. Rock crystal. 20×19. Bore 6 (deeply conical at ends) /1½. YBC 12596.

Spiderlike device (compare 149); disk on pole, spouted vase over squatting pigtailed woman (with rod?), second woman over vase; second "spider;" third woman (with rod?) over another, spouted vase on stand.

151. Pink brown marble. 20×21. Decayed. NBC 9328.

Row of vertical lines before squatting figure with raised arms; repeated twice (chipped behind third figure).

Amiet, 275, p. 104, from Susa, shows a horizontal loom — or is it a vertical loom viewed sidewise?

152. Gray brown limestone. 23×24. Bore 9 (conical at ends) /2½. Decayed. NBC 10982.

Loom (?) with two attachments between two squatting women, third woman amid containers (?).

On presumed scenes of weaving as in 152–53 see *Amiet*, 320, p. 104.

147

149

150

151

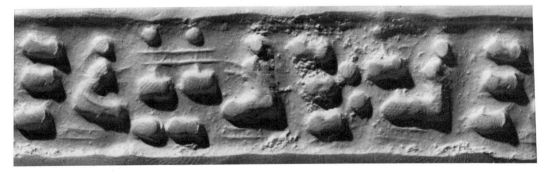

152

153

154

155a

155b

153. Speckled gray serpentine. 17½×19. New impression. *Newell* 31. *Amiet,* 319.

Two women operating loom (?), third woman.

154. Dark green serpentine, speckled. 15× 14½/13½(irregular). Worn. YBC 12832. Said to be from Western Iran.

Probably: four pigtailed women, each with arms raised toward knobbed pole.

For possible Uruk subjects see *Amiet,* 302, 304–08, 310, also *UE* 10, 543 (found out of context).

155. Black limestone. 25×25. Bore 10 (conical at ends)/5/3 (inside). (a) Impression, (b) Shape. NBC 9132.

Ten pigtailed women with joined arms.

Compare the rows of figures in two registers of Protoliterate *UE* 10, 29.

FIGS. 153–155

FIGS. 156–159

156. Gray and light brown alabaster, pink tinged. 21×17. Not bored through. Chipped. YBC 9683.

Insectlike device between two "eye"-lozenges, second row of same, deep vertical terminal.

On an Uruk date for seals like 156–58 see *JAOS* 87 (1967), p. 535. The early date proposed in the last article for some of the material from the deep pit at Tello may have to be extended to include much material still regarded there as Jamdat Nasr, since most of the cylinder seals (except probably pl. 39.3a, 3c, 4b) could be of Uruk date; see under 141–55 above.

157. Green calcite, white streaked. 32×22. NBC 3968. *Yale Library Gazette* 35 (1960), p. 24, no. 4.

Four fish between two rows of connected "eye"-lozenges, horizontal strokes above and below.

158. Brown limestone. 28½×11. Chipped. NBC 9128.

Two fish, lattice borders.

For the design compare *Amiet*, 502, for the style *OIP* 72, 13. A similar, but much later, version of the subject appears in the Mitannian seal, *Ash C*, 951.

159. Black serpentine. 30×14½/13½ (irregular). Worn. NCBS 853.

In vertical bands: (above) dot, lozenge, lattice (?), dot, lozenge; (below) two dots, lizardlike shape, scratched vertical, horizontal oblong, scorpion, linear borders.

Compare somewhat *UVB* 16 (1960), pl. 25b, p. 47, dated Jamdat Nasr, but verbally reported by J. van Dijk to be more likely from an Uruk IV context.

156

157

158

159

160

161

162

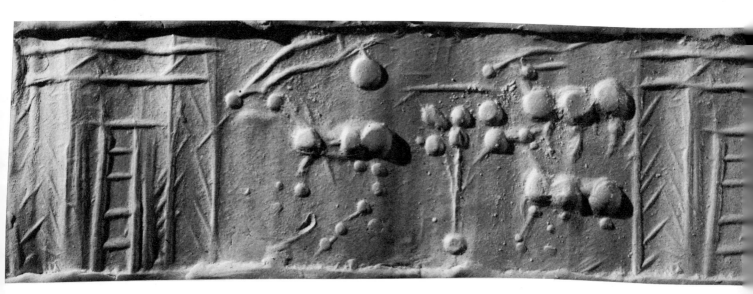

165

BROCADE STYLE

Unquestionable Sumerian seals appeared in the Jamdat Nasr period of Uruk III mixed with Akkadian ones until the latter became dominant after the Ur III Dynasty, toward 2000 B.C. Similarly the development of Proto-Elamite in Jamdat Nasr times reached into Southern Iran as far as Tepe Yahya above the southern bend in the Persian Gulf (Lamberg-Karlovsky, *Iran* 10 [1972], p. 89). The shift from Proto-Elamite to Old Elamite in Southwestern Iran about Susa became significant approaching the Old Akkadian period, until Old Babylonian and to a minor extent Sumerian also became important factors.

The style in 160 recalls Warka IV but should belong to a somewhat later period. This is even more true of 161. Fully Jamdat Nasr pieces featuring horned animals and temples appear in 162–68, 180, without temples in 169–79, 181–82. In the following period, Early Dynastic I, especially in its Brocade phase, animal scenes with other accessories are shown in extremely simplified but often complicated forms, 183–91. A number of seals with animal subject matter, 192–96, may be of similar date, if not earlier, but vary greatly in style. At least three seem to be nonrepresentational, 197–99.

160. Creamy brown marble, mottled. 29×23/22(irregular). Decayed. YBC 12624. *Yale Library Gazette* 35 (1960), p. 24, no. 2.

Sheep with rosette on stalk bent over it; lying ram (?) above sheep protruding from byre topped by ends of reed bundles (?); tasseled standard; rosette on stalk bent over sheep.

The rosettes have been cut in low relief about a central drilling. For rather similar rosettes with sheep, compare the Warka IV piece, 133. In design 160 resembles an impression said to be from Warka III by findspot and style, *UVB* 18, pl. 19j, p. 21. However, the theme apparently goes back to Warka IV; see the impressions presumably from IV: *UVB* 5, pl. 25d, p. 43 = *Amiet*, 186; *UVB* 20, pl. 26k (= 28e), p. 23. Compare *Amiet*, 628–29, 632, all of which show enough degeneration of Uruk style engraving to suggest that they may belong to the earliest phase of the following period.

161. Creamy brown marble, mottled. 24½×25. Bore only at bottom. NBC 9141.

Handled vase and thick line above bull, second line under it, vase in front; byre (or crib?) with side supports; vase before bull, handled vase on thick line over it, line through drilling below.

162. Creamy brown marble. 25×22. Not bored through. Decayed. YBC 12762. *Yale Library Gazette* 35 (1960), p. 24, no. 3.

Bush, tree, ibex, and stag beside shrine; stream below.

For similar scenes see *Amiet*, 382, 390, 393, 625. Compare the stream in 193, 197 below.

163. Creamy brown tinged marble. Not bored through. 36×33. *Newell* 27 (shape fig. 2, p. 4, marked 24). Not shown.

Shrine, bush, two goats.

164. Material like 163 with dark mottling. 41×34. *Newell* 28. Not shown.

Ibex, antelope, shrine.

165. Creamy limestone, brown mottled. 41×33. Not bored through. Decayed. NBC 2577. *BIN* 2, pl. 76d, p. 60.

Shrine, antelope, tree, antelope above gazelle (?); drillings and strokes in field.

It has been suggested that the total of seven drillings at the branches and "root" of the tree in 165 had magical significance, E. Van Buren, *AfO* 13 (1939–41), p. 280. This seems no more likely than in the case of the same total on one of the three floral elements in 169, or the uncertain number on the tree in 162. Similarly, the shrine in the latter bears fourteen dots, or twice seven, but that in 163 has no more than ten, and 168 ten over five.

166. Creamy brown tinged marble. 42×37. Small drilling in bottom. *Newell* 24 (shape fig. 2, p. 4, marked 27). Not shown.

Shrine, three antelopes.

167. Pale brown marble, dark mottling. 23½ ×16. *Newell* 25. Not shown.

Shrine, columns of goats, drilled objects, fish.

168. Light tan limestone, brown mottled. 43× 38. Not bored through. NBC 2591. *BIN* 2, pl. 74g, pp. 58f.

Shrine, lying antelope above goat to left, two lying antelopes above two goats to right; terminal: one spouted pot above another.

169. Light brown marble, dark flecked. 38×30. Not bored through. NBC 5989.

Three ibexes above goat, antelope, and oryx; floral standard before each pair.

170. Creamy limestone, brown mottled. 28× 23. Not bored through. NBC 2580. *BIN* 2, pl. 75a, p. 59.

Four antelopes, star above each of first three.

168

169

170

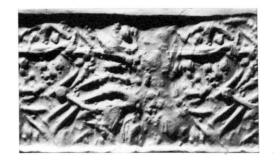

171

173

174

175

171. Shell. 22½×10½. Corroded. NCBS 791.

Two (?) antelopes, dots above; top border: linear device enclosing dots.

Compare *OIP* 72, 43, Protoliterate C.

172. Pale gray marble, spotted. 19½×13. *Newell* 26. Not shown.

Column of antelopes, pots.

173. Reddish brown limestone. 21×21. Bore 6 (conical at ends)/4. Worn. NBC 2587. Bought Baghdad. *BIN* 2, pl. 76b, p. 60.

Two antelopes, two goats (?); ladder device over each, small and large drilling over first and third.

Compare *Amiet*, 377–81, 384, pl. 21 bis D; cf. his p. 76. Of these the closest to 173 in style is 380 from Susa (= *Louvre S.*, 276; see *S.*, 274–75, 277 in contrast). The same flatly cut, rather simplified animal bodies occur in two definitely peripheral seals with this subject: *Ash C*, 716A, which probably has a conoidal top, and *Aulock*, 251, doubly loop-bored. Such evidence, though it is slight, suggests that 173 may have had a peripheral origin.

174. Black limestone. Mark of wear on one side of perforation. 38×21. New impression. *Newell* 57.

Goat, antelope, pots, rosette, fish.

175. Light brown calcite, whitish spot. 17× 14½/13½(irregular). NBC 3165.

Three goats, horns differ, foreleg of each extended, plant through first and third, crescent above.

The motif, a plant through an animal, in 175 and 177 derives from earlier, more naturalistic designs like *Amiet*, 171 (from Warka IV), 397 and 412. It continues into Early Dynastic glyptic, see 235, 254, 331 below. For the posture of the animals in 175 compare *OIP* 72, 460, 790–91, 847; however, the last has been classified as post–Jamdat Nasr in *Amiet* (his 740). In these, and in the first animal here the trunk of the body has been rendered in the tubular fashion much favored in Jamdat Nasr seals. However, the treatment of the bodies of the second and third animals in 175 somewhat suggests the curvilinear outlines so common in the following period.

The crescent, as in 175–76, does not seem to be attested in Uruk period designs. Nor was it part of the usual Jamdat Nasr repertory. When it does occur in Jamdat Nasr or post–Jamdat Nasr seals, it looks more like an added filler than an object of heavenly significance; see, for example, *OIP* 72, 455, 257 (reversed), 467 (both ways). It is therefore possible that the convention of depicting the moon as a crescent grew out of what was originally an aesthetic device. Compare, however, A. Falkenstein, *Archaische Texte aus Uruk,* Berlin, 1936, sign 305, of Warka IV, which looks like a crescent standard, though Falkenstein (p. 60, n. 4) relates it to a sun disk group. See also his sign 301, likewise of IV.

FIGS. 171–175

FIGS. 176–179

176. Creamy limestone, brown mottled. 17×11. NBC 9329.

Lying goat, one foreleg extended, crossed lines behind it, crescent over two strokes above.

Compare the Jamdat Nasr seal *UE* 10, 77, which has a standing animal, its trunk compactly drilled as here, with a crescent above it and a reversed one below.

177. White marble, brown flecked. 48×18. Decayed. NBC 5988. Van Buren, *AfO* 11 (1936–37), p. 7, fig. 10. *Amiet*, 398.

Plant in container (?), one branch extended behind neck and over back of bull.

The authenticity of 177 has been doubted, especially because of the awkwardness of the bull and the vertical branch, R. Boehmer, *BJV* 1 (1961), p. 201, pl. 14, 6 (add to the list of related fakes there: *Brussels Suppl.*, 671, p. 22; probably 1480, p. 23). However, comparable awkwardness occurs in *Basmadschi*, 260, presumably an early Jamdat Nasr seal. It is true that some details in 177 appear to have been crudely reworked, like the rather inept drilling of the scratched eye of the bull. Possibly such questionable areas simply indicate an early date for the reworking. Nevertheless, the genuineness of the piece must be regarded as doubtful.

178. Black limestone. 33×12. NBC 6005.

Running antelope (body cut in three broad segments), tree.

For the same schematic style as in 178–79, but cruder, see *OIP* 72, 191 (Jamdat Nasr).

179. Pinkish brown limestone. 26×12½. Bore 6/4. YBC 12767.

Running antelope, two stars before it, "eye"-lozenge above.

62

176

177

178

179

180

181

182

180. Pinkish brown marble. 36×12/12. New impression. *Newell* 62. *Frankfort,* p. 40, n. 1 (Early Dynastic I).

Shrine, antelope.

181. Glazed (green traces) composition. 35× 12/11(irregular). YBC 6958.

Reversed branch, standing antelope, two adjoining "eye"-lozenges above it.

For typical Jamdat Nasr designs in composition materials see *OIP* 72, 39, 55.

182. Black mica-schist. 54×16½. YBC 12750.

Bird, spouted pot and fish before it, hatched "eye"-lozenge above it, spouted pot (reversed) under it.

Compare *OIP* 72, 201 (Jamdat Nasr) for the pots and for the wings and feet of the bird.

FIGS. 180–182

FIGS. 183–189

183. Green glazed "steatite." 45×16/14(bottom broader than top). NBC 9330.

Lying ibex with clawlike feet (toe and hoof sidewise?), accidental gouge below it; stroke in angle above "eye"-lozenge above curved shape.

For the Early Dynastic I (Brocade) style in 183–91, see *Amiet,* 682–92; for the design in 183 compare *Ash C,* 81–88 from Kish; for a seal tapered like 183 but the other way, see *Ash C,* 94.

184. Dark green basalt. 30×11. Worn. YBC 12501.

Claw-footed lizardlike shape; crossmarked blob above scorpion; strokes in field.

185. Black serpentine. 32×7½. Worn. NBC 3286.

Antelope, scorpion (?) over scorpion, strokes in field.

186. Shell. 26×10½/9(concave). Worn. NCBS 814.

Two horned (?) animals, three birds (?) above.

187. Nephrite. Bottom broken. 23(ext)×8½. *Newell* 64. Not shown.

Three goats, strokes.

188. Gray black limestone. 42×13½/15(convex). *Newell* 63. Not shown.

Two goats, strokes.

189. Black serpentine. 32×10½/9(irregular)/11(convex). Chipped. NCBS 842.

Two antelopes, tête-bêche; added strokes.

Compare *OIP* 72, 233, added tree (Early Dynastic I).

183

184

185

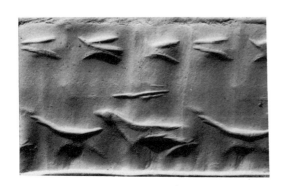

186

189

190

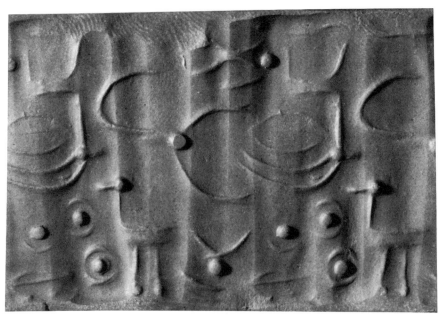

191

190. Black serpentine. 86×11. NCBS 856.

Antelopes as in 189, fish (?) and bird between them; added strokes.

Compare *Berlin,* 65 (top broken).

191. Light and dark brown mottled marble. 47×11½/13½(convex and irregular). Edges chipped. NBC 3983.

Above: horizontal wavy line, sidewise human figure (?) (left side chipped) above scorpion, reversed ibex with bisected ellipse inside horns; below: bird, shape with curves and dot, bisected ellipse, three encircled dots.

For animal legs ending in dots, like the bird's here, see *OIP* 72, 304.

FIGS. 190–191

192. Creamy light brown alabaster. 23½ (ext)×14. Bottom broken off. YBC 12587.

Eagle above goat of unusual type, part of second one, cracked area below.

Compare the eagle in *OIP* 72, 821, post–Jamdat Nasr.

193. Light brown limestone, pink tinged. 37× 12. YBC 13061.

Bird, star and two adjoining "eye"-lozenges above it, three fish in field, all over stream.

For the style of cutting compare *OIP* 72, 625 (goats), 885 (bird); both post–Jamdat Nasr.

194. Pink limestone. 25×12/10(ends cut back). Decayed. YBC 12590. *Yale Library Gazette* 35 (1960), p. 24, no. 5.

Two lines, not quite vertical, connected at bottom (?) (perhaps both once cross hatched, if so possibly trees) above four superimposed curves (hill?), swirl of four birds' heads to left, antelope to right.

The otherwise more naturalistic design with animals (*UE* 3, 239, probably Early Dynastic I) contains stylized hills resembling those depicted in the middle here.

195. Translucent, mottled green talc-schist. 21×13½/12½ (irregular). NBC 9134. *Yale Library Gazette* 35 (1960), p. 24, no. 6.

Antelope, two birds; seven drillings (one with two projections) in field.

192

193

194

195

196

197

198

196. Cloudy agate, brown streaked. 36×14½/13(irregular). Worn. YBC 12826. Said to be from Western Iran.

One animal over another above seven dots; goat over another animal (?) above four dots; vertical stroke above crescent.

The poor condition of 196 makes it difficult to appraise. Its material and quite small perforation point to a late period, but comparisons for the design suggest that it should be of Jamdat Nasr times. The crescent and dots appear to have heavenly significance, which would fit a late date, but it is possible that a similar meaning applied to archaic designs, however infrequently or however conventionalized (see under 175). A number of Jamdat Nasr designs, somewhat resembling that in 196, have dots, usually arranged around a central dot; but the number of dots varies, they are not always in the "sky," and they often look more like mounted rosettes, as in 169, than like stars, *Amiet,* 293–94, *Brussels Suppl.,* 1418 (p. 46), *OIP* 72, 28 (Piedmont Jamdat Nasr).

197. Green serpentine. 26×18. NCBS 869.

Two trees, two bushes (?), obscure object and two spouted vessels among them; stream below.

Compare 162 for the trees or bushes and the stream.

198. Shell. 21×15/14(ends irregular). NBC 9251.

Broken up design: drillings, branches, "ladders," strokes, some connected; terminal "ladder."

For a variety of broken up designs see *OIP* 72, 150–58.

199. Pale brown mottled marble. 25×18. *Newell* 69. Not shown.

Cross shapes separated by "ladders" and a vertical divider.

FIGS. 196–199

FIGS. 200–206

The class here described as Piedmont Jamdat Nasr is especially found in Susiana and Northern Mesopotamia, coming largely from the hilly section of the country. One group shows very stylized geometric forms, 200–08. Others offer animal shapes of considerable variety, 209–12. One definitely Proto-Elamite in style from the region of Susa presents wildlife and floral motifs in a highly sophisticated manner, 213.

200. Glazed (now brown) steatite. 45×13. Some glaze in design. NBC 8145.

Hatched arch, floral fill; top border: triangles and "ladder."

Compare *OIP* 72, 102 (shown with border at bottom), *Ash C,* 74, *Louvre S.,* 99.

201. Glazed (now white) limestone. 21½×8. *Newell* 66. Not shown.

Curved diagonal-filled lines set in triangles.

Compare *OIP* 72, 113, 123.

202. Light green faience. 40×12. NBC 12011.

Alternating concentric triangles twice set in thick borders, separated by heavy band containing triangles; linear borders outside.

203. Brown limestone, discolored. 22×15/16 (convex). NBC 12008.

Alternating triangles, oblique linear fill (once horizontal), thick double linear borders.

204. Gray brown limestone. 19×12/13(convex). NBC 12002.

Thick connected oblique "squares," both obliquely hatched, one of them in linear border, horizontal lines as fill.

205. Light brown limestone. 29×21/23(convex). NBC 12003.

Two continuous angled lines with doubled horizontal lines as fill, set in linear borders having oblique lines on both sides.

206. Light brown limestone, dark spots. 25½×10. NBC 11045.

Pair of "ladder" crosses enclosing solid triangles, set in linear curves, oblong shapes between.

Compare *OIP* 72, 153 (glazed steatite).

200

202

203

204

205

206

207

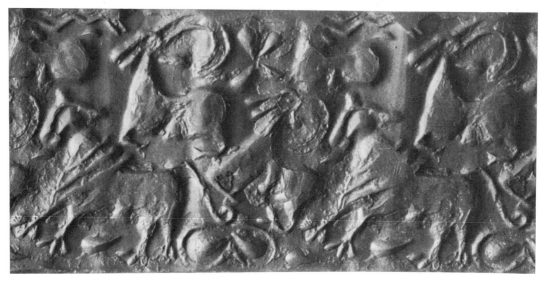

209

208

210

207. Black limestone. 30×11. Ends worn. New impression. *Newell* 68.

Crude "eye"-lozenges with linear fill.

208. Bone. 29×8. Broken at top. New impression. *Newell* 70 (called ivory).

Columns of triangular crosses and alternating triangles, latter in border above, lines below.

Compare *Louvre S.*, 46–47, *MDAI* 43, 103.

209. Glazed (now brown) steatite. 49×16. Worn. YBC 12658. *Yale Library Gazette* 35 (1960), p. 24, no. 8.

Lying ibex over bull beside second ibex, angled lines above, floral elements in field.

Compare *OIP* 72, 54.

210. Olive brown limestone. 51×9/10(convex). NBC 9133.

Goat, star about encircled dot, four encircled dots; chevron borders.

Compare the schematic designs in glazed steatite, *OIP* 72, 78–80.

211. Creamy brown mottled marble. 54×19/20(convex). NBC 9130.

Young creature behind goat, chevron divider, zigzag below, linear borders.

212. Black glazed composition. 26×13. (a) Impression, (b) Shape. YBC 12599. *Yale Library Gazette* 35 (1960), p. 24, no. 7.

Two birds, bird's head, rosette.

For the rosette in relief compare *OIP* 72, 32; for the row of birds, but in drilled style, *OIP* 72, 843; for clawlike feet, *OIP* 72, 882.

213. Light green composition, some dark glaze especially in design. 37×27/26(oval). Bore 10 (conoidal), 3½(inside). Cracked and worn. YBC 12582.

Two rearing ibexes, head turned back, alternating with floral devices; fill of crosses and three-part triangular gouges.

Compare *Louvre S.*, 254. For the range of Proto-Elamite style see *Amiet*, pls. 32–38 bis.

211

212a

212b

213

214a

214b

215

216

217

218

219

Many pieces must be of peripheral origin, including an Iranian four-lobed seal presenting a man in one lobe, beasts in the others, 214. More varied but simpler are animal forms, 215–18, and grotesque shapes, 219–20. Even simpler are some in relief, some with loopbore, some very rudimentary, 221–33.

FIGS. 214–219

214. Four-lobed, deeply pointed hole in each lobe at both ends, inlay perhaps in two of the holes. Dark gray mica-schist. 15×15. (a) Impression, (b) Shape. YBC 12786. Said to be from the Zagros Mountains, Western Iran.

A: Male with one arm raised, bird (?) before him; B: lion reversed over ibex; C: perhaps two sheep, one reversed; D: ibex reversed over antelope (?), added stroke.

For the male figure compare *Ash C*, 721, 756–58. For the inlay holes see 143 above. *OIP* 72, 879, a cylinder of normal type, but with encircled holes about its perforation, contains a figure with an upraised arm. Another figure in it with long hair, standing above an ibex, is of a type attested in prehistoric stamp seals from Gawra and from the Zagros region; compare the ibex-headed demon in 70.

215. Black serpentine. 21×8. NBC 12010.

Goat, young animal above, small shape (?), lion (?), young animal above; divided line borders.

Compare *Ash C*, 713, 715 (both peripheral Jamdat Nasr).

216. "Steatite." 17×16. Worn. NBC 11073.

Scorpion (?) above horned (?) animal with plant (?) behind it, column of three blobs, ibex, T-shape made up of strokes, horned (?) animal with tail (?); line at top.

217. Dark gray serpentine. 18×19. New impression. *Newell* 32.

Two horned animals (second reversed), jagged fill.

Compare *Carchemish* 2, pl. 25b.1; uncertain early context.

218. "Steatite." 16×12½. Cementlike dirt in designs. NBC 12066.

Two schematic creatures.

Compare *Louvre A.*, 61, 12.

219. "Steatite." 35(ext)×17. Worn, broken at top. Bore 6(top)/3. NBC 11075.

Scorpion, forepart (scratchy) at face of lizard (upper forepaw mostly lost); in field: five drillings, obscure objects.

220. Mica-schist. 21×22/21(irregular). Worn. (a) Impression, (b) Shape. NBC 10951.

Design of spirals and vases (all recut?).

For spirals in relief as here compare *Ash C*, 725, 746.

220x, NCBS 716, a very worn "steatite" cylinder, 16½×13/11(irregular), probably had spirals in relief.

221. "Steatite." 17½×10/8(irregular). (a) Impression, (b) Shape. NCBS 714.

Shown sidewise: linear border, horned animal (?), reversed animal (?), angled shape, linear border.

Compare perhaps the "three line inscription" impressed on a tablet, found at Babylon, believed to be late, Eilers *AfO* 10 (1936), pp. 359f.

222. Brown limestone. 18½(face 13½)×20. NBC 11091.

Two spiral twists with thick line between.

223. "Steatite." 28½(top 4)×13½/12(thinner below top). (a) Impression, (b) Shape. NCBS 833.

Irregular groove at top, festoon band above zigzag over small crosses in festoon band.

Compare the more regular design in *Louvre S.*, 24.

220a 220b

221a 221b

222

223a 223b

224a

224b

225a

225b

225c

226a

226b

226c

224. "Steatite." Limestone deposit in part of design. 56(design 40)×22/19(irregular). Bore 7/5. Rounded ends. (a) Impression, (b) Shape. NBC 9362.

Tree (?) between two spiral devices; linear borders.

Compare *Louvre S.,* 114, *Ash C,* 740.

225. "Steatite." 18×18. (a) Impression, (b) Base, (c) Shape. NBC 11074.

(a) Two triangular pointed shapes with blob between, at side cross-hatched oval; (b) dot-filled cross.

226. Dark gray mica-schist. 28(design 22)×17/16 (tapers to top). (a) Impression, (b) Base, (c) Shape. YBC 12496.

(a) Row of framed lozenges, floral (?) device in one, encircled deeply pointed holes as fill; (b) three encircled dots.

Two cylinders with loop on top and design on base, *OIP* 61, fig. 381.3–4, the first with face and the second with base like 226, both probably of Amuq G (mostly Jamdat Nasr). Compare the tapered cylinder with loop on top, possibly Early Minoan geometric design on base, *Troy 3,* p. 298, 35–478, survival in later level 6.

FIGS. 227–229

227. Loopbore at top. Dark gray "steatite." 32×23. (a) Impression, (b) Oblique. New impression. *Newell* 650 (fig. 2, p. 4).

Blobs beside encircled rosette; column of blobs set in animal (?) shape, linear cross with pair of vertical lines on either side.

228. Dark gray "steatite." 22×12/10½(irregular, ends cut back and broken). Chipped. (a) Impression, (b) Shape. YBC 12648.

"Tree," deeply cut vertical with three dots on either side; linear borders.

For the "tree" see *Ash C*, 744, classified as peripheral Jamdat Nasr.

229. Dark gray serpentine. 23½×9/11(convex). NBC 12009.

Twisted upright (snake?), column of bent curves, tree; heavy linear borders.

227a

227b

228a

228b

229

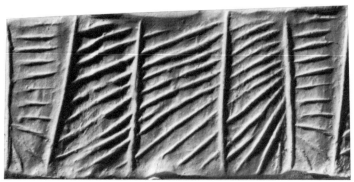

230a

230b

231

232a

232b

233

230. Dark gray serpentine. 38(seal 28)×14½/ 17(convex). Thin loop on top, scratched cross on bottom. (a) Impression, (b) Shape. NBC 12014.

Four vertical lines with irregular horizontals between.

231. Light green alabaster. 20/19×12½/ 11(irregular). NBC 9346.

Two groups of horizontal lines separated by two pairs of vertical dividers; linear borders.

232. Dark gray "steatite." 21×11/10(irregular). Bore (off center, worn to one side) 3/2½. (a) Impression, (b) Shape. NBC 10963. Said to be from Tepe Giyan.

Diagonal lines; linear borders.

That 232 was intended for a bead is indicated by the coarse impression it makes; that it was so used is suggested by the worn perforation.

233. Baked clay. 43×29. NBC 12007.

Crude lattice.

FIGS. 230–233

Early Dynastic I

A few seals may be of Early Dynastic I, though they lack the Brocade mannerism common to the period. Early variants include the sexual suggestiveness of 234 featuring scorpions and a lizard; the floral decorative style of 235 including rosettes, sheep, and insects; the simple treatment of animals in 236–38, more varied in 239, the splendor of contrasted beasts in 240; finally 241, perhaps of slightly later date, a man seated before a bull.

234. Green gray speckled serpentine. 19×11/9½(irregular). YBC 12627.

Scorpion facing down, vertical shape with two angled strokes at each end, scorpion facing up, lizard shape with short projections (hair?) on head, vertical shape, scorpion facing down, vertical line.

For the scorpions compare some early impressions from Ur: *UE* 3, 42, 259–63, 267–73. Of these designs, 42 and 268–70, the last containing also a lizard, show as their central figure a woman in a spread-legged position, suggesting both conception and birth. The same idea was probably evoked in *UE* 3, 283, but with a froglike figure replacing the woman; *UE* 3, 282, apparently a stamp seal impression like the last, may belong with these designs, since it may depict the mating of frogs; compare the similar scene but with more human figures in a hemispheroid found out of context, *Gawra* 1, 3. In this type of design where an animal is the central figure, its head might be mistaken for human. This could apply to the curious lizardlike design in the stamp seal 74 above. In any case the subject matter, and to some extent the composition, of many of these seals sufficiently resemble the design in 234 to suggest that the latter was concerned with fertility also. See *JAOS* 87 (1967), pp. 275, 279.

235. Pink brown limestone. 55×15½. YBC 12760.

Nine-petal rosette between two ten-petal ones, each with central encircled dot, 18 dots (?) (one worn) in field; two-line divider; three lying sheep, each with plant bent behind it; two-line divider; lizard shape between tails of two confronted scorpions.

On the plants behind the sheep see 175 above; for the curious rendering of the sheep's feet compare the "clawlike" ones of the ibex in 183; for the drillings in the bodies of the scorpions see the animals in 168. The rosettes resemble *Amiet*, 703, less so his 705, 707, all dated Early Dynastic I. However, similar rosettes also occur much later, being especially favored in the peripheral style chiefly known from Brak of Early Dynastic III; see *Amiet*, 980, 982–83, *Ash C*, 806–07.

Banquet scenes in early Dynastic III traditional style also present plants growing behind sheep in 331, in 332 a row of striated animals, in 333 a hatched animal contest. Though in a more sophisticated manner than 235 such pieces show the persistence of earlier traits.

236. Dark gray serpentine. 17½×9½. Badly cracked. NBC 11034.

Antelope (?), lion.

237. Shell. 12×7. Worn. YBC 12507.

Lion, goat (?), tree.

Compare *Ash C*, 109–10, pp. 22, 25; see also the Jamdat Nasr seal, *Ash C*, 26. For an interesting version of the subject, probably of Early Dynastic I, see *Parrot*, 59, with a young one under the pursued animal.

234

235

236

237

238

239

240

241

238. Pale brown limestone. 25×15. Very worn. NCBS 819.

Lion (?), sheep (?), floral motif (?).

Compare *Ash C*, 111, possibly of Early Dynastic I.

239. Pale green calcite, some brown limestone deposits. 25×11½. NBC 11053.

Two rows of four horned animals, first at top has young below; crosses and blobs as fillers; hatched band divider.

Contrast the simple alternation of vertical and horizontal stripes in the animals' bodies with the jagged vertical markings in *OIP* 72, 315 from an Early Dynastic IIIa context.

240. Pale green calcite. 37×21. New impression. *Newell* 681 ("doubtful because of eagle"). *Fauna*, p. 83 ("Uruk IV"). *Amiet*, 762 (transition to Early Dynastic).

Crouching ibex over animal leg, leaping lion over lying bull; spread-winged eagle over lying bull and ibex, in latter's horn animal leg, erect dagger outside, lying horned animal above.

Compare *Brussels Suppl*, 1477 (p. 21), said to be from Nippur.

241. Pale brown limestone, green stains. 20×11/10(irregular). YBC 13062.

Seated man holding branch by stem, crescent (?) above; bull, scorpion over it, plant behind.

Despite many differences the design in 241 recalls scenes among the early impressions from Ur, probably of Early Dynastic I, which feature a seated man with a pot and an animal emerging from a byre, *UE* 3, 337–48. As in 241 such designs often contain floral motifs and animals like the scorpion. For a man seated before a bull, holding a branch by the stem, see *Louvre S.*, 468, which is quite naturalistic in manner, peripheral in style, and probably late Early Dynastic in date.

FIGS. 238–241

Early Dynastic II

FIGS. 242–245

In Early Dynastic II, despite a relatively short life about 2700 B.C., a completely new style emerged, dominated by grotesque human shapes, often imaginary, with interwoven animal forms. In 242 a warrior attacks a bull offset by a reversed eagle. Seal 243 presents facing seated figures beside a monster, a hero, and crossed animals, while 244 places a hero between groups of beasts, all beside a reversed creature over a human scene depicting anal sex. 245–47 feature a hero partly in long underwear between lions and goats, and 248–58 show virtually naked beings in conflict with various beasts. Multiformed monsters combined with more conventional conflicts in 259–60, a hero on one knee controls a beast on either side in 261–66, while 267–68 show only beasts in conflict.

242. Light brown composition, traces of light green glaze. 28×22/19(oval ends; whole shape irregular because of deep cutting). Decayed. YBC 12653. *Yale Library Gazette* 35 (1960), p. 25, no. 18.

Hero with upright hair (?) prodding bull with rosette (?) above; two hatched semicircles over reversed full-faced (?) lion-headed eagle.

For the eagle in a double arch compare *Amiet*, 1296 and *OIP* 72, 269, both of about the same date as 242 or slightly later.

243. Pale green calcite, brown markings. 36× 27. Worn. YBC 6962.

Inscription above small seated figure, holding rectangle-topped rod, before larger seated figure holding long staff; scorpion above goat's head; two tall monsters with serpentine trunks held by full-face nude belted hero between them, dagger (?) and snake (?) (broken) under the hero's arms, the second monster also held by hero in fringed kilt who has goat's head behind him; he looks left grasping goat crossed by bull; vertical streamer on short pole before the hero.

244. Pale brown limestone, 26½×18. YBC 12825.

Nude belted hero, looking left, holding: to right, tail of lion crossed with goat; to left, mane of lion crossed with lion; reversed bull (?) with head turned back above scene of anal intercourse.

The hero has a lock of hair curved down to right. The projections on his head (and in 241, 245, and 260) are perhaps also locks of hair rather than horns; compare the careful rendering of horns on the bullman in 253. If intended for locks of hair, it could be that they were deliberately arranged to look like horns as well. The deeply cut body of the reversed "bull" recalls that of the more simply rendered bull in 243. On "anal" intercourse see 515.

245. Light brown marble, darker mottling. 23×18. YBC 13048.

Reversed lion above goat's head; two rampant bulls with head turned back, between them hero wearing long open robe, tucked up in front.

The garment worn by the hero has been described as if it were of one piece, but in the more detailed renderings of 246–47, 255 it seems to consist of at least two, a skirt and a folded up undergarment; see also *Ash C*, 149A of similar date.

242

243

244

245

247

248

250

251

246. Creamy marble, brown mottled. 19½×17. *Newell* 80. Not shown.

Hero in flat cap and long open robe upending lion on either side by leg, long curved line under each arm; both lions grasped by tail and stabbed by similarly clad heroes (one to left worn); dagger.

247. Light brown marble. 22×16. Chipped. NBC 6008.

Hero clad as in 246, holding: to right, goat crossed with lion, to left, rampant goat with head turned back; horn of the latter in grasp of one-eyed full-face nude belted "monster" with upright curls, who stabs rampant lion; the latter held by nude hero in flat cap (?) (chipped), who also grasps the lion of the original group; erect dagger in field.

The "monster" seems to be one-eyed, resembling the figure in 146 vaguely.

248. Light brown limestone, darker mottling. 29×12. Worn. YBC 9686.

One of two crossed lions held by bullman, facing left, his other arm raised; rampant goat (?) with head turned back, held (?) by nude belted hero whose other arm is raised toward lion of original group; vertical line and dagger (?) in field.

249. Brown limestone. 28×14. *Newell* 78. Not shown.

Two nude heroes holding pairs of crossed ibexes and crossed lions.

250. Light green calcite. 26½×11. YBC 9677.

Nude belted hero between two erect goats with head thrown back, each attacked by one of two crossed lions.

The rendering of the goats with their heads pointing up is quite common in late Early Dynastic glyptic; see 298. In Early Dynastic II seals, however, heads are normally placed so that, though twisted, they return to the line of the composition as in 260.

251. Corroded limestone. 18½×10½. NCBS 745.

Two crossed goats; two crossed lions, one held by hero wearing dagger.

Compare *Amiet*, 926.

252. Pale brown marble, mottled. 29½×16. *Newell* 81. Not shown.

Uncertain crossed animals held by full-face bullman and hero who also hold crossed lion and bull; erect dagger in field.

Compare *Amiet*, 903.

253. Brown alabaster, red streaked. 33×21/20(concave). NBC 9125. *Yale Library Gazette* 35 (1960), p. 25, no. 16.

Lion rampant beside nude hero with long hair who holds tail of upended lion that bites leg of bullman with two horns, the latter grasps the lion's leg on one side and one of two crossed lions on the other; inscription above ibex. Perhaps recut; as suggested by muscular legs and a tendency to equal width of lines.

254. Pale green calcite. 23×14/13(irregular). Worn. YBC 9990.

Nude hero with upright hair grasping leg of upended lion, other leg held by nude hero who also grasps rampant gazelle, plant behind back of latter perhaps confused with dagger wielded by nude hero with upright curls who probably holds the gazelle's tail; latter confused with upright dagger; inscription above plant (?) (or scratches).

255. Green glazed composition. 30×23. Bore 6/4. Worn. NBC 9101. *Yale Library Gazette* 35 (1960), p. 25, no. 27.

Hero, clad as in 247, perhaps grasping tail of rampant lion (area chipped and worn), the latter leans forward to seize tail and horns of upended ibex (blood from mouth below it), which is also attacked by second lion, lower foreleg of latter crosses (?) horn of goat's head in field, second goat's head above the lion's tail.

256. Dark mottled, light brown marble. 16×10. *Newell* 86. Not shown.

Two bullmen stabbing backs of lions with heads turned back, reversed ibex under the lions; eagle at end above.

Compare *Amiet*, 869.

257. Light brown limestone. 23×17/16(irregular). New impression. *Newell* 79.

Lion attacking goat with head turned back, which is held by full-face hero, the hero menaced by feline to right, by scorpion and rampant goat to left; in field: obscure object, bull's head.

For the curious treatment of the lion's paws compare 258; see also *OIP* 72, 282, from an Early Dynastic II context, though possibly of I by style.

258. Green serpentine, creamy mottling. 28×15/14½(irregular). NCBS 867.

Seated figure with one arm raised, standing male with bent arms; rampant lion attacking one of two adjacent goats, the other held by original figure; in field: crescent, star, two scorpions, angled lines.

253

254

255

257

258

259

260

261

262

259. Limestone. 36×27/26(irregular). Decayed. YBC 12623. *Yale Library Gazette* 35 (1960), p. 25, no. 15 (plate).

Upended antelope, scorpion (?) above neck; hero with horn bent forward, bull's head below arm, stabbing one of two lions that form lower limbs of monster with human torso, shown full face with upright curls.

Compare the monster in the impression from Kish, *Ash C,* 146.

260. Pale green calcite. 26×20. New impression. *Newell* 77. *Amiet,* 912.

Hero holding turned-back heads of ibexes, dagger on either side of the hero; lion with head turned back, monster whose tails end in feline heads turned back in the monster's grasp, goat's head below, scorpion behind.

261. Green calcite, creamy patches. 22×14/13(ends oval). Worn. NBC 9349.

Nude belted hero, two projections on head, on one knee between two plants, his raised arms holding on either side foreleg of rampant bull with head turned back, the bull's horns held by bullman.

262. Light brown limestone. 38×23/20 (warped). Split and badly decayed. NBC 9366.

Nude belted hero with upright hair on one knee grasping upended antelope to right and upended lion to left, scorpion above the animals' confronted heads.

FIGS. 259–262

263. "Steatite." 25½×15/13(irregular). *Newell* 76. Not shown. *Frankfort,* pl. Xb. *Amiet,* 853.

Hero on one knee holding leg of antelope and of lion.

264. Creamy brown limestone. 22×10/9½(irregular). YBC 12631.

Nude belted hero on one knee holding: to right, upended ibex; to left, bull, latter crossed with lion attacking original ibex.

265. Light green calcite. 15½×12. Bore (off center; larger at top) 4/3/2½. Gimbel Collection 1.

Nude belted hero on one knee holding upended goat (?) on either side, spread-winged eagle at the goats' heads; ground line.

266. Brown limestone, limestone deposits in design. 31×16. Chipped. NBC 11049.

Three pairs of crossed lions (?), kneeling hero grasping throat of lion in two of the pairs; inscription; two-line divider; similar scene below but with walking goat instead of inscription.

267. Brown limestone. 28×13/12(irregular). New impression. *Newell* 72.

Crossed lions attacking ibex with head turned back on one side, reversed antelope on other, goat's forepart (?) attached to the ibex's neck.

268. Light brown limestone. 27×14. NBC 9102.

Full-face lion with foot against and bending over to bite upended goat (?); group: scorpion between two crossed lions which attack bull (tail between legs) to right and goat to left; dagger (?) between legs of goat. Possibly recut.

264

265

266

267

268

269

270

271

272

275

276

Early Dynastic III

ANIMALS

With Early Dynastic III the extraordinary character of the previous period was transformed into a more conventional guise. Crossed animals are the dominant but relatively uninspired theme of 269–79, eagles becoming the chief motif in 280–87 while the serpents of 288 offer a contrast. Human figures, often in a secondary role, are nevertheless important in 289–301, becoming more significant, though sometimes of monstrous form, in 302–16.

FIGS. 269–276

269. Black limestone. 32½×17/16(cut back at signs). Bore (conical at ends) 9½/5/4. NBC 9350.

Lioness (?) attacking gazelle with head turned back which is also attacked by one of two crossed lions, other lion attacking ibex with head thrown back; inscription. Of the inscription, the upper sign has been added over one horn of the ibex and the tail of the lioness, the one below over the lower part of the ibex.

The conical holes at the ends of the perforation may have once held inlay as in the case of *Ash C*, 160.

270. Gray brown limestone, darker mottling. 26×16. Worn. NBC 5997.

Two crossed lions, attacking ibex (?) to right; gazelle (?) to left, latter also attacked by panther (?) (dotted body); crescent.

On the spotted feline as probably a panther see *Fauna*, p. 11, n. 7; compare 296, 298, 308–09 below.

271. Pale brown limestone. 20×11. Corroded. NCBS 772.

Two crossed lions attacking bull (?) (long tail) to right, antelope to left; indeterminate marks above.

272. Shell. 23×11½. Worn. NCBS 801.

Two crossed lions attacking antelope on either side.

273. Olive brown limestone. 43×25/21(irregular). Corroded. *Newell* 647 (impression and shape). Not shown. *Amiet*, 999 ("Royal Cemetery style, archaizing").

Crossed full-face lions attacking bull and ibex, full-face lion attacking crossed human-headed bull.

274. Shell. 33×17. Worn. *Newell* 49. Not shown. *Amiet*, pl. 77 bis F ("Royal Cemetery style").

Crossed lions attacking horned animal on either side, spread-winged eagle over horned animals, animal below.

275. Olive brown limestone. 27×12/11(irregular). Corroded. NCBS 830.

Two crossed lions attacking goat (?) with head turned back to right; upended sheep to left; scorpionman, small scorpion (?) before it.

For the scorpionman see 345 below.

276. Gray brown limestone. 16½×11½. NBC 11048.

Two crossed lions attacking horned animal on either side, three horizontal strokes as terminal.

277. Brownish limestone. 24×12½. *Newell* 65. Not shown.

Crossed animals with other on either side.

Compare *UE* 10, 70, shell, unfinished.

278. Shell. 27×11/10(irregular). NCBS 823.

Lion crossed with bull (?); rest unfinished.

279. Lapis lazuli. 23×10½/7(cut back on one side). Worn. NBC 5940.

Erect lion, upended goat, bull crossed with human-headed bull (head cut almost flat).

Perhaps the present design represents a late Early Dynastic reworking of a worn older piece.

Two very worn seals probably show animal contests: 279x, NCBS 719, limestone, 14½×8½; 279xx, NCBS 812, shell, 23×16/14(irregular).

280. Pale green calcite. 21×14. Chipped. NBC 6000.

Spread-winged eagle (head broken) between lying quadruped and ibex.

If the badly worn device above the quadruped is in fact a wing, possibly a winged lion (see *Amiet*, 1276–80) was meant to be represented here. However, both the posture and a single wing are unusual, so perhaps only extended horns were intended.

281. Pale brown limestone, 21×12. *Newell* 44. Not shown.

Spread-winged eagle, on either side goat with forefoot on mound, terminal: axe (?).

282. Light brown limestone. 34×18. *Newell* 50. Not shown.

Spread-winged eagle with goats, their heads turned back on either side, scorpion below; two crossed lions (?).

283. Light brown limestone. 26×12/11 (irregular). *Newell* 51. Not shown. *Amiet,* 1229.

Spread-winged eagle, to right: gazelle with head turned back, to left: lion with full-face head down; below: four gazelles.

284. Black serpentine. 15×9. New impression. *Newell* 670 ("forgery because of eagle"). *Amiet,* 1230.

Lion-headed eagle holding weapons (?) over backs of lion and bull, antelope over line to right of the eagle, triangle to left.

285. Black "steatite." 29×10. Bore (to one side at bottom) 4×2½. Gimbel Collection 3.

Two spread-winged two-headed eagles, each over lion with head turned back, scorpion facing down; linear divider; four birds, crescent over three of them.

An eagle with two lions' heads appears in an impression from Nippur, *Philadelphia*, 46, Early Dynastic III. Those in 285 are perhaps more likely related to linear renderings of the lion-headed eagle as in *CANES*, 57, Early Dynastic II, where the bisected lion's head of the eagle points to our design.

The birds in the lower register of 285 resemble those in *Boehmer*, 631–33, all probably late Early Dynastic, though the last may be Early Akkadian. In these pieces the birds have short vertical strokes over their backs; in 285, crescents. Furthermore *Boehmer*, 632 shows a use of hatching and of linear-outlined forms comparable to those here.

286. Light brown limestone, darker mottling. 23/22×12/11½(irregular). Bore (crooked) 4/2½. NBC 9344.

Spread-winged eagle above festoon, below lying goat, its head turned back on line.

For a similar scene compare *UE* 2, 85 (=10, 97).

278

279

280

284

285

286

287

288

290

291

292

294

287. Impression on jar sealing with rope marks. Seal 26 (ext). YBC 13070. Nippur D 101b. Found with 288 in a later context.

Crescent above spread-winged eagle between two quadrupeds facing away.

Compare *Boehmer*, 87 Akkadian Ib (=*Parrot*, 11, Ur III).

288. Impressions on jar sealing with rope marks. Two rollings almost certainly of the same cylinder. Seal 16 (ext). YBC 13069. Nippur D 101a. Same findspot as 287.

Head of serpent (?), head of scorpion, intertwined serpent design.

For the serpent design see *Amiet*, 1247–48; compare the scorpion beside an intertwined serpent design in an archaizing Early Akkadian seal, *Boehmer*, 664.

289. Lapis lazuli. 15½×8½. *Newell* 113. Not shown. *Amiet*, 971 ("Early Dynastic III, archaizing").

Erect ibex held by hero who leads (?) bull, on the latter small animal stabbed by bullman.

290. Corroded limestone. 29×20/18½(concave). Worn. NCBS 863.

Two heros grasping tails (?) of crossed sheep (?) and rampant lion (?); between them, floral motif.

Compare *Ash C*, 122–28 (Early Dynastic II–III). *Amiet*, 972 ("Early Dynastic III, archaizing").

291. Light brown limestone. 18×10½. NBC 11047.

Two crossed lions attacking antelope with head back on either side, hero raising weapon (?).

292. Shell. 19×12½. Cracked to left. YBC 12642.

Hero raising dagger (?) and holding bent staff; two crossed lions attacking goat to left, gazelle to right.

293. Pale brown limestone. 15×9. *Newell* 75. Not shown.

Crossed lions attacking horned animal on either side, hero wielding dagger (?) and goats' horns (?).

294. Dark greenish brown mottled serpentine. 21½×11. Worn. NCBS 779.

Two crossed lions attacking horned animal on either side; hero protecting ruminant to right, third lion attacking ruminant to left; crescent above.

As usual the hero or bullman is not threatening the ruminant he protects, but menacing its lion adversary with a weapon.

FIGS. 287–294

295. Light brown limestone. 35×18. Chipped. Gimbel Collection 2.

Two full-face lions attacking upended goat between them, the second lion crossed with gazelle (?), before which nude hero threatens the lion with dagger while holding the gazelle's leg; eagle or lion-headed eagle above two horizontal lines.

296. Pale brown limestone, dark flecked. 24½× 15. NBC 9359.

Nude hero with upright hair (in bandeau?) holding bow and stabbing at reversed panther (?) which is crossed by bullman with two horns (?) and long hair, that curves back over one of the panther's legs; the bullman stabs at turned-back head of lion crossed with reversed bull, a leg of which it bites; scorpion.

297. Light brown limestone. 37×22. Bore 7/5. Worn. New impression. *Newell* 73. *Amiet,* 1013 ("Royal Cemetery style").

Hero holding dagger and grasping stag (?), crossed by lion that attacks antelope, the horns of which are held by bullman wielding dagger, who is crossed by human-headed bull; secondary: inscription, two-line divider, two full-face lions' heads, two-line divider, two winged lions under crescent.

For the winged lions in the secondary scene compare *Amiet,* 1276–80.

295

296

297

298

300

301a

301b

298. Light brown limestone. 38×25. Decayed. NBC 2585. *BIN* 2, pl. 75 d, p. 59.

Group: lizard under two crossed lions that attack ibex with head up on either side; to right, nude bearded hero holding bow (?) and brandishing dagger (?); to left, bearded bullman with thick streaming hair (trace of horn, ear, and tail), holding a tail of the ibex and brandishing dagger, erect panther (by dots) behind him.

299. Shell. 49½×16½. Worn. *Newell* 38. Not shown.

Struggling human figures and animals in two registers.

300. Lapis lazuli. 38×13. Bore 4/1½ (irregular). Worn and chipped. YBC 13053.

Animal with head turned back, another with head up, rampant animal, another with head turned back held by bullman (?), gazelle (?), hero with upright hair brandishing dagger; three-line divider; symbol (or ligature of inscription); animal with head turned back attacked by lion (?), two animals, hero with upright hair, gazelle (?).

301. Lapis lazuli. 38×7½. Probably remains of pin inside. Worn. (a) Impression, (b) Shape. YBC 12633. *Yale Library Gazette* 35 (1960), p. 26, no. 27.

Hero between two gazelles, lion on either side, second hero between two antelopes; two-line divider; hero between two gazelles, lion and gazelle reversed, hero holding gazelle attacked by lion; two-line divider; hero between two gazelles, lion on either side, lion attacking antelope.

In three registers *Amiet,* 1127 (late Early Dynastic).

FIGS. 298–301

302. Black serpentine. 24×13½. New impression. *Newell* 85.

Full-face hero clasps on either side full-face human-headed bull attacked by lion, the lions' tails connected by horizontals.

The jagged appearance of the mouth of the human-headed bull to the right, coming above a chipped area, suggests recutting. The use of small drillings throughout differentiates it from the similar scene in *Amiet*, 1023 ("Royal Cemetery style").

303. Black serpentine. 25×17. NBC 3216. *Yale Library Gazette* 35 (1960), p. 26, no. 24.

Four erect human-headed bulls with heads turned back, full face; first and fourth each held by full-face bullman, third by full-face nude hero in horned crown; inscription over two horizontal lines, small bearded figure holding adjacent tails below.

304. Impressions on tablet. Seal c. 24. (a) Reverse, (b) Drawing. NBC 5823. *BIN* 8, 47, pl. 160 A (poor). *Yale Library Gazette* 45 (1970), p. 55, no. 1 (drawn).

Full-face lion attacking bullman (also twice upper edge) with arm before face, nude belted full-face bearded hero (also reversed far right) grasping erect full-face human-headed bull with head turned back, two horizontals above small belted male in hat (?), nude full-face bearded hero (also edge below) with long tress on either side, wielding dagger and holding (?) horn of bull with head back (dagger and back of bull also lower far left), snake (?), nude male figure (upper far left).

The style is close to that in *Frankfort*, pl. 12b, late Early Dynastic; see also *Amiet*, pl. 82–85. The horns suggested for the second full-face hero are doubtful; so is the interpretation of the small figure (compare perhaps *Amiet*, pl. 77 bis H). Here the figure seems to be wearing a hat with a brim, an odd detail for Early Dynastic glyptic.) A bull with its head back as drawn has few if any parallels in Early Dynastic cylinders (*Ash C*, 791 is very doubtful), but they are well attested in Akkadian seals.

302

303

304a

304b

305

306

307

309

310

305. Lapis lazuli. 19×9. NBC 3291. *Yale Library Gazette* 35 (1960), p. 26, no. 23.

Bullman clasping human-headed scorpion in horned crown; kilted hero with upright hair holding gazelle to left, stag to right, latter attacked by full-face lion, which is stabbed and its tail held by nude hero.

In small scale and rather meticulous style 305 is comparable with a group of peripheral seals known especially from impressions found at Brak in the upper Khabur valley; see *Ash C*, pp. 144f., especially seals 794, 807. For the "scorpionman" see *Amiet*, 1245, pp. 133f.

306. Black serpentine. 18×10. NBC 9358.

Nude hero with upright hair holding antelope to right, ibex to left, lion attacking from either side; between the lions' tails, man holding objects on head, two horizontal lines on either side of him; below: lionserpent (?) to right, vertical serpent to left.

307. Light brown limestone, stained. 29½× 16½. Cracked (burnt?). New impression. *Newell* 74.

Hero as in 306 clasping antelopes attacked by lion (?) on either side, each lion has drilling at back, man with flat object on head.

The man holding an object on his head in 306–07 recalls by his gesture the scorpion-man in 275 and 345, but also suggests the row of men carrying building material in the lower register of 341. The antelope to the left is apparently urinating.

308. Lapis lazuli. 31×18/17 (irregular). *Newell* 83. Not shown.

Central design as in 306 but with full-face lions; panther (?) attacks stag protected by bullman.

309. Lapis lazuli. 37×20. NBC 2588. *BIN* 2, pl. 75b, p. 59. *Amiet*, 1121 (late Early Dynastic).

Panther attacking one of two gazelles held by hero, bird at tail of the gazelle to left, branch above; full-face lion attacking stag held by bullman.

310. Lapis lazuli. 25½×17. Worn. NBC 6004.

Stag with head turned back, speared (?) by bullman; nude hero between two goats, lion attacking on either side.

FIGS. 305–310

311. Lapis lazuli. 17×8½/8(irregular). Very worn. NBC 5931.

Group of nude hero with upright hair between two goats (?) attacked by lion on either side; the lion to right restrained by hero (?) grasping tail, the one to left menaced by bullman with arm raised, long hair (?), tail between legs.

312. Dark green serpentine. 22×12. YBC 8940.

Nude hero with upright hair (?) (head broken), holding goat to right, gazelle to left, lion attacking on either side, tail of the lion to left held by second hero; vertical snake.

Compare *Boehmer,* 28; placed in his earliest Akkadian phase, but very possibly still Early Dynastic.

313. Lapis lazuli. 17×11. New impression. *Newell* 87. *Boehmer,* 18 ("Akkadian I a").

Bullman holding staff and tail of lion from group as in 306.

The design under the horizontals in the terminal (a disk in crescent above) may be a ligature for the sun god; compare the possible ligature in 300.

314. Brownish limestone. 23½×16. Worn. *Newell* 88. Not shown. *Boehmer,* 19 ("Akkadian Ia").

Group as in 306, tail of lion to left held by stabbing bullman.

315. Pale brown marble. 21×16. Chipped. New impression. *Newell* 678 (p. 11, "condemned by technique"). Heidenreich, *AfO* 10, (1935–36), p. 371 (genuine).

Hero grappling lion attacking goat, hero holding long pole (?), hero protecting goat from lion held by hero, tree.

Compare *Ash C,* 184 (uncertain phase of Early Dynastic III).

316. Pale brown alabaster. 19½×12. Worn. NCBS 785.

Goat (?) with head turned back; two heroes with ruminant (?) and lion (?) between them.

311

312

313

315

316

317

318

319

320

321

322

323

Human figures present the central subject in other Early Dynastic themes. The earliest of Early Dynastic II (317–18) or perhaps slightly later (319–25) show seated couples, usually with one or more attendants. In Early Dynastic III the same subject appears normally in one principal register, the other register usually devoted to animal contests or other subjects (326–38). Building operations, probably all of III, are also shown in one of the two registers of 339–42, while 343–44 are devoted to chariots. Boats with human prows packed with other details are featured in 345–48, simplified boats in 349–50. A hero is centered in 351, while rows of men occur in 352–53. A purely geometric design fills 354.

317. Rock crystal. 25×19. Bore (deeply conical at ends) 5½/2. YBC 9991. *Yale Library Gazette* 35 (1960), p. 25, no. 19.

Female and male attendant before seated male with cup, cross in disk above; spray hanging down; seated female with cup, stand, male attendant, rosette (in relief) above; inscription above small seated female with cup.

318. Light gray green calcite. 25×14. Decayed. YBC 13040. Said to be from Western Iran.

Seated female raising cup (?), seated male (?), kilted attendant.

319. Creamy marble, brown mottled. 28×15. Chipped. YBC 12616. *Yale Library Gazette* 35 (1960), p. 25, no. 20.

Seated female and male, each holding wavy object; between them enclosed seven-petal rosette with central encircled dot above zigzag band over two connected arches, each containing thick vertical stroke; shrine.

For earlier rosettes see 235 above; for later ones, resembling that in 319, compare *Ash C*, 133, *Amiet*, 935, 1378, all probably Early Dynastic II. The arches between the figures could depict a kind of table, or they may represent low niches which, combined with the zigzag band and the rosette above, formed part of the decoration of a temple.

320. Light yellow alabaster, brown streaked. 24×10. Chipped. YBC 12625.

Two seated figures, each holding spray, plant between them; shrine.

321. "Steatite." 14½(ext)×10/8½(irregular). NCBS 720.

Two figures seated back to back, attendant before each, tree.

322. Pale green calcite. 22×11½/10(irregular). Worn. NCBS 783.

Two seated figures, attendant between them gesturing toward the one to left who holds cup.

323. Pale brown alabaster. 17×10½/9(narrow bottom). NCBS 753.

Two seated figures, one to right holding cup (?); attendant with raised arms between them.

324. Pale brown alabaster. 22×13. NBC 6007.

Attendant with arms raised toward hands of two seated figures who have long arm in common behind them.

325. Shell. 22×13½. New impression. *Newell* 34.

Attendant with arm raised between two facing seated figures, vessel above, crossed animals.

326. Pale brown limestone. 36×12. Bore 7 (top)/5/3. NBC 11081.

Two seated figures (one to right reversed) reaching toward tubes from vessel between them, two-line divider; two seated figures grasping inner of two tubes rising from each side of vessel which has tube (stirrer?) above and flat cover.

The scenes above and below are so placed that the position of the figures varies slightly. Consequently they must be repeated to clarify their somewhat different relationship, a common feature whenever a seal has two similar registers.

327. Green calcite. 50×26. NBC 5987.

Attendant before seated male with cup; similar group, but with seated female facing other way; cupboard before seated male with cup; two-line divider; one of two crossed lions attacking upended antelope, other lion menaces twisted goat which is held by nude belted hero with upright hair on one knee, who grasps goat with head turned back, the latter attacked by one of second pair of crossed lions, the other lion at rear of original antelope.

324

325

326

327

331

332

333

334

328. Shell. 28×8½. Split twice across. *Newell* 40. Not shown.

Seated figures with attendant before each; two-line divider; lions attacking goats, male on one knee.

329. Lapis lazuli. 33×9½ *Newell* 39. Not shown.

Seated figures, attendant and mounted vessel with pipes; two-line divider; eagle between goats.

330. Shell (top broken). 21(ext)×12. *Newell* 43. Not shown.

Upper scene as in 329, two-line divider, eagle between rear ends of goats.

331. Black mica-schist. 49×14. Bore (worn to one side) 5/2. YBC 13047.

Seated female with added stroke on arm (second arm?), attendant, crescent above, stroke before him, plant before seated figure; two-line divider; two hobbled sheep, plant behind back of each.

For a presumably hobbled animal compare *Ash C,* 106.

332. Creamy brown limestone. 27×11. Chipped. NBC 1200.

Two seated figures, each holding tube from vessel between them; two-line divider; two sheep (?).

The animal row resembles those in *Fara,* pl. 61c.

333. Light green calcite. 29×12. Worn. NBC 5972.

Two seated figures, vessel with tubes between them, attendant at cupboard; two-line divider; gazelle with head turned back attacked by one of two crossed lions, other at rear of falling antelope, plant.

334. Creamy brown limestone. 26×11. Worn. YBC 8941.

Two seated figures drinking from tubes from vessel on stand between them, bearded full-face head with bull's ears and horns; two-line divider; lion-headed spread-winged eagle at rear of confronted gazelle and antelope.

For the seated figures compare *OIP* 72, 334 (Early Dynastic III).

335. Pale brown limestone. 22½×10. Worn. NBC 12006.

Two seated figures holding different objects (musical?) before them, bowl with three tubes between them, goat; line divider; intertwined coil.

336. Shell. 23×8. Worn. NCBS 792.

Two seated figures holding tubes from vessel between them; two-line divider; same scene.

337. Shell. 30×8. Worn. NCBS 816.

Seated figure, attendant, arm raised toward each other, female (?) attendant; two-line divider; two seated figures holding tubes from vessel, crescent above, female attendant.

For the hair of the lower female attendant compare *Boehmer*, 664–65 ("Akkadian Ia, Tigris group").

338. Lapis lazuli. 37×13. Bore 2½, probably remains of pin inside. NBC 2589. *BIN* 2, pl. 74e, p. 58. *Amiet*, 1180.

Nude hero holding two antelopes, lion attacking from either side; between the lions, second hero with arms raised stabbing at them; two-line divider; seated male, vertical stroke, crescent standard with two dotted pendants on animal-footed stand, seated female, plant, attendant, star.

For the stand with animal feet see *Amiet*, 1180, p. 165.

339. Shell. 71×25. New impression. *Newell* 37. *Amiet*, 1460.

Lying antelope with head turned back, spread-winged eagle holding tails of lying lions with head turned back; two-line dividers containing row lozenges filled with big drillings; shrine, six men, their arms up and down, drilling in field.

Von der Osten's suggestion that the row of men below hold daggers cannot be accepted since it conflicts with related scenes of building, *Amiet*, 1441–64. The gesture of the men here, one arm up, the other down, is most unusual in Babylonian glyptic, see post–Jamdat Nasr *Ash C*, 92. It may possibly be peripheral as in *Ash C*, 770 or *OIP* 72, 897 (Early Dynastic I–II).

The crosses and dots of the middle register in 339 recall the rosettes in 235, but can also be compared to *Amiet*, 1054, 1058, 1061 (all regarded as of "Royal Cemetery style").

335

336

337

338

339

341

342

343

340. Shell. 38½×20. *Newell* 46. Not shown. *Amiet*, 1461.

Eagle at rear of gazelles, line divider, triangular building with worker on either side, four men beyond.

341. Gray brown limestone. 45×20. Bore 6/3. Decayed. YBC 9717. *Yale Library Gazette* 35 (1960), p. 25, no. 21. *Amiet*, 1453 (cited as BM because listed first in *RA* 46 [1952], p. 66, n. 2, fig. 2, there followed by YBC 9717).

Eagle between two squatting antelopes, lion attacking on either side, hero stabbing (?) and grasping tail of the lion to right; two-line divider; man with arms before him; three men, each carrying object on head; two men working on building between them, seated figure raising cup.

342. Black serpentine. 32×19. Worn. New impression. *Newell* 42.

Above: doorway, squarish structure with enclosure beside which figure is seated; two horizontals, two men approaching round object with worker on either side, three balls above, three below, those in middle probably encircled; below: striding man with arm forward, two (or three) balls in field, canopy over bull with head down as if eating, T-shape, striding man, man with hand raised behind bull which has head down as if eating, canopy above.

For the structure before the seated figure above compare *Amiet*, 1338–43. It is unlikely that driven animals are depicted below as in the superficially resembling piece *OIP* 72, 914.

343. Shell. 32½×18½. Worn and broken. New impression. *Newell* 41. *Frankfort*, p. 79, n. 2. *Amiet*, 1215.

Driver in four-wheeled chariot with basket-like sides, enemy under "horse," long fringe forms forepart of harness.

The suggestion (Heidenreich, *AfO* 10 (1935–36), p. 370) that this shows a two- (not a four-) wheeled chariot cannot be maintained if other examples are compared, see *Amiet*, 1213, 1217. However, Woolley was doubtless correct, in regard to the famous Standard of Ur, that the high fronts of the chariots there are shown in faulty perspective, incorrectly on the same plane as their sides (*UE* 2, pl. 92, p. 269); see the chariot fronts similarly misplaced in 343–44, 363, 370 here. He was probably also right to treat the animals as onagers rather than horses, *UE* 2, pp. 271ff. On the problems of early "chariots" compare Nagel, *BBV* 10.

FIGS. 340–343

344. Gray brown limestone. 22½×12½. NBC 11052.

Driver in four-wheeled chariot, twisted gazelle with head back between two heroes; below reversed: two seated figures holding tubes from vessel between them, attendant behind each, to left two confronted figures, terminal: scorpion, plant (?).

345. Pale brown marble, darker mottling. 30×17. New impression. *Newell* 47. *Frankfort,* pl. 15j, pp. 67ff. *Amiet,* 1427, pp. 179f.

Above: foreparts of gazelle attacked by lion, plow, forepart of goat, eagle, forepart of antelope; below: scorpionman, crescent, and dots at tail, sidewise pot over bearded "lion," disk between hind legs, worn in front, seated god with sprouts between horns rowing boat, sprouts in front of lap, forepart of boat consists of rowing god with sprouts between horns.

For similar scenes see *Amiet,* 1405–48. For the scorpionman compare 275. On the role of this creature in relation to the heavens see *Amiet,* pp. 133ff.

346. Light brown limestone, darker mottling, green stains. 28×17. Decayed. NBC 9119.

Twisted serpent with three dots above running goat (?) with head turned back, plow and vessel above bearded lionlike monster, crescent-topped (?) pole used by bearded (?) human prow of boat in which figure is seated, lines for stream below.

347. Shell. 29×12. New impression. *Newell* 48. *Frankfort,* p. 69, n. 1. *Amiet,* 1423.

Above: lion, branch extended by human prow of boat which contains plant before seated human figure; below: gazelle and ibex, their heads turned back, spread-winged eagle clutching the animals rears, symbol (or sign) to right below.

344

345

346

347

348

349

350

351

352

353

354

348. Shell. 32×19. Worn. NCBS 864.

Two crossed lions attacking horned animal on either side, under the lions knobbed rod in loop (?); terminal: trace of boat with human prow, two-line divider, two men at rear of the horned animals.

349. Shell. 19×8. New impression. *Newell* 35.

In boat two seated figures holding tubes from vessel, tree.

Compare *Amiet,* 1204–06 (probably Early Dynastic III).

350. Dark gray serpentine. 19½×8. New impression. *Newell* 36. *Amiet,* 1132.

Boat loaded with material on curved "waves" with tree at peak, hatched below, crescent above.

Compare *Amiet,* 1133–34 where a bird is perched on the material in the boat, possibly Post-Akkadian.

351. Light brown alabaster. 38×22/20(edges cut back). Bore 6/4½. Decayed, YBC 12761. *Yale Library Gazette* 35 (1960), p. 26, no. 25.

Viewed sidewise: nude bearded hero full face, on line, extended arms joined to angled lines which may be connected with lower of two snakes (rather than horns or hair) above, sidewise animal perhaps to right, inscription between legs.

Compare *Amiet,* 1284, 1287–95.

352. "Steatite." 21½×9½/9(irregular). Worn. NCBS 742.

Row of four men, disk in crescent over small male.

Compare the figures in the lower register of *Boehmer,* 631, in the upper register of *UE* 10, 129, and in the middle of *OIP* 72, 568, all late Early Dynastic III.

353. Hematite. 20×10/9½(irregular). Perhaps old seal recut. NCBS 748.

Row of four men, last attacking the one before, all on line.

This somewhat resembles *OIP* 72, 557 (Early Dynastic).

354. Lapis lazuli. 30×7. New impression. *Newell* 67.

Two connected lozenge patterns with fill of lines and dots.

On an Early Dynastic III date for this type of design, especially if in lapis lazuli, see G. Herrmann, *Iraq* 30 (1968), pp. 33f., confirming the views already expressed by *Amiet,* p. 60 (1053–61) and in *Ash C,* pp. 41, 43 (227).

FIGS. 348–354

FIGS. 355–360

Peripheral subjects combine odd diversity with a few well-integrated but simplified groups. Animal forms are featured in two early pieces, 355–56. A larger group, some perhaps of Early Dynastic II, present very similar grotesque human and animal forms, 357–63, the last being an odd chariot scene. Inexplicable men with twisted arms occur in 364–65 of similar early date. Possibly as early is a confused scene especially featuring eyes, 366. On a smaller scale, particularly noteworthy at Brak in Northern Mesopotamia, comes a group mostly of Early Dynastic III showing human and animal heads, 367; human figures in an animal contest, 368; animal sacrifice reversed over humans with weapons, 369; a crude chariot scene, 370. Various subjects include figures and curious objects, 371; lions in contest with other animals, 372; various creatures and animals in grotesque conflicts, 373–74; a coarse male in animal contest, 375; very simplified figures and animal, 376; even cruder female and other subjects, 377.

355. "Steatite." 17×11. NBC 11043.

Lizard, fish, bird; herringbone borders.

For subjects in a small space with notched or herringbone borders, as in 355, 368–69, see *Ash C,* 750, 753, 808, 811, all from Brak. The fish here resembles the one in 365 below.

356. Black serpentine. 18×10/9(irregular). Bore 4/3 (cut obliquely). YBC 12634.

Foreparts of five ibexes under twisted ladder shape; below: prone human figure between two rosettes, bird with head turned back.

The human figure and the heads of the animals resemble details in *Louvre* pl. 37.11, Moussian 2 (Piedmont Jamdat Nasr variant); but the figure, the rosettes, and the "ladder" device also recall various crudities in *UE* 10, 141 (Early Dynastic I–II). Animal heads were common in the early seal impressions from Ur, as in *UE* 3, 186–88.

357. Gray "steatite." 37×14. New impression. *Newell* 58. *Brett,* p. 1 (Archaic North Syrian).

Yale Library Gazette 43 (1968), pl. I.2, p. 92–93.

Rampant antelope, full-face bullman, erect lion; linear filling motifs.

358. Dark gray serpentine. 26×12. New impression. *Newell* 60.

Antelope, bird and other marks above it; coarse vertical mark; bull, scorpion above it; male figure, right arm raised, dot above it.

The incorrect description of the man as an ostrich has been copied in *Fauna,* p. 87, n. 8. For the style in 358–63 compare *Ash C,* 767–75 (Early Dynastic II).

359. "Steatite." 32×17. *Newell* 59. Not shown.

Scorpion, human figure with one arm up, other down, gazelle, bull with bird on back.

360. Brown composition. 21×12/11(irregular). NBC 10983.

Erect snake, male figure, left arm down, blob and dagger before him; two gazelles, back to back in opposite directions, reversed bird over blob and two coarse strokes.

355

356

357

358

360

361

362

363

364

361. Decayed limestone. 29×14½/14 (irregular). NBC 11061.

Spray under mouth of antelope attacked by lion; male figure, right arm outstretched, left arm down; star above bird over scorpion (?); notched border above.

Compare the similar scene with a notched border but more elaborate, *MAM* I, pl. 67.368.

362. "Steatite." 30/26×15/13(irregular). Bore 5½/4½(ends differ)/3½. NBC 9247.

Tree, bull, scorpion above it; lion, star above it; male figure, right arm up as well as down, other arm down, pullet behind head.

Compare *Amiet,* pl. 85 bis C.

362x, NCBS 799, speckled dark serpentine, 24½×10/8 (distorted), crude antelope, male figure.

363. "Steatite." 22½×14/13(irregular). NCBS 697. *Yale Library Gazette* 43 (1968), pl. II.1, pp. 94f.

Quadruped drawing chariot (two wheels shown), walking male with right hand stretched out as if holding rein going up and back from animal's mouth; crescent (?) above "tree."

On the front of the chariot shown sidewise see 343 above.

364. Light brown marble, gray mottled. 33×29. NBC 2590. *BIN* 2, pl. 75c, p. 59 (bought Baghdad 1904). *Amiet,* 1335.

Attendant holding cup in left hand which extends in long curve behind back, seated figure with beaker; hero holding antelope to right, lying ibex to left; scorpion (?) below to right, tree (?) to left; above and behind the ibex three more horned animals; line border above.

Compare the simpler, presumably earlier style of *Ash C,* 721.

365. "Steatite." 28×13½. NBC 9244. Could be from the Levant.

Spread-winged eagle, head right, facing snake (?); lion, snake (?) above, fish below, hero carrying weapon(?).

For a coarser version of the style in 365 see *Ash C*, 766 (=*Amiet,* pl. 85 bis i); compare perhaps Ravn, *Copenhagen,* 118, 122, stamped on jar sherds from a late third millennium context at Hama.

366. "Steatite." 43×15/11 (misshapen by deep carving). Worn. NCBS 858.

Hero between two animals, holding the one to left, eye shape with (?) striated vertical appendage (probably reversed); dotted line divider; animal contest (probably reversed and crossed), eye shape as above.

Compare Amiet, *Syria* 40 (1963), pl. VI. 1–3, fig. 21, pp. 72–74 (Archaic Syrian).

367. Limestone. 20½×12. YBC 13076. Gift Harald Ingholt (probably from Beirut).

Full-face bearded heroic head, dot enclosed in irregularly dotted circle with three curved ends, grotesque shape over sidewise head, ibex head and forequarters, dotted head over antelope head; triple lined herringbone divider; grotesque shape above over lying animal, stag (?) head above bucranium beside ibex head, animal head above odd shaped object, vertical odd shaped object, dot enclosed in irregularly dotted circle.

368. Red brown serpentine. 16½×7½. New impression. *Newell* 295.

Hero holding bull with head turned back, its forelegs against back of lion with head turned back which attacks crossed gazelle held by seated figure, branch; notched borders.

Compare *Ash C,* 790, 794 for the scale and style of the figures.

365

366

367

368

369

370

371

372

373

369. Dark gray "steatite." 26×12/11(irregular). Worn. NBC 10984.

Figure pushing sheep toward altar over which second figure reaches, bird (?) on stand, seated figure, tree; notched divider; (reversed) scorpion, schematic bird (?), figure with one arm raised holding tree by other together with second figure who also grasps big dagger pointed down, along with another figure, scorpion.

For scenes of animals presumably led to sacrifice see *Amiet*, 1324–27, pp. 165f., in the last of which there is a bird on the stand before the seated figure.

370. Dark greenish brown serpentine. 19×8. YBC 12603.

Above: crosslike device, two figures on line approaching tree (?), seated figure (?) with two dots about it, two vessels (?) behind; below: two asses, one behind the other, drawing chariot carrying driver, walking figure behind.

The stunted figures here somewhat resemble those in the lower register of Amiet, *Syria* 41 (1964), pl. IX.2. For peripheral chariot scenes with a following figure see *CANES*, 1081–82, compare 363 above.

371. Speckled brown marble. 31×19/18(irregular). Bore 5½/4½(ends differ)/4. Worn. NBC 9103.

Woman in shrine (or under canopy?), vessel (?) behind her, tree and offshoots, all on line; two confronted scorpions above; irregular row of six (?) human figures above three bushes (?), branch (?) bent about seated human (?), rosette-topped (?) bush.

372. Light brown limestone. 17×8½. NCBS 699.

Two crossed lions attacking antelope (?) and stag with head turned back, curved line between them.

Compare the seal with two registers from Chagar-Bazar, *Amiet*, pl. 85 bis L.

373. Creamy brown marble. 30×17/16(irregular). Worn. New impression. *Newell* 82.

Creature held at hind legs by hero, crossed animals, crossed animals held by bullman (?) between them, object (?) held by animal.

FIGS. 369–373

374. Pale brown limestone. 19×9½. Worn. NCBS 698.

Hero on one knee (?) shooting bow (?) at lion rampant over upended sheep (?), small figure before large one.

Compare *Amiet,* pl. 85 bis J.

375. Light brown limestone. 25×11½. Worn. NBC 9364.

Full-face (?) hero with arms raised toward two goats with head back, each attacked by one of two crossed lions; linear borders.

376. "Steatite." 26×12/11(irregular perhaps because of recutting). NBC 9097.

Seated figure, one arm bent up, the other down; lion (?) attacked by full-face bullman (?).

For the seated figure compare *OIP* 72, 720 from a Larsa context but of uncertain date and probably peripheral origin. The bullman here could be a crude version of those in Early Dynastic I–II pieces like *OIP* 72, 799.

377. Clay. 36×21/19(irregular). Ends concave. Corroded, broken. NCBS 862.

Female figure with streaming hair and long robe (?), hands at waist, crossed animals (?), and lizard (?) to right; monstrous shape (?) and eagle over crossed animals (?) to left.

374

375

376

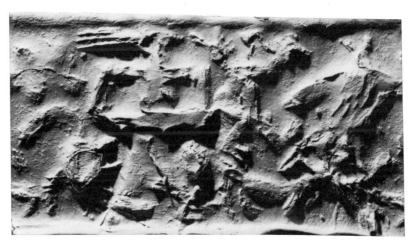

377

378

379

380

381

382

384

385

Early Akkadian

The rather conventional representations of Early Dynastic III were eventually superseded by the dynamic style of the Akkadian period. The earlier and simpler phases of the time feature lions in contest with other animals, 378–84; human figures may be added as a central feature in 385–97. Not much later, the groups, 398–430, tend to be separated into gods or heroes or bullmen, each opposed by a horned animal or a lion, the latter especially against the bullman. These scenes seem to emphasize the power of individual creatures, stressing their overwhelmingly human aspect even if they were depicted as divine.

378. Dark gray serpentine. 15½×7½. NCBS 724.

Tree between two goats, one attacked by lion with long looped tail.

379. Dark green serpentine, brown mottled. 20×11. NCBS 757.

Two lions attacking two antelopes between them, triangle (schematic plant?) under the antelopes; "starspade" (perhaps intended for the sungod, ^{d}UTU).

For 379–80 compare *Boehmer*, 81–82 (Ib). Although doubt has been expressed that the "starspade" stood for the sungod (*Frankfort*, p. 92), the weight of evidence indicates that such must have been its primary meaning (*Boehmer*, p. 85, n. 132–38); see below 386, 391, 445, 450.

380. Dark green serpentine. 20×10. NCBS 764.

Two lions attacking two goats, plant between latter; vertical line.

381. Shell. 26½×13/12(concave). Worn. NCBS 850.

Two lions attacking two crossed bulls (?), disk (?) above; terminal: crescent (?).

382. Shell. 28×16. Worn. New impression. *Newell* 111. *Boehmer*, 335 (Ib).

Two lions attacking two crossed bulls; crescent (?).

383. Diorite. 25×14. *Newell* 110. Not shown. *Boehmer*, 363 (Ib/c).

Two crossed lions attacking two antelopes, lion with head turned back to right.

384. Diorite. 30×18/17(concave). Bore 6/3. Chipped. NBC 3214.

Lion with head turned back grasping bull with head up, lion attacking bull with head back, tree.

385. Lapis lazuli. 15½×8½. NBC 11046.

Hero in kilt and vertically lined conical cap protecting bull attacked by one of two crossed lions, other attacks goat, dot between them, two horizontals.

For the conical cap see *Boehmer*, 50, for the kilt perhaps *Boehmer*, 46, both Ib. Otherwise the style more resembles that in *Boehmer*, 16–18 of Ia.

386. Shell. 33×20½. New impression. *Newell* 112. *Boehmer,* 275 (Ib).

Hero protecting antelope attacked by one of two crossed lions, the other attacks second antelope which has star under head, star on top of pole with triangle in middle, and blunt point in line below.

387. Black serpentine. 16×8. YBC 9669.

Nude hero holding two gazelles, one of two crossed lions attacking from either side.

For the animal style in 387–89 compare *Boehmer,* 39, 45 (Ib).

388. Dark gray serpentine. 20×10. Worn. NCBS 765.

Hero in kilt between two gazelles (?) attacked by lion on either side.

389. Shell. 21½×11. Worn. NCBS 778.

Like 388 plus tree (?).

390. Diorite. 24½×13. *Newell* 106. Not shown. *Boehmer,* 78 (Ib).

Hero between two antelopes attacked by lion on either side.

391. Dark green serpentine. 24×12. Worn. NBC 6678.

Like 388–90, but with nude hero, his hair upright (?); standard with star and "spade."

392. Lapis lazuli. 17×10. YBC 8942.

Like 391 but hero wears flat cap; terminal: two horizontals with scratch (?) above, dagger below.

Compare lower registers of *Boehmer,* 20 (Ia), 60 (Ib).

393. Pale yellow calcite. 19×11. *Newell* 91. Not shown. *Boehmer,* 81 (Ia).

Like 391 but hero has folded hair, is perhaps bearded.

394. Dark green serpentine. 25×13½. New impression. *Newell* 90. *Boehmer,* 248 (Ib).

Like 391 but bearded hero wears horizontally marked cap and thick belt.

386

387

388

389

391

392

394

395

396

397

398a

398b

398c

399

395. Lapis lazuli. 23½×8. Chipped. NCBS 793.

Two lions menacing nude hero in flat cap and antelope between them, cross (?); two-line upper border topped by four hoof(?)-tipped angles.

396. Diorite. 19×9. New impression. *Newell* 89. *Boehmer*, 166 (Ib).

Hero in belt and kilt protecting two antelopes, one to right attacked by lion, crescent over tree.

397. Dark green mottled serpentine. 30×17½. NBC 9111.

Lion with head turned back bites at full-face human-headed bull held by hero in flat cap, goat with head turned back attacked by lion.

398. Impressions all over tablet. Seal ext. 20. (a) Reverse, (b) Left edge, (c) Drawing. YBC 11232. Dated Ibbi-Sin 3. *Yale Library Gazette* 45 (1970), p. 55, no. 2 (drawn).

Bearded god, hair down back, end of belt shown, holding gazelle, its head turned back, attacked by full-face lion; full-face human-headed bull menaced by bearded hero in multihorned crown, end of belt shown; inscription (probably over outside of hair down back of god to left) above two crossed bulls.

The evidence suggests that the Neo-Sumerian inscription was a later addition. It is unusual for the actors in contest scenes to be depicted with the horned crown of deity, particularly if they date as late as Neo-Sumerian, see once in *Ash C*, 439, twice in *Philadelphia*, 142. Earlier, as in Early Dynastic 303 above, the horns were probably meant to suggest supernatural powers rather than to identify specific deities. The multihorned crown worn by the hero to the right in 398 recurs especially in scenes of gods in combat. Such scenes were quite well attested in late Early Dynastic times, see *Boehmer*, 282, probably 284–89, and continue at least as late as the reign of Manishtusu, an early Akkadian king, *Boehmer*, 330. In *Boehmer*, 310, a god in a multihorned crown grasps one horn and one arm of a creature probably a bullman. The group somewhat resembles that to the right in 398 and tends to confirm the early Akkadian date suggested for the latter by its quasi-naturalistic detail.

399. Rock crystal. 22×12. New impression. *Newell* 677. *Boehmer*, 211 (Ib/c).

Full-face lion grappling with bullman, hero holding bull attacked by full-face lion; inscription above two horizontals over ibex.

The identification of the bullman as Enkidu and the hero as Gilgamesh is still subject to dispute; see *Frankfort*, pp. 62ff.; Garelli, ed., *Gilgameš et sa légende*, Paris, 1960; *Amiet*, pp. 169ff.

400. Dark green serpentine. 39×24/23(concave). Bore 6½/4½. Shallow circle around each end of bore. Worn. NBC 2581. *BIN* 2, pl. 76a, pp. 59f. *Boehmer,* 32 (Ia).

Two human-headed bulls, their heads adjacent, each held by nude belted hero; lion in grasp of bullman; all heads full face except the lion's.

401. Lapis lazuli. 19×9. *Newell* 101. Not shown. *Boehmer,* 304 (Ib).

Full-face bullman holding gazelle attacked by lion in grasp of full-face hero who is back to back with ibex; two trees in field.

402. Impression on oblong, cushion-shaped clay strip. Seal c. 27. YBC 13115.

Erect bull with head up, full-face bullman grasping lion by paw and tail, kilted hero in vertically marked conical cap holding bull with head turned back, kilted hero grasping original bull (?).

403. Shell. 34×22. Much brown limestone deposit. New impression. *Newell* 679 ("fake because design shows no signs of wear"). Heidenreich, *AfO* 10 (1935–36), p. 371 ("false"). *Boehmer,* 104 (Ic).

Hero in kilt holding goat, bullman struggling with lion, hero in kilt and striated cap holding bull.

404. Dark green mottled serpentine. 37×24/23 (irregular). Bore 6/3½. Worn. NCBS 857.

Bull, its head up, in grasp of bearded hero in kilt and long cap; bullman grappling with lion; hero (?) holding animal.

400

402

403

406

407

408

411

412

413

405. Light green nephrite. 22×10. Half split away. *Newell* 102. Not shown. *Boehmer, 420* (Ic).

Oryx, head back, in grasp of hero with vertically marked conical hat, back to back with similar hero (?).

406. Green serpentine. 37×26/24(concave). NBC 3965.

Two bulls with head up, back to back, each attacked by full-face lion, the second lion in grasp of kilted bearded hero.

407. Rock crystal. 22(ext)×16/15(concave). Bottom broken off. YBC 12510. From Fulton collection, Medical School Library.

Hero holding bull, bull attacked by lion; inscription.

Compare *Boehmer, 270* (late III).

408. Green nephrite. 20×10/9½(concave). NCBS 773.

Bull held by kilted hero in flat cap; kilted hero grasping human-headed bull, its head turned back; terminal: axe.

The bull is urinating, like the buffalo in 415 and apparently both creatures in 431.

409. Green nephrite. 23×14/12½(concave). *Newell* 103. Not shown. *Boehmer, 146* (II).

Hero holding ibex, lion in grasp of bullman, bush underneath; empty frame.

410. Speckled dark gray serpentine. 25×14½. *Newell* 100. Not shown. *Boehmer, 496* (II).

Hero struggling with lion, buffalo held by second hero; inscription.

411. Shell. 27/29 (bottom end expanded)×18½. Worn. NCBS 852.

Hero grasping lion, buffalo (?) held by hero.

412. Flecked dark gray serpentine. 28×16/15 (concave). Bore 6/3½. Worn. NBC 6018.

Lion held by kilted belted hero, second hero holds bull (?).

413. Dark green serpentine. 32×22/20(concave). NBC 6006.

Lion held by bullman, human-headed bull with head turned back, hero grasping bull with head up.

FIGS. 405–413

414. Green nephrite. 23½ × 12½/11½(concave). Split at inscription. *Newell* 99. Not shown. *Boehmer,* 662 (III).

Hero holding bull, eagle below, lion struggling with second hero.

The tails of both animals were lost when the inscription was cut.

415. Green nephrite. 24 × 15/14(concave). YBC 9718.

Nude belted bearded hero in vertically marked cap stepping on upended lion, urinating buffalo with head up held by bearded hero in kilt and belt; inscription (worn) over gazelle.

416. Dark flecked green nephrite. 22 × 12. New impression. *Newell* 98. *Boehmer,* 169 (III).

Bullman grasping lion, buffalo over bush held by hero, the "men" look at each other.

The bush under the buffalo here recalls the one under the lion in 409.

417. Rock crystal. 32 × 22½/20(concave). New impression. *Newell* 95 (shape fig. 2, p. 4). *Boehmer,* 175 (III).

Full-face hero holds buffalo, lion struggles with full-face bullman, inscription over goat.

418. Mottled dark green serpentine. 30 × 16/14 (concave). YBC 12622.

Full-face hero holding buffalo, lion in grasp of full-face bullman; inscription.

419. Green nephrite. 29 × 17/15(concave). Chipped. NBC 9361.

Inscription, full-face hero holding buffalo, end of inscription, lion in grasp of full-face bullman.

The deep cutting of the design suggests that the tails of the lion and the bullman deliberately had been omitted, presumably to make room for the inscription.

415

416

417

418

419

421

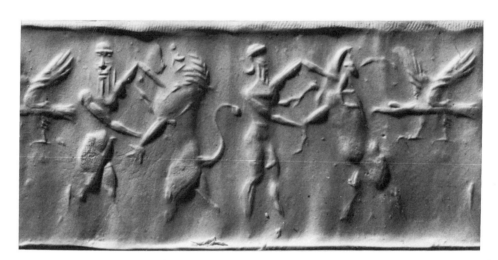

422

423

420. Pale brown limestone. 27½×17/15 (concave). *Newell* 92. Not shown. *Boehmer*, 594 (III).

Full-face bullman with lion, buffalo with full-face hero, worn inscription.

421. Light green brown mottled nephrite. 34×23/21½(concave). One third broken. NBC 11033.

Full-face bullman holding lion, buffalo in grasp of hero (?).

Perhaps by the same artist as *Boehmer*, 198 (III).

422. Black serpentine. 36½×22/21(concave). Worn. New impression. *Newell* 673 ("recut"). *Boehmer*, 186 (III).

Full-face bullman fighting lion, kilted hero grasping buffalo, flying eagle.

423. Light brown limestone. 28×18½/16½ (concave). Worn. New impression. *Newell* 96. *Boehmer*, 189 (III).

Bearded hero in flat cap, belt, kilt, shoes with turned up toes, grasping bull with head up, tree, full-face bullman fighting lion; inscription.

The inscription cut away much of the hindleg of the hero and most of the tail and hindleg of the lion, while part of it appears before the foreleg of the lion.

FIGS. 420–423

424. Impression on oblong cushion-shaped clay strip. Seal 26. MLC 1946.

Full-face bullman grasping lion, bull with head up, held by full-face hero; inscription.

425. Impression with writing over it on oval piece of clay having smooth rounded bottom. Seal c. 35. NBC 10590. Nippur 6 NT 1156 (also 5 NT 653 = NBC 11341). Hallo, *JNES* 31 (1972), p. 95 addendum. No context recorded.

Legs of rampant lion held by full-face bullman, inscription over bull (?) (trace of head to right), full-face hero with side curls holding rampant bull (?).

426. Dark mottled green serpentine. 26×16/15 (concave). Broken. New impression. *Newell* 94. *Boehmer*, 245 (III).

Full-face elaborately bearded hero holding tail before him of full-face erect lion behind whose head he grasps the lion's spread paw; on either side bearded hero struggling with erect bull.

424

425

426

427

428

429a

429b

427. Impressions on sloping sides and narrow top of sealing, basket marks on flat base. Seal c. 26½. NBC 3795.

Hero, facing left, spiral-tipped tassel between legs, holding leg and tail and stepping on up-ended buffalo, other hindleg of latter held by nude belted bearded full-face hero with side curls, who also grasps leg of buffalo in similar scene to right, hero of which (impressed on other end) looks toward original hero; inscription.

428. Gray green nephrite. 25×16/15(concave). Traces of broken bronze mount at top. New impression. *Newell* 97. *Boehmer*, 218 (III).

Full-face nude bearded hero with side curls grasping leg and horn and stepping on buffalo before body of which he stands, similar hero with foot on lion to the right, both animals reversed, cross beside the lion's head, two crossed snakes under inscription.

429. Impressions on faces and edges of thin tag, string hole in broken bottom edge. Seal ext. 32. (a-b) Faces. NBC 4142.

Inscription between two bulls (?), each crossed by full-face hero with side curls who holds their tail.

Compare *Boehmer*, 206 (III).

FIG. 430

430. Impression on both faces of thin tag, string hole (?). Seal c. 35. (a-b) Faces. Goucher 883.

Backs of two rearing bulls (?), inscription between them, under it bull (?) (trace of head to left in "a").

430a

430b

431

432

433

Parallel to the rendition of personalized might are scenes depicting quite realistic action of a divine character.

The fanciful mountainous terrain inhabited by monsters, 431, well illustrates the elaborate style that developed. Even earlier, however, the attack on an armed god is vigorously depicted, 432. Somewhat later and more restrained are the combats of the gods in 433–44, becoming more elaborate in 435–41. Two gods hold an eagle between them in 442. In all Akkadian periods may appear the sun god rising between attendants, 443–47. An early piece shows an attended bull with a winged shrine on its back, 448, later 449. A gatepost is held on either side of a shrine, 450; an early seal shows an eagle above a liongriffin, 451; later appears a god with a whip on a liongriffin, 452; of uncertain date are mounted figures, 453; an attendant pours a libation before a god in 454–55; earlier comes a plowing scene, 456; later a hunter attacking a lion in the midst of other animals, 457.

An early scene presents a prone female with a scorpion under her couch over date-laden trees, 458. Also early, but perhaps later recut, is a group of standing and seated figures, 459, which may be compared with females, one an enthroned goddess, who could be about as early, 460. Of later date are seated males and females with intervening attendants, 461–63, two seated face to face holding tubes, 464, while two more, one of which is a snake god, confront each other, 465. An enthroned god with saw is presented singly or in groups, 466–70; enthroned gods are amidst streams and fish accompanied by various attendants, 471–72; a god of vegetation goes with scenes of husbandry, 473; while another god confronts one standing with a plow, 474. Enthroned with attendants are a goddess, 475, gods, 476–80, and one worn human, 481.

431. Impression on long thin clay strip with rounded bottom. Seal 35 (with cap marks 37). NCBT 2281. Possibly recent impression rolled with ancient original.

Inscription behind monster (?) (antlered) climbing triangular "mountain," line projecting down from creature's mouth to top of hill on which tree grows, lion (?) descending other side, tail straight out, line projecting down from mouth ending below in spiral (which may also connect along side of hill with projecting line above), the "lion" speared by full-face bearded nude hero, with side curls, before the spear bird of prey.

"Bearded very hairy oxen" have been described as bisons, *Boehmer*, pp. 43f. The creature on the left here seems to be bearded and may have been hairy. Nevertheless it must be taken for an imaginary monster since its horns look like antlers. The other creature appears to be a lion, though its tail is not as sinuous as in most representations, while its legs somewhat resemble the other monster's. Both creatures seem to be urinating as is sometimes true of oxen in Akkadian seals; see 408, 415. "Bisons" appear rearing against the sides of small thinnish "mountains" in *Boehmer*, 250–51 (III), 263–64 (his late III, but perhaps Post-Akkadian). In his 263 at least one of them is urinating. For the bird of prey compare the eagle in 422.

432. Grayish brown limestone. 28×16. Chipped. YBC 12763. *Yale Library Gazette* 35 (1960), p. 26, no. 29.

Nude belted bearded god, rays from legs, grasping beard and arm of falling nude belted god, who holds broken weapons, his other arm and one horn (?) in grasp of nude bearded god with hair down back; goddess (?) in long pleated skirt grappling with nude belted god, each holding horn of other, between them small female (?) raising curved staff (?) against the god; mace.

For transitional scenes of gods in combat see *Boehmer*, 282–91, of which only the last two are certainly as late as Akkadian. The small, possibly female, figure to the right here is roughly paralleled in *Boehmer*, 284 probably late Early Dynastic, in 294–95 Early Akkadian, and somewhat later in 326–27; see *Boehmer*, p. 50, n. 7.

433. Gray green serpentine, mottled. 34×19. NBC 7918.

Two contending gods, hero attacking falling (?) hero in flat cap; all figures bearded, nude, belted.

Compare *Boehmer*, 297 (Ib/c).

434. Dark green serpentine, brown mottled. 21×11/10(concave). Worn. NBC 4953.

God in long open robe, mace in right hand, other at head of falling god, worshipper with kid, female attendant with pail.

435. Dark mottled green serpentine. 35×23/21 (concave). Bore 6/3½. Chipped. NBC 5994. *Yale Library Gazette* 35 (1960), p. 26, no. 31.

Kilted belted god with adze attacking fallen god in long skirt, god in long off-the-shoulder garment with horned crown topped by crescent, all gods bearded, lion in grasp of full-face bullman.

The apparent tress down the back of the god with adze was probably produced by a slip of the tool. Men and gods rarely have long tresses in Akkadian glyptic; but compare transitional 432 above. The main exception is provided by some of the figures at the gates in scenes with the sun god like *Boehmer, 394*.

The use of the adze in battles of the gods is rare; see *Boehmer, 851 (Ib/c)*.

The standing god with crescent-topped crown can be compared with *Boehmer, 725–26 (III)*, in which such a figure is seated. It could be that our seal, like *Boehmer, 726*, came from Ur, the great center of the moon god. For a similar representation of later times see a fragment of wall painting from an Old Babylonian palace, *MAM* II, 2, pp. 76f., fig. 59.

436. Speckled dark gray serpentine. 32×21. New impression. *Newell 154. Boehmer, 339 (III)*.

God with foot on stand leaning on mace and wielding one, god with rays holding tail of full-face bullman, mace, god with rays stabbing demon with lion's head and paws, latter grasps the god's leg, mace; the gods wear long open robes with turned up underwear in front.

The three maces in the field need have no connection with the action, even when leaned on by the god to the left.

437. Black serpentine, speckled green and red. 25×15/14(concave). Chipped. NBC 3210. *Yale Library Gazette* 35 (1960), p. 26, no. 30.

Birdman grasping god collapsed on mountain who is also held and stepped on by second god, dagger at waist; tree.

The birdman appears to be very like the one depicted as a prisoner before the water god in 471 below. Scenes like the latter occur from Early Akkadian glyptic on (*Boehmer, 493–521*), but the birdman here seems closest to those in *Boehmer, 509–10 (III)*.

The theme of 437 must be related to that in numerous seals showing a god with rays attacking a god seated on a mountain, as in 438. The main difference is that here the attacking god lacks rays. Curiously, the birdman seems to be the second attacker. Apparently this would not be the crime for which the birdman is led before the water god, since he is not so depicted in *Boehmer, 305*, a seal suggesting a favorable relationship between the worship of the water god and the attack on the god on the mountain. It must be assumed that the crime of the birdman somehow differed.

438. Gray serpentine, brown mottled. 29½×17½. New impression. *Newell 153. Boehmer, 892 (III)*.

Nude god on mountain attacked by two gods, "saws" at their belts, the one to right has shoulder rays, grasps his adversary by the beard and places one foot in his lap; belted god with dagger, all gods bearded, tree.

434

435

436

437

438

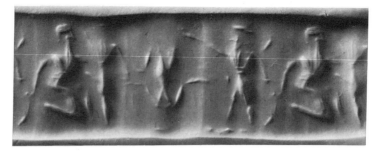

440

441a

441b

441c

442

439. Black and brown serpentine. 23½×13/11½(concave). *Newell* 151. Not shown. *Boehmer,* 909 (III).

Two gods each on one knee attacked by adversary on either side, scorpion added between the two on right.

440. Hematite. 22×12. Bore 4/3, crooked. Worn. YBC 12837. Said to be from Western Iran.

Male figure in flat cap, on one knee, holding scimitar behind him, stepped on by full-face (?) male, who also holds one of outstretched arms of upended male, one of whose legs is bent, other in grasp of hero (?) in flat cap (?), ray (?) (or scratch) at shoulder; all figures nude, belted, and bearded.

441. Impressions all over tablet case. Seal 22. (a) Reverse, (b) Left edge, (c) Drawing. YBC 10978. Dated Shulgi 33. *Yale Library Gazette* 45 (1970), pp. 55f., no. 3. (drawn).

Bearded god in kilt, end of belt shown, menacing with mace, holding (?) horn of and stepping on nude (?) god on one knee, the latter's right arm dropping weapon (?) raised toward the mace; nude bearded god, end of belt shown, arms bent forward, bestride fallen full-face god on "mountain," star above; inscription (left frame over top of the fallen god).

It appears that the Neo-Sumerian inscription was a later addition. The scene to the right is comparable with that in *Boehmer,* 378 (III), in which, however, a goddess takes part by grasping the foot of the fallen figure. *Boehmer,* p. 66, n. 11, 22, maintains that the goddess has weapons at her shoulders against *Frankfort,* pl. 19b, pp. 106, 116 who saw her as a goddess of vegetation. It is probable that she was aiding in the attack on the fallen figure; an attack by others depicted or implied in 437–41. It is curious that when standing the goddess should often be shown with vegetation at her shoulder (*Boehmer,* 381), while when seated it would seem she always has weapons (*Boehmer,* 384). It is possible that at this stage the goddess, presumably Ishtar, could have been depicted in either aspect, but it is perhaps more likely that two different goddesses were intended. Unfortunately, the character of the objects at her shoulders often cannot be determined.

A battle of gods also appears in a very corroded limestone seal, 441x, NCBS 729, 16½×10.

442. Dark brownish green serpentine. 28×17/15(concave). Bore 6/3. Worn. NBC 9116.

Two gods mastering bird of prey between them, plant on line under the bird's neck, second plant behind it; two verticals rise from right arm of the god on right, diagonal before the one on left; tree.

Compare *Boehmer,* 323–25 (Ib/c), 334–36 (II). Of these 334, like 442 here, shows plants under the bird of prey, which according to *Frankfort,* p. 134, the bird is seizing. Such scenes hardly confirm this explanation; in fact the usual absence of plants from similar designs makes a necessary connection with a myth of vegetation doubtful. It is also doubtful that the role of the bird of prey and of the birdman in presumably mythological scenes can be equated, as *Frankfort* suggests. Certainly there is no visual connection between the birdman in 437 and the bird here, except that the former is birdlike from the waist down.

443. Light green serpentine, dark flecked. 23×13. Worn. NBC 1517.

Mounted standard with ball (?) and pennant at top, held by kilted god with one foot on animal, his head turned left (scratch behind it) toward head turned back of nude god who holds mace on shoulder and another behind (?) him, the latter touched by god with rays who rises between two peaks, his other hand at mace that extends before (but is not shown held by) nude god who shoulders another mace (?).

For the god with rays between peaks, his arms turned down, and an attendant with a weapon, see *Boehmer*, 398 (Ib/c). Probably neither there nor in 443 were the armed attendants regarded as enemies of the god.

The standard recalls the crescent standard with streamers in 338 (Early Dynastic III). The standard and the god with one foot on an animal are comparable to *Boehmer*, 437 (III); a somewhat similar standard with pennant appears in *Boehmer*, 548 (III).

444. Dark green serpentine. 31×19/17(concave). YBC 9682.

God with saw and rays standing on line between two peaks, second line below at either end of which is gate held by divine attendant, each looking back toward the other.

The use of lines to connect the peaks and the gates is quite common, especially in early designs; see *Boehmer*, 401, 409, 411 (Ib/c).

445. Shell. 37×22/21(irregular)/20(concave). Worn. NCBS 859.

God with saw and rays between two peaks connected by line, his right foot on one peak; gate on either side, that to left held by attendant who looks back; terminal: starspade.

Compare *Boehmer*, 404 (Ib/c).

446. Brown limestone, red streaked. 25×14/13½(concave). Worn. YBC 9999. Said to be from Kerkuk.

God with rays, one foot on stand, holding weapon behind him and raising saw (?); gates with divine attendants as in 444.

443

444

445

446

448

450

451

452a

452b

447. Dark green serpentine, brown mottled. 21×11½/10½(concave). Worn. *Newell* 167. Not shown. *Boehmer*, 438 (late III).

God with saw, one foot on "mountain," attendant with gate looking back, worshipper.

448. Greenish brown limestone. 23×11½. Bore 5/3(crooked). Worn. YBC 12586. *Yale Library Gazette* 35 (1960), p. 26, no. 28.

Human figure (three holes in head accidental?) in long skirt holding staff (?), other arm raised toward nude god (?) holding hatched rope (?) from winged shrine on back of bull, other end of rope held by attendant in long skirt who reaches toward the bull.

For an early version of the shrine on a bull, probably late Early Dynastic, see *Boehmer*, 589, found out of context at Nippur; compare his 590 which may be Early Akkadian. In style, 448 seems closest to linear Early Akkadian pieces like *Boehmer*, 593, *Ash C*, 295–96.

449. Light brown limestone. 28½×18/16(concave). Chipped. *Newell* 648. Not shown. *Boehmer*, 1396 (III).

Seated figure grasping horn of lying bull with winged gate on back, rope from latter held by attendant, tree.

450. Shell. 32×18/17(ends irregular). Bore 6½/4. Decayed. NBC 9241.

Shrine, on either side gatepost with hourglass-shaped top and ring below held by nude bearded hero in cap (?) and belt on one

knee, each looking back toward the other; crescent above two horizontals, starspade below.

Compare *Boehmer*, 525 (III). Attendants with similar gateposts are often placed on either side of the watergod; *Boehmer*, 518, 520 (III), *Ash C*, 349–50.

451. Olive brown limestone. 22×12. YBC 12769. *Yale Library Gazette* 35 (1960), p. 27, no. 39. Festoon, eagle and crescent above it, plant (?) and liongriffin spitting fire below.

The wings of the liongriffin are placed near the middle of its back, a rendering apparently typical of Early Akkadian versions of the subject, see *Boehmer*, 363; compare the fully developed rendering in which the wings spring from the shoulders, as in *Boehmer*, 371 or in 452 below. For the liongriffin, or perhaps winged lion, in Early Dynastic times see *Amiet*, 1276–77.

452. Impression on reverse of four tablets. Seal 25. (a-b) Photographs of two tablets. NBC 5812 (= a), NBC 6861 (= b), also on NBC 5859, 5908; respectively 284–85, 274, 283 in *BIN* 8, pl. 160B (poor drawing), Hackman p. 8 (placed in group dated to the Akkadian period, though all written in Sumerian).

Figure in long garment raising arm in worship; bearded god in long garment end of belt shown, holding vertical object (mace?) in right hand, shouldering whip and standing on liongriffin; inscription; worshipper with kid led by goddess (?) (same as original figure?).

453. "Steatite." 25×13. Worn. NCBS 805. Probably Early Akkadian.

Lines before figure with outstretched arm on back of broad-horned, long-nosed, full-face bovine creature; figure on back of bovine creature with very long neck, pointed nose, dot-in-circle eye; trace of figure on back of bovine creature with long neck and open jaws.

Compare the long-necked "dragons" in drilled style, *Amiet,* 1391 (late Early Dynastic III), also the variations in the serpentdragon, *Boehmer,* 565–72 (III). The serpentdragon has been called the lionbird by *Frankfort,* p. 121.

454. Dark green serpentine. 29×18. Worn. NBC 3212. *Yale Library Gazette* 35 (1960), p. 26, no. 32.

Protective deity in long robe, end of belt shown; worshipper with kid in pleated kilt, two horizontals, nude male pouring libation into vessel; god in long robe, holding cup, enthroned on dragon with long neck and serpentine head and tail; small erect long-eared animal with dagger, god in long garment holding mace.

455. Dark green mottled serpentine. 31×20. YBC 16396. Gift Mrs. A. K. Sibley.

Two bearded gods, positioned frontally, wearing caps with flare toward the top and long four-tiered flounced skirts, tied with a belt in the waist, each holding with both hands two long staves. Before the gods a priest in a fringed skirt pours a libation from a goblet into an hourglass shaped offering stand over which hangs a strand of beads. A large dagger or ritual knife is placed between the priest and a worshipper who brings a sacrificial goat, followed by a woman who carries a pail. Both wear fringed garments; inscription.

The cylinder is vigorously carved with a very obvious symbolism such as the knife placed before the goat most probably thought to be sacrificed with such a tool. A parallel for the frontally positioned gods with staves is seen in a worn cylinder in *CANES,* 200 where one such figure appears. That cylinder should be dated early in the development of Akkadian glyptic style (Akkad Ic according to *Boehmer,* 496, p. 88). Another example which shows a god with only one staff and in sideview (*Boehmer,* 304) points to a slightly later date. Thus an origin in or before the middle of the Akkad period, c. 2260 B.C. for 455 is indicated by the parallels cited as well as by the form of the fringed garments worn by the human figures on the cylinder.

456. Shell. 35×22/20(concave). Bore 6/4. Worn. NBC 5990. *Yale Library Gazette* 35 (1960), p. 26, no. 33 (plate). *Boehmer,* 712 (I).

Nude belted male at plow drawn by ox, second male bestride the plow shaft, his right hand on seed feeder (?), third male shouldering whip behind the ox; above: star (?) and scorpion over bird, crescent, three birds.

For plowing scenes of varied design compare *Boehmer,* 711–15a. The sacred character of 456 is indicated by the scorpion, for in another such scene, *Boehmer,* 714, a scorpion forms part of the arm of the predominant god. The same thing is suggested here by the manner in which the lower part of the man with a whip is assimilated to the rear of the ox, giving him the look of a bullman. Compare *Boehmer,* 156 (II) in which a bullman is joined to the rear of a bull.

453

454

455

456

457

458

459

457. Black serpentine. 32×19/17½(concave). New impression. *Newell* 680. *Boehmer,* 723 (III).

Small bearded attendant in kilt bearing salver (?) before him, bearded hunter in kilt spearing lion over dead antelope; inscription; above: ibex, stag, ibex; second row: gazelle, fox (?); below: ibex, ostrich.

458. Shell. 61×21/22(convex). Cracked. NBC 8956. *Yale Library Gazette* 35 (1960), p. 26, no. 26 (plate). *Boehmer,* 690 (Ia, Tigris group).

Female on couch with bull's legs, scorpion below; four different vessels; divider (two lines enclosing two hatched bands); two intergrown (?) palm trees with suspended date clusters; on either side rampant goat (?) with head turned back, small tree, shrine; borders of two hatched bands.

On the archaizing Early Akkadian "Tigris" group see *Boehmer,* pp. 80f.; add *Ash C,* 288, probably 289. For the scene in the upper register of 458, compare the Protoliterate impression, perhaps showing lower right a woman on a couch with a bull's head, *Ash C,* 3, p. 6; possibly also the female bust over a couch with bull's legs in a seal perhaps of Iranian origin, Porada, *Ancient Iran,* p. 41, fig. 16, which by its linear outlined bodies and archaizing drilled detail may be of the same Early Akkadian phase as 458. That the scene can be called the setting for a sacred marriage is shown by *Boehmer,* 691, in the lower register where a human pair is coupling in the "normal" position, i.e., the female prone, the male above her, on a couch with bull's legs, a scorp-

ion perhaps below, a column of three scorpions to the left, and to the right a kneeling figure possibly holding the woman's legs. The same subject, similarly treated, recurs in seals at least as late as the second half of the second millennium, see Seyrig, *Syria* 32 (1955), pl. 4.3, pp. 38f., a Levantine cylinder, where bull's legs and a scorpion below appear just as in 458. Otherwise on positions in copulation see under 515 below.

459. Dark green serpentine, brown mottled. 36×21/19(concave). Chipped. NBC 7917. Lately recut?

Figure with outstretched arms (position not clear) and second one behind seated bearded figure holding cup (?), bearded attendant, second seated figure, star above.

For the high-crowned hats worn by the figures compare *Boehmer,* 53–57 (Ib), 105–06 (Ic). However, long garments trimmed below as here usually have a thin vertical line of trimming above as in 461. It seems probable that 459 was originally the work of the same artist as *Ash C,* 291 (Early Akkadian). But there are certain differences. The added eyes are like those in 478 and other crude pieces. Odder is the rather disjointed rendering of most of the arms as two lines in the first figure, though this also occurs with two of the crudely cut figures in *Berlin,* 219 (= *Boehmer,* 976 Ib/c). One explanation might be that the seal was recut or at least retouched in recent times. However, *BN,* 53 (= *Boehmer,* 1592 I) shows a very similar design and comparable, if somewhat different, crudity, yet its authenticity cannot be questioned.

460. Light green composition. 28½×9/8(concave). Worn. YBC 12764.

Three female attendants, second looking back at first, only one leg of third shown, seated goddess with cup; crisscross below set in three lines at top, two at bottom.

For the attendant showing only one leg compare the goddess in *Boehmer*, 377 (II), the musician in *Boehmer*, 390 (Ib). For the style compare the upper register *Boehmer*, 60 (Ib) and the figures in *Boehmer*, 635 (I).

461. Dark green serpentine, brown mottled. 27×15/14(concave). NBC 6017.

Seated male and female figures, each holding cup, female attendant between them, two crescents above: tree.

See *Boehmer*, 673 (III, better), 675 (late III, cruder).

462. Black serpentine. 29×18/16(concave). NBC 6012.

Seated goddess, side curl below chin, female attendant before her, crescent above; "star" above seated bearded god, starspade.

The side curl of the goddess is unusual. It may represent an attempt to depict the ever-present curls over the shoulders of full-face goddesses, as for example in *Boehmer*, 380.

463. Shell. 51×20. NBC 5991. *Yale Library Gazette* 35 (1960), p. 27, no. 37.

Seated bearded god, star above, bearded attendant god, attendant goddess, goddess seated on two geese, tree; two-line divider; seated female and male figures, each with cup, between them female attendant holding date cluster, second female attendant at date palm.

Compare *Boehmer*, 651 (III). For goddess seated on bird in or beside boat see *Boehmer*, 479–80 (III).

460

461

462

463

464

465

466

467

468

464. Black serpentine. 27×17½. New impression. *Newell* 683 ("doubtful"). *Boehmer,* 1613 (III).

Two seated figures, each shouldering rod, their forward hand grasping tubes from vessel between them, crescent above; tree.

See *Boehmer,* 677–82 (III).

465. Shell. 28×13. Worn. NBC 11086.

Snake god, arm outstretched, facing seated bearded (?) figure, arm outstretched, crescent above, inscription.

The snake god without an altar, *Boehmer,* 587–88 (III).

466. Mottled brown green serpentine. 24×11/10(concave). NBC 9123. *Yale Library Gazette* 35 (1960), p. 27, no. 34.

God with saw, seated on "mountain," his feet on platform, crescent above; inscription.

For a god with vegetation seated on a "mountain" see *Frankfort,* pl. 20 i (= *Boehmer,* 791, late III).

467. Greenish black serpentine. 16×8½. Worn. YBC 12816.

Worshipper, offerings on stand (?), seated god with saw, rays at left shoulder, three plants (?).

468. Dark green serpentine, brown flecked. 36×24/23(concave). Bore, conical at ends, 8/4. Decayed. YBC 9676.

Male in flat cap, god led by goddess with head turned back, male in flat cap, arms folded at waist, enthroned god with saw and rays, mace, tree.

469. Dark gray brown limestone. 33×20/18 (concave). Worn. NBC 6011.

God shouldering mace, led by second god, seated god with saw, rays at left shoulder, before him god with right hand extended, branch in left.

470. Shell. 32×19/18 (concave). Decayed. NBC 9127.

Gatepost held by divine attendant, head turned back, god led by second god with head turned back, left hand extended, seated god with saw and rays.

Compare *Boehmer,* 451 (III).

471. Shell. 34×21/19(concave). Bore 6/4. NBC 5992. *Yale Library Gazette* 35 (1960), p. 27, no. 35.

Seated god with streams from shoulders, pronged container (?) above to left, two fish to right, male attendant with whip over shoulder, birdman with rope at neck, one end hanging in front, the other end held by male attendant with star between his arms, fish above.

Compare *Boehmer,* 512–13 (III).

469

470

471

472

473

474

475

472. Black serpentine, green mottled. 33×19. New impression. *Newell* 668. *Boehmer*, 1164 (II).

Attendant with pail, worshipper with kid led by two-faced god, seated god with streams at shoulders, fish above; inscription.

473. Black serpentine. 32×20/18(concave). Bore 6/3½. NBC 3170. *Yale Library Gazette* 35 (1960), p. 27, no. 36.

Seated god holding three ears of grain, goat rearing before him, worshipper with kid; above: four goats emerging from enclosure on line; below: goat with pail under it, three seated men, the first milking, the second perhaps playing on pipe, the third holding vessel.

For the principal theme compare *Boehmer*, 561 (I). Dairy scenes as in the secondary of 473 commonly occur in designs which show a male figure, apparently not divine, who is carried upward by an eagle, a theme generally believed to depict the myth of Etana, *Boehmer*, 693–703a (III), pp. 122f. Taken together these representations suggest that the man on an eagle was the principal actor in an Akkadian myth dealing with life on farms and perhaps with the wilder country nearby. Dairy scenes and maybe scenes of hunting (compare *Boehmer*, 718a–23 with 699) could have evoked the whole myth. In any case a connection of the Akkadian myth with the later Etana story rests entirely on their one common element, a man carried on an eagle.

474. Dark green serpentine. 35×20/19(concave) Bore 6/3½. NBC 3285.

Enthroned god, god holding plow who leads another looking back, human with arms folded at waist; inscription.

Compare *Boehmer*, 533 (III).

475. Dark grayish brown mottled limestone. 29×19. NBC 6016.

Seated goddess, crescent above "star" over arm, bearded worshipper with kid between two female attendants with pails, small female worshipper under arm of the male.

The "star" may stand for the god sign, thus identifying the seated female as a goddess. For the style compare *Boehmer*, 648 (III).

FIGS. 476–481

476. Shell. 36×20. Worn. *Newell* 115. Not shown. *Boehmer,* 1516 (III).

Worshipper, attendant with pail, figure stretching arm toward bearded seated god (?) holding cup under crescent.

Compare *Boehmer,* 659 (III).

477. Shell. 41×25/23(concave). NBC 5993. Van Buren, *AfO* 11 (1935–36), fig. 34 (p. 21), for lizard p. 26, n. 217. *Boehmer,* 539 (III).

Seated god, crescent above, two gods with outstretched hands, star above lizard between them, scorpion, male worshipper, tree.

478. Green serpentine, dark mottled. 36×22½/20(concave). Worn. YBC 9707.

Attendant god behind seated god, inscription, three gods.

The adjacent hands of the gods beside the inscription were probably turned back to make room. Compare *Boehmer,* 627–28 (III).

479. Shell. 36×21/19(irregular). Decayed. NBC 11071.

Seated god, god leading female (?), worshipper in flat hat.

For a god leading a worshipper see *Ash C,* 383 (III).

480. Rock crystal. 19×11. Chipped. NBC 5958.

Figure with left arm at side; two worshiping figures, first in broad-trimmed hat, seated god (?).

The coarseness of the design is probably due to poor mastery of the material as well as wear.

481. Shell. 33½×19½. *Newell* 671 ("doubtful"). Not shown. *Boehmer,* 1565 (III?).

Two figures behind seated figure, two figures in front.

Two worn shell seals: 481x, NCBS 860, 37×22/20(concave), with seated god (?), two worshippers and starspade; 481xx, NBC 6013, 36×21, with figures but no recognizable design.

477

478

479

480

482

484

485

486

488

Post-Akkadian

The brilliant achievements of the great Akkadians (2350–2200) were succeeded by the rather stodgy work of their followers rather mixed with that of Gutian invaders from the north. Later and more important came a Sumerian revival in the south (2150–2000).

Post-Akkadian, perhaps somewhat later, a series of seals shows an eagle between animals, mounted on a hill, or shown separately, 482–91. Scorpions separated from birds are presented in 492; figures, probably female, appear above the birds in 493;

rows of females and males predominate in 494–97. Mythological figures of diverse character center about a holy image in 498–99, the latter probably a fake. A bull bearing a winged temple squats beside a goddess in 500–01, while a chariot perhaps driven by a deity is followed by three figures with symbols in 502. A man rides a quadruped in 503, and two men sit sideways on goats in 504. Gods or heroes struggle with deformed animals in 505–06; in 507 crude creatures are mostly hidden by cuneiform, while heroes contend with animals in 508–10.

FIGS. 482–488

482. Dark "steatite." 25×14. Worn. YBC 12643.

Spread eagle between two lying goats with heads turned back; ball staff, vessel and star (?) above.

Compare *Parrot*, 10, 12–16, Post-Akkadian (11 possibly earlier); *OIP* 72, 641 (called late Agade findspot), 683 (Gutian-Ur III findspot).

The early ball staff, with the "ball" centered on the staff as here, has a rare Akkadian appearance in *CANES*, 190 (= *Boehmer*, 456, III); or apparently even earlier in *CANES*, 84 of Early Dynastic III, but like other filling motifs there it seems to have been a later addition.

The later ball staff, with the "ball" on one side, occurs infrequently before late Neo-Sumerian when it replaced the early type; for rare Ur III examples see *CANES*, 284, *Aulock*, 281; also *Kültepe 1949*, 662, the seal of a servant of Ibbi-Sin reused on a Cappadocian case. After being very popular in Old Babylonian glyptic, the ball staff disappeared from the Babylonian repertory, but it sometimes appears in later peripheral seals, especially in Mitannian (e.g. NBC 9136).

483. Dark "steatite." 24×12½. Worn. *Newell* 52. Not shown.

Theme as in 482; crescent above.

484. Dark gray serpentine. 20×10. NBC 9139.

Spread eagle, scorpion; star above.

485. "Steatite." 26×11. NBC 9121.

Vertically marked festoon, spread eagle above it; below: angled stroke over dots on top of horizontally marked "hill."

Compare *Parrot*, 6–7, Post-Akkadian.

486. Dark "steatite." 23×12½. Chipped. NBC 5963.

Like 485, but top of "hill" lacks dots.

487. Yellowish "steatite." 25½×13/12 (irregular). Worn. *Newell* 55. Not shown.

Like 485, but with hatched line as festoon, star and crescent above.

488. Black limestone. 18×9. New impression. *Newell* 54.

Two-line festoon with reversed eagle on either side.

489. "Steatite." 21×9. *Newell* 53. Not shown.

Reversed eagles; star, crescent, two dots as fill.

Compare *Parrot*, 9.

490. "Steatite." 11×6. *Newell* 45. Not shown.

Two eagles.

Compare *Parrot*, 8 (reversed eagles).

491. Dark gray serpentine. Boss at each end marked by stepped concentric circles. 24 (seal 15)×13. New impression. *Newell* 185 (photograph of shape, drawn fig. 2, p. 4).

Spread eagle, on either side disk containing eight-pointed star centered on dot; inscription.

492. Black serpentine. 44×8/11, irregular. NBC 1493.

Two scorpions, three-line divider, two water birds over two wavy lines.

Compare *Parrot*, 18–20.

493. Impressions of two seals on tablet with pinched corners and sloping sides (obverse smaller than rounded reverse). Height A–22, B–28. (a-b) Left and bottom edges with A, (c) top edge with B. YBC 10534. Date not identified. Tablet Old Babylonian.

A–Woman facing left, hand raised in wor-
ship; second one, hands at waist; (traces on reverse: seated figure, attendant; two-line divider; at least two water birds. B–Stag with head turned back, snake (?) (or blood) under mouth; back of erect lion; (trace of at least one human figure on obverse).

For A compare *Parrot*, 30–38, *UE* 10, 247–56, Post-Akkadian or Ur III. For the style in B compare 309 above of Early Dynastic III.

494. Light green nephrite. 26×8. NBC 9345.

Four women, tree; two-line divider; woman grasping date cluster on palm, two more women, ground line.

For various similar Post-Akkadian designs see *Boehmer*, p. 125, n. 6; compare *UE* 2, 188, which by its more careful detail should be late Akkadian.

495. Lapis lazuli. 27×7/9½, convex. Worn. YBC 12630.

Female worshipper behind and three more in front of seated goddess; two-line divider; seated deity (?), two female worshippers, palm with date clusters.

496. Brown glazed composition. 18½×8½. (a) Impression, (b) Shape. YBC 12628.

Four women, hands at waist, blob above; two hatched bands as borders.

491

493a

493b

493c

492

494

495

496a

496b

497

498

499

500

501

502

497. Dark gray agate, brownish chalcedony inclusions. 26½×13. NBC 9351.

Five men (?) in vertically pleated (?) garments, hands at waist; five "stars" over two lines above.

For similar designs, probably Neo-Sumerian, with comparable engraving see *UE* 10, 548–49, perhaps 550.

498. Dark "steatite." 23×11. YBC 12745. *Yale Library Gazette* 35 (1960), p. 27, no. 41.

Nude male worshipper holding upended animal with hatched body and long snout over uncertain object; second worshipper holding vase with libation pouring from spout; goddess in doubled niche.

For Neo-Sumerian variations of the subject see *Philadelphia*, 156, *UE* 10, 223–24, *Louvre A.*, 960 (latter presumably recut).

499. Dark green serpentine. 15×9. YBC 12579. *Yale Library Gazette* 35 (1960), p. 27, no. 42.

Snake god, his left arm fused with right arm of standing figure in long garment whose left arm is raised in worship, female (?) worshipper with kid, nude male with cup (?), nude figure in niche.

For a comparable Neo-Sumerian rendering of the snake god see *Fauna*, fig. 107. However, in 499 the treatment of all parts of the design may be questioned: the arm that the snake god and the next figure seem to have in common, the worshipper with a kid, probably female, the male with a cup (?), the feature-

less deity in the niche. Then too, the engraving can hardly be paralleled. It must be regarded as very probable that the design was copied.

500. Dark brownish green serpentine. 21×12. NBC 9138, *Yale Library Gazette* 35 (1960), p. 27, no. 38.

Winged shrine on back of lying bull, seated goddess with outstretched hand (chipped), crescent above.

Compare *Boehmer*, 615–19 and related pieces, p. 107, dated late Akkad III, but more probably Post-Akkadian, except perhaps no. 1403 (= *OIP* 72, 584) which presumably had an "Early Agade" findspot.

501. "Steatite." 17×8½/8, irregular. Worn. NCBS 744.

Seated goddess holding angular ropes from lying bull with winged shrine on its back, tree.

502. Dark "steatite." 25×13. Worn. YBC 12583. *Yale Library Gazette* 35 (1960), p. 28, no. 47. Buchanan, *Iraq* 33 (1971), pl. Ic, pp. 3, 17.

Ass(?)-drawn chariot with winged (?) deity (?) as driver; three figures each holding standard, on first, spread eagle, on second, water bird, on third, probably snake with pin through it, first two figures in long garments, the smaller third perhaps belted nude.

The so-called ass may be a crude version of the serpentdragon as in Akkadian 454. For a chariot scene with a beast and driver recalling 502 see *Parrot*, 250, Post-Akkadian.

503. Impressions all over tablet. Height 19. (a) Reverse (partly shown), (b) Drawing. NBC 2200. Shu-Sin 9. *BIN* 3, 253 (poor drawing). Same seal: *Brussels*, 58, pp. 132f. Drehem text.

Perhaps: standing figure holding head of long-tailed quadruped with man bestride it holding whip (?) in right hand, his left resting on (?) back of the animal (this arm partly coincides with frame of inscription into which rear of the animal projects); to right, male in rounded wide-brimmed hat holding scimitar (?).

Irregularity in the frame of the inscription suggests that the design had been cut previously.

For other Neo-Sumerian scenes showing a human bestride an animal see *Philadelphia*, 154 with a quadruped perhaps as in 503, *UE* 10, 270 with a mount like a serpentdragon, *Parrot*, 50 with a bovine mount. Heroes appear bestride a beast in Akkadian designs like *Boehmer*, 294 of I, 211–13, 237 of III; while in *Boehmer*, 720 of III there is actually a man riding a horselike creature.

For early horseback riding see P. R. S. Morey, *Iraq* 22 (1960), pp. 36ff., also Farkas, *Persica* 4 (1969), p. 58, n. 5, which cites the "horses" in *Louvre A.*, 861, probably a Cappadocian cyl-

inder of early Old Babylonian times, also *CANES*, 517, though the creatures there, added in crude Old Babylonian style, are not certainly horses, and the terracotta, *BM* 22958 (= *Opificius*, 638, p. 174), which seems to show a dog and was so described in Van Buren, *Clay Figurines*, p. 159, no. 757.

504. Dark "steatite." 22×12. YBC 12614. *Yale Library Gazette* 35 (1960), p. 28, no. 48.

Two goats, each with man seated sideways on it, crescent and star above.

Compare the more mannered goats in *Ash C*, 822, *Louvre S.*, 255, both Provincial Elamite.

505. Green nephrite. 15½×8½×8(concave). NCBS 700. *Yale Library Gazette* 43 (1968), pl. II.2, pp. 94f.

God with axe attacking lion demon on one knee, its head turned back, in grasp of second god.

Compare *Boehmer*, 344, late Akkad III.

506. Dark "steatite." 23½×11½. NBC 9112. *Yale Library Gazette* 35 (1960), p. 27, no. 43.

Kneeling hero in wide-brimmed cap, grasping legs of bull with head turned back, one horn of which is held by hero in fringed (?) kilt; star and crescent above.

503a

503b

504

505

506

507

508

509

510

507. Impression. Height ext. 27. Reverse shown. YBC 13483. Ibbi-Sin I.

Top: hero in long open robe facing right, inscription (first line), erect lion attacking erect bull with head turned back (horns visible in obverse), inscription (third line), figure facing left (?) in tall hat (?) and long garment, inscription (second line), figure in long open robe (?), one arm bent forward, his back to the first figure; bottom same but begins with the last two figures cited above.

For attenuated figures in an Early Akkadian seal see *Boehmer,* 48 in which much Early Dynastic detail still appears. The inscription in 507 has been added in summary fashion to what must have been a very worn design. Perhaps at the same time there was some attempt to restore part of the latter. This would account for the presumed long garments, an odd detail in an early contest scene, if the original design was such.

508. Green serpentine, dark flecked. 23×15/14 (concave). NBC 6675.

Two erect buffalos with heads up, back to back, each held by hero; third buffalo.

Coarsely engraved throughout. Notice how the headdress of the heroes is like that of the female figures in 494–96; see also the female attendants in Akkadian 461–63.

509. Pale yellow alabaster. 19×13/12 (concave). Worn. NBC 5970.

Hero grasping bull with head up, lion held by second hero; starspade.

For Post-Akkadian contest scenes with two contending pairs see *Parrot,* 90, 92, 94–95, dated Ur III; probably most of *Boehmer,* 266–70 called late Akkad III; compare *Frankfort,* p. 144, n. 1, including *YOS* 4, 196 (drawn = YBC 1282).

510. Pale brown limestone. 17×10. Worn. NBC 5959.

Nude hero grasping bull, lion, second hero; animals' heads turned back over starspade into which their tails extend.

Compare *OIP* 72, 696, Post-Akkadian (*Boehmer,* p. 44, n. 183).

FIGS. 507–510

CONTESTS

One aspect of the Neo-Sumerian phase is a stress on contests of heroes and animals. A few continued the old scheme of conflicts in which each human aggressor fought an animal, the latter back to back, 511–14. Erotic themes feature but do not predominate in the conflict of a lion with a bullman and a hero, 515. It is probable that a similar relationship of beast and warriors without the erotic element held for 516–17. A two-headed male stands beside two heroes mastering a reversed bull in 518. A lion facing right is in conflict with a hero on either side, 519–25; in the latter the hero on the side wears a feather crown while before it comes a scene showing an eagle above flowing waters. In 526–31 a lion facing left or in contorted positions struggles between two warriors while in 532 the creature in conflict is a liongriffin. The lion or liongriffin is placed between a contender in 533–35. Palm branches in a largely geometric setting, 536.

511. Impressions of two seals on both faces of tablet. Height A–ext. 18; B–ext. 22. Reverse shown. YBC 1203. Shu-Sin 2.

A–Worshipper led by goddess, enthroned goddess, inscription. B–Inscription, nude belted hero on either side, each grappling with lions back to back.

The use of two or more seals on an Ur III tablet or its case seems to have occurred relatively late in the dynasty: *Louvre T.*, 140–44, 181–84, 192, 194, 198 (the earliest, Amar-Sin 7); *ITT* 2, pl. II 4266, *ITT* 3, pl. II 6638; *Philadelphia*, 275–76; *Ash C*, 439; below 525, 673 (late Shulgi or more likely Ibbi-Sin); also 511x, NBC 7766 (unpublished case with two worship scenes, Ibbi-Sin 2).

Two or more seals sometimes occur in Ur III bullae, perhaps not before Amar-Sin; *Louvre T.*, 219–22; *Brussels*, 75, pp. 151ff. (see under 643 below). Two possibly contemporary inscriptions appear on the same seal, 580.

512. Impressions all over case (unopened). Height 25. (a) Reverse, (b) Left edge, (c) Right edge. NCBT 2248. Shulgi 47 or Amar-Sin 3.

Inscription over liongriffin (?) (one wing visible); on either side, nude bearded hero, full face with side curls, grappling with erect lion; between pair to right, crescent above antelope with head turned back; between pair to left, water bird above small worshipper in long garment; spread eagle above the lions' tails.

513. Brownish limestone. 43×26. Unperforated. Probably unfinished and discarded. *Newell* 93. Not shown.

Two full-face heroes; two inscriptions (one worn).

514. Impression. Height ext. 26. Reverse partly shown. NBC 2356. Shulgi 38.

Inscription squeezed into open space between belted full-face bullman and nude belted hero, full face, bearded with side curls; each grasping animal.

A similar design appears on both faces of the tablet, 514x, YBC 9805, height 29; inscription.

511

512a

512b

512c

514

515

516

517

515. Mottled dark green serpentine. 27×15. Worn. YBC 12637.

Belted full-face bullman grasping neck and tail of lion, forelegs of which are held by nude belted hero in vertically marked headgear, crescent above arm, water bird below; inscription (second line), erotic scene ("anal" intercourse) above another (female on male); inscription (first line).

The secondary motif here is unusual, since it consists of two erotic scenes that have not so far been found together, one of human congress from the rear, here most likely "anal" intercourse, above one with the woman in the superior position. The combination is doubtfully suggested by the squatting spreadlegged female above a scene of fully clothed "anal" intercourse in a Syrian seal, *Moortgat Festschrift*, pl. 33.4, Porada, pp. 234ff. On the other hand, "anal" intercourse appears with "normal" in a number of seal designs; see *UE* 10, 374, Neo-Sumerian, in the secondary as here; or from the archaic period: *UE* 3, 368, very probably *OIP* 72, 340, perhaps *Ash C*, 254. On normal and "anal" intercourse in the Persian Gulf and Indian spheres c. 2000 B.C., see *Studies Landsberger*, p. 206, n. 14.

So-called "normal" intercourse has been the standard position throughout the course of Western history at least since classical times, certainly since Christianity became dominant. In it the male covers the female, a relationship based on the penis entering the vagina from above. It is very possible this was also true of the ancient Near East, but there "normal" sexual relations were largely private and not commonly a subject for art. It seems first attested in *OIP* 72, 796, of post-Jamdat Nasr at the latest and in *UE* 3, 367–68, 385, early impressions from Ur, though it is possible that an earlier version of such a scene was depicted in the Protoliterate impression, *Ash C*, 4. For further Early Dynastic examples see under *Ash C*, 254.

Some of the not very numerous later representations of the "normal" position in ancient Western Asia are cited under 458 above, with one conspicuous exception. The Assur expedition found a number of lead objects of the thirteenth century that are undoubtedly erotic in character; Andrae, *WVDOG* 58, pp. 103f., pl. 45, 46n. It is true that one (pl. 45c) seems to be of "anal" type, but the most explicit are clearly "normal" (pl. 45a-b, 46n). Their setting is a kind of altar, but they can hardly be called sacred; at least one (pl. 45b) with three actors is clearly obscene. It looks like blatant advertising of temple prostitution contrasting with the more discrete earlier scenes.

Human congress from the rear, commonly anal, is depicted as the central theme, or as part of it, in Neo-Sumerian seals: Parrot, *MAM* 2, 3.949, *Louvre D.*, 148, *Art Bulletin* 13, (1931), plate D (p. 223), 14b (p. 224), pp. 232, 234 ("Selucid"); also in Cypriote of ca. 1300 B.C.: Porada, *AJA* 52 (1948), pl. X.39, p. 191, n. 86; *BM* W 138 (not illustrated); compare the Early Dynastic II version in the secondary of 244 above; and, even earlier, in impressions, perhaps of Early Dynastic I, from Ur, *UE* 3, 368–70. Prehistoric examples are cited below. In other art forms, notice the quite common occurrence of the "anal" theme in Old Babylonian terracottas, many of them unpublished; see *Opificius*, pp. 166ff.

It is very possible that, by the position of her left arm, the bent over female in the "anal" scene of 515 here was thought of as drinking by a tube from a vessel. If so, her action is one commonly depicted with a theme of this type. In *UE* 3, 368, probably the most instructive of our early examples, the act of drinking may be implied by the pots over which the woman bends. The scene in this impression also has a suggestion of violence against the woman. In 515, too, violence is expressed by the way in which the man grips the woman's right arm. Similar violence in various forms often appears in erotic scenes. Thus in 515 the great length of the penis suggests a possibility much more explicitly displayed in a few other glyptic designs; for example: *Brussels Suppl.*, 1583, p. 80, an early Old Babylonian seal, is called a curious contest; while in *Frankfort*, pl. XXIIIh, p. 132, Akkadian (= *Boehmer*, 808) said to depict a killing, the gigantic member held by the waiting man on the right is certainly not a club.

The Ur impression, *UE* 3, 368, shows the woman fully clothed as in the Syrian seal cited at first, thus dissociating the action from ordinary sexual intercourse. On the basis of the more carefully depicted nude representations, the term *anal intercourse* seems to be the most generally appropriate for scenes showing one human figure behind another in an erotic posture. It is called "anal," but in some cases depending on the angle of approach, the actual contact may have been with the vagina. Unfortunately such a distinction is too difficult to discern in the scale of our seals. Consequently the adjective "anal" remains the most acceptable. It has sometimes been suggested that a homosexual relationship was depicted here. However, in all reasonably clear renderings, the forward member of the pair appears to be female. The position may have been adopted in a fertility ritual, because of the great efficacy thought to derive from an act simulating animal copulation; or it may have been favored by women of whom ritual intercourse was required.

For the lower scene in the secondary of 515, with the woman in the superior position, compare *Louvre T.*, 88, *Parrot*, 259, both Neo-Sumerian, both having an element of violence which is missing in the equivalent part of 515, perhaps for lack of space. This scene has been interpreted as depicting the attack of the female demon who draws off a sleeping man's strength, Contenau, *La magie*, p. 94. However, this suggestion becomes hardly tenable in view of the combination of scenes in 515. It is more likely that both scenes here deal with ritual intercourse. Since 515 and the two other examples cited, showing the woman in the superior position, are Neo-Sumerian, it may be that the position came into temporary favor at this time. However, its later occurrence may be indicated in two Old Babylonian terracottas, *OIP* 78, pl. 137.6 (both cited there).

Perhaps the earliest ritual scene so far known on seals is that with "dancing" figures in the stamp seal impression, *Gawra* II, 92 from the well of level XIII. Somewhat later, probably from level XIA, are two impressions with a figure at an altar, *Gawra* II, 82–83 (same seal), 85; and two with erotic scenes, one "anal," the other facing seated on an altar, *Gawra* II, 86–87. Two erotic scenes respectively of the same type were found on impressions from level VIII, *Gawra* I, 41, 40; while on one from level XI there is a seated erotic scene without an altar, *Gawra* II, 88. Seated facing intercourse is also depicted in the early Ur impressions, *UE* 3, 365–66, probably of Early Dynastic I. Prehistoric stamp seals showing intercourse also include: the facing creatures, presumably standing, in the carinated hemispheroid 73; the "anal" scene in the convex handled seal, *AMI* 5, p. 88, fig. 14, TG 2362 (collected Tepe Giyan); the similar scenes showing "quadrupeds" in the hemispheroids, *Giyan*, pl. VI 4 (top = 35.5), 38.24 (see *JAOS* 87 [1967], p. 275).

516. Impressions on both faces of tablet. Height 19. Reverse partly shown. NBC 3249. Shulgi 34. Same seal on YBC 732, YBC 1226. Jokha texts.

Erect lion (?) (accidental winglike strokes) in grasp of full-face bullman; inscription; nude belted full-face hero also (?) grappling with the lion.

517. Like 516. Height 25. Reverse partly shown. NBC 3641. From Amar-Sin 7 or later.

Trace of hero (?); inscription; nude hero, full face with side curls, holding rampant bull.

518. Dark "steatite." 23×12. NBC 4952. *Yale Library Gazette* 35 (1960), p. 27, no. 44 (plate).

Nude male with two heads; nude belted full-face hero on either side of upended bull, upper body of which they grasp, the right hero stepping on the bull's head; inscription.

An upended buffalo between two heroes occurs in a seal of Gudea of Lagash, Porada, *Andrews University Seminary Studies* 6 (1968), pp. 140f., pl. I.2; see also the contest scenes *Boehmer,* 272–73, p. 165, belonging to a son and a grandson of Gudea.

For a two-headed male receiving worship see *Louvre A.,* 251, late Neo-Sumerian; compare the small one in *UE* 10, 475, Old Babylonian. The figure probably derives from Usmu, the two-faced divine attendant of the water god in Akkadian seals (*Boehmer,* pp. 88ff.); see also the four-faced bronze figures of a god and a goddess, probably Old Babylonian, *OIP* 60, pl. 77–81, pp. 21f.

519. "Steatite." 21×10. Top broken. NBC 2594.

Two nude heroes grappling with lion between them; inscription.

520. Pink limestone, red mottling. 25×13. Worn. NBC 6009.

Like 519; inscription.

521. Brown limestone, pink mottling. Bottom half broken off. 11½(ext)×11½. *Newell* 108. Not shown.

Like 519; inscription.

522. Like 516. Height ext. 20. Reverse partly shown. NBC 318. Shulgi 34.

Like 519; inscription.

A similar design on reverse of tablet, 522x, YBC 13219, Shulgi 38, or Shu-Sin 4, height ext. 29; inscription.

523. Like 512. Height ext. 20. (a) Reverse, (b) Top edge. NCBT 2247.

Like 519; inscription.

A similar design on fragment of case, tablet not impressed, 523x, NCBT 1382, Shulgi 37, height 18; inscription.

518

519

520

522

523a

523b

524

525a

525b

526

525c

528

529a

529b

524. Dark green serpentine. 24×11. New impression. *Newell* 104.

Like 519, but linear stylized; inscription.

Compare the lion in the curiously mannered "Ur III" seal, *CANES*, 271; also compare the liongriffin in 578 below.

525. Impressions of two seals on tablet. Height A–19½; B–21. A–reverse (a), top and right edge; B–obverse, left (b) and bottom edge; (c) Drawing. NBC 9265. Ibbi-Sin 2 (?).

A–Spread lion-headed eagle, facing right, holding at an angle on either side small goat with folded legs, above double line of streams that arch over two small men who hold vase between them from which the streams flow, double zigzag line (water) below; bearded hero in high vertically marked hat grappling with rampant lion, head and tail of which are held by second hero.

B–Inscription; two-line divider; small kilted man, one arm raised, other holding notched pole; on either side (visible in obverse) erect lion (?).

The eagle holding goats in A recalls the one in *Ash C*, 419, where it apparently is restrained by two heroes. The vertically marked hat worn by the bearded hero here resembles the more conical-shaped one in 627, less so the hat of one of the heroes in *UE* 10, 561 (Neo-Sumerian). It could represent a feather crown as possibly in *Ash C*, 290 and 409.

A crown of feathers, rather than vegetation, may be worn by a "dancer" in a terracotta, perhaps late Neo-Sumerian, *Opificius*, 568, pp. 158, 232; compare the tall headgear, apparently shaped to look like a feather crown, in *Opificius*, 576. Though such examples show how uncertain possible representations of the feather crown may be, it is very likely that one appears in *Ash C*, 438.

525x, *UDT* (= NBC) 18, on case like 512, drawn, height ext. 23, Amar-Sin 6, Tello text; traces of spread eagle before erect lion between full-face bullman and hero, inscription.

526. Dark gray serpentine. 23×11½. NCBS 800.

Lion held by two nude heroes, spread eagle in front of it; inscription.

527. Shell. 20½×9½. *Newell* 107. Not shown.

Lion, its head pointing up, in grasp of hero on either side, crescent above, scorpion to right, mace to left; inscription.

528. Impressions all over tablet case (fragment). Height 26. YBC 13112. Shulgi 33 (inside of case). Jokha text.

Lion with head turned back in grasp of two nude belted heroes; inscription.

529. Impressions all over case (unopened). Height 20½. (a) Reverse, (b) Left edge. YBC 1759. Shulgi 30. Jokha text.

Like 528, but with lion other way; inscription.

530. "Steatite." 25½×11½. Bore 6/3½. NCBS 829.

Like 529, but with heroes in broad-brimmed flat caps; inscription.

531. Dark red serpentine. 19×10. Crude. *Newell* 109. Not shown.

Like 529, but hero to left in flat cap and long robe, cross before him, vertical object behind.

532. Dark "steatite." 28×15. *Ward,* 187a. *Newell* 105. Not shown.

Liongriffin held by full-face bullman and nude belted god; inscription.

533. Impression. Height ca. 25. (a) Left edge, (b) Drawing. YBC 1668. Shulgi 27. *YOS* 4, 248, drawn (bent arm of hero confused with liongriffin's foreleg).

Hero (?) grasping foreleg of erect lion, its head back, foreleg up (trace on obverse), holds foreleg of liongriffin, its other foreleg extended; inscription.

For the liongriffin in Neo-Sumerian contests with two contending pairs see *Louvre T.,* 51 (drawn), 72–73; between two heroes, *Louvre T.,* 74, *Parrot,* 69, *Ash C,* 417–18; with only a bullman, *UE* 10, 213.

534. Impressions on both faces of two tablets. Height 24. (a-b) Reverses partly shown, (c) Drawing. NBC 3262 (= a), YBC 897 (= b), also NBC 3247. Amar-Sin 7, 6, 2. Jokha texts.

Full-face bullman grasping foreleg of erect lion on either side, the lions' jaws agape, tails curling between their legs; small suppliant goddess facing right; inscription with two geese (?) under it.

Compare *UE* 2, 332, *Parrot,* 93; for a hero between two lions see *UE* 2, 382; all Post-Akkadian.

535. "Steatite." 22×10. New impression. *Newell* 158. *Frankfort,* p. 142, n. 1 ("Guti"); p. 146, n. 2.

Standing female with hands at waist, erect lion on either side as if attacking, scorpion beside the female; terminal: goose on pole.

536. Impression on both faces of tablet. Height ext. 31. Reverse partly shown. YBC 14697. Shulgi 47.

Deity seated on throne (?) (traces), two palm branches in tall vessel over alternating triangles; inscription below oblong object (twist?) (length uncertain because of overlapping rollings).

See the date palm with clusters in 550, 676; or placed in a vase, 576, 680–90.

530

533a

533b

534a

534c

534b

535

536

537a 537b

538

539

540

WORSHIP SCENES

One group consists of a lone figure, 537; a scene showing a goddess leading a worshipper before an enthroned god, the seal naming the early Neo-Sumerian ruler, Gudea of Lagash, 538; several seals featuring a worshipper before a seated goddess, 539–42; or with an added worshipper, 543–47; or with one figure leading another plus a worshipper, 548–49; or a worshipper led before a goddess, 550–61; partly Post-Akkadian, partly Neo-Sumerian, especially early. A large Neo-Sumerian group features a suppliant goddess and a worshipper led by a goddess before another seated goddess, 562–64; without the suppliant goddess, 565–85; with the enthroned goddess holding a crescent standard, 586. A goddess appears full face in 587. A worshipper is led by a goddess before a seated goddess with weapons at her shoulders, 588, seated on geese or with geese before her, 589–93. Seal 594 shows a worshipper before an enthroned goddess (unfinished).

537. Green mottled, black serpentine. 18×9/8½, cut back in area of figure. NBC 9383.

Crisscross in linear borders, "god" with saw (?) enthroned on line.

Compare the seated figure with saw in *OIP* 72, 690, *UE* 2, 259, both Post-Akkadian. As often in this period, the "god" lacks a horned crown. In 537 he has probably been added to an originally all geometric Jamdat Nasr seal like *Ash C*, 69–70. Crisscross patterns do occur from Early Dynastic on, but normally in a register separate from the main theme as in 459 above.

538. Green nephrite. 26×15/14(concave). Cracked. YBC 9685. Seal of servant of Gudea, ensi of Lagash.

Worshipper led by goddess who wears three neck rings over crossed shoulder straps above pleated skirt, long tress of hair at back; god enthroned on platform; inscription.

The headdress of the worshipper looks as though it might be a skull cap which would compress the hair and give the bald effect favored for Ur III worshippers; compare the bulging look of the possibly similar device in 550, or its length at the back, as if for a woman's hair, in 565. A truly bald head can hardly be recognized in the small scale of the seals, but the effect of such is very common in mature Neo-Sumerian style.

An important exception is provided by *CANES*, 274 of the time of Gudea, showing a bearded worshipper with a high mound of hair apparently banded; see *CANES*, p. 35 on this representation as a possible survival of Akkad traditions at Lagash; compare the uncertain rendering in *Berlin*, 250 from Ashur.

For a less elaborate tress than that worn by the goddess see 547. Neck rings also appear on various goddesses in 553, 563–64. Compare the four rings with a pendant attached in *UE* 10, 423. In this rendering it is clear that the rings form a pendant and are not part of the garment. The rings may be fastened to the long ribbon or tassel down the back sometimes worn by suppliant goddesses as in 621; see Spycket, *RA* 42 (1948), pp. 89ff.

A pleated skirt alternates with a flounced one as the favored garment of the leading goddess. Usually it has a broad border at the bottom as here; for exceptions see 554, 582, 582x. The latter probably reflects the somewhat more common Akkadian practice of wearing pleated skirts without bottom trim. The same influence may explain the unusual instances in which this goddess has a fringed robe: 552, 583.

The crossed shoulder straps resemble those of the leading goddesses in 581 (pleated skirt), 553(?), 583 (fringed), 550 and 592 (flounced); see also *CANES*, 274 (pleated), *Berlin*, 250 (fringed). The use of cross straps is rare compared with the usual practice of covering the left shoulder and leaving the right bare; this is reversed for figures facing right as often in Akkadian glyptic. In late Neo-Sumerian seals cross straps are sometimes worn by the leading goddess, *CANES*, 304, *Ash C*, 450; in Old Babylonian they appear quite often on the full-face war goddess, occasionally on other deities.

Seals like 538 naming Gudea of Lagash include *Louvre T.*, 108 (drawn), *CANES*, 274, *Boehmer*, 439. As a group they show features like those cited above, which are generally early in character; also survivals with Akkad traits like the bearded worshipper already mentioned or the use of a god, instead of a goddess, to lead the worshipper as in the last two. For the latter feature, see also *ITT* 5, pl. 1.10051, undated, or *RA* 23 (1926), fig. p. 35 (drawn), naming Ibbi-Sin. The seal of a son of Gudea, *Parrot*, 131, is too obscure for details to be made out, though the seated goddess is said to hold a cup. This is true of many seated deities in Akkadian seals, but quite rare in Ur III (see perhaps 579, 605).

Compare *Southesk*, Qa36 for a seal in "green stone" almost certainly by the same artist as 538; the first two figures are very alike; see also the exaggerated size of the open palms of the facing deities.

539. Impressions all over case (tablet not impressed). Height c. 21. Left edge shown. NBC 7768. Ibbi-Sin 3.

Worshipper with left hand over table having offerings on top; crescent above right arm of goddess on throne with low back; ball staff above vase.

For the design, especially the stand, see *UE* 10, 282–83, Post-Akkadian. Few seals in mature Neo-Sumerian (Ur III) style show only a worshipper before a deity; see *Berlin*, 265, 267.

540. Impressions all over tablet. Height 22½. Obverse partly shown. NBC 7804. Shu-Sin 8.

Worshipper, left hand before face; spread eagle above extended right arm of goddess enthroned on platform (trace on reverse); inscription.

In simple crudity 540 somewhat resembles *OIP* 72, 585, said to be from an early Agade findspot but found in an open area.

541. Impressions all over case (unopened). Height ext. 22. Reverse partly shown. Worn. NCBT 2251. Shulgi 47 or Amar-Sin 3.

Worshipper, right hand before face, left at waist; spread eagle above two-legged stand topped by two incurving volutes; seated goddess; inscription.

Compare the more carefully executed figures with nothing between them in 541x, *UDT* (= NBC) 23, drawn, Shulgi 47.

542. Dark gray serpentine. 18×11. *Newell* 170. Not shown.

Bird above scorpion, worshipper before enthroned goddess holding lionscimitar, vertical snake monster with pigtail.

543. Dark gray "steatite." 27×13½. Worn. NCBS 841.

Worshipper, left hand extended; stand with offerings before crescent over seated goddess (?); worshipper, right hand raised in worship.

For the stand, compare 545, 554.

544. Impressions on both faces and short sides of tablet. Height 18. Reverse partly shown. YBC 11244. Shulgi 43.

Suppliant goddess(?) in fringed mantle, hand before face; inscription (third line); goddess on throne with low back and angled top, suppliant goddess; inscription.

The inscription, undoubtedly added, is crowded by all the figures.

A comparable grouping, but without horned crowns, appears in *UE* 2, 262, Post-Akkadian. On the suppliant goddess see 547.

545. Dark gray serpentine. 28½×15/14(concave). NCBS 848.

Female worshipper with hands at waist, second one with left hand raised, crescent above stand with offerings, seated goddess.

That the seated figure is a deity must be assumed, though she does not wear a horned crown. This is also true of a number of Post-Akkadian seals in which the headgear is reasonably clear; see 546, 557, 560–61.

546. Rock crystal. 29×12. *Newell* 186 (boss with concentric circles at each end). Not shown.

Two worshippers, their left hands raised (the first one chipped), seated goddess, frame for inscription, linear borders.

Compare in rock crystal the crude seals, possibly Post-Akkadian, 549, 555, 560, also the better Ur III piece, 596.

547. Impressions on two tablets (chosen from two dozen with same seal). Height 26. (a-b) Reverses (partial). NBC 8094 (= a); YBC 919 (= b), drawn *YOS* 4, 146; compare *YOS* 4, 85 (= YBC 1037); *BIN* 6, 229, 236, 262 (= NBC 2072, 3449, 2087); *Ash C,* 440. Dates on the numerous tablets with this seal range from as early as Shulgi 35 (*BIN* 5, 227) to at least Amar-Sin 5 (*HUCA* 14). Jokha texts.

Worshipper, right hand at waist, left before face; suppliant goddess, tress (two lines) at back over shoulder; inscription; enthroned goddess, right hand extended, feet on low stool.

The suppliant goddess can be identified as the goddess Lama; Spycket, *RA* 54 (1960), pp. 73f. The inscription was cut after the design, as is shown by the curve in the left frame before the raised arms of the goddess. The unusual placing of the figures, as though facing the inscription, can be accounted for if the latter was cut over a third standing figure or some other subject.

548. White streaked, light brown marble. 30×21/20 (concave). Chipped. *Newell* 116. Not shown. *Ward,* 480. *Frankfort,* pl. 25a ("Guti").

Worshipper, cross, goddess led by goddess before seated goddess holding cup, crescent above, date palm.

549. Rock crystal. 21×11. Unfinished? *Newell* 138. Not shown.

Figure led by second figure, worshipper before seated deity.

550. "Steatite." 31×16. Bore, off center, conical at ends, 7/4/3½. YBC 13063.

Worshipper led by goddess towards goddess seated on "goose" (both goddesses wear crossed shoulder straps above flounced skirts), crescent above; palm with date clusters.

For presentation scenes with a similar tree see *OIP* 72, 689, *Parrot,* 217, or with the goddess on a "goose," but no tree, *Berlin,* 273, *CANES,* 260 (p. 32), all Post-Akkadian.

541

543

544

545

547a

547b

550

551

552

553

555

553

557

551. Dark gray serpentine. 21½×9½. NBC 9117.

Worshipper led by goddess toward seated goddess.

Compare *UE* 10, 288, Post-Akkadian, from a "Sargonic" grave. In it the horned crown of the leading goddess is simply but clearly rendered.

552. "Steatite." 28×14/13, concave. NCBS 827.

Theme of 551; crescent above, frame for inscription.

Traces of the same theme, 552x, NCBS 822, dark gray serpentine, 27×11½, broken.

553. "Steatite." 30×14. New impression. *Newell* 674 (incorrectly "forgery"). Buchanan, *JAOS* 74 (1954), p. 148, n. 5.

Theme of 551, spouted vessel and crescent in field; inscription (mostly enclosed).

554. Pale brown mottled marble. 22×11. *Newell* 122. Not shown.

Theme of 551, crescent over stand with loaves, platform under the seated goddess.

555. Rock crystal. 20×11. Worn. NBC 5974.

Theme of 551, crescent above.

556. Dark gray serpentine. 28×16. *Newell* 114. Not shown. *Frankfort,* p. 142, n. 1 ("Guti").

Seated goddess, crescent, goddess leading worshipper, tree.

For the headdress of the worshipper compare the heroes on the right in *Boehmer,* 107–08, Akkad Ic.

557. "Steatite." 23×11½. Bore (conical at ends), 5/3/2½. NBC 2593.

Goddess on low-backed throne, goddess leading worshipper, cross (star?) above.

FIGS. 551–557

558. Impressions on both faces of tablet. Height 19. (a) Reverse, (b) Drawing. YBC 1636. Amar-Sin 1. Jokha text.

Theme of 557; the goddesses in flounced garments; the throne two concentric squares; no star; inscription.

A different seal of the scribe Daga, 558x, *BIN* 5, 239 drawn (= NBC 3282), Amar-Sin 4.

For other Ur III examples of the seated goddess on the left see *Nikolski,* pl. III, 175, Shulgi 34; *ITT* 4, pl. II, 7479, Shu-Sin 8; add 558xx, NBC 351, tablet like 558, Amar-Sin 9, Jokha text, height 26, crescent above, small suppliant goddess probably before the seated goddess(?), inscription.

559. Like 558. Height c. 22. Reverse (partial). YBC 1559. Shulgi 38 or Shu-Sin 4. Jokha text.

Enthroned goddess, blob (crescent?) above, goddess in posture of one leading worshipper; inscription.

A bulge in the area of the inscription suggests that it was deeply cut, erasing the worshipper to be expected.

560. Rock crystal. 21×12. Chipped. NBC 2600.

Theme of 558.

561. Lapis lazuli. 37×11½. New impression. *Newell* 118.

Theme of 558, goddess on double platform; inscription; three-line divider; four swans in water.

Compare *UE* 10, 249 (= *Museum Journal* 20, pp. 297–99), time Amar-Sin (number confused).

562. Dark green serpentine. 42(face 33)×18/17(concave). Ends rounded to thin groove (10) around bore (7/4). Worn. (a) Impression, (b) Shape. NBC 6010. *Yale Library Gazette* 35 (1960), p. 27, no. 45. Cites *šakkanakku* (military governor) of Umma.

Suppliant goddess, worshipper led by goddess, goddess enthroned on platform; inscription; double-lined borders.

The shape probably copies Ur III cylinders the ends of which have been cut to resemble metal caps; see 491, 546, *Ward,* 17, *Ash C,* 420g, *Brussels,* 606 (pp. 84, 138).

A design probably like that of 562 is partially rolled on the tablet, 562x, NBC 1316, *BIN* 2, 30, pl. 66 d, pp. 47f.

558b

558a

559

560

561

562a

562b

563a

563b

567

564

570

571

572

563. Impressions all over case (unopened). Height 20, with cap marks c. 26. (a) Obverse, (b) Bottom edge. NBC 28 (= *UDT* 28, drawn). Shulgi 47. Tello text.

Suppliant goddess, worshipper led by goddess, lion-headed spread eagle above small suppliant goddess; enthroned goddess with three neck rings, stalks of grain at shoulders (clear on reverse); inscription.

Typical examples of the Akkadian grain goddess appear in *Boehmer,* 541–42. That the eagle, as in 540–41, 565–71, has no necessary connection with the enthroned deity is suggested by the specific identification of the latter as a vegetation goddess here; also by the multiplication of animal elements in designs like *ITT* 3, pl. IV, 4790, in which the eagle appears before a god seated on a bull-throne, while there is a liongriffin over the inscription; or by an unusual combination of elements, as in *ITT* 3, 5967, where, before a goddess, the eagle looms above a horned serpentdragon; the latter, not very common in Ur III glyptic (see it winged in *Louvre T.,* 108, naming Gudea) is normally associated with gods (*Frankfort,* pp. 121f.), or is part of the throne, *Louvre T.,* 111, naming Shulgi.

Small human figures, most often the suppliant goddess as here, occur quite frequently in Ur III seals. More unusual is a detached human head in profile before a deity in *ITT* 5, pl. I.10052; thus anticipating a popular motif of Old Babylonian and peripheral glyptic.

564. Impressions on both faces of tablet. Height 31. Obverse shown. NBC 3344. Shulgi 35.

Suppliant goddess, worshipper led by goddess, star-disk in crescent, goddess enthroned on platform (trace reverse), small worshipper with hands at waist on line above bull's head (body of latter perhaps under inscription). Both the suppliant and the seated goddess wear neck rings.

565. Brownish "steatite." 33×15. *Newell* 124. Not shown.

Worshipper led by goddess, snake between them, spread eagle above bird on line over scorpion, goddess with symbol (?) extended into throne; inscription.

566. "Steatite." 29½×17/15, irregular. Worn. *Newell* 121. Not shown.

Worshipper led by goddess, vessel between them; spread eagle, spouted jar, enthroned goddess.

The stroke behind the worshipper is a scratch. The framelike appearance of the eagle's tail can better be seen in 567. It suggests a part of the temple furnishings rather than a real bird.

567. Dark gray serpentine. 27×15. New impression. *Newell* 140.

Male worshipper led by goddess, spread eagle, enthroned goddess on platform; inscription.

The worshipper must be male since he wears an open robe which shows a thick curve across the front and a faint vertical fringe before him; see also 628, 638. The meager evidence suggests that the open robe is relatively late.

568. Dark gray serpentine. 25×12½/11(irregular). *Newell* 117. Not shown.

Theme of 567, spread eagle above "monkey," inscription.

The worshipper probably wears a skull cap as proposed for the one in 538. On the "monkey" see *Newell,* p. 105; called perhaps a mongoose, *CANES,* pp. 38f. (no. 307), 41. A mongoose or monkey appears in the unusual Ur III worship scene, *OIP* 78, pl. 118.7. See also the "monkey" on a stick in 630.

569. Dark green brown serpentine. 26×14. *Newell* 128. Not shown.

Theme of 567 (worshipper almost lost under inscription), spread eagle above water bird on line.

570. Impressions all over case. Height c. 26. Left edge shown. *UDT* (= NBC) 2, drawn. Shulgi 49. Tello text.

Worshipper led by goddess, crescent above lion-headed spread eagle facing left, goddess enthroned on platform (trace reverse); inscription.

See also 570x, *UDT* (= NBC) 29, Shulgi 41, with eagle's head turned right as is more usual.

571. Like 570. (Tablet not impressed.) Height 25. Left edge shown. NCBT 2244. Shulgi 42. Probably same as *Ward,* 228.

Theme of 570; spread eagle above; inscription.

Compare 571x, *UDT* (= NBC) 19, 22 (height 25, Shulgi 47, lion [?] below eagle); also 571xx, NBC 1838, tablet like 564, Shulgi 47, height 16½ (with cap marks 21), spread eagle above; inscription.

572. Impressions on both faces of tablet. Height 20. Reverse partly shown. YBC 1704. Shu-Sin 4. Jokha text. Drawn *YOS* 4, 194, 205, 225 (= YBC 1749, 904, 3883), Shu-Sin 3, 7, 6; quite good rollings on YBC 1280, 14699, NBC 730, 3265, 3643 (similar dates).

Theme of 570; star disk in crescent above lion facing left seated on edge of platform; inscription.

573. Like 572, also left edge. Height 23½. Reverse partly shown. NBC 3409, Shu-Sin 3.

Theme of 570; star disk in crescent above rampant lion; inscription.

A split dark gray serpentine cylinder, 573x, NCBS 855, 25½×(ext)12, shows the edge of an inscription frame, a worshipper in a fringed garment led by a goddess in a pleated one, trace of a spread eagle over a lion as in 573; inscription.

574. Like 572. Height 19½. Obverse partly shown. NBC 645. Amar-Sin 4.

Theme of 570; star disk in crescent above lion lying on rectangular shape (horizontal lines above, vertical below) mounted on short pole; behind goddess vertical snake; inscription.

575. Like 572. Height 25½. Reverse partly shown. NBC 4373. Shulgi 42. Seal names an ensi of Umma. Worshipper led by goddess, in same seal, NBC 676 (Shulgi 43).

Enthroned goddess, small nude (?) attendant holding standard topped by standing lion on tasseled platform; inscription.

576. Dark "steatite." 31×16. Worn. NBC 6015.

Theme of 570; scorpion before the worshipper; between the goddesses, crescent above date palm in stand; throne broken; inscription.

577. Dark gray serpentine, brown mottled. 28×15/14½, area outside main theme cut back. Worn. YBC 12604.

Theme of 570; worshipper's belt hangs down; goddess enthroned on platform, crescent above; probably added: inscription, crude figure in long garment (?), snake.

578. Black limestone. 23½×12. New impression. *Newell* 119.

Theme of 570, crescent and water bird before the seated goddess, winged liongriffin.

The exaggerated torsion of the liongriffin and its rather crowded position suggest that it could be of Isin Larsa origin; compare 524.

573

574

575

576

577

578

580

581

582

583

584

585

586

587

579. Dark gray limestone. 24×12. Scratched. *Newell* 120. Not shown.

Theme of 570; the seated goddess holds cup, water bird before her, scorpion over bull on double line.

The scorpion over an animal recalls the curious secondary in 585.

580. Dark green brown serpentine. 26×15. Worn. NBC 5953.

Theme of 570; inscription added over forward arms of the goddesses; second inscription ending back of throne.

The writing of the two inscriptions is sufficiently alike to suggest that they are contemporary. They may have been added in a document for two participants who were without seals and who wanted or were required to have their names impressed on it. If so, this probably occurred late in the period, since during most of Ur III only one name was usually impressed on a tablet, generally that of a scribe; see 511 for relatively late Ur III examples.

581. Brown mottled, green serpentine. 26×13. New impression. *Newell* 131.

Theme of 570, star disk in crescent before the seated goddess on platform; inscription.

The worshipper seems to be bearded. His headdress may be a loose version of the proposed skull cap in 538. The stroke below his left arm remains inexplicable. The leading goddess has crossed shoulder straps also as in 538, implying a comparably early date for the seal. It may be a peripheral product as is suggested by its inscription and the rather peculiar simplified engraving of detail.

582. Green mottled, black serpentine. 25×12/11, cut away in area of inscription. NBC 9126.

Theme of 570; crescent above dot (accidental?) between the goddesses; trace of platform under throne; inscription.

The cut back area for the inscription, bulging when impressed, suggests that it was a later addition.

The same theme occurs in 582x. NCBS 846. black serpentine, 28×16/14½(concave), worn.

583. Dark gray serpentine. 24½×12. Worn. NCBS 810.

Theme of 570; the goddesses wear crossed shoulder straps and neck rings; crescent; frame for inscription.

The vertically trimmed edges of the skirts of the first two figures are unusual in the period.

584. Impressions on both faces of big tablet c. 135×75. Height 19. One of the two areas with clear impressions on reverse shown. YBC 7087. Amar-Sin 5.

FIGS. 579–587

Theme of 570; reversed bird (?), crescent; throne with high back (curved top?) on platform; inscription; ground line.

Worn seals, 584x, with the theme of 570, inscription mostly lost; except for the last, a crescent appears at the top: ("steatite") NBC 5996, 24×12, NBC 5939, 29×15; YBC 9986, 23×12; NCBS 734, 20(bottom lost)×14; NCBS 737, 21×11; NCBS 804, 23½×11½, two blobs; NCBS 807, 23×11, scorpion (?), lionscimitar; NCBS 809, 23×11½; NCBS 818, 27½×13, vessel with spout; NCBS 840, 26×13½(12½); (shell) NCBS 790, 25×13.

585. Black limestone. 16×11½. NBC 11042.

Theme of 570; crescent; throne on platform; mounted tree (?), scorpion, meaningless lines.

586. Dark "steatite." 23×13½. New impression. Worn. *Newell* 126.

Worshipper led by goddess, seated goddess holding crescent standard, scorpion above water bird; inscription.

Compare *Louvre T.*, 121, worn; see also the standing god in 666 below.

A broken corroded limestone seal 586x, NCBS 803, 25(ext)×21/20(concave) shows a crescent standard before the seated goddess, and a spray over the forward arm of the leading goddess.

587. Impressions on both faces. Height 24. Reverse partly shown. NBC 320. Amar-Sin 1.

Full-face goddess with neck rings, tress to each shoulder, rod in outstretched hand (?), enthroned on platform; inscription.

The full-face seated goddess occasionally appears in Ur III scenes of presentation: *ITT* 5, pl. I.10020 (p. 66); *UE* 10, 400, compare *UE* 10, 398 in which she sits full face on a "mountain" opposite a water deity. In Akkadian seals the seated full-face goddess always appears with weapons at her shoulders, *Boehmer*, 384–85, 387, 389. When standing she sometimes has rays or vegetation there, either with or instead of weapons so that her warlike and her fertility aspects may be combined; see *Boehmer*, p. 67. One seal, showing her standing with apparently all types of weapons on her shoulders, has been called Neo-Sumerian by *Frankfort*, pl. 25f., p. 144 (= *Boehmer*, 274). However, it is executed in fully developed Akkadian style, while the two-headed eagle under the inscription is unlike the usual Neo-Sumerian rendering with lion's heads as in 646 below.

588. Impressions all over case (tablet not impressed). Height ext. 30. (a) Reverse, (b–c) Right and bottom edges (all partial). YBC 11243. Shulgi 33. Same seal on case *Ash C,* 434 (description corrected here).

Bearded worshipper in cap with rolled brim (see "b") led by goddess, star disk in crescent above date palm in vase; goddess with broad vertically lined shoulder band, long tress over each shoulder (one to left curled), arrows and mace at shoulders, on throne with inset seated lion (?), inscription above standing lion (see "a").

Compare the Akkadian seated goddess in profile with weapons at her shoulders, *Boehmer,* 383, 386, 388.

589. Dark green serpentine, lighter flecked. 22×12. NBC 6022.

Worshipper led by goddess, star disk (?) (worn) in crescent above vessel with covered tubes (?), goddess seated on goose, lion-headed eagle above second goose over traces of inscription.

Compare the goddess presumably on a goose in 550. For Akkadian scenes showing the goddess on a goose associated with boats see *Boehmer,* 478–80 (of III). The vessel with tubes is presumably a variant of the spouted type in 553, 566, 619, and 643.

590. Like 588. Height 27½. Reverse shown. NCBT 2250. Probably same as *Ward,* 231.

Worshipper led by goddess, scorpion between them; star disk in crescent above scorpion, thin double convex shape, and vessel; goddess over two geese back to back, her feet on the first, the second part of her throne; inscription.

588a

588b

588c

589

590

591a

591b

591c

592

593

591. Like 588. Height 24. (a) Bottom edge, (b) Reverse, (c) Drawing. *UDT(*= NBC) 6(drawn). Shulgi 47. Tello text.

Worshipper led by goddess, goose above goddess enthroned on platform; inscription above worshipper before enthroned goddess (right frame of inscription behind this group).

592. Like 588. Height 19. Left edge shown. NCBT 2252. Shulgi 47. Probably same as *Ward*, 234.

Worshipper led by goddess, crescent above goose on pole, enthroned goddess; inscription.

593. Dark green serpentine, brown mottled. 27×14/13½, cut back at end figure. Worn. NBC 9099. Ellis and Buchanan, *JNES* 25 (1966), pp. 192ff.

Belted male figure on line in wraparound kilt and vertically marked cap, engraved over worn inscription, the right frame of which he grasps; bearded worshipper in similar cap led by goddess with crossed shoulder straps, crescent; goddess on cushioned throne on line, her feet on goose.

Some features in the design suggest that the seal may have been partly recut at the time the first figure was added. A goddess seated on a cushioned throne is unusual but does occur in Ur III times, *UE* 10, 423; for a god on such a throne see 606, 624.

594. Green jasper, light and dark mottling. 40×25/23½(concave). Unfinished. No bore. *Newell* 172. Not shown.

Worshipper, goddess on throne.

FIGS. 595–602

The presentation of a worshipper led by a goddess before an enthroned god distinguishes 595–607. The enthroned god holds a flowing vase in 608, while he extends a ring in 609; a presented couple is led to a seated god with perhaps a flowing vase before him in 610; the god extends a bent weapon in 611, possibly a mace in 612; he flourishes a mace and a broad scimitar in 613, holds a scimitar while seated on a "mountain" throne in 614. A suppliant goddess precedes a presented couple before an enthroned god bearing a weapon, 615; shouldering a scimitar, 616; with feline heads at his shoulders, 617; before the god a lion-topped pole, 618–20. A suppliant goddess, a worshipper, a seated god, all before small subjects, 621; the worshipper not attested, 622; a presented couple and a seated god before a standing goddess, 623; a seated god and a standing goddess, 624; a seated god with lionclub before him, 625; a suppliant goddess, a worshipper, and an enthroned god, 626; finally a man on a stand, a worshipper, a suppliant goddess, and a seated god, 627.

595. Black serpentine, greenish brown mottling. 29×16/15(concave). YBC 12605.

Worshipper led by goddess, god enthroned on platform; inscription.

596. Rock crystal. 35×19/18(concave). Worn. *Newell* 135. Not shown.

Theme of 595, star in crescent; inscription.

Impressions on both faces of tablet, 596x, NBC 1423, height 19, theme of 595, crescent, inscription, ground line, Shulgi 49, *BIN* 5, 117 (drawn), Jokha text. The same theme but with some obscure detail occurs in the impression, 596xx, NBC 3407, height c. 21, Amar-Sin 9, inscription.

597. Impression on both faces of tablet. Height c. 23. Reverse partly shown. NBC 3505. Amar-Sin 9.

Theme of 595; crescent above squatting lion (?) before the god, winged liongriffin set in throne, niched platform; inscription.

598. Like 597. Height 22. Reverse partly shown. NBC 577. Ibbi-Sin 2. Jokha text.

Theme of 595; star disk in crescent (blurred); the god on high-backed throne with curved top and sidearms; inscription.

599. Like 597 (also right edge). Big tablet, c. 115×50. Height 26. Open area on reverse shown. NCBT 2241. Shulgi 41.

Theme of 595; scorpion (?) before the god's legs; high-backed throne with curved top and inset lion leaning on foreleg, niched platform; inscription.

600. Like 597. Height 20½. Reverse partly shown. NBC 690. Shu-Sin 3.

Theme of 595; star disk in crescent; squatting lion set in throne; ground line under first two figures; inscription.

601. Like 597 (also right side). Height 25. Reverse shown. NBC 2783. Shu-Sin 2. Same seal on NBC 974, 1956, 2784, 2790, of similar dates.

Theme of 595; star disk in crescent above palm in vessel before the god; behind him standard topped by walking lion, jaws agape, on vertically lined platform; inscription over walking lion, jaws agape.

Compare the lion standard on the tablet tag, 601x, *BRM* 3, pl. III.24 (= 129, Shu-Sin 1); see also 601xx, *BIN* 5, 200, Amar-Sin 5 (= NBC 1542).

602. Like 597. Height 24½. Reverse partly shown. NBC 2815. Shulgi 26, 45 or Ibbi-Sin 3 (more likely). Same seal and date on NBC 658. Jokha texts.

Theme of 595; crescent; behind the god small erect lion holding standard with seven dots; inscription.

A standard, usually with five dots rather than seven, is quite often held by a lion in Ur III worship scenes: *Louvre T.*, 112, 213 (eagle above = *Brussels*, 12, pp. 149f.); *Revue Archéologique* (1909), pl. XIII.1 (before the god); *UE* 10, 381 (four dots); see 685 below (three dots?); *ITT* 3, pl. III. 6631 (but held by small bullman). The standard also occurs on the ground or in the field: see 605 below; *Berlin*, 268; *ITT* 2, pl. III. 4210 (see *ITT* 5, p. 66, 10029); *UE* 10, 534 (three dots). That the standard may be a decorative tree is suggested by *ITT* 3, pl. III. 6646, 6663, where, behind the deity, a "tree" with many dots stands on a hill and is "held" by an erect goat.

595

597

598

599

600

601

602

603

604

606a

606b

606c

607

603. Like 597 (also on three edges). Height ext. 24. Reverse partly shown. NBC 9268.

Worshipper probably led by goddess, enthroned god; inscription inside which small nude hero holds lower right frame.

Compare *ITT* 5, pl. II. 10082 for a long-robed deity who perhaps holds the lower right frame of the inscription; see also the "tree" and goat in the right frame of the inscription, *ITT* 3, pl. III. 6646, 6663. For various elements well inside the inscription see: *ITT* 5, pl. VI. 10073 (mace); pl. IV. 10057b (eagle), 10029 (p. 66– eagle with four more under the inscription); pl. II. 9774 (p. 65– worshipper on stand); *Iraq* 21 (1959), pl. VI. 12, p. 24 (hero– perhaps of late Ur III, compare *UE* 10, 428–31, 435–36).

604. Blue glazed composition. 20×11. Bore off center in area of inscription. Chipped and cracked. NBC 9254. Said to be from Western Iran.

Male worshipper in short pointed beard and striated cap, led by goddess, two dots (?) in crescent above spouted vessel, god holding vase enthroned on niched platform; inscription (lower right sign out of frame) over plant (?) and two rampant liongriffins holding long mace between them.

For the striated cap of the worshipper compare that worn by the beardless one in 630, also the first two figures in 593; see *CANES*, pp. 35, 37 (seal 294).

605. "Steatite." 28×15. Worn. *Newell* 129. Not shown. *Frankfort*, p. 146, n. 1 ("poor Ur III").

Worshipper led by goddess, five dots on pole between them, crescent above scorpion, enthroned god; spread eagle over worn inscription in panel.

606. Impressions all over case (tablet not impressed). Height 29½. (a) Reverse (partial), (b) Left edge, (c) Bottom edge. YBC 4758. Shulgi 46. Jokha text.

Worshipper led by goddess, god on cushioned throne enclosing winged dragon; inscription.

607. Dark "steatite." 26×13½/12, cut back for added inscription. Worn. NCBS 838.

Worshipper led by goddess, mace between them, disk (?) in crescent before god on cushioned throne; inscription.

608. Like 606 (unopened). Height 27. (a) Reverse, (b) Right edge. *UDT* (=NBC) 8 (drawn). Shulgi 47. Tello text.

Worshipper led by goddess, god on altar-throne holds vase from which two streams and three plant shoots emerge; inscription.

In *Louvre T.,* 108 (drawn), a seal of Gudea (see 538), the water god holds two vases and sits on more; the one held as here is also supported by the presenting god who has dragon heads at his shoulders. For later less complicated Ur III examples of the water god see: *ITT* 3, pl. IV. 6641 (his feet on goat); *Frankfort,* pl. XXVd (similar god with worshipper only); *Louvre T.,* 116 (no plant shoots, small deity above the vase), 117, and 119, the vase held by a goddess.

609. Broken tablet. Height c. 20. NBC 11314. Nippur text (5NT 531.)

Enthroned god holding ring with irregular double line attached; inscription.

610. "Steatite." 28×15. Bore 7(worn to one side)/4. Worn. *Newell* 132. Not shown.

Theme of 608 with the god perhaps holding a flowing vase, spread eagle above.

611. Impressions on both faces of tablet (probably also all sides). Height c. 20. Reverse partly shown. YBC 1498. *YOS* 4, 126 (poor drawing).

Theme of 608 with the god holding bent object (throw stick?), dagger at waist; inscription.

A similar bent object is held by the god, doubtfully in a feather crown, seated on a "mountain" throne (see 614), in the presentation scene of Unger, *Beginn,* pl. XIII. 26, pp. 42ff.

612. Like 611. Height 18. Reverse partly shown. NBC 4261. Amar-Sin 8. Same on NBC 5782 (Amar-Sin 7).

Theme of 608 with the god holding mace (pear-shaped head?), enthroned on line; double-convex shape above lion walking on separate line; inscription.

613. Like 611. Height 19½. Obverse partly shown. YBC 9816. Amar-Sin 1. Jokha text.

Worshipper led (?) by goddess, seated god, holding round-headed mace and shouldering lion-headed (?) scimitar with broad blade, on throne with back curved at top; inscription.

For the scimitar compare 616.

At least two other seals were used by the scribe, Ushmu: (1) 613x, *YOS* 4, 103 (= YBC 571, Shulgi 44), 181 (= 1751, Amar-Sin 2), both drawn, presentation to goddess; (2) 641 below.

614. Like 611. Height 23½. Reverse partly shown. NBC 4331. Amar-Sin 2.

Worshipper led by goddess, ground line; star disk in crescent, god shouldering scimitar as in 613, on "mountain" throne on platform; inscription.

608a

608b

609

611

612

613

614

615a

615b

616

617a

617b

618a

618b

615. Impressions on faces and long sides of triangular tag. Height 19 (with cap marks 22). (a–b) Faces (partial). YBC 1302. Mid-Shulgi by inscription.

Suppliant goddess, worshipper in round cap with narrow brim led by goddess; god, perhaps in open robe, shouldering curved weapon on throne on line; inscription.

The robe of the god could be like that of the figure in a conical hat and open robe in 627; while his weapon may be a "throw stick" as in 611, but pointed.

616. Like 611 (also right edge). Height 26. Reverse partly shown. NBC 3615. Amar-Sin 9. *BIN* 3, 548. Drehem text.

Suppliant goddess, tress over shoulder; goddess (leading worshipper?), star disk in crescent above seated lion, god shouldering lion-scimitar enthroned on platform; inscription.

The head of the scimitar is taken to be a lion's, but it may be a panther's (*Frankfort,* p. 143).

617. Impressions all over case. Height 28. (a) Obverse, (b) Bottom edge *UDT* (= NBC, drawn) 26. Probably Shulgi 48. Tello text.

Suppliant goddess, worshipper led by goddess, spread lion-headed eagle, god with feline heads at shoulders enthroned on platform; inscription above plant (?) and boar (?); ground line (?).

Examples of an eagle before a god in simple scenes of presentation: 617x, *UDT* (= NBC) 14, drawn, Amar-Sin 1; 617xx, NCBT 2234 Amar-Sin 3 (?).

The feline heads at the god's shoulders recall those with forepaws in *Louvre T.,* 110 (drawn; same name *Louvre T.,* 109, Shu-Sin 2) in which similar heads appear on a scimitar and a fanlike object, compare also a two-headed lioneagle and lions in and under the throne. For serpentdragon heads at a god's shoulders see *Louvre T.,* 108 (cited 608) and *OIP* 72, 709, which names two late Neo-Sumerian rulers of Eshnunna; compare the god seated on a serpentdragon with apparently two of the creature's tails at his shoulders, *Louvre T.,* 111, naming Shulgi.

For the group under the inscription compare perhaps the boar and tree in *Ash C,* 319, Akkadian.

618. Impressions on both faces of two tablets. Height 17 (with cap marks 20). (a–b) Reverses. YBC 1067 (= a), Shulgi 34; YBC 9807 (= b) Shulgi 35. Same on YBC 14700, date of "a," NBC 1438, date of "b." Jokha texts.

Suppliant goddess; worshipper led by goddess, god enthroned on platform; before the god, pole topped by lion on oblong shape; inscription.

619. Like 617. Height 20 (with cap marks c. 23). (a) Top, (b) Left edge, (c) Drawing. YBC 6765. Shulgi 40. Same on YBC 1641, Shulgi 45. Jokha texts.

Theme of 618; before the worshipper disk in crescent above lizard; before the god spouted vessel as in 553 beside pole as in 618 but shorter and with projecting line under rear of the lion; inscription.

620. Like 611. Height 24. Reverse partly shown. YBC 1296. Shu-Sin 4. *YOS* 4, 201 (drawn). Same *YOS* 4, 66, drawn, Shulgi 45 (= YBC 1396). Jokha texts.

Suppliant goddess in simple horned crown, long tress down back; worshipper led by goddess in elaborate horned crown; lion on line on short pole with pennant at front of platform with enthroned god; inscription.

621. Impressions all over tablet. Height c. 23. Reverse shown. NBC 5592. Shu-Sin 2. Jokha text. Doubtfully same as *HSS* 4, 129, 158 (Amar-Sin 4, 5), drawn with worshipper led by goddess.

Suppliant goddess with "ribbon" down back; worshipper (seems to have right hand before face, left at waist); god enthroned on platform (?); inscription; under it small suppliant goddess, "ribbon" down back, facing similar one (?), object (?) between them.

For other examples of the rare Ur III designs showing a ribbon or tassel down the back of the suppliant goddess see: *Louvre T.*, 217 and 219, naming Shu-Sin; *UE* 10, 435, naming Ibbi-Sin; 649–50 and 673 below.

622. Like 611. Height ext. 23. Reverse partly shown. NBC 4290. Shulgi 34. Jokha text.

Enthroned god; inscription, under it two small gods with pole, topped by scorpion on line between them; suppliant goddess (?) facing right, gap.

623. Like 611 (also one edge). Height 20½. Reverse partly shown. YBC 579. Shulgi 45. Jokha text.

Worshipper led by goddess, enthroned god; goddess with right hand raised, left at waist; inscription.

619a

619b

619c

620

621

622

623

624

625

626

627a

627b

624. Like 611. Height 25. Reverse partly shown. YBC 1652. Shu-Sin 4. Jokha text.

Crescent (?), god on cushioned throne on platform, suppliant goddess; inscription above walking lion; gap.

625. Like 611 (also one edge). Height c. 27. Reverse shown. NBC 486. Shulgi 35. Seal names ensi of Umma. Same on *Nikolski*, pl. II, 188 (Shulgi 36).

God on cross-lined (?) throne with sidearms and low back on hatched platform, his forward foot on cross-lined stand; above the foot, lionclub with notched staff and pointed base; inscription; worshipper, right hand at waist (trace obverse); gap.

626. Impression of two seals on flat base of bulla, traces on other sides. Height 28. MLC 2658. *BRM* 3, pl. VII. 58. For same two seals on other bullae: *BRM* 3, p. 35, under the scribe Ur-Nungal (dates: Amar-Sin 8 to Shu-Sin 6, designs not shown). Jokha texts. Same top design as 626 on tablet YBC 1300 (*YOS* 4, 155, Shu-Sin 6, poor drawing).

Suppliant goddess with three or more neck rings, worshipper; ground line; star disk in crescent, god enthroned on platform; inscription above lion (?). Poor traces of the second seal appear below.

A different seal of Ur-Nungal: 626x, YBC 1367, presentation to king, Shu-Sin 6, named on seal.

627. Impressions all over two bullae. Height 28. YBC 3653 (= a), YBC 3675 (= b); also on bullae YBC 3676 and MLC 2336. *BRM* 3, 71 (= pl. II. 15); Amar-Sin 6, 4, 6, 7. Drehem texts. Later seal of same man: 647x.

Male figure in high conical hat and long open robe, left hand raised, right at waist, on low stand; worshipper, hands at waist; suppliant goddess; god enthroned on platform; inscription.

The robe of the male figure, only one side fully visible, resembles that usual for standing deities, commonly gods, with one foot forward; see 658, 660–61, 666–74. It is perhaps worn by the seated god in 615. His hat may be an imitation of a feather crown as in 525.

A distinctive feature is the placing of this figure on a low stand. In Old Babylonian glyptic, the priest was often similarly placed, sometimes the personage with a mace, the effect desired being presumably to raise them to the level of the gods and at the same time to differentiate them from such. Perhaps the same effect was intended here. In any case it is unusual for a god to be so raised, but see Kupper, *Amurru*, pl. V. 27, IX. 48 (drawn), p. 20(3), where in both cases the god is on a stand. As is very common the male figure wears a high hat as here; perhaps it is even feathered, *Amurru*, p. 37.

FIGS. 628–636

After the concentrated presentation of the goddess, secondarily the god, in Ur III seals the depiction of the seated king follows. First, a worshipper is led by a goddess before a seated king with a cup, 628–38; then a suppliant goddess precedes but the king does not hold a cup, 639–40; or the suppliant goddess stands behind a king who extends a cup, 641, or a flowing vase, 642. A suppliant goddess behind a worshipper confronts a seated king with cup, 643–49; in addition the worshipper holds a kid, 650. The king is beardless, but otherwise with his usual setting in 651–52, except that in the latter he has an offering table before him. The enthroned king faces a worshipper holding a staff in 653, but in 654 the enthroned king with the usual cup simply confronts an unadorned worshipper.

628. Hematite. 26×14½/13½, concave. Bore off center because seal is cut back for added inscription and adjacent objects. NCBS 849.

Worshipper (rear bottom cut away) in cap and open robe, led by goddess wearing neck rings and bracelets, star between them, ground line; star disk in crescent above goose; king with cup, wearing bracelets, on cushioned throne on niched platform (rear cut away); lion-headed spread eagle above goat rampant against inscription.

The king is clad in the flounced robe of deity, as in 630, 632–33, 638–39, rather than in a fringed garment as is more usual. In all the scenes before the king the leading goddess wears a flounced robe as here, except in 634.

629. Hematite. 25×14/13½, cut back at secondary motifs. YBC 9673.

Theme of 628; the goddess wears neck rings and bracelets; star disk in crescent above water bird before the king who has bracelets at wrist, feet on low stool on plain low platform; over traces of worn inscription: bowlegged dwarf and nude male in caps on line over squatting dog (?) facing seated mongoose (?) on line.

The secondary motifs over the worn inscription are Old Babylonian.

630. Hematite. 34×20. NBC 9106.

Theme of 628; the worshipper in striated cap, mongoose (?) on pole before him; scorpion, snake, star disk in crescent, and water bird before the king, second snake and lizard behind him; inscription (erased?).

It is possible that the striated cap of the worshipper and the crowded animal figures are late Neo-Sumerian additions.

631. Dark gray limestone, olive mottled. 29×17. YBC 9665.

Theme of 628; crescent above goose before the king (beardless); inscription.

The king seems to be wearing a chin strap resembling that on a warrior's head of alabaster, Parrot, *Mari*, fig. 107. Curiously enough the faces of the two men are also very similar. No beard is visible on the king in 635, 651–52, but no chin strap either. See, however, 632.

632. Dark gray serpentine. 30½×17. *Newell* 136. Not shown.

Theme of 628; serpent between first two figures; disk in crescent (or full circle?) above, erect lion with staff before the king (beardless) wearing a chin strap as in 631; inscription over opposed scorpions.

633. Dark gray serpentine. 25×14. Worn. *Newell* 134. Not shown.

Nude full-faced hero holding vase at waist from which streams flow to vases on either side; theme of 628.

634. Shell. 26×13. Bore 6/4½. Chipped. NBC 9110.

Theme of 628; crack under star disk in crescent (compare 584); secondary: nude hero on one knee on line, holding flowing vase at waist; below: worshipper (cracked), left hand raised, right at waist, facing goddess, on two lines.

635. Impressions on jar sealing. Height ext. c. 23. Nippur 5 NT 34. No context. NBC 11198.

Theme of 628; the king is beardless; secondary: two crossed bulls on line over full-face hero with side curls on one knee holding flowing vase at waist.

636. Impressions all over case. Height 26. Left edge shown. Ibbi-Sin 3, named on seal. YBC 13286.

Theme of 628, star disk in crescent, inscription.

The same theme on a triangular tag. Height ext. 22. Presented to *šakkanakku* (military governor) by Ibbi-Sin. 636x, NBC 11193. Nippur 5 NT 13. No context.

628

629

630

631

634

635

636

637

638

639

640a

640b

637. Impressions on both faces of tablet. Height ext. 23. Reverse partly shown. YBC 294. Amar-Sin 9, but seal already names Shu-Sin. *YOS* 4, 101, drawn. Drehem text.

Theme of 628; the king holds handled vase; inscription.

For other examples of a tablet written in the year a king died, but already impressed by a seal with the new king's name, see Oppenheim, *Eames*, p. 4. For the handled vase see 638.

638. Like 637. Height 27. Reverse partly shown. YBC 1170. Also YBC 1245, 1627 (=*YOS* 4, 195, poor drawing), YBC 1628, 1688, 9812. Shu-Sin 5, 4, 6, 6, 4, 7. Jokha texts.

Worshipper in open robe led by goddess, ground line; king with handled vase on high backed throne, rounded top, side arms curving over inset lion, its tail up, on platform; inscription above hero with flowing vase as in 635.

For the throne and the vase compare *UE* 10, 428–31, naming Amar-Sin (changed to Shu-Sin in 430). There the worshipper's right hand is raised as usual, but his left at the waist brings the straight edge of his robe or shawl toward the middle, partially covering the leg revealed in 638. For the robe arranged as in

638 see *UE* 10, 433, probably naming Shu-Sin; compare *Berlin*, 253, naming Shu-Sin; *BRM*, 3, pl. VII. 55; *ITT* 5, pl. I. 10041, p. 67; all presentations.

639. Impressions all over case (unopened). Height 19 (with cap marks c. 25). Top edge shown. NCBT 2249. Amar-Sin 1. Seal names Shulgi. Possibly same as *Ward*, 52.

Suppliant goddess; theme like 628, but king does not hold cup; inscription.

A similar design with the king probably not holding a cup: 639x, YBC 13111, case unopened, Amar-Sin 4 (?), height ext. 23, names Shulgi.

See *Wiseman*, 40 for a presumed king without a cup, seated on a throne with curved back and sidearms, bull's legs at its rear, in a presentation like 639–40, but naming Ur-Nammu, first Ur III king.

640. Like 637 (two tablets). Height 16 (with cap marks 22). (a) Reverse, (b) Obverse (partial). NBC 2023 (= a), no date; 3401 (= b), dated Shulgi 43 (= *BIN* 5, 122, drawn). Same on YBC 1761, NBC 2872, NBC 3644; dated Shulgi 38, 40, 46. Jokha texts.

Theme like 639, but the king sits on an altar throne as in 639 without a cup; inscription (last sign behind the throne).

641. Like 637. Height 27. (a) Obverse, (b) Reverse (both partial). YBC 1261. Shu-Sin 4. *YOS* 4, 148 (drawn). Same on YBC 771 (= *YOS* 4, 314), Shulgi 46 (?); NBC 2314, Shu-Sin 4. For other seals of Ushmu see 613.

Theme like 628; star disk in crescent; suppliant goddess behind the king; inscription (first frame empty; next three inscribed, of which the first is long; the next two short– over small worshipper, hands at waist).

642. Like 639 (tablet not impressed). Height c. 25. (a) Left edge, (b) Reverse (partial). YBC 3905. Amar-Sin 5. Seal names Shulgi. Drehem text.

Suppliant goddess in simple crown and pleated skirt, worshipper with hands at waist, king on cushioned throne holding flowing vase (compare god in 608); suppliant goddess in elaborate crown and flounced skirt; inscription.

A similar design without the goddess in the rear occurs in *Nikolski,* pl. I. 435 (Shulgi 35). The careful distinction in crown and garment between the two goddesses here may be significant, perhaps suggesting that the one more simply arrayed was an ordinary suppliant goddess, while the other had a special relation to the personage near whom she stood, in this case a king.

643. Impressions all over bulla. Height 29. MLC 2338. *BRM* 3, 31, pl. II. 10. Amar-Sin 5. Names Shulgi. Legrain, *TRU,* 122 (same date, drawn); *Brussels,* 75, pp. 151f., seal 2 (inscription C–D), one of five different seals on bulla, showing a vertical serpent before the suppliant goddess. Drehem text.

Worshipper in open robe, star disk in crescent above spouted vessel; king with cup on cushioned throne, his feet on low stand, on two-tiered platform; inscription; suppliant goddess.

644. Impressions on both faces of tablet (fragment). Height 23. Reverse shown. NBC 3271. Same on *YOS* 4 159 (= YBC 995, Shu-Sin 6), 161 (= YBC 601, Ibbi-Sin 1), both drawn. Jokha texts.

Suppliant goddess, worshipper, ground line; star disk in crescent above small suppliant goddess, king with cup on cushioned throne, foot on low stand on platform; inscription above walking lion.

641a

641b

642a

642b

643

644

645

646a

646b

645. Like 644 (also one side). Height c. 20. Reverse partly shown. YBC 1374. Shu-Sin 5. Jokha text.

Theme of 644; star disk in crescent; inscription above lion-headed eagle.

646. Impressions on two tablets. Height 27. Reverses shown. NBC 638 (= a), Shu-Sin 9; *UDT* (= NBC, drawn) 167 (= b), Ibbi-Sin 1. Drehem text.

Theme of 644; ground line under standing figures; two star disks in crescents side by side above double lion-headed eagle; inscription.

The two-headed eagle appears especially in the designs of seal impressions from Tello: *Louvre T.,* 110; *ITT* 2, pl. III. 3911; 3, pl. III. 6631, 6651; 5, pl. IV. 6954.

647. Impressions all over case (tablet not impressed). Height c. 24. (a) Bottom edge, (b) Reverse (partial). YBC 3918. Ibbi-Sin 1. Names Shu-Sin. Drehem text.

Theme of 644; star disk in crescent; platform made up of three rows of dots ("hill" marks); inscription.

The same theme with a ground line under the first figures and two rows of dots on the platform: 647x, Goucher 884, bulla fragment, height 23, names Shu-Sin; also on bulla, *Louvre A.*, 257.

648. Impressions on three sides of bulla. Height 20 (with cap marks c. 23). YBC 3648. Names Shulgi. Same on bulla fragment YBC 3649, probably Amar-Sin 2. Drehem texts. Same on bullae MLC 1818, 1819, 2340, 2343.

Theme like 644, the worshipper in cap; inscription.

The theme of 644 also appears in 648x, NCBT 2307, triangular bulla impressed all over, measure like 648, Shu-Sin 3, names Awilaša, ensi of Kazallu, Kutscher, *JCS* 22 (1968–69), pp. 63–65 with photographs.

647a

647b

648

649

650a

650b

651

649. Like 647 (fragment). Height 25½. NBC 6645. Letter. Names Ibbi-Sin.

Theme like 644; suppliant goddess has ribbon down back; star disk in crescent; stepped platform with two rows of niches; inscription, section behind king unframed.

A similar platform occurs in 649x, YBC 11681, dated Shu-Sin 9 (also named in seal); the design shows presentation to a king. For a ribbon down the back of the goddess see the Ur III worship scenes, *OIP* 78, pl. 118. 19, 119. 4.

650. Like 646 (two tablets). Height 17½ (with cap marks 23½). Reverses partly shown. NBC 4405 (= a, *BIN* 3, 550), 2688 (= b, *BIN* 3, 436). Both Shu-Sin 1, drawn. Drehem texts.

Suppliant goddess with ribbon down back, worshipper with kid, king as in 644; inscription, line behind the king partly framed.

It is unusual in this class of seal for part of the inscription to overrun its frame as in 649–50; normally the inscriptions were very carefully placed.

651. Like 644. Height 22. Reverse partly shown. YBC 14698. Shu-Sin 3. Seal of A-a-kal-la, ensi of Umma, "servant" of Shu-Sin. Chosen from over 60 examples in the Collection; see *YOS* 4, 193 (= YBC 1500); *BIN* 5, 64 (king by mistake drawn as a god), 82 (= NBC 2079, NBC 3405), all drawings poor; design good in YBC 1348, YBC 11815; dates Shu-Sin 2, 4, 2, 3, 4. Another seal of same man in 652.

Theme like 644; star disk in crescent; the king beardless; inscription.

It seems possible that the cylinder seal used to make 651 is the one of which more impressions have been found than any other. Its nearest numerical rival in Ur III may be the earlier seal recorded under 547. This was also from Umma, but belonged to a scribe. However, the excavations at Ras Shamra in Syria have yielded a serious contender for the most used seal on record in the numerous impressions of a "dynastic" seal found on texts in which the kings of Ugarit of the fourteenth and thirteenth centuries B.C. appeared as witness or agent, Nougayrol, *PRU* 3, pp. XLf., pls. XVI–XVII.

The design of the latter closely follows the basic formula for depicting the worship of an enthroned king as in 643–51, and need not be much later. The design is almost exactly the same as in 649 of the time of Ibbi-Sin, even including a ribbon down the back of the suppliant goddess, though this feature becomes more common slightly later. The "dynastic" seal of Ugarit shows minor variants like the platform with only one row of niches or the king's feet on a low stand both as in 628 and elsewhere. It is true that a ground line runs under the whole scene, which again suggests a slightly later date.

The inscription of the "dynastic" seal is neither as neatly framed nor as carefully written as is generally the case in 643–51. It may therefore be a much later addition, perhaps added about as late as the time, probably well after 1500, when a copy very like the original seal was made.

FIGS. 649–651

652. Like 644. Height c. 20. Reverse partly shown. NBC 4288 (= *BIN* 3, 554, poor drawing). Shu-Sin 2. Seal of same ensi of Umma as in 651.

Worshipper, hands at waist; star disk in crescent above stand topped by horizontally marked, oblong shapes (pile of cakes?), king as in 651; inscription.

A similar seal with a beardless king but without the offering table: *JCS* 19 (1965), p. 29 (fig.), item d, seal presented by Ibbi-Sin to official, case dated Ibbi-Sin 1. In it the king may hold a seal instead of the usual cup (*JCS* 19, p. 30).

653. Impressions on both sides and edge below. Height 22 (with cap marks 24). Reverse partly shown. NBC 5607. *BIN* 3, 608 (drawn). Ibbi-Sin 2.

Worshipper holding staff in folded arms, perhaps extended behind him, star disk in crescent, king with cup on cushioned throne; inscription.

654. Impressions all over bulla. Height 38. Side without added writing shown. MLC 1822. Shu-Sin 6. *BRM* 3, 37, also 38 (MLC 2339) = Sollberger, *JCS* 19 (1965), p. 29, item b, incorrectly dated year 7. Drehem text.

Worshipper, hands at waist; king with cup on cushioned throne, inscription.

652

653

654

655

656a

656b

656c

656d

656e

All of these seals present human or divine figures, exclusively in standing posture, some quite early, even Post-Akkadian, others Neo-Sumerian, even later. The first group shows a worshipper before a deity, simply in 655, separated by a mound of snakes in 656, by hills and a palm in 657, by a mace standard in 658. Next come worshippers confronting an unidentified deity, 659; or a diety holding a lionclub and a scimitar, 660–61; while in an early scene a deity (?) faces two worshippers, 662. Later a god confronts a presented pair, 663, while somewhat earlier a similar pair faces a goddess, 664–65. More developed amidst elaborate tables, a pair stands before a feather-crowned god holding a crescent standard, 666, while in 667 a worshipper confronts a god grasping a tree. A worshipping pair salutes a god grasping a scimitar before a lionclub in the hands of monsters, 668; a similar grouping shows the god with a plow (?), 669; carrying a scimitar, 670; a mace and perhaps a bow, 671; a three-headed mace, 672; a group in

which suppliant goddess is separated from a god bearing a multiheaded mace and a looped weapon, 673; crudely executed, the usual couple face a god, 674. The couple are before a bird, over a bull, 675; the bull is held by a god, 676, no rein being visible, 677; gap after the worshipper before a god with club on a bull, 678. A winged god, a goddess holding streams of rain above her, and a god on a liongriffin constitute a powerful, perhaps unique, scene, 679; compare a worshipper, a palm in a vase, and a standing god as above, 680. Also unique is a group showing powerful personages beside a palm in a bowl, on either side of which a rock-clad god emerges from rocks across the base, 681. Worshippers are beside a palm in a vase, 682–85; a worshipper and monsters, 686; with an added contest, 687; an extra worshipper, 688; a scimitar held by two heroes beside a palm, 689; finally a lionclub stands between two worshippers, 690; a crescent standard is in a similar setting, 691–92; an early standard in 693.

FIGS. 655–656

655. Speckled dark gray diorite. 25×14. Bore, off center, 5/3. Worn. NBC 6003.

Worshipper, crescent, goddess (?); inscription.

The fringed garments have the crude simplicity of those on the standing figures in 544.

656. Impressions all over case (unopened). Height 24. (a) Reverse, (b-d) Right, top, and bottom edges, (e) Drawing. NBC (*UDT*, drawn) 27. Amar-Sin 3. Tello text.

Worshipper in suppliant attitude (both hands before face), goddess with right hand raised; between them, crescent above inverted crescent (?) over one or more snakes on mound; scimitar-mace standard; inscription.

The snakes on, or perhaps emerging from, a

mound recall, and may even derive from, the similar motif in an Akkadian seal found at Mari, *Boehmer*, 552, in which, however, the possible serpents have heads somewhat suggesting birds, while a god sits on the hill from which they rise. There are also attendant goddesses of vegetation, the lower part of whose body merges with streams of water, and a god who holds a spear pointed at one of the streams, perhaps to open a way for it, perhaps to protect the waters from the "serpents."

Which relation the snakes on a mound have to the rest of the scene here cannot be determined, except insofar as they add an element of supernatural power. The character of the so-called inverted crescent remains enigmatic. Could it be like the object, perhaps a throw stick, that is held by the god in 611?

657. Like 656. Height ext. 21. (a) Reverse, (b) Left edge. NCBT 2243. Shulgi 46. Probably same as *Ward,* 663.

Worshipper, right hand before face, lion-headed spread eagle above two hills with ornamental palm between them, god in flounced skirt, his right hand before him, his left at waist (defect); inscription.

On the ornamental palm tree the presumed date clusters have been transformed into volutes as in 680–89; see Lambert, *Iraq 28* (1966), p. 71, no. 37. Undoubtedly, like the lion-headed eagle and the hills, the tree had become conventionalized. Akkadian designs like *Boehmer,* 432 show the sun god rising between two mountains, and there is often an associated tree. Perhaps the mountains and the tree imply that the sun god is also represented here.

658. Like 656. Height c. 23. (a) Obverse, (b) Left edge. NCBT 2253. Shulgi 47. Probably same as *Ward,* 1305b (p. 401).

Worshipper, right hand before face; crescent over mace standard (length uncertain), god in long open robe, right leg forward, shouldering lion scimitar (?), end of belt (?) with vertical stroke (compare 581) near it; inscription.

659. Olive serpentine. 25×11. Worn. NCBS 820.

Worshipper, left hand raised; inscription over second figure with left hand raised; water bird, goddess (?) in flounced skirt; indeterminate vertical object.

Compare 547, 580 for inscriptions over older designs; see also *OIP* 78, pl. 110. 11 with an inscription over part of a contest scene and a seated figure.

660. Impressions over round bulla. Height c. 20. YBC 3647. Names Shulgi. Drehem text. Same on MLC 2351.

Suppliant goddess; worshipper in cap, right hand before face; god in long open robe, end of belt shown, right foot forward, holding lionclub and shouldering lionscimitar, on niched platform; inscription.

For the headdress of the worshipper, compare the so-called skull cap in 538.

661. Impressions on both faces of tablet. Height 23½. Reverse partly shown. NBC 4393. Shulgi 45. Jokha text.

God in long open robe, end of belt shown, right foot on small stand, holding lionclub before and scimitar behind; inscription.

657a

657b

658a

658b

659

660

661

663a

663b

666a

666b

666c

667b

667a

667c

662. Black serpentine. 15×6. Worn. *Newell* 197. Not shown.

Standing deity (?) before two worshippers, all with hand at face.

663. Like 661. Height 23. Reverses partly shown. (a) NCBT 2268, (b) NBC 4277 (both Shulgi 49). Also NBC 4348 (Amar-Sin 1). Jokha texts.

God, hands at waist, in long open robe; crescent above, T-shaped table with two acutely angled short legs (very faint); goddess leading worshipper; inscription.

664. Dark brown serpentine. 18×9. *Newell* 141. Not shown.

Worshipper led by goddess to standing goddess, one hand of all before face; lion-headed spread eagle over bird.

665. Dark gray serpentine. 17½×7. *Newell* 143. Not shown.

Theme of 664; inscription.

The same theme but worn, 665x, NCBS 760, brown limestone, 16½×9.

666. Like 661. Height 23. (a) Reverse, (b) Obverse, (c) Drawing. MLC 1902. Shu-Sin 6.

Worshipper led by goddess, between them enclosed double-convex shape on vertical double-convex shape; to right enclosed double-convex shape perhaps holding fish mounted on oblique square before god in feather crown and long open robe, holding crescent standard, right foot on pile of rocks, left arm behind holding scimitar before frame of inscription.

The two double-convex topped objects may both have been a kind of table. On the god's feather crown see 525. In the presentation scene of Post-Akkadian *OIP* 72, 778 the seated goddess holds a crescent standard. See also *OIP* 72, 438, perhaps by the same hand as the last, in which the seated deity holds a branch (?); compare 667 below. For the crescent standard held by a seated goddess, see 586 above.

667. Like 661. Height c. 20. (a) Reverse, (b) Obverse (partly shown), (c) Drawing. YBC 1341. Shulgi 46–47 or Amar-Sin 2–3. Jokha text.

Tree held by god, right foot on pile of stones; inscription; worshipper; gap.

668. Dark gray diorite. 26×15. Gimbel Collection 4.

Bearded worshipper in cap led by goddess; crescent beside lionclub on obliquely hatched staff between two erect liongriffins; god holding lionscimitar, right foot on small mound, on line; crescent in frame of worn inscription; ground line.

669. Brown mottled, speckled gray serpentine. 26×14/13, cut back at inscription. Worn. NBC 11013.

Worshipper without beard or cap led by goddess, goose between them; lionclub above right foot on stand of god shouldering plow (?); inscription.

The added inscription is partly over the worshipper. See *UE* 10, 334 for a presentation to a seated goddess holding a plow before her.

670. "Steatite." 23×11½. Worn. *Newell* 127. Not shown.

Worshipper led by goddess, crescent above spread eagle, standing god in tunic holding lionscimitar; inscription.

671. Impressions on both faces of tablet. Height 19½. Reverse partly shown. NBC 264. Goetze, *JCS* 2 (1948), p. 168. Shulgi 36. Jokha text.

God holding mace, right foot on stand, bow over left shoulder; inscription; worshipper led by goddess (?).

Compare *UE* 10, 434, Shu-Sin 7; Parrot, *MAM II*, 3, pl. XXXIX. 759 with worshipper, table and god with mace; *ITT* 5, pl. III. 10033, mace held by nude male in cap, though the bow, an unusual feature carried by the god in 671, is missing.

672. Impressions all over case (unopened). Height c. 25. Left edge shown. NCBT 2263. Shulgi 47 or Amar-Sin 3.

Worshipper (faint) led by goddess, god in ascending posture holding three-headed mace; inscription.

Compare *ITT* 5, pls. I and VI. 10017, p. 65; *Weber*, 442a; *Parrot*, 151 (seated god). The standing god in *Parrot*, 183 most likely holds a lionclub and has a plow before him.

673. Impressions of three seals on case (fragment). Tablet not impressed. Height A–ext. 15; B–ext. 23; C–ext. 13. YBC 13463. B also on *ITT* 3, pl. II. 6637 (shows god's foot on low cross-lined stand); 5, pl. I. 9921; both dated: MU SI.MU.RU.UM^ki[BA-H]UL, i.e. Shulgi 26, 45, or Ibbi-Sin 3 (probably the latter). Tello text.

A–Suppliant goddess with ribbon down back, worshipper led by goddess, deity on throne with inset animal (?), inscription, perhaps liongriffin under it.

B–Suppliant goddess in pleated skirt, worshipper led by goddess in flounced skirt; god in long open robe, shouldering "weapon" with two small loops enclosed by large oval one, holding standard topped by swirl of seven small maces over right foot in ascending posture; lion-headed spread eagle over inscription.

C–Faint traces contest.

The ribbon down the back of the suppliant goddess in A (see 621) and the use of three seals on the tablet (see 511) suggest a late date for the piece; this is to some extent confirmed by the alternative Ibbi-Sin date for the Tello texts on which B appears.

The multiheaded mace standard in B recalls the fanlike object held by the seated god in *Louvre T.*, 110 (see 617 above). The same type of "weapon" is apparently held by the warrior stepping on a captive in *Philadelphia*, 239, possibly of late Ur III since the warrior is beardless as in 651–52 above of the time of Shu-Sin and wears a tunic somewhat like the figure with the cup, presumably a king, in *UE* 10, 438, naming Ibbi-Sin.

674. "Steatite." 23×13. Worn. *Newell* 142. Not shown.

Worshipper led by goddess, scratch under raised left arm of goddess, standing bearded god with foot on platform, weapon at shoulder; inscription.

675. Dark gray limestone, brown tinged. 25×15. Chipped. NBC 6023.

Worshipper led by goddess (?), crescent beside goose over bull; inscription.

676. "Steatite." 23½×10½. Worn. NCBS 806.

Worshipper led by goddess, crescent above god holding rein from bull on which he stands, date palm with clusters.

Compare *UE* 10, 468–70; see also *OIP* 78, pl. 111. 5 with a standard between the worshipper and the god on a bull.

668

669

671

672

673

675

676

677a

677b

678

679

677. Impressions all over tablet. Height 22½. (a) Left edge, (b) Reverse (partial). NBC 9223. Shu-Sin 9.

Theme of 676; crescent; no rein from bull is visible; inscription.

678. Impressions on both faces of tablet, (also one edge). Height ext. 21. Reverse shown. NBC 1007.

God with lionclub in right hand, left at waist, legs blurred, standing above tail over bull's back; inscription; worshipper, right hand before face; gap.

679. Impressions all over case (tablet not impressed). Height 21. Reverse shown. NBC 5613. *BIN* 3, 627 (drawn). Shulgi 43 or Amar-Sin 6 (probably the latter). Seal of scribe of an ensi of Simurrum. Buchanan, *Iraq* 33 (1971), pl. Id, pp. 3–4, 17.

God in skull cap (?), below which hair extends backward, wearing tunic with thick edging, double-lined belting with end shown, two horizontal wings behind his shoulders, right hand at waist, in left hand scimitar held before him below waist; full-bosomed goddess in long open robe, hair straight out over left shoulder, holding above her head streams with looped top; star disk in crescent above god in long open robe, end of belt shown, right hand before him, left at waist, right foot on small stand on back of fire-spitting lion-griffin; inscription.

Some Neo-Sumerian scenes with a deity on a liongriffin: *ITT* 3, pl. II. 5979, worshipper before goddess, and a god on monster much as in 679; *ITT* 2, pl. II. 4292, presentation to the god; *UE* 10, 467, worshipper before the god; *Ward*, 135a, worshipper before deity thought to be a goddess; perhaps *RA* 23 (1926), p. 35, presentation to a king in which the leading deity, a bearded god, apparently steps on a lying liongriffin, inscription names Ibbi-Sin. Notice that the deity always stands behind the wings of the monster in contrast to the Akkadian version in which he stands between them.

For Akkadian scenes with the theme see 452 above, also *Boehmer*, 115, 333, 345, 362–71; in *Boehmer*, 372–74, the god rides in a chariot drawn by the monster. The goddess appears holding streams of rain in *Boehmer*, 333, 367–68, 373, or symbols thereof in 372, or standing amidst the rain in 369. In all except 369 she is on a liongriffin and usually her bosom is well rounded. The winged god, the first figure in 679, may perhaps be related to the hero walking before the deities in *Boehmer*, 367, or to the god killing a bull under the rain in *Boehmer*, 369.

680. Dark gray green serpentine. 20½×11½/11(concave). NCBS 701. *Yale Library Gazette* 43 (1968), pl. II, 3, pp. 94f.

Worshipper, date palm in vase, star disk in crescent above god as in 679, but in tunic and shoes with turned up toes; inscription.

For shoes with turned up toes see Akkadian 423.

681. Impression on two fragments probably from same jar sealing and part of scene on small tablet. Height 25. (a) NBC 11330 (Nippur 5 NT 593), (b) Drawing. Also NBC 11331 (5 NT 597), NBC 10539 (6 NT 27), NBC 11199 (5 NT 35), NBC 11333 (5 NT 622). Buchanan, *JNES* 31 (1972) pp. 96–101, pl. 1; Hallo, *JNES* 31 (1972) pp. 87–89. No context.

High official pouring libation on date palm in vase over which full-face goddess extends ring and rod; all over mountain from each end of which god holding bowl emerges, tree growing before one to left; inscription.

The ornamental character of the mountain and its gods contrasts with the pseudo-naturalism of the numerous Akkadian scenes in which there is a deity in or on a mountain. Only *Boehmer*, 433 is to some extent comparable, where a winged Shamash with a saw climbs between two mountains while looking at a god, man above, mountain below, who stands immediately before him.

Somewhat suggestive of the mountain gods in 681 is a group of seals, largely of Syrian origin and of Old Babylonian times, which feature divinities merged with the end of a stream, Amiet, *Syria* 37 (1960), pp. 215ff., figs. 1–3.

682. Dark gray serpentine. 19×10/9½(concave). NCBS 739.

Date palm in vase between two worshippers.

The theme is very common in Neo-Sumerian seals, sometimes with distinct variations in the design as in 657, 686–89. Seals like *UE* 10, 254, 265, or *Philadelphia*, 169 are certainly Post-Akkadian and may suggest a similar date for many of the rest. An early date is also indicated by the crudely pleated skirt with pronounced edge as in 682–83. It is curious that in two instances, *UE* 10, 270, *Parrot*, 50, the theme is combined with the rare Neo-Sumerian examples of a rider (see 503).

The same theme and material, but with traces of a worn inscription in 682x, *Newell* 159, 27×9/7, irregular.

683. Dark gray serpentine. 17×8. *Newell* 160. Not shown. *Frankfort*, p. 142, n. 1 ("Guti").

Like 682; mace standard and crescent on either side of plant; inscription.

684. Dark "steatite." 19×10/9(irregular). NBC 9135.

Theme of 682; secondary: crescent mounted on back of goose above scorpion, ground line.

685. "Steatite." 17×8. Worn. NBC 9353.

Theme of 682; secondary: standard topped by three dots (?) (top one faint) with goat on one side, lion (?) on other, goose above.

The "lion" is stylized rather like the one in 524.

686. "Steatite." 25×12. Worn. YBC 13042. Said to be from Western Iran.

Erect liongriffin, worshipper in fringed mantle, date palm in vase, erect lion, vertical snake.

Compare the lion in 685 and the liongriffin in 578.

680

681a

681b

682

684

685

686

687

688

689

692a

692b

693

687. Black serpentine. 18×10. Worn. NBC 11037.

Worshipper, date palm in vase, two heroes in contest with lion.

Compare the date palm in a vase beside a typical contest scene as here: *UE* 10, 206.

688. "Steatite," with brown inclusions. 27×12. Worn. YBC 12784. Said to be from Western Iran.

Worshipper perhaps led by goddess, date palm in vessel, goddess (?); inscription.

Compare the different arrangement of the figures in the upper register of *Parrot*, 38, Post-Akkadian.

689. Pinkish brown limestone, gray mottled. 17×8. NBC 9120. *Yale Library Gazette* 35 (1960), 28, no. 49 (probably not late Neo-Sumerian).

Lionscimitar with two streamers between two heroes (one reversed); date palm in vessel; reversed weapon (?) beside it.

Compare the hero grasping a lionscimitar beside a worship scene (perhaps reworked) in *Parrot*, 211.

690. "Steatite." 18×9/8(irregular). Worn. *Newell* 253. Not shown.

Worship of lionclub, shoot at side.

Infrequently an object of worship; compare *Louvre A.*, 339; *UE* 10, 485 (worshipping deities).

691. Light brown glazed steatite. 18×9. Worn. *Newell* 187. Not shown.

Worship of crescent standard, lionscimitar at end.

Compare the worship of the crescent standard in *UE* 10, 488–89, 492, 509–10, 512–14; also the presentation to a crescent standard in *UE* 10, 520. All are crude and simple, like most of those featuring a date palm in a vessel, and like the latter probably mostly early. The theme was especially favored at Ur, only very few have come from other sites; see *OIP* 72, 713, *Parrot*, 49 (from Tello), both variants of simple worship.

Similar scenes with two worshippers occur in impressions: 691x, NBC 2296, *BIN* 3, 165 (drawn), Amar-Sin 8, height ext. 15, inscription; 691xx, NBC (= *UDT*) 10, Shulgi 44, Tello text, height ext. 15, inscription. A corroded limestone seal perhaps shows a figure holding a flowing vase before a crescent standard: 691xxx, NBC 5962, 30×14.

692. Impressions on both faces of tablet. Height c. 23. (a) Reverse, (b) Drawing. NBC 1857. Dated Shu-Sin 3.

Worshipper (led by?) goddess (?), crescent standard, god; inscription.

693. Corroded limestone. 16×9½/8½(irregular). Worn. NCBS 715.

Deity holding lionscimitar (?) over table, worshipper, crescent mounted on two supports.

FIGS. 694–700

The Late Neo-Sumerian period, often called Isin-Larsa, refers to the time when Sumerian was largely replaced by the phase of Akkadian best known as Old Babylonian. Most conspicuous are the seals showing a worshipper led by a goddess before a seated deity, usually a goddess, sometimes a king, 694–95, also a warrior, 696, a personage, 697, a dog with a crook, 698–99, a liongriffin, 700–01. A deity (?) is touching the shoulder of a worshipper with a kid, who stands before a seated goddess holding a crescent standard, 702. A suppliant goddess behind a worshipper who confronts a seated deity, 703; the latter may be a king holding a cup, 704–06, with personage to right, 707–08. A worshipper stands before a seated king, 709, with attacked captive to left, 710, lion to right, 711. The usual couple face a standing king with cup, 712, while in 713 a worshipper confronts two gods with different insignia. Two worshippers face a god, 714–15, or in 716, a man with a cup. Between two worshippers is a god (?) facing left, 717; or they confront each other, a man in tunic being beside them, 718. In 719 three different figures face left; in 720 a man and a woman have three monsters between them, while in 721 they are accompanied by a dog with a crook. A worshipper and a bullman are in reversed position to a personage and a goddess (?), 722; two nude men hold weapons before and behind them, 723; three full-face heroes, 724; two full-face heroes and a god are accompanied by symbols, 725. Holy figures are presented on either side of a crescent standard, 726–28; in 729 they hold it dancing, in 730 only the crescent is over the dancers' opposed arms. Two pairs of dancers (?) recur in 731; a worshipper accompanies a similar group in 732; three varied figures appear in 733; a nude female and a bowlegged male with accessories are shown in 734; compare a bowlegged man with objects on his head and a warrior attacking a lion in 735. Two men spear a lion swallowing a man in 736; heroes and lions, some reversed, occur in 737. A personage and a goddess (?) adjoin a bull and a bullman in 738, while a hero wars with a lion and a bull with a bullman in 739.

694. Dark green serpentine; remains of creamy brown glaze (?). 20×11/10(irregular). Chipped. NBC 5961.

Worshipper led by goddess, crescent above enthroned deity, row of lines below (?).

The crude marks on the bosom of the leading goddess probably stand for crossed shoulder straps, see 538. Seals in a similar, or even coarser, style were common in the Diyala region; see for example *OIP* 72, 734, 737, 742–43, all "Early Larsa" (*OIP* 88, p. 261, n. 113, and ff.).

695. Hematite. 16×8. NBC 7927.

Theme of 694, but with feet of the enthroned goddess .on platform; inscription; ground line.

Compare the short pointed beard of the worshipper with the more careful rendering in 604. For broad stumpy figures as here see *CANES*, 309, 335–39.

Thinner figures with the same theme occur in 695x, NCBS 751, worn hematite, 16×7½, inscription, ground line.

696. Hematite. 24×13. *Newell* 123. Not shown.

Presentation to goddess holding vase (?) (or scratch); in field ball staff and vessel; ground line (?); warrior shouldering axe. The worshipper and the warrior are both bearded.

697. Hematite. 21×10. Worn. *Newell* 125. Not shown.

Presentation to goddess holding vase, before her dot in crescent and monkey (?), before the worshipper vessel above ball staff, ground line; to the left personage with mace (?).

698. Hematite. 20×11. *Newell* 139. Not shown.

Presentation to god holding scepter, behind him dog with crook on head; in field: ball staff, star, crescent, and vessel; ground line.

699. Light brown limestone. 22×12/11(concave). YBC 13052.

Presentation to enthroned "king" with cup, crescent above bow-legged dwarf; ground line; lionscimitar behind dog with crook on head.

694

695

699

700

The same theme and material but much worn occurs in 699x, *Newell* 137, 18×10, presenting king with cup, star, and crescent in field.

700. Impressions in reserved areas on faces and sides of case (tablet not impressed). Height 23½. Obverse partly shown. YBC 11164. Simmons, *JCS* 14 (1960), pp. 50f., no. 70; 13 (1959), pp. 78f., Harmal text from archive of time of Sumu-la-el of Babylon.

Erect liongriffin holding staff, dot between wings, worshipper, right hand before face, left at waist, star above; goddess posed as if leading worshipper but with right hand turned back; crescent above vessel; enthroned "king" with cup, support at back; ground line.

For the style compare *OIP* 72, 732, 737 from an early Larsa context; see also *Ash C,* 458.

701

702

704

706

707

701. Black limestone. 29×15/14(concave). NBC 3016.

Rampant liongriffin, vertical line below foreleg; inscription on either side of worshipper who is connected by line with shoulder of worshipping goddess; enthroned goddess, her feet on line.

The curious stroke before the left arm of the worshipper may be the remains of an older design. The line below the foreleg of the monster could be a survival also.

For the style compare *Berlin*, 318, late Neo-Sumerian, from Warka.

702. "Steatite." 27×14½/13½(irregular). YBC 9674.

Deity (?) with hand at shoulder of worshipper with kid, enthroned deity holding crescent standard; spade above bowlegged dwarf, crook, lightning standard over goat fish.

Compare the heavy linear style of *CANES*, 312, p. 39, which like 702 should perhaps be placed later.

703. Brownish limestone. 22×12. Worn. *Newell* 175. Not shown.

Suppliant goddess, snake, worshipper, enthroned deity, lionclub (left side worn – dot for mace); ground line (?).

704. Light brown limestone. 25×12. NBC 5957.

Suppliant goddess, star above scorpion, worshipper, crescent above lion-headed snake, enthroned "king" with cup, lionclub on notched pole; ground line.

705. Lapis lazuli. 15½×7. *Newell* 181. Not shown.

Theme of 704; two drillings, star above vessel, crescent above ball staff, crescent on notched pole; ground line (?).

706. "Steatite." 21×10½. Worn. NCBS 780.

Suppliant goddess, small animal (?), worshipper, crescent above "mongoose," enthroned figure with cup, lionscimitar with pennant (?).

707. Dark gray serpentine. 21×11. Chipped. NCBS 741.

Personage with mace; theme of 706, all in fringed garments.

708. "Steatite." 20×9. Worn. NCBS 776.

Unfinished personage, worshipper, suppliant goddess, crescent above animal (?), enthroned "king" with cup.

709. Brown streaked, grainy hematite. 26×15/14(concave). Scratched. YBC 9721.

Gatepost, topped by human head in peaked hat, held by erect lion, star disk, worshipper, crescent above goose, enthroned "king" with cup; ground line; inscription.

The head on a gatepost recalls seals, mostly Syrian, that show a standard with two heads, sometimes topped by a bird, Seyrig, *Syria* 37 (1960), pp. 233f.

710. Hematite. 24×15. Chipped. NBC 5979.

Worshipper in short pointed beard, crescent, enthroned "king" with cup, his feet on niched stand, worshipper (reversed), nude bearded hero in belt, holding rod, and brandishing scimitar, one foot on captive.

For the hero stepping on a captive, see *Philadelphia*, 239 (Ur III style); *UE* 10, 557, 561 (late Neo-Sumerian); *Parrot*, 260 (c. 1900 B.C.); *Louvre D.*, 128; *OIP* 72, 907; *CANES*, 382; *Berlin*, 292; *Ash C*, 467 (Early Old Babylonian).

711. "Steatite." 14×6. Worn. *Newell* 211. Not shown.

Erect lion, worshipper, crescent, seated king, vessel above ball staff.

712. "Steatite." 18×8. Worn. YBC 13044. Said to be from Western Iran.

Worshipper led by goddess, vessel above ball staff between them; crescent above "mongoose," vessel held by "king" with short pointed beard in bordered tunic; inscription; ground line.

Compare *CANES* 542–43, late Neo-Sumerian.

Very worn, darkish serpentine, 712x, *Newell* 145, 17×9, lionscimitar, worshipper led by goddess, vessel over ball staff between them, crescent (?) above scorpion, vessel (?) held by striding figure.

713. "Steatite." 26×11. Decayed. YBC 12626.

Worshipper, fish, god in schematic horned crown holding saw (?), nude male on one knee before god with leg forward who holds ball-topped rod with streamers; ground line.

Compare the even cruder style of *OIP* 72, 739 ("Early Larsa"; see 694 above).

714. Grainy granite. 17×8½. Worn. NCBS 718. Fake?

Dog with crook on head, worshipper, male worshipper in tunic, crescent above crook (?), deity shouldering weapon (?); inscription (upside down).

715. Dark "steatite." 17×8. NCBS 768.

Suppliant goddess, lionscimitar standard with pennants, worshipper, goddess (?), vessel above ball staff; ground line.

716. Brown mottled buff limestone. 19×9. Chipped. YBC 12822.

Worshipper, goddess (?) with outstretched arms, male figure in tunic holding cup; inscription.

Compare *Louvre T.*, 206, *CANES*, 541.

708

709

710

712

713

714

715

716

718

719

720

721

723

724

725

726

717. Dark olive limestone. 18×9. *Newell* 201. Not shown.

Two worshippers on either side of god (?) with short pointed beard wearing tunic and striated cap (back of head chipped) holding (?) crescent, behind him vessel above ball staff, before him crook; terminal: lionclub on twisted pole; ground line.

718. Brown mottled, dark gray limestone. 22×13. NBC 6021.

Dog with crook on head between two worshippers, crescent above bird, male figure in tunic; ground line.

Compare *OIP* 72, 772, late Neo-Sumerian (?).

719. Hematite. 16×7. YBC 9699.

Personage (without mace), crescent above crook, worshipper, star, hero in tunic; inscription.

Compare *OIP* 72, 774, *CANES*, 551–53.

720. Dark brown serpentine. 23½×11/10(irregular). Worn. NCBS 824.

Lionscimitar (?) on pole, sitting dog, male figure in tunic facing female worshipper, between them fishman (?) above sphinx (?) above lion with jaws agape.

Compare *OIP* 72, 933.

721. Hematite. 16×8. NCBS 721.

Dog with crook on head, male figure in tunic, crook, worshipper; ground line.

722. Dark gray serpentine. 23×13. Worn. *Newell* 144. Not shown.

Worshipper in tunic, disk in crescent above seated "monkey" with staff (?) on head, mace standard held by full-face bullman; reversed: crescent above schematic human head, goddess (?), personage with mace.

Normally the personage holds his mace in the left hand as in 707, but see the second figure in *OIP* 72, 939, "Isin-Larsa."

723. Dark "steatite." 22×10. Worn. YBC 12629.

Two nude (?) males with mace (?), standard between them, each holding lionscimitar; small animal.

724. Dark "steatite." 24½×12. Bore, conical at ends, 5/4/3½. Worn. NBC 9104.

Nude full-face bearded hero with double-marked belt, hands at waist, dog with crook on head, hero like first, bowlegged dwarf, gatepost held by bullman.

Bodies rendered like those in 724–25, tall with thin waists and well-muscled legs, appear in *OIP* 72, 900, Early Larsa, but with the heroes in profile.

725. Light green, glazed composition. 28×13. Some glaze in design. YBC 9684. *Yale Library Gazette* 35 (1960), p. 28, no. 51.

Two nude heroes, full face with side curls, holding spade standard between them; crescent on notched pole with supports held by god in schematic horned crown, one leg forward.

A spade standard held by a hero and bullman occurs in *Philadelphia*, 455, 471.

726. "Steatite." 16×10½. Worn. NBC 5937.

Liongriffin (?) grasping ball-topped standard, worshipper, notched crescent standard with pennants (?), suppliant goddess, lion; ground line.

Compare the worship of a crescent standard in *OIP* 72, 713.

727. Dark gray serpentine. 15×9. *Newell* 208. Not shown.

Worshipper on either side of notched crescent standard, goat rampant against pole; ground line.

728. Dark "steatite." 17×8. YBC 12612. *Yale Library Gazette* 35 (1960), p. 28, no. 50.

Two dancers (?) in flat caps, axe above scorpion between them, notched crescent standard.

For similar figures, but with the more usual triangular chests, see *Brussels Suppl.*, 1629 (p. 173).

729. Dark gray serpentine. 18×10. *Newell* 148. Not shown. *Frankfort*, pl. 29c (Old Babylonian).

Liongriffin, two dancers hold crescent staff between them over bird with (small) head turned back; ground line.

For typical late Neo-Sumerian, or perhaps slightly later, dancers with one leg crossed over the other, see: *Brussels*, 472 (p. 206); *Brussels Suppl.*, 1630 (p. 142); *Ash C*, 472; *Louvre A.*, 341, 455, S., 532; *CANES*, 555–56, *Parrot*, 219.

730. Impressions on case fragment (two other seals impressed elsewhere on case; tablet not impressed). Height c. 20. (a) Obverse (partly shown), (b) Drawing. NBC 5382. *BIN* 7, 86 (drawn along with the two other seals, both mature Old Babylonian). Simmons, *JCS* 13 (1959), p. 116, no. 33; pp. 72, 76 (Harmel text, probably c. 1800 B.C.).

Two facing dancers, forward hands raised to crescent, outside arm beside body, fly (?) between them; ground line.

An impression perhaps all over tablet, 730x, NBC 8596, height 20, Rim-Sin 58; dancers, probably as in 729, but with outside arms bent to waist, inside bent down, on line above lion (?) on line.

For examples of dancers in the secondary of mature Old Babylonian seals see *CANES*, 467, *Berlin*, 358.

731. Olive limestone. 24×13. Worn. *Newell* 150. Not shown.

Dancing (?) men; one pair has hand on staff between them.

732. Light brown calcite. 19×11. Worn. NBC 11087.

Lionscimitar, worshipper, ball staff, two dancers (?) (or fighters), crescent above, vessel between them.

733. Light brown limestone. 18×11. Corroded. YBC 9671.

God (?) in tunic holding bent rod, vessel (?) above crook beside two-legged (?) stand, personage, obscure objects, bowlegged figure, spread eagle above ball staff (?), lightning symbol.

Compare *OIP* 72, 927 (Isin-Larsa).

734. Hematite. 11½×8½. *Newell* 261. Not shown. *Frankfort*, 150, n. 2 (Old Babylonian).

Nude female and bowlegged figure both looking right, crescent standard like 726, but mounted on three-legged stand, lightning symbol, spade standard.

735. Shell. 15×16. Worn. *Newell* 162. Not shown.

Hero spearing erect lion, crescent above, bowlegged dwarf holding loaded tray in upraised hands.

736. Dark gray serpentine. 21×11. New impression. *Newell* 147. *Yale Library Gazette* 43 (1968), pl. I. 3, pp. 92f. (incorrectly described).

Two heroes in striated caps spearing lion that is swallowing man (head down, arms spread); in field: lionscimitar standard, crescent, gazelle nibbling plant on line above scorpion, spread eagle above "mongoose."

737. Brown limestone. 21×12. Worn. *Newell* 146. Not shown. *Frankfort*, p. 174, n. 1 (Old Babylonian).

Hero, hands at waist; reversed lion; belted hero holding bent weapon in either hand, throw stick before him; reversed hero (like first), lion.

The heroes all wear garments over their shoulders and probably tunics.

738. Hematite. 20×9. YBC 9679.

Personage, crescent, goddess (?), lightning symbol, bull held by full-face bullman, small personage between them.

739. Dark "steatite." 26×14. Worn. YBC 9998.

Nude belted hero grasping lion, bull held by full-face bullman and attacked below by small bearded hero in flat hat holding scimitar before him below waist; inscription.

Compare *Berlin*, 466, more mannered, but late Neo-Sumerian at the latest by the ball staff in its design. The full-face head of the bullman in 739 resembles the full-face heads in a cylinder of c. 1900–1850 B.C. from Acemhöyük in south central Anatolia, N. Özgüc, *Anatolia* (Anadolu) 10 (1966), pp. 38, 50, pl. XIV. I.

728

730b

732

730a

733

736

738

739

740

742

745

746

748

749

Early Old Babylonian

Early Old Babylonian cylinders commonly show a suppliant goddess and a worshipper facing an enthroned king with cup, 740–44, to which may be added contending beasts, 745, a warrior attacking a prone foe with a whirling mace, 746, a hero shouldering an axe, 747, a personage on a stand, two reversed figures, and in the middle a worshipper with kid, 748. A similar worshipper with kid between a suppliant goddess and an enthroned god, 749; a goddess and a worshipper before an enthroned goddess complete the series, 750.

740. Light green composition. 22×13. NBC 2601.

Suppliant goddess with ribbon down back, vessel above ball staff, bearded worshipper in striated cap, hands at waist, star disk in crescent, bearded full-face head, scorpion, bearded king with vessel on cushioned throne on low platform; lionclub on twisted pole in oblong enclosure with twisted sidepieces; ground line.

741. Hematite. 23½×15. *Newell* 174. Not shown.

Figures and disk in crescent as in 740; low stand for feet, niched platform below; inscription.

742. Hematite. 24×13/12½(concave). NBC 2578.

Like 741 except worshipper seems bald; inscription.

743. Carnelian. 23×11½. *Newell* 178. Not shown.

Like 742 except for simple platform; inscription.

744. Hematite. 21×11½. *Newell* 173. Not shown.

Like 742 except for vessel over ball staff, "mongoose," inscription over lion, not on ground line.

745. Lapis lazuli. 22×13. NBC 3288.

Like 742, but with inscription before the enthroned king, erect lion in grasp of full-face bullman.

746. Hematite. 23×15/14(concave). Worn. YBC 9689.

Like 742 except for simple platform, no crescent, and the enthroned king's vessel, latter partly covered by added inscription which fills the two spaces between the principal figures; kilted hero raising dagger, holding multiple mace before him with one foot on prone captive; no ground line.

Beside worship of king, added full-face Ishtar, weapons at shoulders, one foot on lion, wielding multiple mace, 2184A, left edge envelope, *AJSL* 24 (1913), p. 203 (drawn *CT* 45 [1964], pl. I, 82050), Sumulael, 2nd Old Babylonian king (c. 1850 B.C.).

747. Hematite. 17½×9. *Newell* 179. Not shown.

Like 743 except for bearded worshipper in striated cap, vessel over ball staff, crescent, niched platform; hero in striated cap, belted kilt, axe on shoulder.

748. Lapis lazuli. 22×11/10(concave). Worn. NBC 9149.

Personage in kilt with mace (?) held at waist on rocklike dais, suppliant goddess, male head over blob, worshipper in hat with kid, ground line under last two figures, star disk in crescent above blob, bearded king with vessel on cushioned throne on niched platform; reversed: full-face ithyphallic bullman over small male worshipper.

A similar scene shows a worshipper with kid while at the side a hero attacks a lion from the rear (compare the lion and bullman in 745), *CT* 45 (1964), pl. I, bottom obverse, Sumulael (c. 1850 B.C.).

749. Hematite. 25×14. YBC 9720.

Suppliant goddess, bowlegged dwarf in striated cap, worshipper, perhaps bald, holding kid, leg with kilt exposed, cross in disk in crescent over crook, enthroned god; inscription; ground line.

750. Hematite. 28×18. *Newell* 177. Not shown.

Suppliant goddess with ribbon down back, "mongoose," worshipper in cap, crescent above bowlegged, phallic dwarf, enthroned goddess, her feet on low stand, space; ground line.

Old Babylonian

PSEUDO-REALISTIC STYLE

This style begins shortly after 1900 B.C. and ends c. 1740. First a pair of fishmen, 751; then two groups of figures, 752–53; all of Sumuel, Larsa. Worshippers plus a small figure with kid before an enthroned king, both of the latter figures on a platform, 754; a ruler on a throne beside a reversed bullman, 755; three fragmentary sealings showing worshippers before enthroned kings, 756; a dancing (?) man with other figures, 757, all of Sumulael, 2nd king of Babylon. A seated god with small goddesses behind him, Nur-Adad, Larsa, 758; varied figures, Sin-iddinam (?), 759; two bulls, one with figure on back, 760; a personage on dais, goddess, worshipper with kid, and armed goddess, 761, Sin-iddinam, all of Larsa. Contorted man in grasp of god, Eshnunna ruler, 762; snake goddess with back to acrobatic god, Warad-Sin, Larsa, 763; god holding flowing vase, Apil-Sin (?), Babylon, 764; hero fighting bullman, 765; various figures, 766; deities with sacred objects, 767; personage facing goddess with small nude female between them, 768, last four Naram-Sin, Eshnunna; personage facing goddess, An-am of Uruk, probably late 19th century. All the above seals belong to the 19th century.

Rim-Sin of Larsa, 1822–1763 B.C., is represented by numerous sealings. The first shows a worshipper with kid before an enthroned god, 770; then a personage between two worshippers, 771; a man with kid before a god with saw, 772; a suppliant goddess, 773; a god with saw and a priest, 774; a personage with mace, 775; an enthroned king with cup, 776; two rows of figures beside a reversed goddess, 777; numerous figures include a hero holding a flowing vase and an armed goddess, 778. One section of 779 shows a god, perhaps in a coffin, and various other holy figures. Contending figures recur in 780; more complicated heroes, demons, and animals in 781; flowing vases are held by a goddess and a hero in 782; two rows of creatures struggle behind a goddess in 783; a personage confronts a deity in 784; small objects and a figure occur in 785; worshipper with kid faces the sun god in 786. Rim-Sin I (or perhaps II, of the time of Samsuiluna) could belong to 787, showing a personage facing a goddess, or 788: two goddesses on either side of an inscription. Impression of a nude female and personages, Sinmuballit 8 (or 5), 789; worshipper with kid before a deity, other holy subjects, Hammurabi 1, 790; personage, goddess, each with inscription, 791; contest of heroes and animals, 792–93; row of holy figures, 794; personage facing full-face goddess, 795; a hero with bow strangling male with hands tied, 796; a worshipper with kid before a seated god, symbols on side perhaps Neo-Sumerian, 797; contending figures, Hammurabi 41, 798; a personage before a goddess, Eshnunna king, first half of 18th century, 799; gods in conflict (?), Eshnunna king, 800.

Under Samsuiluna of Babylon Rim-Sin II ruled for an uncertain time in the south; a leading goddess before a seated goddess, 801, and a suppliant goddess before an inscription, 802. During the early years of Samsuiluna the pseudo-realistic style persisted. Rows of divine or ministering figures appear in 803; a personage facing a deity, both on lions, 804; worshippers before seated deities, 805; personages with inscriptions, 806; among many impressions, one; perhaps Cappadocian in style, shows worshippers before a seated deity and, reversed, warriors on a prone enemy; two, contending heroes; three, a number of sacred figures and animals, 807; an attenuated female, a personage, and perhaps a goddess, 808; different impressions, a personage, a row of holy figures, inscription, and a goddess, 809; confronted pairs with a little warrior between

751

752a

752b

752c

753a

753b

them, 810; priests grasping bucket above man assaulted by dragon 811; holy figures in related groups, 812; religious group, bull equipped with sacred trappings behind which a personage confronts a goddess, 813; inscription with added figures,

their back to a worshipper, 814; below a guilloche, separate humans attacked by lion and dragon, 815; the god with a saw, 816; a row of sacred figures within guilloches, 817.

751. Small oblong tablet. Very worn impressions. Height 26½. Bottom edge. NBC 5500 (*BIN* 7, 126). Sumuel 4 (1891 B.C.), 7th king of Larsa.

Under the inscription, fishman with human erect body, hand before face, tail opposed to similar tail in other direction; ground line.

An Isin-Larsa cylinder shows a fishman almost prone on an inscription. In it there is the presentation to a two-headed god, *Louvre A.*, 251. A subsidiary motif in Old Babylonian seals is a fishman with erect human body, *Louvre A.*, 305, *Philadelphia*, 260.

752. Small oblong tablet. Probably all im-

pressed except right edge. Slopes in to obverse. Height 22½. (a) Reverse, (b) Bottom edge (both partial), (c) Drawing. NBC 5410 (*BIN* 7, 108). Sumuel 13 (1882 B.C.).

Inscription, priest with pail and sprinkler, human figure (trace – see drawing), . . . god with right arm extended, in long robe with bare right leg; ground line.

753. Flat clay strip. Height 27. (a-b) Impressions. YBC 13113. Servant Sumuel.

Worshipper, king with cup on cushioned throne on platform, inscription, personage with arms to middle, perhaps holding staff like worshipper in 653.

279

754b

755

754a

756a

756b

756c

756d

754. Long tablet, probably impressed all over. Height 24. (a) Left side, (b) Drawing. MLC 1218. Oath by Sumulael 6 (1875 B.C.). 2nd Old Babylonian king.

From bottom up: uncertain hand holding star disk standard, suppliant goddess, gap (?), worshipper with hands at waist, star disk in crescent, small worshipper with hand before face, holding kid, on edge of niched platform with king apparently on cushioned throne, ground line.

755. Quite thick tablet, slightly cut back to face, impressed all over. Height 21½. Left side shown. MLC 1688. Compare Sumulael 26, perhaps c. 1855 B.C.

King (?) on cushioned throne, his feet on low stand on niched platform; in reverse: full-face bullman holding flat-topped gate post standard; normal: suppliant goddess with ribbon down back.

756. Envelopes (tablets not impressed). Height: A–20, B–19½, C–16½. (a) Top edge, A above B, (b) Left edge, B on either side of A (a-b = YBC 11169), (c) Left edge, C twice above A (YBC 11173), (d) Drawing (A). Simmons, *JCS* 14 (1960), p. 24, no. 48, 13 (1959), p. 78, YBC 11169; 14 (1960), p. 23, no. 47, 13 (1959), p. 73, YBC 11173; from Abu Harmal near Baghdad. Time of Sumulael (1880–45 B.C.).

A–Erect lion, worshipper with hand before face, second worshipper, king with cup on altar throne; ground line.

B–Trace crescent, king in striated hat, right hand extended, on altar throne, inscription, worshipper (?); ground line.

C–Worshipper with hand before face, bearded worshipper in striated hat with hands at waist, crescent above ball staff beside vessel, king with cup on cushioned throne on platform; ground line.

757. Oblong tablet, perhaps impressed all over. Height ext. 14. (a) Left side, (b) Top end. Simmons, *JCS* 14 (1960), p. 27, no. 55, 13 (1959), p. 79, YBC 11158. Source like 756. Time of Sumulael (1880–45 B.C.).

Worshipper led by goddess, nude belted hero, erect lion in grasp of nude belted hero who steps on it with one foot.

758. Squarish thick tablet tag, string holes at upper corners. Height ext. 18. (a) Lower reverse (other impressions omitted), (b) Drawing. NBC 9267. One of the six inscriptions can be of Nur-Adad (1865–50 B.C.), 8th king of Larsa.

Enthroned god holding sword upwards before him, two small facing suppliant goddesses over inscription.

Though the god with saw is customarily seen with one bare leg extended forward (*Frankfort,* pl. XXVI f, l), at least one exception shows him seated (*Frankfort,* pl. XXVII a) as may have been intended here.

759. Long oblong tablet, ends broken or blank, otherwise probably impressed. Height A–23+, B–22. Right side. YBC 4485. Probably Sin-iddinam 5 (1845), 9th king of Larsa.

A (top)–Possibly priest with pail and sprinkler, suppliant goddess with ribbon down back, small framed inscription, worshipper (?).

B (lower three rows)–Worshipper with right hand before face, disk in circle (?) above mongoose (?), god with rod and ring before him, mace in left hand at waist, long robe with right foot before it on small stand, ground line.

A god holding rod and ring is seated before worshippers in *OIP* 72, 712, see p. 50 for a probable reference there to Ibalpiel I, Eshnunna, possibly c. 1900 B.C.

760. Three squarish tablet tags, string holes at upper corners. Height 13½ (with cap marks 24). (a-b) Left side (YBC 4970, YBC 5205), (c) Top edge (YBC 3268), all partial. Sin-idinnam 6 (1844 B.C.). Goetze, *JCS* 4 (1950), pp. 88ff. (tags presumably from Larsa), p. 113 (names Nur-Adad, preceding king); Porada, *JCS* 4, pp. 160–61, fig. 14 (correct reference probably YBC 5205), drawn.

Two facing (?) bulls, on one to right figure in long robe with right leg exposed, right hand forward, other bent to waist; inscription.

761. Envelope (badly broken); tablet not impressed. Height 22½. Blurred. Long side. YBC 5472 (*YOS* 2, 29, undated letter). Seal names ᵈSin-idinnam (1849–43 B.C.).

Personage with mace on cross-lined stand, suppliant goddess with ribbon down back, worshipper with kid, star disk in crescent, full-face goddess with tress over each shoulder, extending lionclub to right, in long robe with right leg exposed, ground line; inscription.

On both edges and faces of tablet a personage with mace on a stand facing an inscription, height c. 18, 761x, YBC 5170 (*YOS* 5, 213), Sin-idinnam 7 (1843 B.C.). A similar figure similarly placed, but without a stand, occurs on an envelope face, 761xx, NBC 6747, Sin-eribam 1 (1842 B.C.).

762. Oblong envelope (tablet not impressed). Height c. 25. (a) Obverse partly shown, (b) Drawing. NBC 7309. Simmons, *JCS* 14 (1960), p. 49, no. 67; 13 (1959), p. 79, Ipiq-Adad II, king of Eshnunna, time of Sabium (1844–31), 3rd king of Babylon.

Goatfish (?) above, man in round cap on one knee, twisted with head turned back, his right hand in grasp of god in high hat with bow over left shoulder, profile head over small priest with sprinkler and pail on niched platform; ground line.

757a

757b

758a

758b

759

760a

760b

760c

761

762a

762b

763b

764a

764b

763a

765b

764c

765a

765c

766

763. Oblong tablet. Height 21 (with mark above 23). (a) Right side, (b) Drawing. Same design on reverse. Impressions of inscription of 2nd seal on other parts except bottom edge. YBC 5698. Buchanan, *Iraq* 33 (1971), pl. Ia, pp. 1, 17, drawn fig. 1, p. 8. Warad-Sin 9 (1826), 13th king of Larsa.

Nude goddess with hair outstretched, hands raised before her, wings behind, her lower body snake coil; god with hair outstretched, looking up in bent over position, his arms up and down attached to wings; ground line.

The snake goddess and the acrobatic god, both with wings, very much alike, except for small differences, occur with similar gods in a cylinder seal, BM 134773, *Iraq* 33 (1971), pl. Ie, pp. 9–11 (in pl. IIa only the principal figures are shown, the normal Old Babylonian filling motifs all being deliberately omitted).

764. Oblong envelope (probably impressed all over); tablet not impressed. Height 23½. (a) Top end (also drawn), (b) Left side, (c) Drawing. MLC 113. Apil-Sin (1830–13 B.C.), 4th king of Babylon.

God extending vase from which stream on either side flows (?) to vase held at waist by nude belted full-face hero on one knee, cow and calf on line above second kneeling hero, (figures drawn below), gap, star disk in crescent before god in ascending posture back to back with suppliant goddess with a ribbon down her back.

765. Oblong envelope (both it and tablet probably all impressed). Height A–22, B–c. 20. (a) Right side, lower half (drawn), (b) Bottom end, (c) Drawing. Other impressions not shown. NBC 5347 (*BIN* 7, 72). Simmons, *JCS* 13 (1959), p. 113, no. 23, Naram-Sin, king of Eshnunna. Time, Apil-Sin (1830–13 B.C.), 4th king of Babylon.

A–Hero contending with bullman, seated "mongoose" between them, star disk in crescent above fish, suppliant goddess; ground line.

B–Goat seated on stand attacked by erect lion that full-face naked hero grasps by neck and leans against with right leg, second full-face hero reversing second lion whose snout crosses the hero's left leg.

766. Oblong envelope (fragment). Height 18½. Left edge. NBC 9762. Simmons, *JCS* 13 (1959), p. 76. Naram-Sin, Eshnunna.

Personage with mace, crescent, suppliant goddess with ribbon down back, worshipper, wing of dragon (?); ground line.

767. Oblong envelope (tablet not sealed). Height 21½. (a) Reverse (partial), (b) Drawing. NBC 8604. Simmons, *JCS* 13 (1959), p. 112, no. 21. Naram-Sin, Eshnunna.

God with crook, goddess grasping ribbed lionclub standard; ground line, streams (at bottom), gap (?), full-face goddess holding lionclub, arrows at shoulders.

768. Oblong envelopes (partly impressed); tablets not impressed. Height A–21, B–20. (a) A, left edge (NBC 6751), (b) A, right edge and (c) B, left edge (NBC 8603), all partial. Simmons, *JCS* 13 (1959), p. 115, no. 31 (a), Naram-Sin, Eshnunna; *JCS* 13, p. 117, no. 36 (b-c), Eshnunna date uncertain.

A–Personage with mace, star disk in crescent above small full-face nude female, suppliant goddess with ribbon down back, ground line.

B–Parallel zigzag pattern, linear borders.

The zigzag pattern is a survival from protoliterate times, see *UE* 3, 7, also 202 above.

769. Carnelian with light translucent streaks. 25×14. NBC 1199. An-àm, king of Uruk, probably late 19th century B.C., *ZZw.* pp. 155f.

Personage with mace, suppliant goddess with ribbon down back, ground line, bull on line with crook on back, over rearing antelopes on either side of tree; inscription.

770. Envelope. Height A–ext. 19, B–ext. 20, C–ext. 22. (a) Left side (A-B), (b) Top end (C), (c) Drawing. YBC 5616. Rim-Sin 4 (1819 B.C.), 14th king of Larsa.

A–Lion (?) attacking man on one knee, right arm down, left up; seated goat in grasp of erect lion.

B–Overlapping trace of suppliant goddess, vertical fish, worshipper with kid, disk in crescent over rod held by god, on altar throne on platform with two tiers of niches, facing left, small worshipper (?) above man with extended arm holding weapon (?); ground line.

C–Suppliant goddess with ribbon down back, mounted lionscimitar, worshipper with hands at waist, disk in crescent, king with cup on cushioned stool on platform.

767a

768a

768b

768c

767b

769

770a

770b

770c

771a

771b

771c

772

773

774

775

776

777

771. Oblong envelope (it and tablet probably sealed all over). Height 18½. (a) Top edge, (b) Right side, both partial, (c) Drawing. YBC 4483. Rim-Sin 5 (?).

Worshipper on line; personage in kilt, leaning on scimitar, dagger at waist on left side; bearded human head facing right, worshipper in long fringed robe, mounted lionscimitar, worshipper with hand before face.

772. Fragment envelope. Height c. 22. Part reverse. YBC 5852 (*YOS* 8, 11, poor drawing). Rim-Sin 16.

God (with saw), bullman in contest, worshipper with kid, god with saw (as before), right foot on stand, rear of bullman (mixed with front of suppliant goddess who on long side of tablet appears behind worshipper with kid).

773. Thick oblong tablet. Height c. 24. Part reverse. YBC 6217 (*YOS* 8, 28). Rim-Sin 17.

God in ascending posture above line, below it worshipper with right hand at waist, left before face, toward them suppliant goddess with ribbon down back (repeats), lionclub (?) on ribbed pole.

774. Thick oblong tablet (probably all except one end impressed). Height ext. 20. Part reverse. YBC 8705. Rim-Sin 19.

Trace worshipper with kid, star disk in crescent, god with saw, right foot on low stand, priest with pail and sprinkler on platform.

775. Oblong tablet (all impressed except one long side, also case with different seal or seals). Height 23. Bottom end (partial). YBC 5668 (*YOS* 8, 10). Rim-Sin 24.

Personage with mace facing (poor) full-face goddess holding lionclub; ground line.

A similar scene with tall thin figures, poorly impressed, appears on 775x, YBC 5696 (*YOS* 8, 170), Rim-Sin 3.

776. Oblong tablet (one end not impressed). Height 30. Left side partial. YBC 5729. (*YOS* 8, 22, poor drawing). Rim-Sin 25.

Star disk in crescent over cup held by king on cushioned stool on niched platform, three dots behind head.

777. Oblong envelope (tablet probably not impressed). Height 22. Right edge partial. YBC 5377 (*YOS* 8, 139). Rim-Sin 26.

Reversed: deity facing left, worshipper with right hand before face, left at waist, suppliant goddess (?); below: trace of figure, suppliant goddess, worshipper with hands at waist; (upside down) full-face (?) goddess with scimitar beside her, arrows (?) at shoulders.

778. Thick oblong envelope, probably all impressed. Height. A–ext. 19, B–ext. 20.(a)Left edge (A), (b) Bottom (B). YBC 12141. Rim-Sin 28 (?).

A–Nude belted full-face bearded hero, stream flows from either side from vase at waist, suppliant goddess with ribbon down back, worshipper with kid in long open robe, full-face goddess with arrows at shoulders and extended curl of hair on either side, holding lionclub and leaning on scimitar, bracelets at wrists, right foot on stand.

B–Suppliant goddess with ribbon down back, personage with mace; goddess with arrows as in (A).

779. Long tablets, impressed all over. Height: A–24 (YBC 4217 = *YOS* 8, 85). B–23 (YBC 4219) with cap marks 26 (latter not shown in YBC 4217). (a) Left side, (b) Reverse (both partial), (c–d) Drawings (c = A, d = B).

A–Rim-Sin 29, B–30. *Yale Library Gazette* 45 (1970), p. 57, no. 7.

A–Full-face, bull-eared god with hands at chest, below elbows frame of enclosure with which body merges, set in low double-lined stand; fly above three fish, worshipper with hands at waist, star disk in crescent before full-face goddess with right hand raised, ground line.

B–God in ascending posture, bowlegged dwarf in lower right of three columns of inscription, under this full-face nude female, monster with weapon, worshipper.

780. Long envelope (and tablet), perhaps impressed all over. Height ext. 20. (a) Obverse (part), (b) Drawing. YBC 4484. Rim-Sin 30.

Full-face bullman in contest, before him small figure; above: worshipper in folded tunic holding rod (?) before seated deity.

778a

778b

779a

779b

779c

779d

780a

780b

781a

781b

782

783

784a

784b

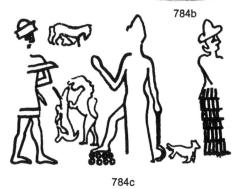

784c

785

786a

786b

786c

781. Oblong envelope. Height 18½. (a) Reverse, (b) Left side (both partial). YBC 5453. Rim-Sin 31 (?).

Liondemon brandishing weapon and holding trident (?) over goat on which the demon places foot, hero with curls down back of head, his hands grasping animal group which (to right and below) shows goats seated on either side of crossed lions beyond which with outstretched hands stands second hero (?), whose back is to the original liondemon.

The worn end of a tablet shows a worshipper with kid, gap (?), personage, bowlegged dwarf, suppliant goddess, inscription: 781x, YBC 5749 (*YOS* 8, 62, poor drawing). Rim-Sin 32.

782. Oblong envelope (and tablet, both impressed). Height 21½ (with cap marks 25). Reverse (partial). NBC 9263. Rim-Sin 40.

Full-face goddess and nude bearded full-face hero both holding flowing vase at waist, personage.

783. Thick oblong envelope (tablet not impressed). Height 21. Bottom edge (partial). YBC 4323. Rim-Sin 40.

Goat with head turned back attacked by winged dragon on line; below: hero grappling with full-face bullman, suppliant goddess, star, ground line.

784. Tablet. Height 26. (a) Bottom end, (b) Top end, (c) Drawing. YBC 8441. Rim-Sin 46.

Personage with mace, right hand across chest, in double lined tunic, cow and calf above seated goat attacked by lion, deity with right leg on pile of stones, holding scimitar in left hand, inscription above goatfish, suppliant goddess.

A personage with his right arm across his chest, an unusual position, occurs in *BN*, 229.

785. Envelope (and tablet, both impressed). Height 23. Part reverse. NBC 8937. Rim-Sin 47.

Fragment deity (?); column: star disk in crescent above man with hands at waist above sidewise goat fish; inscription.

786. Oblong tablet, probably all impressed. Height 25. (a) Obverse, (b) Top end (both partial), (c) Drawing. YBC 4378. Rim-Sin 50.

Worshipper with kid facing god with saw, right foot on human-headed bull the horned crown of which projects into inscription between the figures; ground line.

787. Big oblong impressed envelope. Height 24 (with cap marks 27). Part reverse. NBC 9039. Rim-Sin, 1822–1763 B.C. (or Rim-Sin 2, compare 801–02).

Personage with mace, suppliant goddess with ribbon down back, inscription, ground line.

788. Black green moss agate. 32×18½/17½ (concave). Corroded copper pin. *Newell* 661. Not shown. Rim-Sin (see 787).

Facing suppliant goddesses with ribbons down back on ground lines, inscription between them.

789. Envelope (probably all impressed). Height 23. NBC 7687. Part reverse. Sin-muballit 8 (or 5), 1805 (or 8), 5th king of Babylon.

Full-face nude female, ground line, personage with mace facing suppliant goddess (?), indented staff between them.

790. Thick squarish tablet. Height 24. NBC 8898. (a) Left side, (b) Right side, (c) Bottom, (d) Drawing. Hammurabi 1 (1792), 6th king of Babylon.

Trace of worshipper with kid, star disk in crescent, deity on altar-throne on niched platform, profile human head at back of suppliant goddess, disk in crescent above staff (?) above omega, device above fly, gap (?), personage with mace, three drillings above dotted circle over fish, gap (middle view of objects starting with personage is placed sideways below "a").

791. Envelope. Height c. 30, (first seal includes upper border of cross-hatched triangles). MLC 1220. Hammurabi 18 (1775).

First seal: bearded (?) personage in pointed hat with mace (?); inscription. Second and third seal: suppliant goddess in round hat with ribbon down back; inscription.

787

789

790a

790b

790c

790d

791

792a

792b

793a

793b

793c

794a

794c

794d

794e

794b

792. Oblong envelope (tablet not impressed). Height ext. 20. (a) Reverse, (b) Left side. YBC 7153. Hammurabi 28.

Full-face bullman reversing lion, blur, seated goat attacked by erect lion, hero on one knee struggling with animal. On the reverse a worshipper with kid, a seated deity with rod and ring, and other figures, all rather poor.

793. Oblong impressed tablet. Height 24½. (a) Reverse, (b) Left side, (c) Top. YBC 10486. Hammurabi 38.

Full-face hero with side curls (on poor reverse shown grasping tail of reversed lion and stepping on its head), inscription, erect ibex, its head turned back, attacked by lion, inscription between them, vessel above fly (?),

above ball staff, ground line (in "c" middle part of three figures shown sideways).

794. Oblong envelope and tablet. Height 23. (a) Envelope reverse, (b) Tablet reverse (both partial), (c) Left side tablet, (d) Top tablet, (e) Left side envelope. YBC 4348. Hammurabi 38.

Full-face bullman contending (?) with full-face nude hero, suppliant goddess, inscription, goddess, hands at waist, inscription over small griffin attacking man on one knee (?), full-face goddess with tresses on shoulders holding lionclub mounted on two lions back to back, reclining goat over inscription, bullman as at start. Similar but poorer figures on reverse of tablet and left side of envelope.

795. Small impressed envelope. Height 24. Part reverse. YBC 7758. Hammurabi 39.

Personage with mace facing full-face goddess extending lionclub with lying lion above it and full-face mask (faint) below; ground line.

Similar but poorer diverse figures on obverse and bottom end.

796. Two small impressed oblong tablets. Height 24½. (a) Left side (YBC 4435, Hammurabi 37), (b) Bottom end (YBC 5654, Hammurabi 40), (c) Drawing. *Yale Library Gazette* 45 (1970), p. 58, no. 9 (YBC 8023, adds nothing).

Full-face hero with bull's ears carrying scimitar, hero with bow on back strangling male figure (head like Humbaba mask) with hands tied behind back, cow and calf on line between them, on line above man on one knee holding reversed animal with both hands, small figure with hands at waist under whirling maces held by full-face goddess with ar-rows at shoulders, her right foot on lion, leaning on scimitar; ground line.

797. Oblong tablet, probably sealed all over. Height: A–ext. 18, B–ext. 21. (a-b) Bottom and part reverse (A) (*Yale Library Gazette* 45, [1970], p. 58, no. 8), (c) Top side (B), (d) Drawing (A), (e) Drawing (B). YBC 7150. Hammurabi 41.

A–Man on one knee, head turned back, right arm raised, attacked by winged liondragon; worshipper with kid, goatfish above, god holding stylus on altar-throne, his feet on niched platform, facing right, human head above, worshipper with hands at waist, small kilted male; ground line.

B–Lightning symbol, worshipper, spade, feathers and legs of bird (overlapped by lightning symbol and following).

The symbols here resemble those of 734, late Neo-Sumerian.

795

796b

796a

796c

797a

797b

797c

797d

797e

798a

798b

799a

799b

800a

800b

803a

801

802

803b

803c

798. Squarish envelope, all impressed. Height 25. (a) Left side, (b) Top. YBC 4474. Hammurabi 41.

Full-face bullman contending with nude hero, deity looking other way on either side; ground line.

799. Oblong envelope and tablet impressed. Height: A–18, with cap marks 21, B–22½. (a) Obverse (A), (b) Left side (B, both partial). Repeats and other impressions not shown. YBC 11151. Simmons, *JCS* 14 (1960), pp. 30f. Oath Ibalpiel 2, king of Eshnunna. Impression names predecessor Dadusha. Time of Hammurabi, 1st half 18th century B.C.

A–Inscription with vessel above ball staff in middle, worshipper (?), . . . elbow of personage with mace (?), star disk in crescent above four drillings, above small full-face goddess, suppliant goddess with ribbon down back.

B–Trace human figure, star disk in crescent above full-face nude female, personage with mace facing suppliant goddess, star above notched standard between them; ground line.

800. Small oblong tablet, perhaps not all impressed. Height 22. (a) Left side, (b) Bottom. YBC 11159. Simmons, *JCS* 13 (1959), pp. 75f. Ibalpiel 2, 10.

God with saw (?), his right foot on low stand, god holding lightning fork (?) before him, brandishing dagger above with hooked drilling beside it, before him, bowlegged dwarf; in frame: bowlegged dwarf looking right, holding curved sword, shouldering scimitar (?), below: reversed similar dwarf, figures separated and divided by cross; in next frame: wedge, scorpion (?), fish, mongoose (?).

801. Oblong tablet, cushion shaped, probably all impressed. Height 20 (with cap marks 25). Right side. YBC 7676. Rim-Sin II. Time Samsuiluna.

Goddess, left hand raised, leading worshipper (?); crescent with dot inside, three underneath, "mongoose" below, enthroned goddess on platform.

802. Oblong tablet, probably all impressed. Height 17 (with cap marks 20½). Part reverse. YBC 4234 (*YOS* 8, 54). Rim-Sin II. Time Samsuiluna.

Inscription before suppliant goddess with ribbon down back.

An indistinct tablet, 802x, YBC 4316 (*YOS* 8, 55), lower left reverse, dated Rim-Sin II, shows a weather god on a bull.

803. Oblong envelope (partly sealed, tablet not impressed). Height: A–ext. 15, B–ext. 13. (a-b) Obverse and left side (both partial, A), (c) Top edge, B. YBC 6972 (*YOS* 12, 44). Samsuiluna 2.

A–Suppliant goddess, full-face goddess, her right hand extended, full-face bullman holding kid, god with saw in ascending posture.

B–Priest with pail and sprinkler, suppliant goddess, full-face goddess extending lion-club, arrows at right shoulder, bow at left, bared right leg in ascending posture.

804. Oblong envelope and tablet. Height 23. (a-b) Bottom end tablet and envelope (A),(c) Left side envelope (B),(d) Drawing. YBC 6744 (*YOS* 12, 74). Samsuiluna 3.

A–Deity with right hand forward, right foot on human-headed bull (?), male head facing left above, personage standing on lion, lying lion above lionclub held by deity, right foot on lion, ground line.

B–Suppliant goddess before inscription; struggling animals on reverse of the envelope.

A fragment of a tablet, 804x, YBC 8679 (*YOS* 12, 108) presents on one side: a suppliant goddess, lying lion over vessel, rod and ring held by seated deity, ground line; Samsuiluna 4.

A small square tablet shows a worshipper with kid, inscription, lionclub on stepped stand, suppliant goddess, 804xx, YBC 7972 (*YOS* 12, 123), Samsuiluna 4.

805. Squarish tablet, probably all sealed. Height 26½. YBC 4424. (a) Reverse (part), (b) Right side, (c) Base, (d) Drawing. Hammurabi 3 or 12 or Samsuiluna 5 (probably latter).

Worshipper in high hat, long skirt, seated deity with crook, all on line; full-face bearded hero with arms at waist, belted, enthroned deity with feet on rocky platform; erect dragon and lion attacking man on one knee between them; below: worshipper, hand before face, full-face enthroned deity, all on line.

806. Oblong envelope (tablet not impressed). Height ext. 24 (personage), ext. 20 (suppliant goddess). (a) Obverse, (b) Right edge (both partial). YBC 6232 (*YOS* 12, 153). Samsuiluna 5.

Personage (with mace?) thrice repeated but probably not same, backs to inscriptions, third has crescent and two dots in first column of inscription, suppliant goddess (overlapping last personage) facing inscription.

The top edge of a tablet, 806x, YBC 4209 (*YOS* 12, 186), Samsuiluna 6, height 19½, shows the back of an erect winged dragon, a mounted lionclub, an erect lion attacking a goat on a mound, star above, line across below.

804a

804b

804c

804d

805a

805b

805c

805d

806a

806b

807a

807b

807c

807d

807e

807f

807g

807. Oblong impressed tablet. Height: A–ext. 19, B–ext. 15, C–ext. 16, D–ext. 14. (a) Obverse (right), (b) Obverse (left), (c) Right side, (d) Left side, (e) Drawing (A), (f) Drawing (B), (g) Drawing (C). On one end worn inscription and full-face goddess. YBC 4313 (*YOS* 12, 224). Samsuiluna 7. *Yale Library Gazette* 45 (1970), pp. 58–59, no. 10.

A–Lion crossed by bull on line attached to gate post; below: lion in grasp of hero on line; suppliant goddess; attendants holding structure over mounted tree with erect goat on either side, perhaps two crowned and bearded human headed bulls below; worshipper.

B–Full-face heroes, each with side curls and dagger, linked by arm and leg; above: star over fly, sidewise worshipper and dragon; under double line: four animals.

C–Female in skirt, male in kilt, seated deity (?), all on hatched double line; in reverse: two belted heroes stepping on prone victim, nude belted worshipper (?), all over hatched double line.

D–Same motif as A, inscription.

Two small squarish tablets, 807x, NBC 8556, height 24, and 807xx, NBC 8693, height 19, both Samsuiluna 7, of which the first shows a lionscimitar above seated mongoose (?), a god, all over line, inscription, bullman; the second an inscription, worshipper, crescent above fly (?), god (?), dog with crook seated on altar (?), ground line. An oblong tablet of similar date, 807xxx, YBC 12261, has partial views of inscription, deity holding stylus (?) on altar-throne with curved back facing god with saw, fox (?) above.

FIG. 807

808. Smallish rectangular tablet, probably one seal all over. Height c. 17. (a) Right reverse, (b) Drawing. YBC 6039. Samsuiluna 7.

Full-face female, hands at waist, pleated skirt; ball staff, personage in belt and tunic, small male, goddess (?) with outstretched right arm, left at waist, pleated skirt.

809. Envelope and tablet, oblong, probably impressed all over. Height 20½. (a) Left side envelope, (b) Top edge envelope. Other impressions including four not shown. YBC 4246 (*YOS* 12, 225). Samsuiluna 7.

Trace worshipper with kid, goatfish (?) above; god with saw, right foot on small stand, inscription, suppliant goddess, star disk in crescent above small worshipper on one knee, right hand before face; bull-eared god, full face, holding scimitar; goddess with hands at waist, trace original worshipper (?); ground line.

810. Oblong and small square tablets, both impressed. Height 21. (a) Reverse, left corner (YBC 5910 = *YOS* 12, 236), (b-d) Reverse, right and top edges (YBC 7966 = *YOS* 12, 213), (e) Drawing. Samsuiluna 7.

Worshipper with kid facing god with saw, foot on small stand, star disk in crescent between them; feline animal lying on line, its head turned back, above little man shooting (?) upwards, personage with mace facing goddess holding lionclub, reversed little man between them.

The impression, *Louvre A.*, 508, Rim-Sin 20, shows a little archer shooting at a lying goat above. A perverted version of the same subject may have been intended here. Compare *Ash C*, 492.

808a

808b

809a

809b

810a

810b

810c

810d

810e

811a

811b

812a

812b

812c

813a

813b

813c

811. Oblong tablet, poor traces of two other impressions. Height c. 16. (a) Right side (part), (b) Drawing. NBC 6799. Samsuiluna 8.

Two small men holding handled, two-legged vessel between them, divider; below: small man attacked by two-winged dragon; inscription; personage (?).

812. Thick oblong tablet. Height A–c. 20, B–c. 18. (a) Obverse (A-B top), (b-c) Left side and bottom(A). YBC 7160 (*YOS* 12, 285). Samsuiluna 8.

A–Worshipper with kid facing god with saw, foot on rocky mound, male head probably between saw and mound, dotted disk in circle above; vessel above fly above ball staff; personage with mace facing suppliant goddess with ribbon down back, between them lying animal above two dots, above squatting creature (?), lines under separate individuals.

B–Long robed figure extending cup, dotted circle above, worshipper with hand before face, crescent (?), god in ascending posture, cross design, priest with sprinkler and pail (?), male worshipper, hands at waist.

Particularly on the reverse there are one or two other impressions.

813. Oblong thick tablet, probably all impressed. Height A–18, B–21½. (a) Part left side (A),(b) Part left side (B),(c) Top edge (B). YBC 6083 (*YOS* 12, 300). Samsuiluna 8.

A–Nude female in rounded hat looking left with left hand raised, crescent above spade, worshipper with right hand before face.

B–Inscription before bull from which rein rises to lightning fork, presumably held by god, one of whose feet is visible on the bull, rear of latter probably before personage with mace, disk in crescent above small priest with sprinkler and pail, suppliant goddess, inscription repeated, trace of bull.

814. Oblong tablet, probably all impressed, two (?) not shown. Height 31. (a) Top, (b) Obverse. YBC 6174 (*YOS* 12, 289). Samsuiluna 8.

Inscription; first column: worshipper with left hand before face, on line; second: male head; third: man on one knee, hand raised in worship, on line; facing left, worshipper, right hand before face, on line.

Same inscription on YBC 6003 (*YOS* 12, 219), Samsuiluna 7.

815. Small tablet, probably sealed all over. Height c. 14. (a-b) Left and right end, (c) Drawing. YBC 5998. Samsuiluna 10.

Man walking, female (?); guilloche divider; man, man with head turned back while attacked by erect lion; inscription; female (?); guilloche divider; dragon attacking belted man.

816. Oblong tablet, probably two seals. Height 25. Left side shown. YBC 4214 (*YOS* 12, 323). Samsuiluna 10.

Foot of worshipper with kid (?), reclining sheep above inscription, above full-face bearded head with side curls, god with saw, his foot on stony hill, star disk in crescent above vertical guilloche, deity in long robe with hand extended; ground line. The god with saw in ascending posture coincides with the inscription, ᵈShamash.

816x, YBC 4303 (*YOS* 12, 317), Samsuiluna 10, shows a scorpion, a reclining ibex, and a small man on one knee, all behind a kilted man in pointed hat with hands at waist; oblong tablet, height c. 22, right side, spare linear style.

817. Long tablet with normal Old Babylonian design. Height 13. (a) Bottom edge, (b) Drawing. MLC 1581. Samsuiluna 14.

Seated figure, suppliant goddess (?) with two hands up; personage in kilt, worshipper with hand before face, both facing god, his right leg on incline; guilloche borders.

814a

814b

815a

815b

815c

816

817a

817b

819

820

821

826

828

830

832

The Old Babylonian style produced a number of relatively simple yet sometimes ornate designs, some quite early but many more probably of the first half of the 18th century B.C., especially from the time of Hammurabi. Conspicuous are two showing an enthroned god with a crescent standard, 818–19, both of them more stylish than an ordinary worshipper grasping a crescent staff, 820. Much less complicated is a worshipper beside an inscription, 821–24, the only complexity being repeated males on the other side of the inscription, 825. Suppliant goddesses face an inscription in 826–31; a personage has been added over the inscription in 832, while a worshipper replaces one of the goddesses in 833. The most common scene placed a personage before a suppliant goddess, 834–47, once with their positions reversed, 848. Unusual is a god with a lionclub confronting a goddess, 849; and even more so, worshippers on either side of a full-face head, 850.

FIGS. 818–832

818. Brown mottled pale agate. 19½×9½. *Newell* 264. Not shown. *Frankfort,* p. 178, n. 6, Old Babylonian.

Inscription; crescent standard held by seated god on ground line.

819. Light streaked brown agate. 29×15. Chipped. American Oriental Society (Marsh).

Inscription; design like 818, line under feet.

For the inscription see *CANES,* 573 (Kassite).

820. Pale brown alabaster. 15½(ext.)×9/7½ (irregular). Worn. NCBS 726.

Inscription; crescent staff in right hand of worshipper, ball staff (?) under it, crook above vessel.

821. Oblong envelope fragment. Height 25. Part reverse. NBC 8672.

Inscription; female worshipper on line.

822. Hematite. 28×12. *Newell* 268. Not shown.

Inscription; star disk in crescent above bush, worshipper on line.

823. Hematite. 26×14. *Newell* 235. Not shown.

Suppliant goddess on line; inscription.

824. Pale blue green agate, brown mottled. 22(ext.)×11. *Newell* 230. Not shown.

Lionscimitar, suppliant goddess; inscription.

825. Hematite. 19½×9. *Newell* 273. Not shown.

Small male with arms outstretched on line, repeated underneath; inscription; suppliant goddess on line.

826. Light brown agate, red mottled. 24×14. Chipped. NBC 9107.

Suppliant goddess on line, lionscimitar; inscription; lionclub, suppliant goddess on line.

827. Obsidian. 31×17/16½(concave). Chipped. *Newell* 262. Not shown.

Suppliant goddess; inscription; suppliant goddess.

828. Green jasper. 31×17/16(concave). Chipped. YBC 9664.

Suppliant goddess on line; inscription; suppliant goddess on line.

829. Speckled dark gray serpentine. 27×13. *Newell* 263. Not shown.

Subject as in 828.

830. Mottled pink and white agate. 29×14/13 (concave). Chipped. NBC 5998.

Subject as in 828.

831. Hematite. 27×14. *Newell* 260. Not shown.

Subject as in 828, but without ground line.

Subject like above, but badly chipped, hematite, 26½×13½/13(concave); 831x, NCBS 844.

832. "Steatite." 34×17/15(concave). NBC 2596.

Suppliant goddess, personage with mace over traces of inscription, crook, suppliant goddess.

The personage, more deeply cut, must have been added over the inscription.

833. Speckled dark gray serpentine. 29×14. *Newell* 265. Not shown.

Worshipper; inscription; suppliant goddess.

834. Hematite. 19½×10. YBC 9711.

Personage with mace facing suppliant goddess with ribbon down back, on line; inscription.

835. Brown jasper with quartz veins. 29×17. *Newell* 232. Not shown.

Scene like 834, but inscription almost lost.

836. Hematite. 30×17/15½(concave). Chipped. *Newell* 237. Not shown.

Scene like 834.

837. Hematite. 22½×10. NBC 11038.

Scene like 834, but without ground line; inscription almost lost.

838. Black jasper. 28×16/15 (concave). Chipped. NBC 6677.

Scene like 837.

A scene like above, but inscription lost, 838x, NBC 6014, green black jasper, 29×15.

839. Hematite. 27×14. *Newell* 239. Not shown.

Scene like 838, but goddess has ribbon down back.

840. Mottled dark green agate. 31×16/15 (concave). YBC 9712.

Scene like 839, but with ground line.

841. Pale brown marble. 18½×13. Worn. *Newell* 238. Not shown.

Scene like 840, but figures smaller.

Similar designs but half broken; 841x, YBC 12511, black serpentine, 27×14/13½ (concave); 841xx, NCBS 733, hematite, 20 (ext.)×14.

842. Hematite. 23×12/11(concave). YBC 9672.

Personage with mace facing suppliant goddess, notched lionclub between them, ground line.

843. Hematite. 25½×12½/12(concave). *Newell* 240. Not shown.

Personage with mace facing suppliant goddess, lionscimitar; inscription.

844. Blackish limestone. 28×14. *Newell* 242. Not shown.

Inscription; personage with mace facing suppliant goddess with ribbon down back, on line, goatfish between figures.

845. Dark green mottled serpentine. 28×24/13(concave). Worn. *Newell* 212. Not shown.

Personage facing suppliant goddess, crescent between them; two erect antelopes back to back, their heads adjacent.

846. Hematite. 27×13/12½(concave). Worn. *Newell* 247. Not shown.

Inscription; personage with mace facing suppliant goddess, between them encircled dot in crescent above nude female.

847. Hematite. 24×10. *Newell* 246. Not shown.

Personage facing suppliant goddess, between them crook over nude female, all on line.

848. Hematite. 17(ext.)×10. NCBS 746.

Suppliant goddess with ribbon down back facing personage with mace (to right), between them fox (?) above lightning fork (?); inscription.

849. Hematite. 25×13. NBC 6516.

God leaning on scimitar and extending lionclub, left leg on stand, inscription, suppliant goddess.

850. Hematite. 18×8½/7½(irregular). YBC 12632.

Facing worshippers with arms behind back, between them hatched cross in disk in crescent above full-face male head with curls; to side: hatched cross in disk above three-part twist.

834

837

838

840

842

848

849

850

851

853

854

855

858

860

COMPLEX, FORMAL STYLE

A relatively large group of Old Babylonian seals of approximately the first half of the 18th century represent a great variety in style, often quite complex, but tending to be rather formal though normally in the realistic idiom. Confronted principals show a worshipper and a god, the latter bearing a crook, 851; two worshippers, 852; a worshipper before a goddess, 853; a personage before a deity, 854–56, a woman, 857–59, a worshipper, 860, a deity, 861–63, a woman with a reversed worshipper, 864; finally a worshipper facing a deity, 865–66. Three leading characters include a goddess and a worshipper before a male figure, 867; a personage with two other figures, 868–71; a deity likewise, 872–75. A nude goddess appears with inscription, 876; with a worshipper and holy objects, 877–78; with a personage, 879;

between other figures, 880–81; with a personage and a goddess, 882–86; with a worshipper and a god, 887–88; same figures plus one reversed, 889; with a personage between two females, 890; with a worshipper facing a god holding lightning, 891. Without the nude goddess there appears a god with lightning accompanied by a worshipper, 892–93; and by a god grasping a mounted crescent, 894; a similar crescent between a personage and a female, 895; a worshipper facing a crook in grasp of a god, 896; a female (?) and a personage confronting a god, 897–98; finally a priest with holy vessels is accompanied by sacred figures, 899–900.

A group generally more complex is presented in 901, including a hero with a lightning fork over a captive and another shouldering a bow, while 902–03 more simply show worshippers and deities. Other subjects are presented by a god with lightning on the back of a bull, 904; a god holding lightning forks on a liondragon accompanied by other deities, 905; a hero choking a monster beside a demon lifting up a man, 906; a god in a casket, 907; a deity with crescents before a god in contrast with the smoother style presenting a bull reversed by a hero, 908; a hero mastering a captive beside a sacred scene with a priest in the center, 909. A personage before a suppliant goddess plus other figures, 910–19, may be combined with scenes showing a god with saw, 920–30, a goddess with weapons at shoulders, 931–36, or an attendant carrying a kid, 937–55. Enthroned deities also play an important part in 954, 956–59, as do various figures in 960–66.

851. Hematite. 16½×8. YBC 12797.

Female figure facing god in kilt holding crook with foot on lying goat, spade between them; man on one knee before bull with lightning fork on back, all on double line containing angled hatches; below: erect fish, scorpion.

852. Dark gray diorite. 19×8. Chipped. *Newell* 184. Not shown.

Bull with lightning fork on back, worshipper in hatched cap with right hand before face, crescent above "mongoose," female figure, spade.

853. Hematite. 20×9. Chipped. NBC 5981.

Lightning fork on back of lying bull, female figure (?) facing goddess extending vaselike object, between them crescent (?) above plant, crooks back to back connected by ladder on back of lying ibex.

854. Light and dark mottled green serpentine. 20½×8. Worn. NCBS 777.

Spade, personage in hatched cap facing goddess, between them crescent standard connected with A-shaped object, animal (?) beside lightning fork on back of bull.

855. Hematite. 19×9. NBC 3289.

Personage in pointed hat facing deity perhaps holding object in outstretched hand, between them crescent above fly; inscription.

856. Hematite. 23×11/10½(concave). Worn. *Newell* 651. Not shown.

Personage with mace facing god (?) with saw (?) in outstretched hand, between them scorpion beside sidewise fish above phallic bowlegged dwarf beside seated "mongoose," crescent standard above lionscimitar standard.

857. Hematite. 17×9. Broken. *Newell* 229. Not shown.

Personage facing female figure, between them eagle (?) above vertical fish; inscription (upside down).

858. Limonite. 24×10. NBC 2595.

Personage with mace facing female figure, both in hatched caps; inscription (first frame worn).

859. Dark gray diorite. 21×10. *Newell* 228. Not shown.

Subject like 858, but with ground line.

860. Hematite. 31×14/13(concave). YBC 9985.

Personage with mace facing worshipper with hand before face, between them small priest (reversed) with pail and sprinkler over crook on back of lying ibex, ground line; small man (reversed) dancing over similar figure; inscription.

861. Hematite. 20×12. Chipped. NCBS 735.

Personage with mace facing suppliant goddess with ribbon down back, between them big dot above lionclub with dot at base, ground line, worn inscription, big dot in crescent above, (reversed) phallic bowlegged dwarf.

862. Hematite. 23×11. New impression. *Newell* 234.

Personage with mace in vertically marked high hat facing suppliant goddess with circular knob on crown, small male between them; inscription.

863. Hematite. 24×9. Worn. YBC 9993.

Vase with side arms, personage, bearded god with extended right arm, right leg on stand.

864. Hematite. 18×8/7½(concave). NBC 11039.

Personage facing female figure on line, (reversed) worshipper with hand before face and lionscimitar.

865. Hematite. 20×9½. Chipped. NCBS 771.

Spade, crescent standard above lightning symbol, male figure in kilt, seated "mongoose," reversed bowlegged dwarf, crook beside fly.

866. Brown limestone. 23×11. NCBS 797.

Lionclub on notched pole, man, seated "mongoose," reversed figure with hand before face (?), god with exposed right leg.

867. Hematite. 13×8. *Newell* 163. Not shown.

Suppliant goddess, vessel (?) above ball staff, worshipper with hands in middle, crescent above seated "mongoose," male figure in belt and hatched cap, staff with flat top held by erect griffin, ground line.

868. Hematite. 12½×6½. Worn. YBC 9992.

Personage facing two female figures in hatched caps.

869. Hematite. 16×8. NBC 5982.

Personage with mace, mounted crescent above ball staff above male bust in hatched cap, worshipper with right hand before face, fly above animal-like standard, female figure in pointed hat, ground line.

870. Hematite. 19×8½. Worn. NCBS 759.

Male figure in kilt, personage, deity; inscription.

871. Hematite. 21×10. Worn. *Newell* 219. Not shown.

Male figure in kilt, vessel above ball staff, personage, seated "mongoose," female figure, ground line.

872. Hematite. 18×9. YBC 12635.

Worshipper in hatched cap, with hand before face, "mongoose" (?) above lionscimitar, man in kilt, goddess, rays in back of lying bull above rays beside phallic bowlegged dwarf.

861

862

863

864

865

866

868

869

870

872

874

876

877

878

879

880

881

885

884

873. Hematite. 20×10½. Bore 6/4. *Newell* 190. Not shown.

Worshipper with hands in middle, spade, worshipper with hand before face, star disk in crescent above ball staff, god holding disk (?), ground line, goat fish above phallic bowlegged dwarf on line; inscription.

874. Limonite (fragment). 21×11. NCBS 775.

Front half of bull, crook held by male figure in tunic, worshipper in hatched cap with right hand before face, decorated crescent standard, god with right leg on stand, ground line.

875. Black limestone. 23×11. *Newell* 188. Not shown.

Worshipper with right hand before face, female (?) figure, both wear hatched caps, deity with leg raised in front, ground line.

876. Rock crystal. 24×11. Worn. NBC 10992.

Full-face nude female on pedestal; inscription.

877. Pale brown limestone. 17×8½. Chipped. NCBS 717.

Nude female with head right, star above crook, lightning standard, ball staff, lionclub, lionscimitar, crescent, female figure, vessel, ground line.

878. Hematite. 15½×8½. Chipped. NCBS 769.

Female figure in hatched cap, star, crook on back of lying ibex, vessel above ball staff, "mongoose" above phallic bowlegged dwarf, nude female with head right, circle in crescent over spade.

879. Hematite. 22×11. YBC 9987.

Personage, full-face nude female, fish, crook, fish above fly, vessel above ball staff, lionclub on notched pole, porcupine (?) above phallic bowlegged dwarf in hatched cap, scorpion above "mongoose."

880. Hematite. 18×13½. Worn. NBC 11036.

Belted man in tunic, nude female, star above crook, goddess; all heads hatched.

881. Hematite. 18×10. Pin in bore. YBC 9719.

Suppliant goddess, nude female, bearded full-face god with sidecurls and flowing vase at waist, ground line; inscription.

882. Rock crystal. 19×10. Chipped. *Newell* 244. Not shown.

Nude female on pedestal, personage with mace facing suppliant goddess on line.

Very similar 882x, *Newell* 243, amethyst, 22×12, figures to left not on line.

883. Hematite. 19×9. *Newell* 248. Not shown.

Lionscimitar, nude female, vessel above ball staff, personage, goddess in hatched cap.

883x, *Newell* 251, blackish limestone, 25×12, worn, principals as in 883, vessel over ball staff, crescent over "mongoose."

884. Limonite. 25×11. YBC 9680.

Principals as in 883, lightning standard above lionscimitar, crescent above scorpion, ground line.

885. Hematite. 17×9. YBC 12813.

Principals as in 884, vessel above ball staff, crescent above "mongoose"; inscription.

FIGS. 873–885

886. Hematite. 18×7. *Newell* 256. Not shown.

Principals as in 885, bowlegged dwarf above crook on back of lying ibex, scorpion above cross, crescent standard on tripod (middle held by the goddess).

887. Hematite. 19½×10. NCBS 782.

Nude goddess, worshipper in hatched cap extending vessel, star, god with right leg exposed, scimitar (?) in left hand.

888. Hematite 17½×7. *Newell* 257. Not shown.

Nude goddess, worshipper with right hand before face, god, ground line.

889. Hematite. 19×10. Worn. *Newell* 259. Not shown.

Nude goddess, personage with mace (?), crescent, god, (reversed) figure, frame of inscription behind last two figures.

890. Hematite. 20×12. NBC 5933.

Erect liongriffin, female figure, personage, vessel above ball staff, goddess, nude female.

891. Blackish limestone. 20×10. Worn. *Newell* 255. Not shown.

Nude female, vessel above ball staff, female (?) figure, crook, lightning symbol held by god in tunic.

892. Limonite. 23×12/11 (concave). YBC 12818.

Male figure in kilt and hatched cap holding lightning symbol, spade, worshipper with left hand before face; inscription.

893. Grainy gray black hematite. 25×10½/10 (concave). Worn. YBC 9688.

Kilted god in peaked hat holding lightning symbol, "mongoose" (?), worshipper with left hand before face, ground line; inscription.

894. Hematite. 25×10½. NCBS 828.

Male figure in kilt over worn inscription (?), goddess holding lightning symbol, left arm raised, fly over phallic bowlegged dwarf, decorated crescent mounted on tripod held by god in kilt with left arm raised (overlap with first figure).

895. Hematite. 20×8. YBC 12820.

Spade over crook, personage, decorated crescent standard, female figure with hands at waist.

896. Gray brown agate. 27½×13½. Worn. NBC 11035.

Star on standard, worshipper with right hand before face, crook held by god over back of lying ibex (?), before the god ovoid (?) above twisted object; inscription.

897. Hematite. 16½×8. Worn. NCBS 770.

Female (?) figure, personage, deity holding rod and ring, right leg on stand.

887

890

892

893

894

895

896

897

899

900

901

902

903

905

906

907

908

910

898. Dark green serpentine, brown mottled. 24×12. *Newell* 207. Not shown. Kupper, *Amurru,* p. 20, no. 2a (= fig. 29).

Female (?) figure, porcupine above seated "mongoose," personage with mace, crook held by god with right leg on stand; inscription.

899. Hematite. 21×10/9(concave). NBC 9118.

Priest with sprinkler and pail, worshipper with right hand before face, star, god with right leg on pedestal; inscription.

900. Hematite. 14(ext.)×9. Worn. YBC 12824.

Priest with sprinkler and pail, fly, personage, figure (?); inscription.

901. Hematite. 16×8. YBC 12800.

Personage holding club at rear facing god with right leg forward, holding club at rear, hero wielding weapon in right hand while holding lightning fork over head of captive on one knee on which the hero stands, reversed bird above crook, hero with bow on left shoulder, ground line.

For the subject compare *Louvre A.,* 477, Sumulael 2nd king of Babylon; see also *CANES,* 382. A reversed bird appears in *Berlin,* 415, which is also early Babylonian. Perhaps a similar bird, more schematically rendered, is shown in Neo-Sumerian 585 above.

902. Hematite. 23×12. Worn. YBC 12812.

Two worshippers, hands before faces, deity holding mace, his right leg on two-horned animal, crook held by god in tunic and vertically striated hat.

903. Light brown limestone, mottled cream and red. 23×12. Worn. NBC 5960.

Male and female figures, worshipper with right hand before face, crescent, deity.

904. Dark gray diorite. 27×14/13(concave). Chipped. *Newell* 249. Not shown.

God holding rein with lightning fork from back of bull, personage facing suppliant goddess, ground line; inscription.

905. Hematite. 21×12. New impression. *Newell* 220.

Goddess in vertically striated hat, god holding two lightning forks on back of liondragon spitting blood, lionclub extended by goddess with arrows at shoulders, holding scimitar to left, right foot on striated cushion, star disk in crescent, god holding ring before him, right leg on high striated cushion, ground line.

906. Hematite. 21×11. New impression. *Newell* 157.

Hero throttling bent over monster deity, hands tied behind back, goatfish above, liondemon reversing naked man, god leaning on scimitar, right leg exposed, ground line.

907. Hematite. 19×10. New impression. *Newell* 213.

Worshipper with right hand before face, fly above "mongoose," full-face bearded god in upper half of casket-shaped object, god holding sword, right leg on striated stool, goddess extending dagger, arrows on shoulders, scimitar to left, right foot on animal (?), ground line.

908. Limonite. 23×13. New impression. *Newell* 252.

Deity with crescent crown holding decorated crescent standard, god with right foot on lined stand, worshipper with right hand before face, dot in circle of dots in crescent above nude goddess facing left, bull reversed, one hind leg, its tail and head grasped and stepped on by hero in tunic.

909. Hematite. 22×13. *Newell* 155. Not shown.

Hero in tunic wielding scimitar above, grasping and stepping on captive on one knee, lying ibex on line above, suppliant goddess with ribbon down back, priest with pail and sprinkler on niched pedestal, god with right leg forward.

910. Limonite. 23×11/10(concave). YBC 12766.

Full-face belted nude phallic hero with side curls, personage with mace facing suppliant goddess with ribbon down back; inscription.

911. Hematite. 26×13. Chipped. NBC 2597.

Man in kilt, crook above ball staff, personage with mace, vessel, suppliant goddess with ribbon down back; inscription.

912. Hematite. 18½×11. NBC 3294.

Personage with mace, vessel above ball staff, suppliant goddess with ribbon down back, sidewise lion above sidewise fox (?), god, sidewise goatfish, full-face bullman wrestling with full-face nude hero, porcupine above demonfish between them, ground line.

913. Carnelian. 21×11. Worn. *Newell* 241. Not shown.

Suppliant goddess on either side of personage with mace, ground line; worn inscription.

914. Hematite. 24×11½/10½(concave). *Newell* 254. Not shown.

Principal figures as in 913, but goddesses have ribbons down back, cross disk in crescent, nude female (later addition), ground line.

915. Hematite. 19×7½. Worn. *Newell* 203. Not shown.

Worshipper with right hand before face, cross disk, personage with mace, crescent, suppliant goddess; above: (reversed) figures with hand before face back to back; below: same figures, all four separated by linear cross, ground line.

916. Hematite. 22×10. NBC 5941.

Suppliant goddess with ribbon down back, personage with mace, deity, lionclub on hatched standard.

917. Limonite. 16×7. *Newell* 245. Not shown.

Suppliant goddess, personage with mace, deity, ground line.

918. Lapis lazuli. 18½×9. Chipped. *Newell* 191. Not shown.

Suppliant goddess, worshipper with hand before face, personage with mace; inscription.

919. Hematite. 29×15½. Chipped. New impression. *Newell* 266.

Inscription approached by god, spread eagle (?) above "mongoose" on tail, personage with mace, porcupine, cross disk in crescent above goatfish above small male holding tall vase in right hand looking left like smaller male on one knee on niched pedestal, suppliant goddess.

920. Hematite. 30×15/14(concave). *Newell* 217. Not shown.

Worshipper with right hand before face, star disk on crescent handle over two fish, god holding saw, right leg on cross-hatched pedestal, fly above lionclub above ball staff;

personage with mace, vessel beside three dots above full-face nude hero above ratlike creature, suppliant goddess with ribbon down back, ground line under personage and suppliant goddess, scorpion over goatfish above lizard beside lying animal beside erect goat above phallic bowlegged dwarf.

The first group of figures has exaggerated drill work and is either a later addition or a fake.

921. Hematite. 19×9. *Newell* 221. Not shown.

Male in tunic shouldering bent dagger over worn inscription, suppliant goddess with ribbon down back, personage with mace, star disk in crescent over bowlegged dwarf, god holding saw, his right leg forward.

922. Hematite. 21×10. Worn. NCBS 756.

Suppliant goddess, big dot over lionscimitar, worshipper with hand before face, crescent, god holding saw, right leg on stand, big dot above reversed bowlegged dwarf, sword held by male in tunic on ground line.

923. Coarse dark gray diorite. 31×16. Worn. *Newell* 224. Not shown.

Suppliant goddess, rosette formed of triangular wedges above vase above goat, personage with mace, vase beside seated dog on line above ovoid shape; god holding saw, right leg on stand, vase above ball staff above vase; inscription.

924. Rock crystal. 22×11. Chipped. NBC 9255.

Suppliant goddess, worshipper with right hand before face, god with saw, right foot on stand, "mongoose" above phallic bowlegged dwarf, crook, ground line.

925. Pale pink mottled agate. 21×6½/8(convex). Chipped. *Newell* 189. Not shown.

Female figure, crescent above crook, worshipper with right hand before face, god holding curved sword, right foot on stand.

Principals as in 925 but sword is held out straight, 925x, NCBS 722, hematite, 17×8½/8(irregular).

926. Hematite. 24×13½/13(concave). NCBS 837.

Suppliant goddess with ribbon down back, worshipper with right hand before face, cross disk in crescent, god with saw, right leg on cushion, erect lion attacking ibex with head turned back, ground line.

927. Hematite. 25×16. Worn. *Newell* 192. Not shown.

Principals as in 926, "mongoose," man in tunic facing female figure, below reversed, two phallic bowlegged dwarfs, to side vessel above fish, above ball staff.

911

912

916

919

922

924

926

928

930

931

935

936

928. Hematite. 21½×11½/11(concave). Broken. NCBS 811.

Suppliant goddess, vessel (?) over ball staff, worshipper with hand before face, crescent, god with saw, right leg exposed, crook, phallic bowlegged dwarf over bull.

929. Hematite. 23×12. *Newell* 182. Not shown.

Principals as in 928, vessel over ball staff, cross disk in crescent, (added later) seated god in top hat, ground line.

930. Limonite. 27×15. Chipped. NBC 5932.

Suppliant goddess, male figure holding object in right hand before him, long robe with left leg exposed, disk in crescent, god holding saw, right leg on vertically striated pedestal.

931. Hematite. 28×13. New impression. *Newell* 215.

Suppliant goddess with ribbon down back, personage with mace, crescent over "mongoose," full-face goddess with arrows and long curls at shoulders, lionclub in right hand, scimitar in left, exposed right leg on lying lion; above: nude hero wrestling with bullman, both full face on line; below: lion at back of ibex with head turned back, ground line.

932. Limonite. 24×12/11(concave). *Newell* 214. Not shown.

Suppliant goddess, personage with mace, star, full-face goddess with arrows at shoulders, scimitar in left hand, right leg on sloping platform, ground line; above: nude man facing inscription; below: same figure reversed.

933. Hematite. 29×17/15(cut back in area of the three faked male heads). Chipped. *Newell* 216. Not shown.

Hero and bullman wrestling, sidewise sphinx between them, fish, personage with mace, male portrait head, lionclub held by full-face goddess with arrows at shoulders, scimitar in left hand, right foot on animal.

934. Hematite. 31×17/16(concave). *Newell* 218. Not shown.

Suppliant goddess with hair down back facing god with saw, right foot on cross-lined pedestal, personage with mace, lionclub held by full-face goddess with tress down shoulders and arrows over them, leaning on scimitar to left, right leg on back of lying lion, ground line; inscription.

935. Reddish brown limestone. 30×17/15½ (concave). Corroded. NBC 2583. *BIN* 2, pl. LXXIVf.

Suppliant goddess, personage, and goddess on lion as in 934, except latter holds three-part animal-headed object and has extended belt; nude female; ground line.

936. Hematite. 25×13½. YBC 13075.

Full-face bearded hero holding vessel at waist, cross disk in crescent above (added) cross, scimitar held by god with right leg on cross-hatched pedestal, personage with mace on rocky pedestal, goddess on lion as in 934, priest with sprinkler and pail on two-tiered pedestal.

FIGS. 928–936

937. Hematite. 22½×12. New impression. *Newell* 225.

FIGS. 937–947

Full-face nude belted hero with hatched hair, side curls and beard, hands at waist, god wielding scimitar, holding lightning fork and rein to lying bull on which his exposed right foot is placed, full-face bullman carrying kid, god extending ring, right foot on cross-hatched pedestal, full-face bearded monster with big ears and bird feet, fly, lionclub held by full-face goddess with curl on each shoulder and arrows to left, leaning on scimitar, right foot on lion.

938. Hematite. 26×14/13(concave). *Newell* 205. Not shown.

Personage with mace on three-tiered pedestal, suppliant goddess, worshipper with kid, cross disk in crescent, goddess as in 937 with arrows on both shoulders, god with saw, right foot on cross-hatched pedestal, ground line.

939. Hematite. 26×10½. Broken. *Newell* 194. Not shown.

Suppliant goddess with ribbon down back, "mongoose" (?), worshipper with kid, cross disk in crescent above kneeling animal, god extending clenched hand, porcupine (?) above spade, beside lightning fork over sidewise fly, beside ibex (?) horn, ground line.

940. Rock crystal. 19×11. Worn. *Newell* 198. Not shown.

Worshipper with kid, crescent, god with saw, right foot forward; inscription.

941. Hematite. 25×14½. NBC 2584.

Suppliant goddess as in 939, worshipper with kid, god with saw, right foot on rocky pedestal, ground line.

942. Hematite. 25×11. *Newell* 206. Not shown.

Principals as in 941, the god's foot on cross-hatched pedestal, phallic bowlegged dwarf, cross disk in crescent; inscription; ground line.

943. Hematite. 27½×14/12(oval ends). NBC 7923.

Principals as in 941, the god's foot on pedestal, (reversed) phallic bowlegged dwarf above nude male, disk, ground line; inscription.

944. Hematite. 22×12. Chipped. NBC 7681.

Principals as in 943; winged goat (?) above phallic dwarf beside four drillings; three drillings above reversed phallic bowlegged dwarf, star, reversed nude female.

945. Hematite. 25×15. NBC 7920.

Principals as in 943 with the god's foot on striated pedestal; priest in tunic with sprinkler and pail on two-niched platform, warrior leaning on scimitar to left, right leg exposed, ground line.

946. Limonite. 22×15/14(concave). Chipped. YBC 9678.

Priest with eye shield in tunic with sprinkler and pail (?), vessel over ball staff, worshipper with kid; cross disk above three crude drillings, god with saw, right foot on cross-hatched pedestal, porcupine above "mongoose," nude female, liondragon grasping spade, ground line.

947. Hematite. 22×10½. NBC 3292.

Personage with mace on platform, male profile head, worshipper with kid, cross disk in crescent, god with saw, right foot on pedestal, ground line.

330

937

941

943

944

945

946

947

950

951

952a

952b

953

952c

954

948. Rock crystal. 21(ext.)×16. *Newell* 250. Not shown.

Personage (?) in tunic, cross (?) beside ball staff, worshipper with kid, "mongoose," god with saw, right foot on pedestal, nude female, angular design (?) above small worshipper with hand before face, lionclub, ground line.

949. Hematite. 20×10. Worn. *Newell* 196. Not shown.

Worshipper with kid, front of clothes crooked, crescent, god with saw, foot on hatched pedestal, fly above lightning fork, male figure with arms at sides.

950. Hematite. 29×15. Worn. NBC 7921.

Suppliant goddess, three dots, personage with mace, crook, worshipper with kid, lightning fork (?) over lying goat on line, crescent (?) standard held by goddess; schematic animals (Mitannian addition).

951. Hematite. 26×15/14(concave). Chipped. NBC 8927.

Suppliant goddess, phallic dwarf (?) (head lost) above small nude female, worshipper with kid, lion over lionclub held by goddess, who also grasps ring with chain attached, going over small lying bull, to lion on which the goddess steps, latter full face with arrows at shoulders and scimitar to left, porcupine (?), full-face hero wrestling with full-face bullman, small seated antelope between them.

Very worn, 951x, YBC 9709, hematite, 21×10, shows a suppliant goddess, worshipper, full-face goddess with lionclub and scimitar, priest with sprinkler and pail.

952. Three-sided roughly pyramidal tags, only writing on one face, hole in top. Height ext. 18. a = MLC 959, b = MLC 967, c = MLC 945. See also MLC 941, 946–47, 949–53, 956, 958, 961, 963, 965–66, 968–71. All may have same continuous design and additional writing.

(a) Goddess, arm and feet to left, inscription (first line), worshipper with kid before (?) god, (b) in ascending posture, full-face goddess, right hand raised, (c) inscription (third line), full-face goddess, hands at waist, inscription (second line), ground line (see under "a").

953. Hematite. 25½×13½/13(concave). NCBS 705. *Yale Library Gazette* 43 (1968), pl. II 5, p. 94–95.

Suppliant goddess, cross disk in crescent, worshipper with kid, lying lion above lying goat with head turned back, lionclub held by full-face goddess with curls at shoulders who stands on two lions, full-face male head, full-face goddess, full-face hero grasping leg and tail and stepping on bull's head.

954. Hematite. 27×14/13(concave). Worn. NBC 3218.

Male portrait, personage, cross disk in crescent over inscription, suppliant goddess, inscription, worshipper with kid, lying ball over long ibex head, enthroned god holding stylus on niched platform, full-face male portrait with twists at cheeks above inscription, god with hands in middle.

FIGS. 948–954

955. Rectangular tag, same impression (a-b) on both faces. Height ext. 20. YBC 13216.

Suppliant goddess, full-face bearded head with horned crown above small full-face (?) nude hero with hands at waist, worshipper in tall pointed hat, perhaps carrying kid, gap (?), full-face bearded head, personage in kilt and high rounded hat holding (?) scimitar behind him, left hand at waist, star disk in crescent above small figure (?) with hands at waist, repeat of suppliant goddess.

956. Hematite. 25×13. New impression. *Newell* 180.

Personage with mace, inscription, suppliant goddess with ribbon down back, animal above vessel, above ball staff, worshipper holding vessel before him pouring libation on palm in vessel, cow and calf, enthroned god with feet on lying bull, it and the throne on rocky pedestal, god, sidewise antelope with head turned back, ground line.

957. Roughly rounded oblong tag covered with impressions. Height 18½. YBC 12984. Tags with same impressions: MLC 962, 1173, 1182, 1187, 1189.

Suppliant goddess, vessel above ball staff, worshipper with arms at waist, crescent above "mongoose," enthroned goddess, feet on low stand, male head facing left above lion on line above male head facing right, back of head dotted, suppliant goddess repeated, ground line.

958. Tag roughly like 957. Height c. 20. YBC 13108. Tags with same impression: YBC 13103–07.

Personage with mace (part), star disk in crescent, suppliant goddess, seated dog with crook on head above bowlegged dwarf, enthroned goddess holding rod.

959. Squarish tablet, perhaps all impressed. Height c. 21. Reverse (part). YBC 8615.

Inscription, suppliant goddess with ribbon down back, inscription, worshipper with kid, enthroned deity with feet on human-headed bull, ground line.

960. Rounded triangular tag. Height A–21, B–c. 18½. Reverse (part). YBC 13110.

A–Worshipper, crescent above "mongoose," god with stylus, right foot on stand; inscription; ground line.

B–Personage with mace on stand (on obverse), suppliant goddess with ribbon down back, worshipper with kid, full-face goddess holding lionclub, arrows at shoulders, right foot on lion, ground line (both on obverse).

955a

955b

956

957

958

959

960

961a

961b

961c

962a

963a

964

962b

963b

965a

965b

966a

966b

965c

961. Oblong tablet, perhaps all impressed. (a) Bottom edge, A, height ext. 18, (b-c) Obverse and left side (both partial), B, height ext. 23. MLC 1307.

A–Between two suppliant goddesses with ribbons down back, cow and calf on line above small full-face hero with hands at waist holding cup (?) from which streams flow to either side.

B–Worshipper with kid, full-face goddess holding lionclub and leaning on scimitar, arrows at shoulders, right leg exposed, small male head to left above small priest with sprinkler and pail (?), suppliant goddess; inscription.

962. Small square tablet shaped tag with two different seals. Height: A–18 (a), B–22 (b). YBC 8114.

A–Worshipper with kid, star disk in crescent (?), god with saw, right foot on small stand, inscription, suppliant goddess with ribbon down back, ground line.

B–Deity (part), inscription above lying lion, suppliant goddess with ribbon down back, ground line.

963. Tags with impressions of same seal on both sides. Height 22. (a) YBC 3017, (b) YBC 3008. Also on YBC 3007, 3011–13, 3016, 3019.

Erect liondragon attacking goat with head turned back, seated on mound, staff (?) above vessel above ball staff, worshipper with arms at waist, lionscimitar standard, full-face bullman with kid, porcupine (?) above "mongoose," god.

964. Triangular tag impressed on faces, sides and top. Height c. 24. Goucher 835. Also on Goucher 830–33, 836–37, 840, 842, 872–73, 894.

Repeated parts of worshipper with kid and god with saw.

965. Oblong tablet, all impressed. Height ext. 20. (a) Reverse, (b) Left edge (both partial), (c) Drawing. NBC 8535.

Worshipper with hands in middle, goatfish above vessel above ball staff above small god with crook probably on one knee, personage with mace, animal on line above reversed lion (?) held aloft by male figure, suppliant goddess.

966. Small thick square tablet, one side not impressed. Height 22. (a) Top edge, (b) Bottom edge. NBC 9266.

Worshipper with right hand before face, crescent above indeterminate object, lionclub held by goddess, vessel above ball staff, personage with mace, star disk in crescent above "mongoose" (?), suppliant goddess (?).

An oblong tag, 966x, NBC 8013, height c. 21, reverse and top, shows a suppliant goddess, a worshipper and a god with saw.

An oblong tablet, 966xx, YBC 12248, height c. 18, reverse, presents in the secondary two facing figures.

FIGS. 967–970

The scenes featuring animals, bullmen, and heroes first show conventional patterns, 967–68, then less conventional ones, 969, finally in a quite free style, 970–75. A number present standard groupings, 976–78; some animals only, 979–82.

967. Pale yellow calcite. 21½×13½. Broken. New impression. *Newell* 84.

Full-face human-headed bull with head turned back, held by full-face bullman, vessel between them, ball staff under similar figures in opposite direction, lionclub under the human-headed bulls.

968. Hematite. 21×14. New impression. *Newell* 166.

Scene in middle: crossed lions, two dots between them, the lion's head and tail held on each side by nude belted hero; two human-headed bulls with full-face heads turned back, lionclub under the heads, dots above and below the bull's bodies, two dots over neck of bull to left.

969. Hematite. 23×15/14 (concave). YBC 12748.

Full-face nude belted hero wrestling with lioness, "mongoose" between them, tortoise, lion grappling with bullman, seated dog between them, ibex with head turned back attacked by liondragon, ground line.

970. Oblong envelope, tablet not impressed. Height 17½. YBC 6836 (= *YOS* 2, 147, pl. LVII, both sides shown).

Crescent above fish, goat with head turned back attacked by lion, vessel above ball staff, man on one knee with head turned back menaced by liondragon, ground line.

967

968

969

970

971a

971b

972

973

974

976

977

971. Triangular tag, all sides impressed, no writing. Height ext. 22. (a) Face, (b) Side. MLC no number.

Trace of rampant lion attacking man on one knee, right hand down, left up over big drilling, hero grasping tail and stepping on reversed lion which hero to right also holds, latter menaced by erect lion, ground line.

972. Hematite. 24×15. NBC 6517.

Naked hero, back of head curly, grasping outer leg and tail, while left leg steps between horns of reversed bull being bitten by erect lion, three dots, similar hero holding neck and pressing left leg against back of erect lion that attacks ibex with head turned back seated on layered mound, seated "mongoose" on hatched rectangle above three dots, ground line.

An oblong tablet shows twice on one long side a hero upending a bull beside a full-face goddess (?), 972x, YBC 7700, height 24.

Fragments of an envelope, the tablet not impressed, show an erect lion reversing a small male beside a god with lionscimitar over right shoulder, 972xx, NBC 8236, height c. 20.

973. Hematite. 19×8½. NCBS 766. Unfinished, perhaps fake.

Full-face bullman (?) struggling with hero (?); man on one knee in mid-air, head turned back, attacked by liondragon, seated antelope with head turned back attacked by lion.

974. Hematite. 19×10. YBC 9681.

Liondragon attacking man on one knee with head turned back, lion attacking seated goat with head turned back.

975. Black serpentine. 17×10. *Newell* 161. Not shown.

Crescent over seated "mongoose" (?), man on one knee attacked on either side by liondragon and lion.

Corroded lion and liondragon, both erect, with human figures, 975x, NCBS 732, pale brown limestone, 18½×12.

976. Hematite. 22×11/10(concave). NBC 5980.

Small nude man over phallic bowlegged dwarf, full-face nude belted hero grasping leg and tail while stepping on reversed bull, nude belted hero with animal skin on shoulder (?) wrestling with bullman, both full face, between them porcupine above seated goat with head turned back.

Worn heroes or bullmen separate animal forms, symbols in frames at end, 976x, NCBS 795, hematite, 21½×12.

977. Brownish "steatite." 23½×12/11½(concave). Worn. NCBS 808.

Erect winged liondragon attacking goat with head turned back (?), protected by hero; reversed lion (?) with one hind leg grasped and head stepped on by hero.

978. Oblong tablet. Height c. 16. (a) Reverse (part), (b) Drawing. MLC 1682. Script perhaps Middle Babylonian.

Erect lion attacking goat with head turned back, which is held by full-face nude belted hero, before him twisted bird (?), behind him lion, both small, vessel above ball staff.

An Old Babylonian impression shows two lions attacking a seated goat, while a man on one knee is molested by a liondragon on the reverse of an oblong tablet, height c. 12, 978x, NBC 6187, Nabonidus 16, 540 B.C.

979. Hematite. 18×8. NBC 9113.

Lionscimitar standard, two winged liondragons attacking goat with head turned back.

980. Hematite. 24×13. NBC 3293.

Erect antelope with head turned back attacked by lion, scene repeated, inscription above lioness, ground line.

981. Hematite. 16½×8½. NCBS 750.

Erect lion attacking kneeling bull with head turned back, vessel between them, crescent above ball staff, repeat of bull with forelegs raised, ground line.

982. Bituminous shale. 21×12. Chipped. NCBS 787.

Ovoid above ball staff, winged liondragon attacking seated goat, vessel between them, molested by seated, winged liondragon.

978b

978a

979

980

981

982

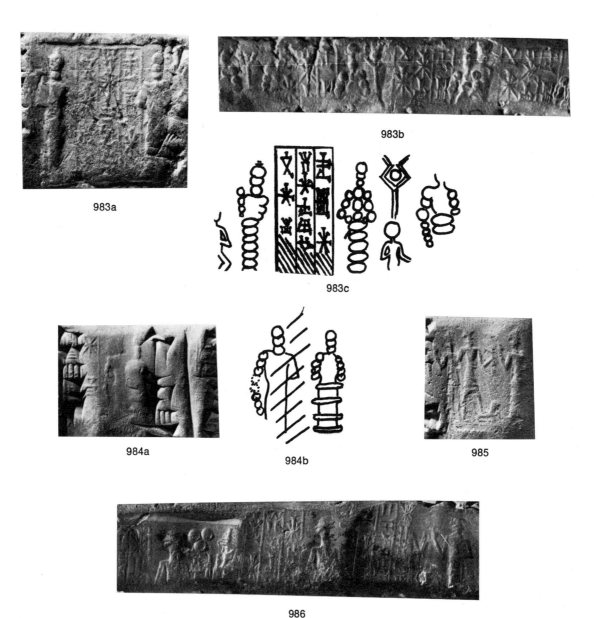

983a

983b

983c

984a

984b

985

986

Late Old Babylonian

TRANSITION TO SCHEMATIC
REPRESENTATION

Shortly before the 20th year of Samsuiluna
a drastic change in the manner of representation began to appear, the modified
naturalism of the older period was replaced, slowly at first, then more dras-
tically, by a definitely schematic style
featuring drilled circles in a kind of curvilinear mannerism. The closest compari-
son in modern times would perhaps be the
shift from naturalism to cubism.

344

The first sign of the early shift in style occurs in the dotted patterns of 983–84, but these are not really comparable with the thin figures of 985, nor even with the large dotted designs of 986–87. A hero is perhaps supported by another in 988, a worshipper with kid faces a god amidst large dots in 989, men occur with simple twisted shapes in 990, while more conventional figures appear in 991.

Abi-ešuḫ, dated c. 1700 B.C., presents in roughly chronological order: two groups of various figures, 992; a deity plus attendants with dots, 993–94; a servant with kid and a god, 995; large circles, one of which serves as the common head of reversed dwarfs, 996. The last three Old Babylonian rulers, Ammiditana, Ammiṣaduqa, Samsuditana, persisted through the 17th century B.C., increasingly stressing simplified linear engraving in which circular forms loomed large. Pairs of religious figures occur in 997; suppliant goddesses appear with other figures in 998; somewhat more traditional subjects are depicted under the pitted arch over a seated goddess in 999; or the god surrounded by numerous varied details in 1000; the confronted deities and heroes of 1001–02, and the suppliant goddess of 1003 are more in the new style. Clearly in the new manner, a god with lightning facing a priest, while a different impression features a god with a lionclub, 1004. A more conventional seated goddess over a much-dotted god with saw in 1005. Contending warriors in 1006, full-face heroes beside a seated god in 1007, bullmen with standard in 1008, gods before worshippers in 1009, beasts in conflict with warriors in 1010, a mounted god with lightning (?) in 1011, various small figures in 1012, sacred pairs in 1013, a mounted deity in 1014, small groups of holy pairs in 1015, all in the advanced style. This is also true of the full-face god, 1016, the opposed pairs, 1017, the archer against a man with shield, 1018, two extreme impressions showing contrasted pairs, 1019, also extreme is a parade of gods with "trees," 1020. A more conventional worshipper in 1021, smaller contenders in 1022, the conventional again in 1023, gods with "trees" and other extreme figures in 1024, advanced impressions showing circular confronted styles opposed to wholly linear figures in 1025, also advanced impressions especially featuring a god in a coffin in 1026, likewise sacred figures facing worshippers with kids in 1027, small holy figures in 1028, and, finally, deities crudely presented in 1029 bring the whole to a stylized climax under the last Old Babylonian king, Samsuditana.

983. Oblong tablets, all impressed. Height c. 23. (a) Reverse, MLC 202, (b) Left side, MLC 610, both partial, (c) Drawing. Also MLC 203. *Yale Library Gazette* 45 (1970), pp. 59–60, no. 11. Samsuiluna 18.

Bowlegged dwarf, suppliant goddess (?), inscription, full-face male with dagger at waist, lightning symbol above small figure, personage.

An oblong tablet, 983x, MLC 1618, Samsuiluna 18, height 23½, shows a god extending a club, his foot on a goat, a crook over left shoulder, inscription before him.

984. Square tablet, all impressed. Height ext. 15. (a) Part reverse, (b) Drawing. NBC 8570. Samsuiluna 19 or 21.

Inscription; personage, gap, full-face figure.

985. Square tablet, all impressed. Height c. 23. Part reverse. NBC 8885. Samsuiluna 21.

God leaning on scimitar (?), holding knob (?)-topped rod, his left foot on lying lion, facing worshipper with right hand before face, ground line.

986. Oblong tablet, probably all impressed. Height A–ext. 13½ (with cap marks 14½), B–ext. 14. Left side. YBC 7743 (= *YOS* 12, 401). Samsuiluna 21.

A–Inscription (three times); personage, three drillings over spade, suppliant goddess.

B–Trace worshipper with kid facing figure with right hand before face.

987. Oblong tablet, probably all impressed. Height c. 17. (a) Reverse, (b) Bottom (both partial), (c) Drawing. YBC 7665 (*YOS* 12, 487). *Yale Library Gazette* 45 (1970), p. 60, no. 12. Samsuiluna 27.

Lying goat above nude female, "mongoose," nude hero holding rod with balls and streamers, worshipper with right hand before face, star (?) disk in crescent over vessel over ball staff, god with open robe leaning on scimitar.

988. Oblong tablet, all impressed. Height ext. 16. (a) Left side, (b) Drawing. NBC 9264. Samsuiluna 27.

Man on one knee, cross disk in crescent above lying lion, hero with head turned back held crosswise by second hero, reversed lion.

989. Squarish tablet, all impressed. Height ext. 21. (a) Reverse (part), (b) Drawing. YBC 4407 (*YOS* 12, 497). Samsuiluna 27.

Human head above big drilling above small man with hands at waist, worshipper with kid, disk in crescent amidst three big drillings and one below, god with saw in ascending posture.

990. Squarish tablet, all impressed. Height ext. 15. (a) Left end, (b) Drawing. YBC 5986 (*YOS* 12, 502). Samsuiluna 28.

Personage, standard held by male figure, crescent above phallic male with hands behind him, lightning symbol.

987a

987b

987c

988a

988b

989a

989b

990a

990b

991a

991b

992a

992b

993a

993b

994a

994b

994c

991. Oblong envelope, all impressed. Height A–20½, B–21½, C–ext. 25, D–ext. 24. (a) Left side A–D, (b) Obverse A and D. YBC 4981 (*YOS* 12, 536). Samsuiluna 30.

A–Third column inscription, full-face goddess in high hat, second column inscription, suppliant goddess, first column inscription, worshipper with hands at waist, priest (part), ground line.

B–Worshipper in long open robe carrying kid (?), god with saw, right foot on human-headed bull, full-face nude bearded hero, drilled curls beside head, ground line.

C–Inscription, trace of personage.

D–Inscription, god brandishing scimitar.

992. Oblong tablet. Height c. 14. (a) Edge, (b) Drawing. YBC 5665. *Yale Library Gazette* 45 (1970), p. 60, no. 13. Abi-ešuḫ "k."

Personage, crescent over reversed omega symbol, suppliant goddess, tree (?), worshipper with hand before face, vessel (?) above ball staff with attached cord, god holding "bouquet tree," right foot on stand, ground line.

An oblong tablet fragment, 992x, YBC 11926, Abi-ešuḫ "h" (?), height c. 15, shows a cow and calf over male figures beside an inscription, plus other impressions.

993. Oblong tablet, all impressed. Height ext. 14. (a) Right edge (part), (b) Drawing. YBC 5939. *JCS* 5 (1951), p. 102. *Yale Library Gazette* 45 (1970), p. 61, no. 14. Abi-ešuḫ "m."

Inscription, star in crescent over solar (?) symbol in grasp of deity.

A fragment of oblong tablet, perhaps all impressed, height ext. 11, left side, 993x, YBC 8458, Abi-ešuḫ "o," shows worshipper with kid, god in ascending posture and other figures.

994. Oblong tablet, all impressed. Height A–ext. 16, B–ext. 15. (a) Bottom, (b) Left edge (part), (c) Drawing. YBC 11990. *JCS* 5 (1951), p. 101. Abi-ešuḫ "p."

A–Suppliant goddess, ribbon down back, three large drillings, full-face hero with curls at sides, arms at waist, worshipper with kid, six dots, bottom three in horizontal lines, god in ascending posture.

B–Two (?) rows of squares with central circles; divided obliquely.

995. Oblong tablet. Height ext. 17. (a) Left side (part), (b) Drawing. Other impressions. MLC 1287. *JCS* 5 (1951), p. 101. Abi-ešuḫ "u."

Trace of suppliant goddess, ribbon down back, vessel over ball staff, worshipper with kid, sidewise lying goat with head turned back below tree standard extended by god with right leg exposed.

996. Squarish tablet, all impressed. Height c. 14. (a) Right side (part), (b) Drawing. MLC 222. *Yale Library Gazette* 45 (1970), p. 61, no. 15. Abi-ešuḫ 28.

Column of four drillings, two dwarfs with arms akimbo reversed about common head; inscription.

A squarish tablet, 996x, YBC 6790, *JCS* 5 (1951), p. 96, Abi-ešuḫ 28, left and bottom edge, height c. 18, shows a man on one knee, and a bullman amidst animals and drillings.

997. Oblong tablet, all impressed. Height c. 20. (a) Left side (part), (b) Drawing. YBC 12983. Ammiditana 3.

God holding bouquet tree (?) in ascending posture, disk, priest with sprinkler and pail; suppliant goddess, vessel above ball staff, worshipper, ground line.

998. Oblong tablet, perhaps all impressed. Height A–ext. 14, B–ext. 15. (a) Bottom, A, (b) Left side, B. YBC 5477 (*YOS* 13, 402). Ammiditana 8.

A–Suppliant goddess with ribbon down back before (?), inscription.

B–Suppliant goddess, trace worshipper with kid, vessel above ball staff, small erect dragon attacking goat with head turned back, reversed legs of same (?) creatures, personage with mace, big drilling.

999. Oblong tablet, perhaps all impressed. Height c. 20. (a) Reverse, (b) Left edge, (c) Top, (d) Drawing. YBC 5920. *Yale Library Gazette* 45 (1970), p. 61, no. 16. Ammiditana 11.

Attendants holding arch over enthroned goddess, all on "mountain" platform, cross disk in crescent, liondragon and lion attacking male with belt on one knee between them.

A broken long tablet, 999x, MLC 1524, height 25, left side, Ammiditana 15, shows suppliant goddess with ribbon down back before inscription.

995a

996a

997a

995b

996b

997b

998a

998b

999a

999c

999b

999d

1000a

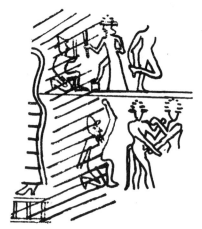

1000b

1001

1002a

1002b

1003

1002c

1000. Oblong tablet. Height c. 25. Other impressions. (a) Reverse (part), (b) Drawing. YBC 12259. Ammiditana 20.

Trace of suppliant goddess with ribbon down back on rear of niched platform; above: double-lined divider, man on one knee attacked by god with right leg on small stand, nude dancer, gap (?); below: bearded man on one knee, bullman and hero in contest, gap (?), worshipper, cross disk in crescent, god with rod and ring, his feet and throne on human-headed bulls, omega shape on long rod held by goddess (first cited), all on niched platform.

1000x, MLC 1214, Ammiditana 20, oblong tablet, left side and elsewhere, height ext. 20, god carrying crescent standard before inscription; reverse, height c. 19, human figures in high hats, other figures and details.

1000xx, MLC 1392, Ammiditana 25, squarish tablet, left side, height c. 16, features full-face hero and personage with mace.

1001. Oblong tablet. Height ext. 19 (plus other impressions). Top edge. YBC 5501. Ammiditana 31.

Trace of worshipper; god in ascending posture, brandishing weapon and extending knobbed mace, dotted fringe of robe below left arm, facing worshipper with hands at waist; worshipper with right hand before face confronting god with saw in ascending posture, star between them, first figure repeated.

1002. Squarish tablet, probably all impressed. Height 23. (a) Reverse, (b) Left edge (both partial), (c) Drawing. MLC 425. Ammiditana 36.

Hero brandishing weapon in right hand and grasping right hand of man on one knee with head turned back, suppliant goddess with hands before face, worshipper with kid before god in ascending posture, right arm extended downward and right leg exposed toward small figure, star above, ground line.

1003. Oblong tablet. Height c. 22. Reverse (part). NBC 1273 (*BIN* 2, 78). Ammiditana 36.

Dot-centered disk with rays in crescent, suppliant goddess with ribbon down back before inscription.

1004. Squarish tablet, probably all impressed. Height A–21, B–ext. 16. (a) Reverse A, (b) A to left, B to right, (c) Drawing A, (d) Drawing B. YBC 4271. *Yale Library Gazette* 45 (1970), p. 62, no. 17 (a-b). Ammiṣaduqa 1.

A–Two human figures, star over line between them, god holding mace and lightning fork, left foot on goat, facing priest with sprinkler and pail, ground line.

B–God with right leg exposed, lying sheep above, god leaning on scimitar and holding lionclub, crescent above, figure (?) below, suppliant goddess with ribbon down back, vase above ball staff, worshipper (?).

1005. Oblong tablet. Height A–26, B–23. Reverse (part). MLC 606 (*YOS* 13, 89). Ammiṣaduqa 6.

A–Enthroned goddess on platform, feet on small stand, scorpion below; inscription.

B–Inscription; gap, trace of worshipper with kid, star (small dots around large), god with saw in ascending posture.

1006. Squarish tablet, probably all impressed. Height ext. 15. (a) Obverse, (b) Left side, (c) Drawing. MLC 1388. Ammiṣaduqa 8.

God with right leg forward, ithyphallic bullman contending with hero, diagonal fish above three dots, reversed lion (?) held aloft by full-face hero on one knee, back of figure.

Oblong tablet, 1006x, YBC 12034, Ammiṣaduqa 8, plus others shows suppliant goddess before inscription.

1004a

1005

1004b

1006a

1004c

1006b

1004d

1006c

1007a

1007b

1008a

1008c

1008b

1009a

1009b

1010a

1010b

1010c

1007. Oblong tablet. Height ext. 18. (a) Top end, (b) Drawing. Other impressions. YBC 4329. (*YOS* 13, 484). Ammiṣaduqa 9.

Full-face hero in worship before god with vase on altar throne, crescent above, full-face hero with hands at waist, long robed deity holding lightning fork.

1008. Squarish tablet, probably all sealed. Height ext. 14. (a-b) Right and left edge, (c) Drawing. MLC 1394. Ammiṣaduqa 9.

Trace of suppliant goddess with ribbon down back, two full-face bullmen holding tree between them, suppliant goddess with ribbon down back facing inscription.

1009. Squarish tablet. Height c. 18. (a) Reverse (part), (b) Drawing. Other impressions. YBC 6769. Ammiṣaduqa 9.

Trace of god, perhaps on animal with head raised, facing suppliant goddess, perhaps on animal with head lowered; drilling behind god with scimitar, extending arm toward kid held by worshipper, star disk in crescent between them, ground line.

In the lower reverse of 1009x, NBC 5575, Alexander, *BIN* 7, pl. LXIX, 207, appears an Ur 3 presentation to a goddess, height ext. 16; otherwise the tablet is late Old Babylonian, dated Ammiṣaduqa 10 (p. 38). It has a tall late figure as in 1021x.

On a long tablet of similar date, 1009xx, MLC 1690, reverse and left side, appear three figures each with an inscription.

1010. Oblong tablet. Height c. 18. (a) Reverse, (b) Left side (both part), (c) Drawing. Other impressions. YBC 9118. Ammiṣaduqa 11.

Vessel, full-face human-headed bull with head turned back in grasp of full-face bullman, fly and fish above, lion (?) reversed by full-face hero who steps on its head, uncertain small bowlegged figures, man brandishing mace.

A broken oblong tablet, 1010x, YBC 11927, Ammiṣaduqa 11, height ext. 20, shows figures composed of dots and lines plus more impressions.

1011. Squarish small tablet, all impressed. Height A–ext. 11, B–ext. 21. (a) Left edge A–B, (b) Drawing A. MLC 828. Ammiṣaduqa 13.

A–God with right leg exposed, worshipper with kid, god holding lightning fork (?) mounted on goat.

B–Personage with mace facing suppliant goddess, star disk in crescent above.

1012. Squarish small tablet. Height c. 16. (a) Left side, (b) Reverse. YBC 5987. Ammiṣaduqa 13.

Two contending heroes, nude female, striding god brandishing mace and extending knobbed mace before worshipper with left hand before face, sidewise lion (?) between them.

1012x, two tablets, NBC 5456 (*BIN* 7, 209) and 5301 (*BIN* 7, 208), Ammiṣaduqa 13, height 22, shows crescent over crook behind god with left hand before inscription.

A squarish tablet with rounded corners, only faces engraved, 1012xx, MLC 446, Ammiṣaduqa 14, height c. 22, reverse, man on one knee before goddess extending right hand, hair down back. For the same shape see 1019x (MLC 455).

1013. Oblong tablet, multiple rollings. Height c. 19. (a) Reverse (part), (b) Drawing. NBC 5355. (*BIN* 7, 210). Ammiṣaduqa 15.

Worshipper with kid, dots above, before god with right leg exposed, worshipper with arms at waist facing god holding lightning fork and leaning on scimitar, star.

1014. Oblong tablet, almost all impressed. Height ext. 17. (a) Left edge, (b) Drawing. YBC 4962. Ammiṣaduqa 16.

Worshipper before god with lightning fork, deity with arrows at shoulders, right leg exposed, holding rein to mounted dragon.

A long tablet, probably all impressed, 1014x, MLC 1564, Ammiṣaduqa 16; reverse, height A–ext. 16, god holding spear point up before inscription; B–c. 19, suppliant goddess, vessel above ball staff, worshipper before deity in ascending posture on bull (?).

1015. Small square tablet, very worn. Height ext. 11. Left side. YBC 7813. Ammiṣaduqa 16.

God facing goddess with striated hair, holding lightning fork between them, god with saw facing worshipper with right hand before face.

1016. Small square tablet, probably all impressed. Height 28. (a) Reverse, (b) Bottom (both part), (c) Drawing. MLC 807. *Yale Library Gazette* 45 (1970), p. 62, no. 18. Ammiṣaduqa 16 (?).

Full-face god holding flowing vase at waist, crescent and star above, ground line.

An oblong tablet, 1016x, MLC 1334, Ammiṣaduqa 17; reverse, A–ext. 20, inscription, personage; B–ext. 16, god, inscription, nude female; plus other impressions including part of 1019(B).

1011a

1011b

1012a

1012b

1013a

1013b

1014a

1014b

1015

1016a

1016b

1016c

1017a

1017b

1017c

1018a

1018b

1018c

1019a

1019b

1019c

1019d

1019e

1017. Oblong tablet. Height ext. 18. (a) Reverse (part), (b) Right edge, (c) Drawing. MLC 2228. Ammiṣaduqa 17+a.

Worshipper with kid facing god with saw, between them lying goat over ball staff, star, god holding curved (?) staff before worshipper.

1018. Small squarish tablet. Height 20. (a) Reverse, (b) Right edge, (c) Drawing. MLC 811. *Yale Library Gazette* 45 (1970), p. 63, no. 19. Ammiṣaduqa 17+b.

God in ascending posture, archer fighting warrior with shield and dagger, crescent between them, tree.

1019. Tablets. Height A–18½, B–17½. (a) Left edge (= MLC 210), (b) Left edge (= MLC 223), (c) Reverse (= MLC 223), (d) Drawing A, (e) Drawing B. B also on MLC 1366, year 14, MLC 1334, year 17 (partial on 1016x), MLC 2587 and MLC 220 (different impression on envelope MLC 219) year 17+b. *Yale Library Gazette* 45 (1970), p. 63, no. 20 (a-b). Ammiṣaduqa 17 (MLC 223), 17+b (MLC 210).

A–Two figures holding "bouquet tree" between them, god with dagger and lightning fork, sword (?) on back, facing suppliant goddess.

B–God, left foot on mound, before worshipper with kid, vessel between them, god with dagger (?) and "bouquet tree," left foot on mound, facing worshipper, ground line.

A thin ovoid tablet, 1019x, MLC 455, Ammiṣaduqa 17+b, shows a male and a female (?) figure holding a "bouquet tree" between them; marked only on two faces like 1012xx (MLC 446).

1020. Squarish tablet. Height c. 15. (a) Part reverse, (b) Drawing. MLC 2212. *Yale Library Gazette* 45 (1970), p. 64, no. 21. Ammiṣaduqa 17+b(?).

Row of gods carrying "bouquet tree," rays (?) at waists.

1021. Oblong tablet, impressed except bottom edge. Height ext. 15. Part left edge. MLC 1331. *JCS* 13 (1959), p. 41. Samsuditana 2.

Worshipper before inscription, beaded border with row of beaded triangles above.

An oblong tablet, 1021x, MLC 1570, *JCS* 13, p. 41, Samsuditana 2, all impressed, with at least three seals, the worshipper on the reverse being very tall, height 26.

1022. Oblong tablet, probably all impressed. Height 16. Part reverse. Another impression. MLC 1742. *JCS* 13 (1959), p. 41. Samsuditana 5.

Personage with mace facing goddess (?), hero upending bull (?), spread-legged man with kid (?).

A squarish tablet, probably same seal all over, 1022x, MLC 1628, *JCS* 13, p. 42. Samsuditana 7, height 17, on reverse and left side various figures including worshipper with kid before god in ascending posture.

An oblong tablet, probably all impressed, 1022xx, MLC 2559, *JCS* 13, p. 42, Samsuditana 10, height ext. 16, on left side deity holding spear pointing down.

1023. Oblong tablet, perhaps all impressed. Height A–24, B–22, C–ext. 23. (a) Left edge A–B, (b) Bottom C (both partial). MLC 644. *JCS* 13 (1959), p. 43. Samsuditana 12. Kish tablet.

A+B–Suppliant goddesses with ribbon down back before inscriptions, ground line under B.

C–Lionclub (?) standard on three-part support, suppliant goddess with ribbon down back before inscription.

1024. Oblong tablet, all impressed. Height ext. 24. (a) Top edge (enlarged), (b) Part reverse. MLC 1656. *JCS* 13 (1959), p. 43. Samsuditana 12.

Ball staff, god with sickle sword above, extending "bouquet tree" which may be held in two hands by attendant, fly (?) between them; same scene all repeated except that attendant raises hands before face; large drilling over obscure god with extended saw, leg forward in open robe, crescent or dot above, obscure "bouquet tree" below, facing "bouquet tree" held in two hands by attendant.

1025. Small squarish tablet, all impressed. Height A–c. 19½, B–13½. (a) Left side A, (b) Bottom A, (c) Reverse B above A, (d) Drawing A, (e) Drawing B. MLC 1604. *JCS* 13 (1959), p. 43. *Yale Library Gazette* 45 (1970), p. 64, no. 22 (a-b). Samsuditana 13.

A–Worshipper before god with saw, right foot over wavy line, star standard above; god raising dagger (?), and holding lightning fork, one foot forward, facing god with dagger.

B–Two male figures grasping star (?) standard between them, ground line.

A small squarish tablet, all impressed, 1025x, YBC 10624, *JCS* 13, p. 43, Samsuditana 14, height c. 20, reverse and left edge, shows a god with crescent standard and other figures.

1020a

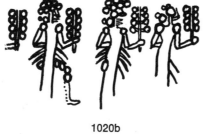

1020b

1021

1022

1023a

1023b

1024a

1025a

1024b

1025d

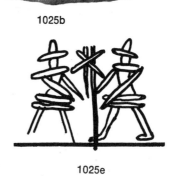

1025b

1025c

1025e

1026a

1026b

1026c

1026d

1027a

1027b

1028

1029a

1029b

1026. Small squarish tablet, all impressed. Height A–ext. 14, B–15. (a) Reverse B, (b) Left edge B–A, (c) Drawing A, (d) Drawing B. YBC 3285. *JCS* 13 (1959), p. 43. *Yale Library Gazette* 45 (1970), p. 65, no. 23 (a-b). Samsuditana 14.

A–Two figures with star standard between them, worshipper (?).

B–God wielding dagger with attachment that hangs from elbow, touching bull-eared god with arms akimbo, lower body in coffinlike frame ending in point, two figures holding star standard between them, ground line.

1027. Oblong tablet, all impressed. Height ext. 18. (a) Left side, (b) Drawing. MLC 1654. *JCS* 13 (1959), p. 44. Samsuditana 14.

Sidewise lion, head down; worshipper with kid facing god holding "bouquet tree," bowlegged dwarf between them; god brandishing dagger and holding lightning fork before worshipper with kid, crescent above bowlegged dwarf.

1028. Squarish tablet, all impressed. Height 13½. Part reverse. YBC 8308. Samsuditana 14.

Personage, spade, nude female, star disk (?) in crescent above vertical fish, long-robed figure, lightning standard, spear (?).

A small square tablet, 1028x, YBC 8691, *JCS* 13, p. 44, Samsuditana 14, shows a row of figures.

1029. Oblong tablet, perhaps all impressed. Height c. 18. (a) Part reverse, (b) Drawing. MLC 1515. Date unassigned, *JNES* 14 (1955), p. 160(a). Samsuditana.

God in high hat, brandishing weapon and holding lightning fork, left foot on lying bull (?), before worshipper with hands at waist; deity extending lightning symbol mounted on dots, two dots above; secondary: two figures on one knee, spread standard between them, on line with verticals below.

FIGS. 1026–1029

FIGS. 1030–1034

From the middle years of Samsuiluna, c. 1730 B.C. until Samsuditana shortly after 1600, the last Old Babylonian ruler, the stylized treatment of art persisted, though fixed dates are lacking.

An armed male in 1030, holy worshippers before gods, 1031–32; a snake (?) goddess surrounded by sacred figures in 1033, seated deities with companions, 1034–35; worshippers with kid and holy figures, 1036–37; various figures in 1038, wrestlers in 1039, seated deities in 1040–41; animals beside tree in 1042, crooks on back of animal in 1043, hero with streams in 1044; goddesses before inscriptions, 1045–48, worshippers likewise, 1049–51, with added animals, 1052; god with lightning, 1053; deity and female, 1054; dwarf beside god on bull (no inscription) in 1055, personages and goddesses, 1056–58; confronted worshippers, 1059; deities and worshippers, 1060–62; dwarf and confronted figures in 1063, personages between females in 1064–65, distorted figures (no inscription) in 1066, fighters with crossed forelegs in 1067, distorted figures in 1068. Two separate groups of figures, 1069; more stylized figures form two human groups, 1070–73; stylized figures and animals in 1074, also seated deities with companions in 1075–77.

1030. Oblong tablet. Fragment of impression around left edge. Height 34 (with cap marks 47). (a) Left edge, (b) Drawing. YBC 6518. *RA* 34 (1937), pp. 184ff. Dura Europos. Ḫammurabi of Ḫana, c. 1700 B.C.

Tall figure in rounded hat, leaning on scimitar (?) to left, dotted edge, and dotted triangular insets at top and bottom.

Oblong tablet, probably all impressed, 1030x, YBC 6785, reads . . . *ta-na* (late Old Babylonian ruler), height 26, reverse, showing personage with mace, other impressions.

1031. Small squarish tablet. Height 19. (a) Top edge, (b) Left edge, (c) Drawing. NBC 6811.

God in two-pointed peaked crown holding crook, vessel above ball staff, worshipper with hands before face, gap, left elbow and foot of figure, three-pointed device above, god (?) extending mace, exposed foot on lying dragon, ground line.

1032. Oblong tablet, probably all impressed. Height ext. 12. (a) Left side, (b) Drawing. YBC 8017.

Ball staff, worshipper with right hand before face, omega symbol above "mongoose," lightning fork above bull, blunt end drilled standard above dagger held by deity.

1033. Oblong tablet. Height ext. 15. (a) Left side (part), (b) Drawing. MLC 1206.

Above: two small men on one knee; below: god wielding dagger while holding whirling maces with cloth attached; full-face goddess with outstretched arms (winged?), coiled undergarment (snake?), ball staff beside her, both over line on back of striding animal; god brandishing mace before worshipper with kid, animal above, between them.

1034. Oblong tablet, probably all impressed. Height c. 15. (a) Reverse, (b) Right side, (c) Drawing. MLC 836.

Nude female above lion with head turned back, attacking animal; enthroned deity holding rod, seated on crosspiece held by figure with outstretched arms; worshipper with left hand before face, vessel above ball staff before god holding bow, arrows at back, grasping scimitar behind him, disk, ground line.

1030a

1030b

1031a

1031b

1031c

1032a

1032b

1033a

1033b

1034a

1034b

1034c

1035a

1035b

1036a

1036b

1037

1036c

1038a

1038b

1039

1040

1035. Squarish quite plump tablet, probably all impressed. Height c. 25. (a) Reverse, (b) Bottom (both partial). YBC 8499.

Seated deity holding "bouquet tree" (?) to right, personage with mace behind small god brandishing dagger (?).

1036. Small square tablet, probably all impressed. Height c. 24. (a) Part reverse, (b) Left side, (c) Drawing. YBC 5295.

Full-face nude belted hero with hands at waist, streams flowing from them to either side, worshipper with kid before full-face god with saw, between them star disk in crescent above inscription; to right personage (?).

1037. Triangular tag, all impressed, no writing. Height 21½. One side shown. YBC 928.

God in ascending posture, right hand raised, lionclub in left, vase before forward leg, full-face nude bearded hero with vase at waist from which stream flows on either side, crescent above, ithyphallic bullman holding kid to left, dotted star above fly, god with right foot on small stand, ball staff, repeat of ascending god, ground line.

1038. Squarish tablet, one edge blank, almost no writing. Height c. 20. (a) Reverse, (b) Obverse. NBC 11431. E. J. Banks, purchased from estate, 1971.

Deity in long robe, exposed left leg forward, vessel, hero with arms at sides from which stream falls on either side, bullman holding kid to left, deity in long robe, exposed right leg forward, ball staff, first deity repeated, ground line.

1039. Fragment of tablet. Height ext. 15. Left edge. MLC 555.

Worshipper with kid before god with extended right arm, disk in crescent between them, full-face hero and bullman wrestling, star between them.

1040. Triangular tag, all impressed, no writing. Height c. 21. Face. YBC 13215.

Deity in long robe facing right, enthroned deity with two horns on peaked hat, personage with mace facing suppliant goddess (?).

1041. Triangular tag, all impressed, no writing. Height ext. 17. (a-b) Faces. YBC 13109.

Ten or more drillings held in extended right hand of seated deity, suppliant goddess with ribbon down back, spade, worshipper with hands at waist, ground line (?).

1042. Fragment of tablet. Left edge, height A–ext. 14, B–ext. 17. MLC 897.

A–Lions (?) on either side of tree, crescent above ball staff; inscription.

B–Suppliant goddess with ribbon down back facing inscription.

1043. Orange carnelian. 14 × 6/8 (barrel shaped). (a) Impression, (b) Shape. YBC 12638.

Star standard, two opposed crooks over back of gazelle lying on cross-hatched pedestal, tree, all on line; inscription.

1044. Hematite. 15×7. Engraved transversely. New impression. *Newell* 336. *Ward,* 204.

Full-face bearded naked hero holding vase at waist, from which streams flow on either side, star above to right, lightning fork to left, dotted line below.

1045. Light brown composition. No bore. 25×11. Worn. NBC 6019.

Suppliant goddess on line; inscription.

1046. White, brown, and bluish sardonyx. 30×17/16(convex). Worn. NBC 5999.

Like 1045; worn inscription.

1047. Brown and white agate, green strained. 30×18. Worn. NBC 6001.

Like 1045; inscription.

1048. Brown glazed composition. Irregular holes at ends; broken pin perhaps inside. 34×13½. YBC 9687.

Suppliant goddess with ribbon down back, ground line, crescent over lionscimitar standard; inscription.

1041a 1041b

1042 1043a 1043b

1045 1046

1044

1047 1048

1049

1051

1052

1053

1055

1056

1049. Light and dark brown sardonyx. 31×14. YBC 12610.

Worshipper with back to inscription.

1050. Pale blue, mottled brown agate. 25½ ×12. Chipped. *Newell* 233. Not shown.

Inscription before worshipper.

1051. Brown and white banded agate. 16×8 /7½(cut back at inscription). NBC 8926.

Like 1050; last line of inscription reversed.

1052. Pale olive to dark brown banded agate. 29×12½/12(convex). Chipped. NBC 11028.

Inscription; lying goat with head turned back, star-tipped rod held by worshipper, column of cross between drilled devices (flies) in frame, two lying antelopes with head turned back in frame.

1053. Brown streaked chalcedony. 27×12. NBC 2582. *BIN* 2, pl. LXXIVb.

Inscription; lightning fork held by god wielding dagger, right foot on bull.

1054. Brown jasper with creamy spot. Chipped. Probably unfinished. *Newell* 258. Not shown.

Bent rod (?), deity holding flat-topped staff with star above nude female; inscription.

1055. Hematite. 21½×9. Chipped. NBC 8928.

Bird (?) above vertical scratch, bowlegged dwarf, lionclub standard, lightning fork held by god on bull, lionscimitar standard, ground line (?).

1056. Mottled light and dark brown agate. 28½×13/12½(cut back at two columns of inscription behind goddess). NBC 8925.

Personage with mace, notched lionclub over lionscimitar standard beside fly, suppliant goddess, ground line; inscription.

FIGS. 1049–1056

1057. Hematite. Remains of copper pin in bore. 25×11. *Newell* 231. Not shown.

Row of five dots, personage with mace, crook, suppliant goddess, ground line; inscription.

1058. Black and cream flecked dioritic stone. 31×15. Chipped. NBC 5950.

Personage with mace facing suppliant goddess, line under figures; inscription.

1059. "Steatite." 25×11. Worn. *Newell* 271. Not shown.

Worshipper with right hand before face, erect snake, inscription, second worshipper, towerlike open structure.

1060. Brown tinged, yellowish agate. 19½×8 /7(bottom narrow). *Newell* 223. Not shown.

Goddess, crescent, male worshipper; inscription.

1061. Pink orange agate. 19½×10. Chipped. YBC 12584.

Deity, vessel over ball staff, worshipper, line under figures; inscription.

1062. Dark brown jasper. 35½×20. *Newell* 269. Not shown.

Worshipper with right hand before face, confronting god with bent object, line under figures; inscription.

1063. Hematite. 24×10. Chipped. *Newell* 267. Not shown.

Phallic bowlegged dwarf, figure, left hand raised, spade, inscription, figure, right hand lowered.

1064. Brownish cloudy chalcedony. 23×12. NBC 5934.

Suppliant goddess, personage, female figure, line under figures (?), two frames for inscription, one sign begun.

1065. Hematite. 21×11½. YBC 12823.

Nude female, inscription, personage, suppliant goddess, worn inscription.

1066. Limonite. 21×8. Worn. *Newell* 210. Not shown. Figures probably later crudities.

Bearded god in vertically striped hat facing worshipper with left hand before face, star over spade between them; crescent over "mongoose" before downward right arm of figure, roughly twisted pole on tripod, ground line.

1067. Hematite. 19½×9/8½(cut back beyond personage with mace). NBC 9242.

Personage with mace, big drilling in crescent over two smaller drillings, above two drillings connected by vertical rod, two contending men with crossed foreleg, the further one holds bent sword behind him, ground line; inscription.

1068. Hematite. 21½×10. Scratched. NCBS 798.

Figure with arms at waist; object (bird?) above object (mongoose?), perhaps worshipper with right hand before face, vessel above ball staff, figure in long pleated robe, inscription beside crook, full-face hero with hands at waist, inscription, ground line.

1069. Hematite. 26×15/14(cut back at two figures to left). Worn. YBC 9702.

Worshipper with kid, lying animal above, goddess with right foot on animal (?), leaning on scimitar to left, suppliant goddess; worshipper with hands before face, two drillings above ball staff, suppliant goddess.

1058

1061

1064

1065

1067

1068

1069

1070

1072

1073

1074

1075

1076

1077

1070. Hematite. 20×11½. New impression. *Newell* 652.

Worshipper, fly, god holding "bouquet tree," right foot on stony mound, vessel on ball staff, god wielding dagger, extending lightning fork connected by line with lying bull on which the god's left foot is placed, worshipper with left hand at mouth, crescent above lionscimitar, worshipper with kid, star, spade, small figure facing left, on one knee over line, ground line.

1071. Hematite. 21×8. *Newell* 204. Not shown.

Worshipper, crescent above, saw held by god, right foot on stony mound; full-face bearded hero with vessel at waist, from which streams flow on either side, dotted rod held by goddess, star above, ground line.

1072. Hematite. 19×8½/8(irregular). Worn. NCBS 738.

Worshipper with kid (?), crescent, saw held by god with right foot on stony mound; two worshippers holding long pole with flat top and bottom between them.

1073. Hematite. 18×8/7½(irregular). Worn. NCBS 762.

Worshipper holding vessel in right hand at waist, left hand bent up, rod with dot at each end held by god with exposed right leg forward, left hand up; above: monster (?) looking back toward lying animal (?), three brackets between them; below: seated dog with head turned back on outstretched leg of man on one knee facing similar man, holding tree with circular dotted top between them.

1074. Hematite. 26½×12½/11(irregular). Worn. NCBS 836.

Personage with mace (?) before suppliant goddess, hero and bullman in combat (?) over animals in opposite directions (?), animal (?) above two erect dogs (?).

1075. Limonite. 19×9. Chipped. YBC 12591.

Worshipper with arms at waist, "bouquet tree" held by seated deity, phallic bowlegged male, lightning fork.

1076. Hematite. 20×9. YBC 12619.

Dagger wielded by god who holds lightning fork attached by line to animal on ground, worshipper; worshipper with right hand before face, "bouquet tree" held by seated god with feet on low pedestal, ground line.

1077. Hematite. 20(ext.)×8/9(convex). No bore. Groove at top perhaps cut away. YBC 12589.

Worshipper with right hand before face, dotted staff with cross on top held by god with exposed right leg forward, vessel over ball staff, nude female, head left, dotted staff with cross on top held by seated god, ground line.

STAMP SEALS OF HISTORIC MESOPOTAMIA

FIGS. 1078–1081

Very few stamp seals later than the fourth millennium and entirely of Mesopotamian origin can be attested. An eagle over goats, probably pyramidal, may be Sumerian but is more likely Post-Akkadian, 1078; a seated figure, its back a rolled top, should be Post-Akkadian, 1079, as is certainly true of a rolled top showing a worshipper making a libation before a sacred symbol, 1080; finally an Ur III hemispheroid presents worshippers before a seated goddess, 1081.

1078. Broken pyramid (?). Light brown limestone. 20×17×ext.8. YBC 9723.

Spread eagle over two goats, one with its head turned back.

1078x, NBC 4011, broken pyramid (?), green nephrite, 22×17×ext. 12, traces of a goat.

1079. Roll handle on stepped base, lengthwise perforation. Black limestone. 20(ext.)×16 (ext.)×10. Face broken. (a) Impression, (b) Shape. YBC 12588.

Seated male, raised arm touched by standing figure.

1080. Roll handle on quite thick base. Black limestone. 17½×15½×10(base 4). Chipped. New impression. *Newell* 521 (on the standard p. 140, drawn fig. 25).

Worshipper pouring libation under crescent before vase mounted on vertically marked rectangle attached to pole set in angular support.

Standards with a striated rectangular platform on top are usually surmounted by a lion, as in 601, 618. A vase-topped standard visibly enclosed by a support as here seems to be unique.

1081. Hemispheroid. Limonite. New impression. *Newell* 171.

Worshipper with right hand before face, suppliant goddess (chipped in front), "mongoose" (?), seated goddess, ground line; design below lost (eagle?).

On the crossed shoulder straps of the suppliant goddess see 538; on the "mongoose" (?), 568.

1078

1079a

1079b

1080

1081

1082

1083

1084

1085

1086a   1086b   1087a   1087b

SEALS FROM OUTSIDE MESOPOTAMIA

Egypt

The earliest cylinders at the beginning of Egyptian civilization (about 3000 B.C.) were under Asian influence. They developed a specifically Egyptian character as time went on only to be transformed by a later Asiatic incursion, particularly in the Sixth Dynasty and the beginning of the First Intermediate period, c. 2350–2150 B.C.

The stylized creatures of this later time, human and animal, were primarily cylindrical in form, 1082–85. A few stamp seals in the collection, vastly outnumbered elsewhere, show captives on top with circular fill below, 1086, and a "negroid" woman on top with maze below, 1087.

1082. Cylinder. Bone. 26×17/16(oval). Bore 13 /9(irregular). YBC 9710. Van Buren, *AfO* 11 (1936), p. 32, fig. 36.

Vertical stroke, sidewise antelope over sidewise bowlegged full-face male, reversed seated monkey over scorpion, bee and male figure with tail (?) (or phallus) over sidewise seated male.

Compare in limestone, Petrie, *Buttons*, pl. VI. 140.

1083. Cylinder. Light brown limestone, dark limestone (?) in design. 25×15/13(oval). Bore 7/6(irregular). YBC 12497.

Monogram of lying antelope and sidewise seated monkey, bull over schematic human figure, crocodile over crescent over beetle.

1084. Cylinder. Greenish black speckled serpentine. 24½×12/11(irregular). Bore 6/4. YBC 12772. Buchanan, *Archaeology* 20 (1967), pp. 105–06, fig. 7.

Lion with uraeus projecting from foreleg above reversed Set animal; Set animal (?) with blobs over it above sidewise human figure; notched ground line under both figures; blob above water carrier (?) over reversed Set animal with uraeus projecting from foreleg.

For the Set animals compare *Frankfort*, p. 298, pl. XLVII.

1085. Cylinder. Dark gray "steatite." 28×15. Bore 8/5. YBC 12600.

Linear outlined animal (?) on line, fused with human figure (?) handling bow (?), followed by human figure, arms raised, in boat (?); all over linear outlined crocodile; running male figure over indeterminate linear shape.

For the running male compare Petrie, *Buttons*, pl. VI.147.

1086. Mounted amulet seal with four bound captives on sloping base (half lost). Green glazed steatite. Probable loop on top broken. 9(ext.)×16×18. (a) Impression, (b) Shape. Yale Art Gallery 36.34. *Pier Collection*, pl. X.3.

Four circles and linear fill before head and forelegs of galloping horned animal (?).

For the shape compare the two figures back to back in Petrie, *Buttons*, pl. I, A2, B2 (= nos. 15, 197, with early button seal designs); A1, B1 (= nos. 251, 128, with later "maze" designs).

1087. Mounted amulet seal with squatting woman holding right breast, child on lap. Perforated. Glazed (now brown) steatite. 11½×(ext.)9×19. Chipped at edge. (a) Impression, (b) Shape. Yale Art Gallery 36.33. *Pier Collection*, pl. XV.7–8.

Maze design.

Indus Valley

Stamp seals originated in the Indus Valley during the second half of the third millennium B.C., a few examples of which were exported to Mesopotamia. The older type with bossed top feature a bull-like creature with an inscription, 1088–89. Somewhat later bossed seals became relatively common on islands in the Persian Gulf, and are also known from Mesopotamian impressions, one with facing seated figures dating c. 1900 B.C., 1090. A cylinder with animals may be of similar source and date, 1091.

1088. Boss (shallow groove across top) on thick base with rounded side (chipped). Dark polished "steatite." 23(face 21)×13. (a) Impression, (b) Shape. New impression. *Newell* 23.

Bull with Indus characters above.

Normally in Indus seals the short-horned bull has a manger before it (Marshall, *Mohenjo Daro*, p. 385), but this is missing in a possible Western imitation of the type (*AS* 16, p. 205, n. 9), which furthermore is engraved in a more linear fashion.

1089. Shape and material like 1088. 22×11. Broken and worn. NCBS 876.

Bird with Indus characters (?) above.

1090. Impressions of stamp seal on tablet. Seal height 24. (a) Left edge, axis of design almost centered in two imprints; two on right edge slightly off center; (b) Bottom oblique; similar one on obverse; (c) Drawing. YBC 5447. Dated Gungunum 10, Larsa, 1923 B.C. (d) Drawing of seal found on Failaka island in the Persian Gulf, *ILN* Jan. 28, 1961, p. 142, fig. 3. Buchanan, *AS* 16, pp. 204 ff.; on the tablet see Hallo, *AS* 16, pp. 199ff. Buchanan, *Archaeology* 20 (1967), pp. 104ff.

Two facing seated figures, each drinking by tube from vessel below; between them: circle with cross-hatched square on either side above bucranium and three horizontal lines.

1091. Cylinder. Blue green glazed composition. 26×13. NBC 9256.

Three antelopes above two bulls.

Animals with dotted eyes and long snouts as in *Weber*, 176, also show a bull with a humped back, *UE* 10, 632, both cylinders.

1088a

1088b

1089

1090a

1090b

1090c

1090d

1091

1092

1093

1093 A

1094

Elam

Elamite cylinders seem to be attested from late Neo-Sumerian times on. Two worshippers before a standing god in the midst of a possible inscription, beside an inscription of normal type, 1092. A seated deity before a worshipper, or worshippers, introduces a series of very varied type, in 1093 an altar lies between the figures, in 1093A two standing and a seated figure face an altar, in 1094 a bird on a stand separates the principals, in 1095 a god with a crook, in 1096 a disk in crescent held by a god, in 1097 vessels between the sacred figures exemplify a group showing close Cappadocian connections; all including the last probably of the early second millennium. Standing figures, a worshipper confronting a god, 1098 of similar date; 1099 in the later stylized manner of c. 1700 B.C.

FIGS. 1092–1094

1092. Hematite. 20×11/10(secondary cutting beside principal figures). YBC 12834.

Suppliant goddess, inscription (?) over fish, worshipper with arms at sides, inscription (?), right hand of god outstretched, right leg on pedestal, inscription.

Close to Elamite style in treatment of figures, odd for fish above, see Unger, *Beginn*, p. 41, no. 8, pl. XI.21, servant of Bur-Sin of Isin.

1093. Shell. 30×15. Worn. NBC 6002.

Deity (chipped) enthroned, feet on platform, curved staff in left hand, crescent above altar with two steps towards the deity, worshipper, right hand perhaps raised before face, other hand may hold rod behind back to left; inscription.

1093A. Black serpentine. NBC 11094.

Two worshippers, foremost of which has left arm bent forward, facing bent right arm of seated goddess, under arms altar topped by horns, below left side scorpion; inscription.

1094. Light brown limestone, with darker spot. 21×10. NBC 5964.

Worshipper with hands extended, bird on stand, vessel (?) held in right hand of deity, other extended, flowers in striated vase.

1095. Hematite. 24×12. YBC 12611.

Worshipper with hands extended, crescent, crook tendered by god on cushioned throne; inscription.

For the gesture of the worshipper with hands extended see *Louvre S.*, 513, *S.*, 524–25, *O.*, 113.

1096. Hematite. 27×10½. Worn. YBC 12771.

Worshipper, right hand before face, misshapen disk in crescent on rod held by god seated on throne with curved back, sickle sword, ground line; inscription.

1097. Bituminous shale. 21×10. Worn. NBC 11010.

Worshipper, hands in middle, crescent above small mouthed, big bosomed vessel, vase held by king on cushioned throne; inscription.

Numerous seals mostly in bituminous composition present similar figures; *Louvre S.*, 492–96; *MMAI* 43, 1825–2014.

1098. Dark gray diorite. 18×7. Worn. New impression. *Newell* 209.

Worshipper reaching for mace held by king, goat between them, ground line; inscription.

A similar scene occurs in *Louvre S.*, 528, of limestone; see also Amiet, *Elam*, pp. 256–57, fig. 186, and *MMAI* 43, 1679.

1099. Hematite. 26½×9. NBC 11093.

Worshipper, right hand before face, mace enclosed by crescent on rod held by god, ground line; inscription.

1095

1096

1097

1098

1099

1100

1102

1103

1104

1106

1107

1108

Cappadocia

CYLINDERS

Cappadocian *cylinder* seals are to be distinguished from the earlier, not very common stamp seals, but even more conspicuously from the numerous stamp seals of 1700 B.C. on. The cylinders, produced from before 1900 to after 1800 B.C., were inspired by Mesopotamian examples, particularly of Assyrian origin, but show a gaucheness that marks them as provincial.

Old Assyrian is among the earliest of these not always clearly differentiated styles, which may present a bull, 1100–03; a god in a boat, 1104; contending warriors, 1105; kneeling heroes and a two-headed antelope, 1106; a row of gods and human-headed bulls, 1107. In 1108 appear crude figures and animals; in 1109 the same but with an altar, perhaps recut.

An early but persisting native style, often designated as Anatolian, shows heroes and animals in conflict, 1110–11; rows of worshippers, 1112–14; the adoration of a bull, 1115–16; heroes fighting lions, 1117; elaborate chariots, 1118–19; and complicated scenes with gods, heroes, animals, and sacred symbols, 1120–23.

Provincial Babylonian or, much less common, Syrianized Colony were probably the latest cylinder seal styles of Anatolia, but early examples are also attested, as in provincial Babylonian 1124, where a worshipper is presented by a goddess to a seated "king." Similarly, but probably not as early, a seated king or god is the central feature of 1125–31. A row of holy figures appears in 1132, culminating in a god, his right foot to the fore, in 1133–37; a goddess (?) standing left in 1138–39; a personage to the right in 1140–41; a god on a bull in 1142–43. Possibly provincial, certainly of Babylonian origin, are holy figures each on a goat, 1144, and a dwarf with animals and a monster, 1145.

1100. Hematite. 20×11/10½(concave). NBC 7821.

Protuberance on back of bull over outlined front-view head; suppliant goddess, vessel above ball staff, lightning fork above male head, crescent on staff held by god with forward leg on pedestal.

1101. Hematite. 15½×9½. *Newell* 280. Not shown.

Erect goat with head turned back, worshipper in striated hat, worshipper led by goddess, star disk in crescent, cup held by enthroned king, protuberance on back of bull over framed enclosure on three circles.

1102. Hematite. 17×9. NBC 8916.

Suppliant goddess, crescent, worshipper, angle, suppliant goddess, vessel above ball staff, trident held by god who stands on attached lying bull, ground line.

1103. Dark brown limonite. 15×9. NBC 8142.

God holding trident attached to lying bull, worshipper, angle, suppliant goddess, star disk in crescent, vessel held by enthroned king.

1104. Hematite. 22×12/11(concave). YBC 12770.

Goddess, angle, god with streams at shoulders standing on boat with in-curved arms, ball staff, worshipper, angle, suppliant goddess, striated disk in crescent, vessel held by enthroned king.

1105. Hematite. 14×8. *Newell* 156. Not shown.

Warrior wielding dagger (chipped) while grasping right shoulder of man on one knee looking back, warrior shouldering axe, ground line.

1106. Hematite. 16½×9. NBC 11030.

Ball staff, two facing men, each on one knee, antelope with two heads on common body.

1107. Hematite. 20×11. YBC 8943.

Full-face bearded belted gods, first grasps spear, second beside spear, third holds human-headed bull, its head turned back against head of human-headed bull held by fourth god, star above reversed human head, erect goat.

For the human-headed bulls see Özgüç, *Seals*, pl. XII. 2A–B.

1108. Reddish brown serpentine. 19×10/9(irregular). Worn NCBS 743.

Lying goat (?), scorpion on back, bull, mace, and male figure on back, two worshippers.

Worn dark gray serpentine, 19×7½/7(irregular) 1108x, NCBS 725, shows three human figures, goat with head turned back, and obscure markings.

1109. Green nephrite. 22×11½/11(cut back in area of altar). NCBS 788.

Male worshipper, angle, crescent above line over enclosed five-level altar containing crescent, crescent above three-angled lines, attendant, two human-headed full-face bearded deified bulls, heads turned back, crescent above each, ground line.

1110. Hematite. 23×13. New Impression. *Newell* 149.

Circle, full-face bearded bullman holding star disk in crescent mounted on striated pole, circle, antelope with head turned back seated on pile of stones, attacked by lion with jaws agape, star disk in crescent above circle, full-face bearded hero, arms at breast, on one knee.

For the scene see Özgüç, *Seals*, pl. 19A; *BN*, 142.

1111. Hematite. 17(bottom lost)×10. *Newell* 169. Not shown.

Lion attacking man on one knee, his head in jaws of liondragon, antelope its head turned back in jaws of lion.

1112. Hematite. 17½×8½. NCBS 703.

Bush, worshipper, crescent, axe held by male, crescent above head, male worshipper.

1113. Hematite. 13×8½. *Newell* 285. Not shown.

Goat monster, two male worshippers with worshipping god between them.

1114. Hematite. 19×9. YBC 9697.

Male worshipper, worshipping god, male worshipper with foot on head of lion.

1115. Pale green limestone. 20½×11. YBC 12831.

Two worshippers, crescent over two vessels on curved stand with two angled legs, ball staff, bull with protuberance on back over elongated rectangle on scorpion, erect snake (?).

1116. Dark brown limonite. 16×9. *Newell* 283. Not shown.

Hero grasping lion by rear foot and tail, his left foot on its head, worshipper, bull with protuberance on back, line beneath.

1117. Hematite. 15×8. *Newell* 286. Not shown. Özgüç, *Anatolian*, p. 45, n. 6.

Two heros, each grasping erect lion.

Worn hematite, 17½×9, 1117x, YBC 12815, scene as in 1117.

1118. Hematite. 23×11. Worn. New impression. *Newell* 282. Özgüç, *Anatolian*, p. 45, n. 6.

Worshipper, ball staff, deity, all over lion attacking goat with head turned back; four animals with reins before and above them, drawing god in chariot with two wheels shown underneath, animal below, crossed goats with animal shapes below.

On the harnessed animals as horses see Özgüç, *Anatolian*, p. 67, n. 4.

1119. Hematite. 23×11. Worn below. New impression. *Newell* 284. Özgüç, *Anatolian*, p. 45, n. 6, p. 67, n. 4, no. 99.

Four animals drawing chariot as in 1118 (wheels ruined); crescent on vase shape, bull with crude cross over back, line below, two full-face bearded deified dwarfs, each on one knee, with angle-topped rod between them.

1120. Hematite. 23½×13. Worn, split through middle. NCBS 870.

Bull altar (?), horizontals at chest, over lying outstretched lion (?); ball staff, seated worshipper, circle, seated monkey (?), all over lying ibex with head turned back; double lightning fork on long rein coming from mouth of winged dragon, on which stands bearded god who grasps the rein near top, ball staff.

1121. Dark gray reddish hematite. 21×9. NBC 8918.

Running male over male on one knee; fly and angle before lying animal over which is bird (?), all over seated animal, and male monster on one knee; seated animal before fly over god on lying animal; lying animal over animal, rod before lying goat with head turned back.

1109

1110

1112

1114

1115

1118

1119

1120

1121

1122

1123

1124

1125

1126

1128

1122. Hematite. 21×9. NBC 7819.

God with knobbed rod before him holding crescent-topped staff, standing on lying animal, crouching animal before him, tall cup held by god standing on hare, bull attacked from below by archer with foot on seated male, animal above gazelle with head turned back on second seated male.

1123. Hematite. 19×10. NBC 7827.

Crescent enclosing animal heads over bracket on pole, held by male with dagger; in field: fish, star, birds, various animals, seated monkeys over each other.

1124. Green jasper. 19×12½/12(concave). YBC 12494.

Worshipper, worshipper led by goddess, star disk in crescent above ball staff beside vessel, cup held by bearded king on cushioned throne, erect goat with head turned back held by nude hero.

Closely resembles the design in Kienast, *Alt-assyrische Texte*, fig. 6.

1125. Hematite. 25×12. Chipped. NBC 6020.

Worshipper, lying goat in outline above sidewise animal, vessel held by seated bearded "king" on pedestal, small male on one knee over upturned bull, hind leg and tail in grasp of full-face horned bearded bullman with right foot on the bull's head, star before, small striding man behind.

1126. Hematite. 23×14/13(concave). NBC 8391.

Worshipper, star over three dots, god, scimitar behind, holding by handle rod topped by bent trident, left foot on crowned dragon, three dots in field, star disk in crescent, vessel held by bearded "king" on throne, full-face bearded hero grasping erect lion (head chipped), two dots between them.

On the Syrianized Colony style see *Kültepe 1949*, IV, pp. 234–36, especially seals 697–700.

1127. Dark brownish limonite. 21×11. *Newell* 183. Not shown.

Personage with mace (?), dot, suppliant goddess, vessel over ball staff, worshipper, lying animal over fish, vessel held by enthroned "king," blunt-ended rod.

1128. Hematite. 20×13. Chipped. NBC 10985.

Worshipper between two suppliant goddesses, angle before each, star disk in crescent, vessel held by seated "king," crossed bulls.

FIGS. 1122–1128

1129. Hematite. 17×12. YBC 9704.

Worshipper holding vase, fly, suppliant goddess, ball staff, worshipper, vessel, vase held by enthroned "king," fish above fish.

1130. Hematite. 20×11. YBC 9667.

Suppliant goddess; male worshipper, star disk in crescent, rod held by "king" enthroned on niched pedestal.

1131. Hematite. 16½×8½. NBC 11041.

Suppliant goddess, worshipper, vase held by "king" (worn hat) on throne.

Similar scene, but with disk in crescent, throne on pedestal, inscription, *CANES,* 878.

1132. Hematite. 21×10. Worn. *Newell* 200. Not shown.

Worshipper, spade, attendant with kid, fly, personage, vessel above ball staff, suppliant goddess.

1133. Dark brown limonite. 18½×8½. *Newell* 193. Not shown. Kupper, *Amurru,* p. 20, no. 2a.

Personage with mace, suppliant goddess, vessel above ball staff, worshipper, star above fish, crook held by god with foot on pile of stones, ball staff with circular center.

1134. Limonite. 26×13. Worn. NBC 12013.

Erect lion in grasp of full-face bearded bullman, male head between them, star above; suppliant goddess, vessel above open-work ball staff, bearded worshipper, rod held by god with right foot on striated pedestal.

1135. Hematite. 19×11. NBC 8408.

Worshipper, sword held by god with right leg raised, suppliant goddess, vessel above ball staff, worshipper, fish, crescent on rod held by god shouldering weapon, his right foot forward.

1136. Hematite. 17½×9. NBC 8915.

Suppliant goddess, three dots, worshipper, two dots, knobbed rod held by god, his right foot on pedestal, star disk in crescent; inscription.

1137. Hematite. 24×11/10(concave). YBC 9670.

Suppliant goddess, star, worshipper, star disk in crescent, sword held by god, his right foot on pedestal, ground line.

1129

1130

1131

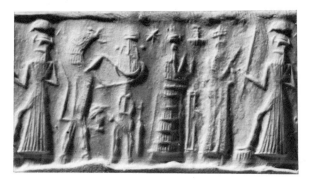

1134

1135

1136

1137

1139   1142

1143

1144

1145

1138. Hematite. 16×8. *Newell* 202. Not shown.

Worshipper, personage, crescent, goddess (?), ground line.

1139. Hematite. 22×8. NBC 3164.

Worshipper, personage with mace, goddess (?) (worn hat); inscription.

1140. Hematite. 21½×9½. *Newell* 227. Not shown.

Personage with mace, bull, crescent, staff held by god, two small worshippers, one over other, ground line; inscription.

For god holding crescent staff, *CANES*, 875–77.

1141. Hematite. 23½×10½. Chipped. *Newell* 236. Not shown.

Personage, crook (on head?) of squatting dog, chipped, small figure; inscription.

1142. Hematite. 25½×12½. Chipped. YBC 12777.

Double lightning fork on long rein coming from mouth of bull on which stands god, who grasps the rein near top while wielding bent weapon, star before it, on either side suppliant goddess; worshipper, vase between volutes on dagger-tipped spear with rein held near top by god, scimitar behind him, his right foot on animal, which has the rein at mouth.

Double lightning fork held by god, *CANES*, 867–68, in latter he also wields bent weapon. For a vase between volutes see Özgüç, *Seals*, pl. XV, B, p. 48.1.

1143. Hematite. 24½×10. Chipped. NBC 5935.

Male head, trident lightning fork attached by rein to bull, also held by god on back of the bull, which is mounted on guilloche; star disk in crescent, worshipping god; small god on one knee, streams from arms at waist, guilloche, facing males their forearms crossed, ground line; inscription (spade in first column, vessel above ball staff in second).

1144. Hematite. 24×13. New impression. *Newell* 226. Kupper, *Amurru*, p. 20, no. 1a, fig. 22.

Phallic dwarf, nude female, head left, crook held by god, crescent over fly, deity, star above "mongoose" (?), worshipper; all four major figures on backs of goats.

1145. Gray brown jasper. 23×13/12½(irregular). NCBS 704. *Yale Library Gazette* 43 (1968), pl. II.4.

Ibex above scorpion, ball staff, lying goat attacked by lion, animal above scorpion beside fly, all above reversed; phallic dwarf, star, feeding humped bull, spade, human monster with legs and fish body, crook, bull, linear borders.

FIGS. 1146–1149

Cappadocian impressions, mostly of cylinder seals (a few with stamp seals), are shown according to their order in the present catalogue, the classification of each indicated separately. 1146, Old Assyrian, A, enthroned "king," B, bull with protruding back; 1147, A, mostly Old Babylonian with probable Cappadocian additions, B, Old Assyrian, enthroned "king" on human-headed bulls; 1148, Old Assyrian, enthroned "king"; 1149, A, Old Babylonian, crossed lions, B–C, Old Assyrian, enthroned "king" . . . goddess; 1150, Old Assyrian, enthroned "king" (four times); 1151–52, Syro-Cappadocian, nude females; 1153, A, Syro-Cappadocian, enthroned winged god, B–D, varied stamps; 1154, Syro-Cappadocian, winged nude goddess and enthroned winged god; 1155, Anatolian, enthroned god with streams; 1156, Old Assyrian, enthroned "king"; 1157, Provincial Babylonian, god on bull; 1158, Old Babylonian, row of divine figures; 1159, A, Old Babylonian with Cappadocian inscription, B–C, Old Assyrian, god holding lightning forks on bull . . . enthroned "king"; 1160, Anatolian, god on bull and enthroned god; 1161, bird stamp seal, Old Assyrian (?), . . . jagged creatures; 1162, Old Assyrian (?), bull on altar; 1163, Anatolian, enthroned "king"; 1164, Old Assyrian, enthroned "king"; 1165, Old Babylonian with Cappadocian inscription, enthroned "king."

1146. Envelope. A–height 16 ext., B–height 18 ext. (a) Reverse below (A), (b) Left side (B). NBC 1845 (*BIN* 4, 161, pl. LXXXIIa).

A–Worshipper, ball staff, god, vase, goddess, small figure above scorpion, vessel held by "king" on cushioned throne, three (?) men on line over three male worshippers.

B–Disk in crescent above small worshipper, suppliant goddess, ball staff, male worshipper with arms at waist; three circles over scorpion before bull with protuberance on back, circle (or two) extending in ropelike semicircle over and behind the bull, all on line over three worshippers, inscription, two erect lions in conflict, staff between them.

1147. Envelope. A–height 18½, B–height 22. (a) Reverse below (A), (b) Obverse below (B). NBC 1846 (*BIN* 4, 110, pl. LXXXId; also pl. LXXXIIc).

A–Lion attacking bull with head up, small male figure reversed over dot, suppliant god, vessel above small worshipper, worshipper with arms at waist, crescent, stand with three angled legs, two circles, vessel held by "king" on cushioned throne.

B–Worshipper with arms at waist, angle, deity, angle, worshipper, vessel above ball staff, all over two lying animals with heads turned back, god wielding sword, two-headed lion beneath, star, bird, pile of loaves on stand with four angled legs, star disk in crescent, angle, vase held by "king" on cushioned stool over two full-face human-headed bulls lying back to back, erect goat.

1147x, NBC 1883, *BIN* 6, 160, pl. LXXX.7, reverse, height 21, Provincial Babylonian, shows a worshipper led by a goddess, suppliant goddess, cross disk in crescent above small figure, deity on altar throne. *BIN* 6, 160, pl. LXXX.5, side somewhat similar, top lost.

1148. Half envelope. Height 23. Face below. NBC 1884 (*BIN* 4, pl. LXXXIb). Also on NBC 1880, 1882, 3729, 3899. *Inscriptions Kültepe* II, Ka 462, p. 39, Old Assyrian, add *Aulock*, 334b.

Small male figures over each other, two angles above two full-face human-headed bulls with heads turned back on line over lying lion; worshipper, star, goddess, angle beside cross disk in crescent above spray, cup held by "king" on cushioned stool.

1149. Envelope. A–height ext. 20, B–height ext. 13, C–height c. 15, (a) Obverse (A), (b) Reverse (B), (c) Bottom (C). NBC 1892 (*BIN* 4, 210, pl. LXXXVc, pl. LXXXIVc. Not shown *BIN* 4, pl. LXXXVc, top reverse; see *Kültepe 1949*, 666, p. 230, "reworked Ur III").

A–Two crossed lions with bull, its head turned back, inscription on either side.

B–Two belted nude full-face heroes with full-face bullman between them, three (?) drillings in field, worshipper, suppliant goddess, star above ball staff over table with offerings (?), cross disk in crescent over cup held by "king" on cushioned stool.

C–Worshipper led by goddess, vessel above ball staff between them, dotted crescent above scorpion, seated goddess, vertical line, two worshippers (second reversed), column with two goat's heads opposed above vessel.

1146a

1146b

1147a

1147b

1148

1149a

1149b

1149c

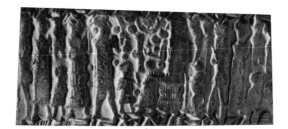

1150a

1150b

1150c

1150d

1151

1152a

1152b

1153a

1153b

1153c

1153d

1150. Envelope. A–height c. 20, B–height c. 16, C–height ext. 15, D–height c. 15. (a) Face obverse (A), (b) Reverse bottom (B), (c) Reverse top (C), (d) Right side (D). NBC 1902 (*BIN* 4, 206, pl. LXXXIIIa). C = *Inscriptions Kultépé* II, Ka 464 B, p. 40, Old Assyrian.

A–Worshipper, two small worshippers one over other, suppliant goddess, god raising sword, star disk in crescent above vessel, beside ball staff over small worshipper, vase held by "king" on cushioned stool, sidewise goat (?) with head turned back above sidewise lion, against upright long weapon with herringbone shapes at top, curved bottom, nude belted hero, ten or more drillings in field.

B–Full-face nude belted hero, ball staff, suppliant goddess, worshipper, hands at waist, second suppliant goddess, star disk in crescent above vessel, cup held by "king" on cushioned stool, erect goat with head turned back.

C–Suppliant goddess, ball staff, worshipper, disk in crescent above small reversed figure, two drillings, cup held by "king" on cushioned stool, inscription.

D–Worshipper, goddess, second worshipper, and goddess, star disk in crescent above ball staff and vessel, cup held by "king" on cushioned stool, snake.

1151. Envelope. Height 20. Bottom shown. NBC 1905 (*BIN* 4, 42, pl. LXXXIVe). *Inscriptions Kultépé* II, Ka 626, p. 51, Syro-Cappadocian.

Two bowlegged dwarfs head to head, nude female facing right, angle above two vertical fish, indeterminate animal above lying goat with head turned back, over lying bull above small lizard (?) over lying lion, bird above ball staff above fish, worshipper in open robe, star, suppliant goddess, star disk in crescent above vessel above scorpion, vase held by "king" on cushioned stool, feet on niched pedestal, vertical snake (?).

1152. Envelope. A–height c. 15, B–height 15. (a) Left side (A), (b) Obverse (B). NBC 1906 (*BIN* 4, 114, pl. LXXXIId).

A–Nude female with pigtail, circle in middle, snake, reverse nude female, circle in middle, suppliant goddess, worshipper, suppliant goddess, star disk in crescent, king with cup on board under right arm on cushioned stool.

See the Syrianized nude female in *Kültepe 1949*, 694, p. 234.

B–Worshipper, suppliant goddess, striated disk in crescent, king with cup on cushioned stool, two birds over male head, scorpion, lying goat with head turned back, lying lion.

1153. Envelope. A–height 16, B–diam. 17/15½, C–diam. 12/9, D–14×12 ext. (a) Obverse top (A), (b) Reverse top (B), (c) Top edge (C), (d) Bottom (D). NBC 1907 (*BIN* 4, 208, pl. LXXXIc (A–B), *BIN* 6, pl. LXXXI.40 (C–D); pl. LXXXI.38 omitted, odd marks).

A–Two small human figures above lying sheep, reversed over full-face bearded head; suppliant goddess with ribbon down back, seated monkey (?) above rampant goat with head turned back, god holding saw and suspended hare, man holding human head in left hand on one knee over object, star disk on crescent over bird, cup held by god with rays at shoulders seated on high-backed altar-throne, inscription.

B–Swirl of five animal-like shapes connected by lines.

C–Four dot-in-circle devices.

D–Four-petal rosette in square.

1153x, NBC 3796, *BIN* 6, 19, height 19, fragment, trace of figure, inscription, worshipper, vessel above stand with three vertical projections, god with weapon on right shoulder, ground line.

1153xx, NBC 3824, *BIN* 6, 10, pl. XLIa-g, height c. 19, all same seal, showing god on lying lion, god on dragon (?), god on full-face lying human-headed bull, bull on line above lying lion over two small worshippers.

1154. Fragment of envelope. Height 17. NBC 3843 (*BIN* 4, pl. LXXXIIe).

Bull with protuberance on back, beside flaming vessel on thick stand, horizontal line with vertical beside small worshipper holding kid, vase receiving libation from worshipper with pigtail, ball staff, nude female looking right holding drapery behind her, seated monkey above rampant gazelle with head turned back over prone man above whom stands god with saw, two circles in field, cross disk in crescent above lying goat (?), over small man with bent knees holding cup (?); god with outstretched right hand, scimitar on left shoulder, high backed altar-throne, star.

1155. Same impression on several envelopes and fragments. Height 20. NBC 3847 (*BIN* 4, pl. LXXXVe, pl. LXXXIVa). NBC 3938 (*BIN* 4, pl. LXXXIVb). Also on NBC 1880, 1882, 3711, 3748, 3887, 3890, 3933, 3936, 3992. *Inscriptions Kultépé* II, Ka 270, p. 35, Anatolian; add *Aulock*, 334a; *Kültepe 1949*, pp. 238f., n. 499, 715; Özgüç, *Anatolian*, V, 14, p. 77.

God with tassel on crown, holding lightning fork and rein from bull on which he stands, star disk in crescent over frog (?), deity in peaked crown with streams to either side coming from vase at chest, seated on cushioned stool over lying gazelle; reversed small male with bent legs under spear, its point down, with crossed parallel lines in right hand of hero with axe over left shoulder, standing on prone captive, square object over fox (?), head down with fish behind it, at bottom human heads and other objects; reversed bull, its leg held by hero grasping dagger, his right leg on its head; two stars, three angles, four drillings in field.

1156. Fragment of envelope. Height 16. NBC 3845 (*BIN* 4, pl. LXXXIIf, *BIN* 6, pl. LXXXI.22 a–b). *BIN* 6, pl. LXXXI.25, like this but with added bull.

Two small worshippers above two more, suppliant goddess, vessel above fish (?) beside ball staff, worshipper, second suppliant goddess, cross disk in crescent above fish, cup held by "king" on cushioned stool.

1156x, NBC 3893, *BIN* 6, LXXXI.32, side, height ext. 15, showing seated "king" with cup, two full-face human-headed bulls with heads turned back held by full-face hero on either side. 6, LXXX.14, face above, height ext. 13, three worshippers; 6, LXXXI.26, face below, height ext. 7, goddess; inscription.

1157. Fragment of envelope. Height ext. 17. NBC 3894 (*BIN* 4, pl. LXXXIVg).

Worshipper with kid before god with saw in ascending posture, suppliant goddess (?), personage, seated monkey above four

drillings, god holding lightning fork and rein of bull on which he stands, ball staff.

1157x, NBC 3895, *BIN* 6, 28, fragment, height ext. 14, showing bull altar on niched platform over lying lion with jaws agape also on niched platform, globular vessel on edge of stand. Shown opposed: *Inscriptions Kultépé* I, LXX C, II Ka 83 B, p. 59; (both shown reversed), Anatolian.

1157xx, NBC 3896, *BIN* 6, p. 4 (6 and bottom, *TMH* I, pl. 32–33, 333 B a.); fragments A–B, height c. 19, worshipper, suppliant goddess, "king" with cup, inscription, two belted men above two more.

1157xxx, NBC 3898. Fragments, *BIN* 6, LXXX.9, height 14 ext., goddess holding rod on cushioned stool, ball staff, suppliant goddess; LXXXI.33, height 8 ext., full-face bearded heroes opposed on one knee. (*Inscriptions Kultépé* II, p. 47, Ka 538, 589 C, 708, Old Assyrian.)

1157xxxx, NBC 3900, *BIN* 6, 4c; NBC 3902, *BIN* 6, 4 a–b, p. 29, height c. 20., poorly shown, worshipper, suppliant goddess, cup held by "king" on cushioned stool.

1157xxxxx, NBC 3981. Fragments, *BIN* 6, 226, LXXX.3 a–b, LXXXI.29, 36, height 11 ext., two worshippers.

1157xxxxxx, NBC 3990. Fragment, *BIN* 6, 27, height c. 18, showing disk in crescent, cup held by "king" on cushioned stool, bull, indistinct objects.

1158. Fragment of envelope. Height ext. 17. NBC 3894 (*BIN* 4, pl. LXXXIVg). *Inscriptions Kultépé* II, pp. 50f., Ka 618, Old Babylonian. Kienast, *Altassyrische Texte*, seal 31, p. 111, fig. 13 (top reverse) — fig 14 (bottom).

Full-face goddess, arrows at shoulders, leaning on scimitar, holding bow at left shoulder and mace at waist, her left foot on head of lying lion; suppliant goddess, worshipper with kid, disk with central circle above saw held by god, his right foot on small stand, priest with sprinkler and pail on platform, ground line.

1158x, NBC 3994, *BIN* 6, LXXX.21, height c. 20, suppliant goddess, worshipper, second goddess, cup held by "king" on cushioned stool over boat; inscription.

1158xx, NBC 3995, *BIN* 6, LXXX.18, height 18 ext., fragment, two worshippers, suppliant goddess, seated goddess (?), bull over two crossed lions.

1158xxx, NBC 3997. Fragments, *BIN* 6, LXXX.17, height 12 ext., inscription, full-face bearded horned bullman, worshipper; *BIN* 6, XXXI.34, height 12 ext., suppliant goddess, seated animal over seated hare (?), worshipper, cup held by seated god.

1154

1155

1156

1157

1158

1159a

1159b

1159c

1160

1161b

1161a

1162

1159. Envelope. A–height 17 ext., B–height c. 13, C–height c. 15. (a) Side (A), (b) Obverse below (B), (c) Reverse (C). NBC 4013 (*BIN* 4, 211, pl. LXXXIIIc, pl. LXXXVa; *BIN* 6, pl. LXXX.13). *TCL* 21, 45, 247B (A).

A–Full-face nude bearded hero with vase at waist from which streams flow on either side, suppliant goddess, inscription (first line mirror writing), worshipper, inscription (second line mirror), cup held by "king" on cushioned stool.

B–Suppliant goddess, worshipper, second goddess, god holding two lightning forks and rein of bull on which he stands, bird with head turned back; angle and seven drillings in field.

C–Bull altar with protuberance on back, star above over oblong shape, below perhaps bullman between two full-face heroes, worshipper facing left, suppliant goddess, vase above ball staff, worshipper, second goddess, star disk in crescent between two angles above scorpion, cup held by "king" on cushioned stool.

1160. Envelope. Height c. 18. Obverse(part). NBC 4014 (*BIN* 4, 209, pl. LXXXVd). *BIN* 6, pl. LXXXI.24 a-b = Porada, *Nuzi*, p. 99, 4 (Anatolian), n. 195 = *Inscriptions Kültepé* I, pl. LXV, 35a C. *BIN* 4, pl. LXXXIVf, height 13 ext., side, three worshippers, bull altar with protuberance. *BIN* 6, pl. LXXX.15, height 10 ext., side, obscure details; pl. LXXXI.37, top reverse, diam. 7, four head (?)-shaped marks.

God whose right hand grasps rein stretched forward to mouth of bull on which he stands, he holds cup in left hand before which are disk in crescent and half-reared goat (?) with head turned back, tall stand before the god, erect liondemon (?) before the bull; worshipper carrying spouted vessel, goat fish above, tall table with offerings before vessel held by god in pointed hat seated on altar throne; god shouldering whip while holding (?) bird with head turned back, on stag with throwing stick (?) above it, animal (?) under its head; angled object on right side of which are four tall linear, thin horizontal projections.

1161. Envelope. A–20×15 ext., B–height c. 12. (a) Side (A), (b) Obverse top (B). NBC 4015 (*BIN* 6, 186, pl. LXXX.16 [A], pl. LXXX.35 a [B]). Not shown BIN 6, pl. LXXX.1 a, bottom obverse, height 15 ext., figures obscure; *BIN* 4, pl. LXXXVb, reverse, height c. 14, worshippers, cup held by seated king, obscure animals.

A–Bird with head turned back, only one leg, ovals at side.

B–Crude figures and animals.

1162. Envelope. Height 15 ext. Obverse below. NBC 4018 (*BIN* 4, 207, pl. LXXXIIb, side; BIN 6, pl. LXXXI.30 a-b). *Inscriptions Kültepé* I, 21 Rev. E. Not shown *BIN* 6, pl. LXXXI.23 a-b, height 20 ext., inscription, deities, details; pl. LXXXL.31 a-b, height 16 ext., obscure details.

Full-face nude belted hero, suppliant goddess, nude female with head left, carrying vessel in each hand, god with saw ascending over prostrate big-headed dwarf, bull on vertical doubly striated altar, ground line.

1162x, NBC 4033, BIN 6, pl. LXXX.11, height c. 15. fragments, suppliant goddess, worshipper, second goddess.

1163. Fragment of envelope. Height c. 15. Obverse. NBC 4034 (*BIN* 6, 223, pl. LXXX.6).

Goddess (leading worshipper?), cross disk in crescent above three drillings, cup held by "king" on cushioned stool on platform, two crossed lions, drilling between them, full-face nude belted hero, erect snake, trace of worshipper.

1163x, NBC 6569, *BIN* 6, pl. LXXX.8, fragment, height 17 ext., worshipper, suppliant goddess, cup held by "king" on cushioned stool, two small worshippers facing crossed lions.

1164. Fragment of envelope. Height 18. NBC 6572 (*BIN* 6, pl. LXXX.2 a-b). *Inscriptions Kültépé* I, LVI 20a, Rev. D, LXXIII, 74a, Rev. D.

Hero holding crescent standard, worshipper led by goddess, vessel above ball staff between them, cross disk in crescent above two drillings, cup held by "king" on cushioned stool, full-face bearded nude hero with hands at waist.

1165. Fragment of envelope. Height 20. NBC 6599 (*BIN* 6, p. 4 [5] = *TCL* 21, pl. CCXXXIII, 46, p. 5).

Full-face nude bearded hero with vase at waist from which streams flow to either side, inscription (first line mirror writing), suppliant goddess, inscription (second line mirror), worshipper with hands at waist, star beside cross disk in crescent above vessel over ball staff, cup held by king on cushioned throne on platform, small worshipper facing left over second one facing right, ground line.

1163

1164

1165

1166

1167

1170

1171

1172

1173

1175

Syria

PROVINCIAL

The group, called Provincial Syrian, may include pieces also derived from Palestine or Anatolia. Their date should be around 2000 B.C. The so-called Levantine cylinders, 1166–67, may be placed in the early second millennium. Those shown feature men and birds. Somewhat earlier are 1168 showing a creature between two figures; 1169, a row of crude men; and 1170, figures and an animal. Also early come 1171–73 with men and twisted animals; 1174–75 show a seated figure drinking before an animal on an altar.

1166. Brown limestone. 14½×8. Chipped. NCBS 752.

Bird over bird, two men with exaggerated right hands, bush between them, linear borders.

For 1166–67 see *JAOS* 89 (1969), p. 761; Alp, *Zylinder- und Stempelsiegel*, pp. 128–30, no. 26–32; to be called Levantine rather than Anatolian.

1167. Brown limestone. 16½×9½. Chipped. NBC 11064.

Bird over bird, vertical line, point at bottom, irregular pole made up of vertical lines and spaced blobs on which rests right arm of figure in striated robe, twisted snake (?), enclosed vertical marked lines, linear borders.

1168. "Steatite." 16½×8. *Newell* 56. Not shown.

Rectangle doubly divided with vertical lines above and below, man holding (?) neck harness of horse (?) with head turned back, man, linear borders.

1169. Dark gray serpentine. 17×10. *Newell* 287. Not shown.

Rider on horse (?), man holding ball-topped pole, man with arms up and down, another man with left arm up (?).

1170. Black serpentine. 15½×9. NBC 12065.

Figure holding spade up, oblong shape (fake cuneiform?) over lying goat before plant, figure.

1171. Dark mottled red serpentine. 22×11/10 (irregular). NBC 10986.

Goat with two heads turned back, common neck but two bodies, heads encircled by jagged lines, jagged line to left, man holding lying goat with head turned back.

For style see *Weber*, 278a, *CANES*, 1091–92.

1172. "Steatite." 16×9. NBC 10952.

Erect animals connected by lines to central line, star behind head of each, man, crescent above mask on pole, second man, scorpion above squatting animal.

Aulock, 273, diorite, seated figure, standing male and animal reversed.

1173. Dark green serpentine. 16×8. NBC 8319.

Two antelope heads looking back on common body, cross disk in crescent between them, male head on either side; spade pointed down on long handle, two worshippers with mask (?) on angle-topped rod between them.

For curved animal heads see Ravn, *Copenhagen*, 141.

1174. "Steatite." 32×15. *Newell* 279. Not shown. *Frankfort*, pl. XL k.

Seated man holding tube to big vessel, vase beside ball staff between them; crescent over hatched bush, bull lying in partly enclosed, doubly lined, vertically marked manger, linear borders.

Of similar design see Dunand, *Fouilles de Byblos*, pl. CXXIV, 2337.

1175. "Steatite." 22½×11. Worn. NCBS 702.

Canopy over animal on multilinear altar, crescent above attendant who holds pipe going from vessel to mouth of seated figure, vessel above ball staff before latter.

FIGS. 1176–1181

Syro-Cappadocian cylinders of early 19th-century date present columns of various creatures, 1176–77; or heads and animals in the two lower rows, while above a prone male is attacked by two lions, 1178; a group of figures centered on a spread-legged female, 1179; or holy figures and a two-headed pedestal beside which stands a deity, 1180. A similar pedestal stands between two figures, 1181; a man grasps an animal, 1182; kneeling griffins are shown in possible combat, 1183–84; warriors, gods, and animals occur in various poses, 1185; finally, a row of worshippers standing before a hero under an arch, 1186.

1176. Hematite. 22×13½. Worn. NBC 10991.

Worn scroll in vertical columns, antelope with head turned back above lying hare beside animal head (?) over bird (?) above lying hare, column of five worn deers' heads, worn column, column of six (?) hares' heads, column of five lions' heads, column of four ibex heads, column of four heroes' heads; linear borders (very worn).

1177. Hematite. 16×9. Worn. NBC 9381.

Column with lying hare over ibex with head turned back, column with lying hares, one over the other, column with bird beside rod with central circle over two lying lions, one over the other, column with two birds, one on the other, over deer with head turned back; linear borders (very worn).

1178. Hematite. 17×11/10½(concave). YBC 12594. *Brett*, 92.

Flying bird attached to tail of lying lion biting at head of prone male attacked at feet by second lying lion, two sections divided in quarters with vase shapes side by side below, linear borders, rope design in middle, linear borders enclose five lying lions (?) between them, dot above four; ten male heads over line below.

1179. Hematite. 24×12/11½(concave). Worn. NBC 7812.

Two demons on knee, each holding rod topped by mace with curved side pieces, winged lying ibex with head turned back, antelope with head turned back, seated spread-legged naked woman holding jagged curve on either side in bent arms, antelope and kneeling winged demon, both with heads turned back; linear border, two rows of horizontally marked circles, horizontal line (worn), six (?) lying animals, nine male heads.

In *Louvre A.*, 931 a spread-legged woman holds jagged curve above, with other figures all below, animals and heads in upper rows.

1180. Hematite. 20×10/9(concave). New impression. *Newell* 312.

Man in long skirt, naked left leg bent forward, star in crescent, facing female (?) figure on niched throne with short thick back; two heads rising from vertically lined pedestal before female figure (bottom of robe flattened); linear borders, rope design in middle, four squatting hares in linear borders, seven male heads on line below; deity with right leg forward, left in long open belted robe.

1181. Hematite. 12½×6. New impression. *Newell* 164.

Warrior holding sword, left leg in long open robe, bare right leg forward, bird, two heads on vertically lined pedestal, female figure, ball staff beside seated monkey over antelope with head turned back, beside rod with mace in middle.

For heads vertically arranged see Seyrig, *Syria* 37 (1960), pp. 233–52 of which three (1, 2, 4) are Syro-Cappadocian, two (14–15) crude Syrian, ten (3, 5–13) good Syrian including 1180–81 cited above. Only one (8) shows a single head.

1176

1177

1178

1179

1180

1181

1182

1183

1184

1185

1186

1182. Hematite. 13×8/7(concave). NBC 7824.

Erect lion, lying hare over lying goat with head turned back, erect lion, animal head (?) below seated animal with mouth and one hand in grasp of man, his right leg exposed, left in long open robe, vertical line with knob at bottom.

1183. Hematite. 13×6½. Gimbel Collection 5.

Belted man, right arm before face, ball staff, facing spread-winged griffin without arms, with kneeling skirted left leg, erect lion, male head before it, long ear over hare's head behind; linear borders.

1184. Hematite. 17×9. Worn. NBC 7818.

Belted man, left hand before face, fish, pick axe raised by warrior, dagger at waist, who holds spear with two ringlets toward bottom, tree with twisted trunk, narrow pine near top, winged griffin on one knee holding spear in right hand, circular blob above seated monkey, linear borders.

1185. Hematite. 19×10. Bore 4½/3, off center. Worn. YBC 12506.

Man with bent legs shooting arrow (?) at seated monkey, menaced by man with axe (?), before him lying winged (?) lion on line attacking ibex; mace with angled sides held by full-face god from which stream flows to animal, on which the god places bare right leg, left in long robe, holding scimitar (?), full-face bearded hero with arms at waist.

1186. Hematite. 14×7. NBC 7530.

Erect ibex with head turned back, two worshippers with right arm before face in long robe, left leg bare, ball staff between them, hero with arms at waist in jagged oval arch on line.

FIGS. 1187–1192

Syrian seals of different dates and miscellaneous types including degraded scenes featuring a figure shouldering a stick, 1187–88; warriors or gods in conflict, 1189–91; warriors facing a griffin, 1192; a seated deity before armed attendants, 1193; groups in combat, 1194–95; warriors struggling over a prone foe, 1196; a row of women, 1197.

1187. Hematite. 16×8. NBC 7820.

Seated winged griffin above seated monkey, two full-face bearded bullmen (chipped above each man's head), nude female with necklace, holding stick behind shoulders between them.

1188. Hematite. 15½×8. NBC 7928.

Two-winged male, figure in long robe, left hand before face, rectangular mass, man with right hand before face, right leg bare, left leg in long robe, rectangular mass above and below, figure with stick behind shoulders, rectangular mass, man in heavy hat, right arm at waist, left leg in long garb, rectangular mass; linear borders.

A stick held behind the shoulders in 1187–88 also appears in *CANES*, 925 (= *Ward*, 882) and *Brett*, 87 (= *Frankfort*, XLII g).

1189. Hematite. 21×9. New Impression. *Newell* 324.

Deity in horned feather (?) crown, head turned back, life sign, striding god in tunic with pigtail, rod raised to right, dagger at waist, chipped by feet; to left, axe, sickle sword, and halter to lying bull, facing winged god, rod to right, dagger at waist, tunic, long skirt to left, ball staff.

1190. Hematite. 20½×8½. New impression. *Newell* 327.

Winged god in horned feather (?) crown, pole on back, axe to left, dagger at waist, tunic, long skirt to right; sickle sword, axe, and halter to lying bull with head turned back, in right hand of horned god with pigtail, raised left arm (chipped), tunic, bird, double twist in two lines, lying winged griffin; linear borders.

1191. Hematite. 15½×6½. New impression. *Newell* 339.

Deity in hat like 1189–90, facing animal, headed (?) axe in right hand, similar hat worn by god, mace (?) in left hand, pigtail, dagger in tunic; two lying hares, divider, bull, linear borders.

1192. Hematite. 17×8½. New impression. *Newell* 315.

Life sign, sickle sword held by man whose left hand at waist holds bent object, crook, man with robe on right leg, left bare, holding reversed hare, winged bird-headed griffin, dotted line to right and left below, linear borders.

1192x, NCBS 731, worn, hematite, 14×7/6½ (irregular), winged griffin (?), two figures.

1187

1188

1189

1190

1191

1192

1193

1194

1195

1196

1197

1193. Hematite. 16×8½. NBC 11051.

Seated monkey, enthroned deity, disk in crescent, staff and spear held by attendants, linear borders.

1194. Hematite. 18½×10½/10(irregular because of deep-cut bodies). Chipped. NBC 10955.

Vertical fish, belted man with spear, V-shape over angled line on base, belted figure in long robe with spear, blob over line with hook, man in long robe, right arm ends in double-lined axe (?), sickle sword raised in left, linear borders.

1195. Hematite. 17½×9. NBC 7826.

Spear in grasp of figure with head turned back, blob at bottom, star, man in tunic holding knobbed rod, mace in ground, figure with hands in middle wearing long robe, spear in grasp of man in tunic, right hand raised by figure in long robe, linear borders.

1196. Hematite. 17½×8½. New impression. *Newell* 152.

Two warriors opposing each other with shields, one to left has weapon above head, other holds weapon behind him, crescent above lying warrior between them; quadruped being shot at by arrow (?) from archer below.

The motif of an animal shot at by an archer occurs in *Ash C,* 492 and *Louvre A.,* 508, while Alp, *Zylinder- und Stempelsiegel,* p. 122, no. 15, fig. 13 shows a bird shot at by an archer.

1197. Pale brown limestone. 23×13½/13(concave). Worn. New impression. *Newell* 222.

Four women looking right, arms at waist; after first, crescent above dot over gatepost (?); after second, goat fish above arms before face over blob; after third, spread-winged eagle above small woman with arms at waist; inscription.

FIGS. 1193–1197

Early or mature Syrian seals should date not later than the 18th century B.C. Two figures kneel on either side of an emblem, 1198; two facing seated figures with crooks beside standing group of three (family?), 1199; holy group, 1200; enthroned figure with vase, 1201; nude female between two seated figures, 1202; enthroned goddess with Egyptian signs, 1203; enthroned figure between Egyptian deities, 1204; attendant with kid before seated figure, 1205; enthroned deity, 1206–10; enthroned full-face god, 1211; armed god on mountains, 1212; god facing scroll with mixed creatures on either side, 1213; full-face god with streaming shoulders, 1214; two holy figures, 1215–17; facing couple in Egyptian garb, 1218; lions and eagle above row of men holding dead animals, 1219; group of three figures of various character, 1220–33; three small figures before obscure facing group, 1234; four holy figures, the last group in combat, 1235–38; full-face "bull"-gods with emblems between them, 1239; nude goddess in garland, 1240–42; winged deities or demons, 1243–47; winged goddess facing human, divine, and animal creatures, 1248.

1198. Hematite. 21×12. Scattered blotches. New impression. *Newell* 165.

Figure in long dress extending handled vase to left, seated on pedestal with three-part vertical sections, facing small long-robed figure; two kneeling figures with necklaces, belts, long robes to rear, facing arms raised, between them disk with cross in crescent over mounted jug with sidewise droplets; faint linear borders.

1199. Hematite. 17½×10. Cracks at left bottom and altar. New impression. *Newell* 656.

Three full-face long-robed belted figures, one to left bearded, one in middle has right and left arms in common with those adjacent; two enthroned long-robed figures extending crooks, between them star over altar; linear borders.

Similar figures with crooks appear in *CANES*, 987.

1200. Hematite. 18×9. NBC 8316.

Worshipper in high hat, right hand at mouth turned left, left hand to right grasps arrows, robe partly open, star, personage with left hand raised, robe partly open, disk in crescent over scorpion, facing suppliant goddess; worshipper before seated figure, attendant behind, scroll between two lines, seated lion attacking seated goat with head turned back.

1201. Hematite. 23×13½. Worn. *Newell* 305. Not shown.

Figure in long robe with left arm raised, marked disk above vertical over horizontal; enthroned figure in long robe holding vase in outstretched left arm, cross disk in crescent, pile of plates on angled stand below bird (?) in outstretched right arm of man with vertically marked tunic, one leg in embroidered robe; scroll over line, disembodied left arm raised, two figures in long robes with adjacent arms crossed.

1201x, YBC 5128, fragment of Nuzi tablet; worship of seated figure, contending men below, inscription, H. ext. 11.

1202. Hematite. 18½×8½. Bore 3½/3 (slightly to one side). NBC 8929.

Spear held upright by full-face bullman, between them line with curved top; on either side enthroned figures in high hats, raised hands, disk in crescent, hand and star before each, one to left shoulders axe, between them nude female facing right, pigtail, left palm turned out; scroll between two lines on each side.

1203. Hematite. 20×9. Blotched at seated figure and signs. NBC 7680.

Figure with vase (?) at waist, left hand before face, in wraparound robe, disk in crescent above life sign, female with right hair coiled down, left hand before face, long robe, star beside disk in crescent, life sign, facing vase held by enthroned goddess on pedestal; Egyptian hieroglyphs.

For different Syrian figures with Egyptian hieroglyphs see *Ward*, 822, p. 273 (= *De Clercq*, 389).

1204. Hematite. 14×7½. New impression. *Newell* 319.

Disk in crescent over head of goddess, left hand raised before face with bird above, before her Egyptian hieroglyph, enthroned figure with right hand at left before face, left hand at waist grasps upbent symbol, feet on niched pedestal, dot in rayed disk in crescent, Egyptian hieroglyph, life sign, right arm extended from uraeus-topped figure in long belted garment, column of dotted scroll in vertical lines, linear borders.

1198

1199

1200

1202

1203

1204

1206

1208

1209

1210

1211

1212

1214

1215

1216

1205. Hematite. 18½×10½. Broken. *Newell* 309. Not shown.

Warrior grasping spear, triple-ringed cup, attendant shouldering crook and carrying kid, triple-ringed cup, enthroned figure with right hand before face, seated dog (?); linear borders.

1206. Hematite. 21×12. Copper pin in bore. Split. YBC 12618.

Enthroned god, palm of right hand shown, on pedestal (?) between two attendants with hand before face; lying antelope with head turned back confronting lying winged sphinx, scroll between two lines, scene as at top.

1207. Hematite. 18×8½. *Newell* 304. Not shown.

Figure, hand before face, in long belted robe, triangle above, oval shape on vertical point below, figure (face marked) enthroned in long robe, extending capped vase, triple-ringed cup over four layers on three-point stand, handled vase in right hand of figure in long robe, rectangle enclosed in lower left hand; dot above bird, scroll, lying rabbit.

1208. Hematite. 16½×9. New impression. *Newell* 306.

Worshipper in long dress holding palm branch, altar, wedge inside crook (?) held by enthroned figure in long dress, pointed top on ball staff, utensil held by figure (head and vicinity chipped) in long dress; bird over dot, scroll between two lines, rabbit (?).

1209. Hematite. 19×10. NBC 7816.

Figure in long dress (feet omitted) holding bent rod, handled vase, double globes over column, vase held by enthroned figure (chipped head) in long dress, double flattened globes on column, double ringed crook held by figure in long dress; bird over bird with scroll between.

1210. Hematite. 22×11. NBC 7810.

Seated griffin over scroll above lying rabbit; figure in long dress with left hand before face, winged disk above bird, vase held by enthroned figure over niched pedestal, palm branch held by pigtailed female, linear borders.

1211. Limonite. 28½×11. Chipped. NBC 11089.

Man with hand before face in long open robe, winged disk over vertically marked dish, cup held by full-face bearded enthroned god with axe (?) at right shoulder, five oval shapes as pedestal, life sign (?), right hand before face of bearded male; nude male on one knee above two facing birds, linear borders.

1212. Hematite. 18×7½. New impression. *Newell* 303. *Ward, 887.*

Suppliant goddess, ribbon down back, circle amidst eight-sided star above fish, man with hand before face in long open robe, disk in crescent above antelope head, spear and axe held by god with long pigtail, under raised left arm holding vase, series of belts over bare legs, each on rocky mount joined in middle, linear borders.

1213. Hematite. 21½×12½. Worn. *Newell* 314. Not shown.

Rod held aloft on right of bearded god extending axe to left, tunic, feet on pile of stones; mixed animals, long scroll, mixed animals and human figures.

1214. Hematite. 17×9. NBC 8409.

Figure in long dress, raised left hand holding vase, bird over notched staff over fish, full-face bearded hero with streams from shoulders to ground, arms at waist, nude legs with outlined fish on either side, crescent before antelope before winged antelope, all over upright spear, antelope with head turned back, kneeling griffin, linear borders.

1215. Hematite. 13×5½. YBC 12580.

Male with right hand to left before face in open robe before god (?) with open palm to right before face; seated lion clawing at lying goat with head turned back, three scrolls, central circle in each, two rabbits, one behind the other.

1216. Hematite. 14×8½. New impression. *Newell* 300.

Man, hand before face, left leg covered (?), scroll in vertical lines, suppliant goddess; facing seated griffins above facing seated lions.

1217. Hematite. 18×10. Worn. NBC 7813.

God with sickle sword in right hand, wearing long open robe, sitting ibex over antelope's head, man with left arm before face to right, in long open robe; gazelle with head turned back, lion, scroll, hawk, sitting winged griffin, bottom edge (in part).

1218. Hematite. 22×15/14 (ends oval). Chipped. NBC 9249.

Crowned goddess with disk in horns, her head turned back, tall vase in right hand, in left undulating stalk topped by blossom, issuing below from coiled snake in crown like the goddess, gazelle's head at top; stalk of lotus flowers held by god in pointed helmet and Egyptian tunic, falcon above and below the lotus, life sign before the tunic; gazelle (?) head over lying humped bull, plant, lion, twist in linear borders, gazelle (?) head over lying stag, plant, lion.

1219. Hematite. 23×11½. NBC 8315. *Ward,* 860.

Kneeling confronted lions, man's head between them, fish, spread eagle (chipped), rabbit; below: three men holding continuous pole by hands behind shoulders, three antelopes tied upside-down in space between; linear borders.

1220. Hematite. 21×12. Faded. Split in middle. YBC 9695.

Confronted women with facing raised hands, between them star disk in crescent over small left-facing male with arms at sides in tunic beside topped oval; lying winged sphinx, seated rabbit, twist with five center dots, two facing humped cattle, rod between them.

1221. Hematite. 22½×10. New impression. *Newell* 298. *Frankfort,* XLIj, pp. 253ff.

Personage with mace at waist; disk in crescent before small suppliant goddess with ribbon down back beside star above antelope's head, all over seated antelope with head turned back attacked by seated lion; suppliant goddess; confronted seated sphinxes, twist with three central dots between vertical lines, confronted seated winged griffins.

1222. Hematite. 20×9. Chipped. YBC 12798.

Worshipper in tall hat, bird (?) above scorpion, god in spiked headdress wearing tunic, holding "bush" in left hand, snake springing from left leg; winged cross disk above angled mark above scorpion, throw stick (?) held by man; squatting winged griffin (?) above scroll with four central dots above lying ibex, ground line, row of six birds.

1217

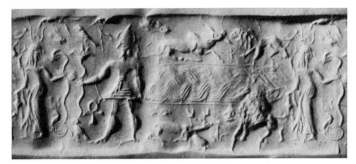

1218

1219

1220

1221

1222

1223

1225

1226

1227

1228

1229

1230

1223. Hematite. 23×13. Chipped. New impression. *Newell* 299.

Full-face bearded hero, stream from left shoulder, suppliant goddess with ribbon down back, crescent above life sign, man with left arm before right face, long open robe on left; squatting sphinx, double globes on column, animal (?), all over line, winged sphinx (?) before goat (?) with head down, all over line, lion on one leg before hump-backed bull.

1224. Hematite. 18×9. *Newell* 332. Not shown.

Figure in long dress, left hand before face, ball staff, woman with long tress, hand and dress as before, fish, long pole with knobbed top held by man in open robe, bird above sidewise antelope with head turned back, linear borders.

1225. Hematite. 17×10. NBC 7811.

Woman, hand before face, star, sickle swords held on opposite sides by men wearing robes, between them seated monkey above antelope's head; seated winged griffin, twist between two lines, lying lion, linear borders.

1226. Hematite. 20½×11½. New impression. *Newell* 316.

Rod held by man in open robe, rabbit head over ball staff over fish, figure in long dress (top and bottom worn), bulging vessel above antelope's head above ball staff, figure in long dress, hand above bulging vessel above ball staff; seated winged griffin, bird above griffin's tail, twist with five central points (?), lying rabbit.

1227. Limonite. 16½×8. New impression. *Newell* 338.

Two women with long tresses, adjacent hands confronted under doubly ringed cup, antelope head before and behind the second woman, palm branch held by figure in long dress; seated winged griffin over line, lying antelope, linear borders.

1228. Hematite. 26½×14. NBC 10990.

Female with long tress holding crook above handled jug, beside doubly oval topped column beside point-topped ring, handled vase held by figure in long dress (defect at base), ball staff, palm branch held by deity in long dress; spread eagle, twist with five central points between two lines, confronted sphinxes; four scattered dots, linear borders.

1229. Hematite. 20×10. New impression. *Newell* 330.

Figure with left hand before face in long dress, pointed dot above ball staff, two figures with hands crossed before faces in long dresses, between them star above column topped by double volute; spread eagle, twist with three central points between lines, lying hare; linear borders.

1230. Hematite. 15½×7½. New impression. *Newell* 317.

Bull demon with bird's head, handled jug above life sign, two men with fists in contact, star above them, two ovals in column below, all figures naked; spread eagle (to right worn), twist with three central dots between lines, lying hare; linear borders (worn).

1231. Hematite. 23×12½. New impression. *Newell* 308.

Suppliant goddess, ribbon down back, cross-hatched dress, fish, intricate design (broken) on rod over right shoulder of figure in elaborate dress (broken below), winged dotted disk in crescent over bird above vertical marks over four (?) loaves on table with horizontal base, god in high headdress and open robe holding sickle sword (?); squatting hare with head turned back attacked by lying winged griffin, twist with three central dots between lines, plant attacked by lion; linear borders (worn).

1232. Hematite. 18½×8½. New impression. *Newell* 307.

Woman in long dress facing woman (face worn) in cross-hatched skirt, handled (?) jug between them, crescent over spear held by bearded hero (worn above) in long vertically marked skirt to left; doubly ringed cup before seated winged griffin, twist with three central dots between lines, bull with head turned down and back.

1233. Hematite. 18×8. NBC 7825.

Man in tall hat, right hand before face to left, open robe, facing man in broad cap, his right hand before face to right, open robe, ball staff between them, god, right hand before face, long dress; seated winged griffin attacking seated ibex with head turned back, twist with three central dots between lines, two figures with confronted hands; linear borders.

1234. Hematite. 22×11. Worn under winged disk. *Newell* 313. Not shown.

Winged goat beside life sign over three attendants in long skirts, eight (?) scrolls in rectangular frame, below hero, left hand before face, tunic, winged disk over animal head beside irregular figure and other strange subjects, dagger over bow held in right hand by man in open robe; linear borders.

1235. Hematite. 19×9½. New impression. *Newell* 333.

Figure in dress, crescent, dagger (?), fish, figures in high hats and long dresses, adjacent hands confronted under cross disk over crescent, crescent to left, scorpion below beside topped tall vase, star over fish, hand before face of deity in pointed hat and long dress, bird over seated hare; linear borders.

1236. Hematite. 20×11. NBC 10956.

Suppliant goddess, ribbon down back, man with right hand before face, open robe, holding in left hand reversed hare, two flattened tips on short rod, attached to semicircle, bent double curves on rod held by man in open robe to left who grasps sickle sword, palmette under which two streams flow from vase held in right hand by god in long dress.

1237. Hematite. 19×10. Worn. *Newell* 340. Not shown.

Man in open robe with left arm raised toward vessel as in 1236, seated monkey underneath, spear held by god in tunic holding sickle sword downward, woman with left arm raised, ball staff, curved rod held by man in open robe.

1238. Hematite. 22×9½. YBC 12779.

Figure in long dress, left hand before face, star above life sign, life sign between two warriors in tunics, raised arms crossed, outside arms pointing dagger at each other, three vertically connected disks, warrior in tunic with kilt below, right arm raised, dagger in left, star in crescent on ridged pole with flat base, life sign below; lines with alternating spaces on each side.

1239. Hematite. 12(bottom lost)×12. YBC 12806.

Full-face goddess with dotted headdress curled at sides, holding in left hand spear topped by twist on each side, figure, hand; full-face heroes with bulls' horns, each holding facing poles with curving tops, between them: fish beside dotted disk over crescent on divided spiral mounted on pole; vertical spiral.

1240. Hematite. 21×10. Worn. NBC 5955.

Figure in long dress holding spear head down, on one side of which is dagger (?), nude goddess with head right, holding up garland behind her, plant, figure (poor) in dress; bird (?) (worn), four-way twist, bird.

1231

1232

1233

1235

1236

1238

1239

1240

1241

1242

1243

1244

1245

1246

1247

1248

1241. Hematite. 17×9. NBC 7814.

Man with right hand left before mouth, in open robe, dagger, bird over each end of garland held up behind her by nude goddess looking left, standing on lying bull, figure in open robe with hand before mouth, left hand crossed toward the bull's horns; lying winged griffin, three-way twist between two lines, lying lion; linear borders.

1242. Hematite. 21×9. NBC 7926.

Leaves at ends of garland held behind her in two sections by nude goddess looking left, wings at shoulders, approached by three men in girdles, arms behind backs, striding legs crossed; linear borders.

1243. Hematite. 16×8½. New impression. *Newell* 320.

Figure in long dress raising left hand, right arm across body holding doubly capped staff, god in Egyptian crown wearing belt and girdle, left arm bent up, small bird, winged deity in long open robe looking right, low standard with four hands (?), male with right arm bent up (scratch behind it), belted with legs nude; vertical scroll with four central and six outside circles, linear borders.

1244. Hard dark gray stone. 18×10. NBC 9368.

Winged liondemon with serpent rising right over head, arms on either side, in girdle with fringes between legs, horned animal head, man in open robe with arm behind him, figure with arm before face in open robe, hare's head, crook held forward by man in tunic, sickle sword down to left, bird above; linear borders.

1245. Hematite. 16×7. New impression. *Newell* 322.

Liondemon holding dagger at right side, two roughly clad legs, down-swept mace (?) at waist, standard with two vertical hands (?), spear with point down held near top by winged god in open robe, sickle sword by left side; figure with angled dress, bird above lying ibex, linear borders.

1246. Hematite. 22×10½. New impression. *Newell* 325.

Man with right hand before face, small animal on left arm, to right open robe, spear point down, held to right by winged god in high vertical and horizontal hat, mace at waist with tunic and fringe to left, vertical double disk, inverted crook held by man in dress; squatting animal (botched) opposed by seated winged griffin above upright antelopes with heads turned back, linear borders.

1247. Hematite. 26½×13. YBC 12775.

Suppliant goddess, dagger beside scorpion, sickle sword (?) to right, carried by winged demon (?) in open robe, holding reversed antelope, crossed disk in crescent, sickle sword (?) to right carried by man with open robe to left; hand over back of lying sphinx, twist with three central dots between vertical lines, hand over back of seated lion; linear borders.

1248. Hematite. 28×16. Cracked in middle. New impression. *Newell* 311.

Goddess with long hair, her wings facing left, above her elaborate hair before animal twist (worn) ending in part rectangle; two winged griffins, each on one knee, one holds spear to left, other crook outward, between them narrow vase with double top, about twelve twists between lines, three men in girdles with crossed legs, two horizontal lines, seated lion; small man in belted tunic beside spread eagle above man holding curved bracket to left, three-leaved plant in grasp of man, both men in open robes, between them life sign.

ANIMALS

FIGS. 1249–1259

A few Syrian seals present only animals, 1249–52, with twists in the last three. A few show human beings as a minor element in animal scenes, scrolls in 1253–55, a divider in 1256, a circular twist in 1257.

1249. Hematite. 17×8½. New impression. *Newell 452.*

Two erect ibexes, their heads turned back, tree between them; seated winged griffin beside fish over lying hare, all over bull, linear borders.

1250. Hematite. 20×10. Worn. YBC 9690.

Four hares, one antelope between them, all lying; fourteen twists between lines; seated winged griffin, small lying animal, seated lion, second griffin, vertical triple disk; linear borders.

1251. Hematite. 19½×9½. *Newell 347.* Not shown. *Ward, 1036.*

Three humped bulls; fourteen twists with dot in center of each between lines; three lions, linear borders.

1252. Hematite. 16×8. *Newell 349.* Not shown.

Two scorpions; eight twists with dot in center of each; bird, two antelopes with heads down; in vertical lines, seven twists probably with central dots, linear borders.

1253. Limonite. 18½(broken below)×13½. *Newell 342.* Not shown.

Small figure, two crouching lions, each with foreleg crossed over male head; fabulous monster, on each side of which is belted man on one knee holding spear downwards, outside of the men, rearing antelope with head turned back; rope pattern between lines; three animals to right, opposing pair to left, birds (?) above, top edge.

1254. Hematite. 18½×8½. New impression. *Newell 346.*

Kid held by girdled man on one knee facing winged sphinx, reversed antelope with neck stepped on by foreleg of lion; on both sides twists, set between upper and lower edges.

1255. Hematite. 19½×11½. Worn. *Newell 344.* Not shown.

Animal(?)-shape, two confronted winged demons, two seated winged beasts; fifteen twists; animal shapes, seated hare, archer on one knee shooting at lion striding over prostrate beast.

1256. Hematite. 23½×13½. New impression. *Newell 348.*

Seated ibex with head turned back, plant, bird, second ibex, sharp wedge above vertical triple disk, between them right leg of sphinx above and below which are bulls' heads, hare's head; divider; ibex, bird (?) above, treelike design, girdled male with arms and legs spread, wedge above animal head, vertical triple disk over charging bull, bird's head, bird; upper and lower edge.

1257. Hematite. 14(about ¼ preserved)×13½. YBC 9705.

Circular twist containing two confronted nude men, seated lion and antelope, lower part of dress.

SYRO-PALESTINIAN

Two seals, probably Syro-Palestinian, perhaps dating from 1700 B.C.

1258. Hematite. 21½×11. NCBS 707. Syro-Palestinian.

Man, life sign, *was*-staff held by falcondemon in Egyptian crown, framed column with two hawks, spray above each, framed column of vertical twist; linear borders.

A similar subject in *Syria* 42 (1965), p. 41, pl. V. 4 (= *de Clercq,* 389).

1259. Dark green jasper. 22½×12½. Corroded. Remains of copper pin in bore. New impression. *Newell* 318. *Syria* 42 (1965), p. 42, pl. V. 7.

Hawk (?) in tunic, poor surface, smaller figure in tunic, bird with Egyptian crown over tree with flowering bush, man facing two falcons, rectangle held by hands of Egyptian woman, vertical twist.

1249

1250

1254

1256

1257

1258

1259

1260

1261

1262

1263

1264

1265

1266

1267

Mitanni

The Syrian style dating to the late 17th century B.C. tends to overlap with developing Mitannian. Heroes, lions, and rich detail fill 1260–61; a male in rosette contrasts with various forms on either side, 1262; joined rotating heroes are set in twists with groups of animals, 1263; embracing man and woman beside hero on back of prostrate bull, 1264; male figures confront each other on either side of twist, 1265; a seated god is set in streams, 1266; men facing each other, 1267; three gods are depicted differently, 1268; a man and a woman beside worshipper, 1269; two holy figures face a third, 1270; two pairs, each different, 1271–72; sacred group, possibly Cypriote, 1273; a dancer before a stirred pot, 1274; five sacred figures in various guises, 1275–77; miscellaneous scenes are built up before a holy pair, 1278–80; diverse rows of five figures, 1281–83; three chariot scenes, mature to late, 1284–86.

FIGS. 1260–1267

1260. Hematite. 18½×8. NBC 9373.

Tree between two erect lions with heads turned back, each in grasp of hero with long hair behind him, wearing girdles hanging in middle, their rear legs crossed, linear borders.

1261. Hematite. 18/17×9½. NBC 9375.

Man in tall hat and open robe with spear head up, reversed lion held and stepped on by bulldemon, Egyptian staff in grasp of bulldemon who holds own tail (?), star above angle, ornamental plant, ground line.

1262. Hematite. 23×13. Worn. NBC 7924.

Rearing animal with head turned back attacked by lion, two ovals on dot over the lion's back, lying animal with raised hair, its head turned back, two ovals on dot over its back, squatting lion and sphinx; rope pattern; man (?), rod on right shoulder of man looking left holding animal, handled pitcher, figure looking right with arms at waist, tall knobbed handle on vase, bull on shoulders of man on one knee looking right with pole on each shoulder, T on top of pole held by haredemon; semicircle of double rosette containing man looking right, arms at waist in long dress.

1263. Hematite. 20½×9. New impression. *Newell* 345. *Frankfort*, XLII m., pp. 264–65.

Four full-face rotated heroes each holding vase in left hand, wrist of which is held by right hand of next hero, all enclosed by twists that join to form continuous line in middle, over which seated lion with head turned back confronts seated winged sphinx, under which two confronted bulls meet, each with bird on back.

For swirls of somewhat similar character see *Ward*, 706 (= *Frankfort*, p. 264, n. 2); Özgüç, *Seals*, pl. XI, C, pp. 54–55.

1264. Hematite. 17(ends broken)×13. YBC 8189.

Man in open robe, his arms crossed with partly nude woman in robe to left and behind her, cross disk in crescent, full-face bearded hero holding horn and hind leg of prostrate bull on whose back the hero curves his leg, squatting winged sphinx (?) facing squatting lion over right hand before mouth of winged god on one knee, who holds spear to left.

1265. Hematite. 18×8½. New impression. *Newell* 334.

All sidewise; god with high hat in open robe, reversed two squatting facing griffins; fourteen twists with lines on either side; man in open robe, reversed seated lion with head turned back facing small figure in high hat; seated lion, linear borders.

1266. Hematite. 19½×10. Worn. NBC 10989.

Man in open robe, central dot with six surrounding in circle, bearded god with streams from shoulders, enthroned on niched platform; reversed lion with head turned back attacked by animal, five-part doubled curves, two seated lions, hare's head between them.

1267. Hematite. 21×10. New impression. *Newell* 331.

Person in robe with pigtail, disk in crescent, man in robe, sickle sword on shoulder; lion (head lost) over prone bull below lying goat (?) with head turned back, eight twists with dots in center, top and bottom lines, facing seated winged sphinxes, ornamental tree with bar divider between them.

1268. Hematite. 14½×7. YBC 12602.

Goddess with horned crown, ribbon down back, vertical jagged line over flaming altar above small animal over back of lying bull, from which rope runs to god's bent right arm holding axe, long curved pigtail, tunic with short divider, mace raised in left arm, seated monkey, bearded god with crescent mounted on hat, mace over left shoulder; linear borders.

1269. Hematite. 14×6. YBC 12774.

God in open robe embracing partly clothed goddess, man with left hand to right in open robe, seated antelope with head back over squatting winged sphinx; linear borders.

1270. Hematite. 14×6. New impression. *Newell* 321.

Goddess with head covering fore and aft, god in long dress, life sign, facing personage with weapon at waist; lying winged griffin, three twists with top and bottom lines, two small figures; linear borders.

1271. Hematite. 28×10. NBC 8930.

Sickle sword held behind back in left hand of man in open robe, who holds other hand with god in ribbed skirt and a bow over left shoulder; two suppliant goddesses, between them elaborate standard topped by cross disk in crescent, life sign on either side; above continuous spiral, below continuous twist with star in each turn.

1272. Hematite. 23×10½. Border broken. NCBS 706.

Suppliant goddess with ribbon down back before god holding flowing vase under life sign, bush, bearded god with mace in right hand, axe and whip (?) in other, two small lying bulls, woman pulling robe aside.

1273. Hematite. 24×10½. New impression. *Newell* 329.

Naked goddess facing left, with long pigtail, diaphanous robe crossing front above belt, held at sides by hands, going behind below, flowering plant, winged liondemon, full-face nude male seated on flowering plant which he holds behind, bird feet, which are held by bulldemon, who wields sickle sword in left hand, star.

1274. Hematite. 22×11. Worn. New impression. *Newell* 335.

Man in tunic, long-haired figure dancing before pot in which stirrer is operated with two hands by man in tunic, seated antelope with head turned back, both horns held by man in robe; linear borders.

1268

1269

1270

1271

1272

1273

1274

1275

1276

1277

1278

1279

1280

1281

1275. Hematite. 20(top broken)×11. New impression. *Newell* 310. *Ward,* 941.

Nude female, head left, arms at breasts, figure holding sickle sword, in robe, life sign, man with pigtail wearing tunic, bearing axe, winged sphinx with snake on head, which is held by cord from right arm of man in elaborate tunic with fringe below; ground line.

1276. Hematite. 21×11½. New impression. *Newell* 337. *Ward,* 944.

Woman holding palm leaf before her, facing god in high hat with crook at chest, wearing open robe; reversed dagger, crook in right hand of man in open robe, reversed spear held by man in tunic, crook in right hand of man on one knee, all between two rows of twists with dot in center of each twist; linear borders.

1277. Hematite. 16×8½. New impression. *Newell* 302.

Suppliant goddess with necklace down back, two crescents above ball staff, mace held aloft by god with spiked headdress and pigtail, naked body (left foot deformed), spear in left hand, two men in high hats with open robes, point before each, bucranium above nude female; linear borders.

1278. Hematite. 20½×11. Worn. New impression. *Newell* 301. *Frankfort,* XLI i, pp. 253ff.

Personage facing suppliant goddess between two rows of seven curves; lion above prostrate man in grip of right claw of winged eagle facing right (worn similar figures on other side), below: god in scaly garb (mountains) carrying small flowerpot, figure in long dress tending

palm in vase, bearded god enthroned on niched pedestal, behind him two gods in scaly garb holding flowerpots.

1279. Hematite. 24×13½/12(concave). New impression. *Newell* 297. *Frankfort,* XLII h, pp. 260ff.

Personage in open robe, winged cross disk above crossed lines over crowned falcon, all beside nude on line beside bird over dot, lion (broken) underneath; two enthroned women each holding vase, between them table with two sets of leaves, five curves with centered dot in each set in top and bottom lines, two birds attacking bull; suppliant goddess with ribbon down back, linear borders.

1280. Hematite. 22×9. Worn. NBC 2598.

Bearded personage in open robe, star above six circles about small seventh, winged disk containing circle over two facing winged griffins, each raising small vase in one hand and suspending heart-shaped vessel in other; woman in dress.

Meek, *BASOR* 90 (1943), pp. 25.4, 27.4, winged disk like 1279, under it facing griffins, but with lion bodies instead of tails, and elaborate symbols instead of containers. *Louvre A.,* 951, winged disk in circle under which two full-face heroes hold a stool with drilled circles.

1281. Hematite. 15½×7. New impression. *Newell* 294.

Four men all in tunics, their left hands raised, the first has right hand at side; crescent and point above, below: two lines pointed up, two down, vertical line, vertically marked vessel; linear borders (some defective).

FIGS. 1275–1281

1282. Hematite. 18½×9½. Worn. NBC 11050.

Five men, all with pointed headdress, long vertically marked dress, four vertically marked vessels (one lost); linear borders (some defective).

1283. Light green turquoise. 19×8½. NBC 8322.

Four full-face women with inscriptions between, linear borders.

1284. Hematite. 19×9. New impression. *Newell* 343.

Two-horse chariot, one acrobat on ground beside it, another above, driver and rider, two marching men behind in tunics, their adja-

cent legs crossed, flying bird over small bird (?); linear borders.

1285. Hematite. 20×11½. NBC 8931.

Chariot and acrobats as in 1284, one driver, two stars above, five-part twist over four marching men in tunics, their adjacent legs crossed; linear borders.

1286. Hematite. 18½×7. New impression. *Newell* 341.

Four groups of seven to nine pellets enclosed in continuous circles, bird, all over two marching men in tunics, their adjacent legs crossed, two-horse chariot with driver; linear borders.

1282

1283

1284

1285

1286

SEAL INSCRIPTIONS

Introduction

More than three hundred of the seals and seal impressions in this catalogue carry inscriptions. These inscriptions are transliterated and, as far as possible, translated in what follows. Here and there, I have permitted myself brief remarks and bibliographical indications designed to throw light on the seal inscription as an inscriptional genre. Little systematic work has hitherto been devoted to this subject for the period in question, although the immediately following period is the subject of a monograph by Limet.[1] To the extent that the inscriptions mention the king, it may be sufficient to refer to my "The royal inscriptions of Ur: a typology," *HUCA* 33 (1962), pp. 1–43, and E. Sollberger and J.-R. Kupper, "L'inscription royal comme genre littéraire" in *IRSA*, pp. 24–36.

Given the large number of seal inscriptions catalogued below, and the rudimentary state of the art, the reader's indulgence may be entreated if a brief typology is attempted here. It is meant to be suggestive, not definitive; that would require incorporating the evidence of hundreds of previously published seal inscriptions. I have, however, availed myself of a mimeographed "Typology of seal inscriptions" prepared by I. J. Gelb for a course in Mesopotamian sigillography (April, 1961; revised 1975). This was based on "only main seal publications" but its statistics are helpful and tend to bear out those below.[2] Throughout the millennium with which we are concerned (c. 2600–1600 B.C.), the seal cutter faced essentially the same two problems: whether to identify the seal with its owner, and if so, how. A distinctive design could accomplish this purpose by itself but there were phases when identical de-

signs were utilized in hundreds of seals; one could put the name of the seal owner (or seal user) underneath its impression as an identifying caption but this usage, though it was introduced toward the end of our period, did not become standard till later. So the addition of an inscription to the design of the cylinder seal itself was the favorite device in most of the millennium, particularly its second half. In keeping with monumental inscriptions generally, the seal cutters evolved a limited repertoire of acceptable formulations answering to the twin requirements of form and function: to identify the seal owner in an extremely restricted space and as concisely as possible.

There were, however, equally compelling reasons *not* to identify a given seal with a particular owner, i.e. to make it available to many different users. The presence of the seal cutter (BUR.GUL) in Old Babylonian lawsuits from Nippur has been interpreted as evidence for achieving the same purpose by other means.[3] It could be inscribed, but fulfilled its function by omitting any mention of a personal name and confining itself to a divine name or names. Thus the initial breakdown of seal inscriptions is according to whether they serve to identify the seal owner or not.

The former category can be further subdivided. In addition to the personal name (PN), the identifying criteria applied in the thousand years at issue can be described as: degree, role, status, and rank. A careful syntax of priorities gradually evolved to prevent confusion among these criteria.

Degree. In Early Dynastic and Sargonic

---

1. H. Limet, *Les légendes des sceaux cassites* (Brussels, 1971); see the detailed review by W. G. Lambert, *Bi.Or.*, 32 (1975), pp. 219–23.
2. Now published as "Typology of Mesopotamian seal inscriptions," *Seals and Sealing in the Ancient Near East* (1977), pp. 107–26.

3. A. Poebel, "Der bur-gul als Notar in Nippur," *OLZ* 10 (1907), pp. 175–81; *BE* 6 /2 (1909), pp. 51–55. So-called bur-gul seals, i.e. cheap stamp seals recarved for each one-time use, are not represented in this catalogue, since they consist solely of an inscription and lack a design. Note however, No. 580, a cylinder seal with what appear to be two separate but contemporaneous inscriptions which may have served a similar purpose.

times, the profession of scribe (DUB.SAR) was simply a role like any other. But with the establishment of the scribal schools at Ur and Nippur under Shulgi (Ur III), the title seems to have become something of an honorific. It is met with more often than any strictly professional name in the Neo-Sumerian seals; it always follows immediately after the seal owner's name, preceding the professional name (so in Nos. 429 and 642), the "rank" (No. 452), and the patronymic (passim); and it is borne only by the seal owner, never by his father in contrast to the professional names frequently attached to the patronymic.[4] In short, the title appears, almost like the modern doctorate, to have identified graduates of the contemporary schools. Since the only known schools of the Neo-Sumerian and Old Babylonian periods were the scribal schools, the only "degree" to which one could aspire was that of scribe.

Role. The actual office held by the seal owner when he commissioned his seal was expressed by a professional name (PrN) immediately following the degree (if any) or the PN (if not a scribe).

Status. It is here contended that the kinship terminology of the seal inscriptions served primarily to indicate status and not necessarily or exclusively real kinship.[5] "Son of PN" was a more specific claim to the generic status of a free man, literally "son of a man" (*mār awīlim*).[6] "Daughter of PN" or "wife of PN" were variations on the same theme. Such designations regularly followed the role (PrN); when the order is reversed it can only identify the "father's" role.

Rank. Rank is identified as a subordinate relationship to a higher authority, and determined by the level of that authority. The relationship is normally expressed by "servant" (ÌR) or "maidservant" (GEMÉ); more rarely by "man" (LÚ, Nos. 414, 532). The higher authority may be another private person, a high official, a queen, a king, a temple, or a deity. Rank is regularly expressed at the furthest remove from the PN, either at the end of the inscription,[7] or by a more complex structure which begins with the higher authority and then identifies the seal owner as "his/your servant."

With these preliminaries in mind, we turn to our corpus.[8] After eliminating 42 texts of doubtful reading (Nos. 112, 266, 269, 300, 351, 415, 420, 465, 530, 533, 568–69, 589, 592–93, 605, 609, 629–30, 666, 668, 714–15, 758, 815, 832, 835, 837, 859, 861, 896, 913, 921, 959, 993, 1042, 1046, 1064, 1095, 1153, 1203, 1283) and 26 which are not republished below (Nos. 788, 806, 818, 823, 825, 829, 836, 839, 843, 844, 846, 862, 898, 918, 934, 1008, 1023, 1050, 1054, 1057, 1059, 1060, 1062, 1063, 1197, 1204) we are left with some 291 items. These may be divided into four general groups and seventy-five more specific types as follows:

    I. Seal inscriptions identifying the owner (Types A–N)
  IA. "Scribal" seal inscriptions (Types J–N)
   II. Seal inscriptions not identifying the owner (Types O–S)

---

4. Note too that, in contrast to true professional names, the designation "scribe" is not normally appended to personal names in the actual text of Ur III tablets. Thus N. Schneider counted only 54 scribes in the texts of the period compared to 464 in the seal inscriptions; see *Or.* 15 (1946), p. 83.

5. Similarly M. de J. Ellis, *JCS* 27 (1975), p. 145, n. 57 for Old Babylonian times and J. Zabłocka, *RAI* 18, p. 210 for Neo-Assyrian times.

6. F. R. Kraus, *Vom Mesopotamischen Menschen*, pp. 65–77, discusses all conceivable constructs with *mār*, including *mār* GN (= geographical name), but not *mār* PN, apparently taking its meaning for granted.

7. Note especially the seals of women, where it is clear that "maidservant (of the deity)" applies to the owner, not the intervening patronymic (Types 36 and 37).

8. Note the following abbreviations:
EOB = Early Old Babylonian
DN = divine name
GN = geographical name
OA = Old Assyrian
OB = Old Babylonian
ON = official name
PN = personal name
PrN = professional name
RN = royal name
TN = temple name
+ = new line (case)

III. Atypical seal inscriptions (Types T–Y)

I. Seal inscriptions identifying the owner.
  A. By name only (PN)
    1. ED II: 243, 253, 254
    2. ED III: 297, 317
    3. Sargonic: 399, 428, 455
    4. Ur III: 527, 688
    5. OB: 745, 961(?), 1065
  B. By name and role (PN + PrN)
    6. ED III: 303
    7. Sargonic: *407, 418*, 427*, 431,* 457, 472, 474(?)*[9]
    8. Ur III: 521(?), 525(?), 587, 675.
    9. OB: 892 (female).
  C. By name, role, and status (PN + PrN + DUMU PN₂)
    10. Late Sargonic: *503, 507*
    11. Ur III: 517, 529, 540, 559*
    12. OB: 799
  D. By name and status (PN + DUMU PN₂)
    13. Ur III: 511, 513, 515, 519, 523, 526, 528, 561, 564, 580II, 581, 588, 607, 628, 631, 659, 665, 670, 674, 677, 678
    14. OB: 709, 739, 793, 820, 996
    15. Elamite: 1093(?)
    16. OA: 1146, 1150, 1159, 1165
  E. By name, status, and "father's" role (PN + DUMU PN₂ + PrN)[10]
    17. Sargonic: 398, 410(?), 424†, 491 (late Sargonic)
    18. Ur III: 512, 520, 522, 524, 536, 567, 576†, 580I†, 591, 612†, 623†, 655†, 669†, 680†
  F. By name and rank
    19. Sargonic (PN₂ + PN₁ + ÌR.ZU): 417(?)
    20. Ur III (PN₁ + ÌR PN₂): 577, 582, 586, 683. 752 may be an OB example of the same type. Cf. also 675.
    21. OA (same): 1136(?)
    22. OB (PN + ÌR DN or [892]GEMÉ DN): 746, 813, 932, 1043, 1067. 441 may be an isolated earlier example of the same type.
  G. By name, role, and rank
    Sargonic:
    23. PN₁ + PrN + ÌR PN₂: 452
    24. PN₂ + PN₁ + PrN + ÌR.ZU: 419
    25. PN₂ + PrN + PN₁ + PrN + ÌR.ZU: 466
    26. PN₂ + PrN + PN₁ + PrN + ÌR.DA.NI: 423
    Ur III:
    27. col. i: PN₂ + PrN; col. ii: PN + PrN + ÌR.ZU: 596(?), 606, 639, 643, 648, 651, 652. In these cases, PN₂ is a royal name

(RN) and the PrN's that follow are the royal titles. In 651, the seal owner is himself a high official. 596 appears to diverge somewhat.
    28. Same as preceding, but PN₂ is a high official: 538, 562, 575, 615(?). The Elamite seal 1093A may reflect the same type.
    29. col. i: PN₂ (= RN) + PrN (= royal titles); col. ii: PN + PrN (in dative) + IN.NA.BA: 653, 654.
    30. (PN + PrN + ÌR DN): 632, 661(?).
    30a. OB (PN + PrN + ÌR DN + ù RN): 760.
  H. By name, status, and rank
    31. Ur III (PN₃ + PrN + PN + DUMU PN₂ + ÌR.ZU): 625
    OB:
    32. PN + DUMU PN₂ + ÌR RN: 753, 761, 769, 787, 791I (adds PrN after PN₂), 802, 899
    33. PN + DUMU PN₂ + ÌR DN: 804, 807, 811, 814(?), 821, 822, 826, 827, 831, 833, 834, 848, 860, 923, 952, 960(bis), 983, 986(?), 991D, 1005(bis), 1045, 1047, 1048, 1049, 1058
    34. PN + DUMU PN₂ + ÌR DN + ù DN₂: 998, 1003, 1056
    35. PN + DUMU PN₂ + ÌR TN: 991A, 991C
    36. PN(female) + DUMU-MÍ PN₂ + GEMÉ DN: 910, 919
    37. PN(female) + DUMU-MÍ PN₂ + GEMÉ DN + ù DN₂: 791II, 876
    "Elamite":
    38. like 33: 1096[11], 1098, 1099
    39. like 36: 1092.[12]
  I. By name, role, status, and rank
    40. Ur III (RN + royal titles + PN₁ + PrN + DUMU PN₃ + PrN + ÌR.ZU): 681
    40a. OB (PN + PrN + DUMU PN₂ + ÌR DN): 828(?)
IA. "Scribal" seal inscriptions.
  J. By name, degree, and status (PN + DUB.SAR + DUMU PN₂)[13]
    41. Ur III: 514‡, 516, 544, 547, 558, 570, 571, 572, 573, 574, 584, 595, 597, 598, 599, 601, 604, 611, 613, 614, 616, 617, 620, 621, 622, 638, 641, 644, 645, 657, 658, 663, 667, 671, 672, 673, 692.
    42. OB: 751.
  K. By name, degree, status and "father's" role (Ur III)
    43. In four or more lines (PN + DUB.SAR + DUMU PN₂ + PrN): 425[14], 534, 563, 590, 618, 626, 640†, 656.
    44. In three lines (PN + DUB.SAR + DUMU PN₂ PrN): 541, 600, 608, 624.

9. * indicates that PN PrN is written on one line or in one case. Italics indicate that PrN (of seal owner) = DUB.SAR (scribe).
10. † indicates that DUMU PN₂ PrN is written on one line.

11. Inserts Akkadian particle *ša* between ÌR and DN.
12. Writes DUMU instead of DUMU.MÍ.
13. ‡ indicates that PN DUB.SAR is written on one line.
14. For the late Sargonic or early Ur date of this seal, see my discussion in *JNES* 31 (1972), pp. 88ff.

45. In three lines (PN DUB.SAR+DUMU PN₂+PrN): 602, 619.
46. In complex form (PN₂+PrN+PN+ DUB.SAR+DUMU.NI): 603.

L. By name, degree, and rank
47. Sargonic (PN₂+PrN, PN+DUB.SAR+ ÌR.ZU): 430.
48. Ur III: 637 (in this case, PN₂=RN and PrN=royal titles), 679. Cf. also 609.

M. By name, degree, and rank (Ur III)
49. Like 47, but adds PrN before ÌR.ZU in last line: 642.

N. By name, degree, status, and rank Ur III:
50. col. i: RN+royal titles; col. ii: PN+ DUB.SAR+DUMU PN₂+ÌR.ZU: 627, 636, 646, 647, 649, 650.
51. same as preceding, but adds PrN after PN₂: 660.
52. OB (PN+DUB.SAR+ÌR DN): 1021.

II. Seal inscriptions not identifying the owner
O. Single divine name (DN)
53. Ur III: 518.
54. OB: 695, 719, 756, 759, 816, 857, 956, 1036.

P. Two divine names (DN+ù DN₂)
55. OB: 942.
56. OA: 1141.

Q. Two divine names on one line (DN DN)
57. OB: 712, 809 (Šamaš Aia).

R. Two divine names on two lines (DN+DN₂) OB:
58. Šamaš Aia: 741, 742, 744, 749 (Aia+Šamaš), 940, 980, 1149.
59. other male/female pairs: 743, 779(?), 784, 785, 838, 858, 870, 873, 885, 1061.
60. others: 900, 911, 943, 1068.
61. Elamite: 1097(?).
62. OA: 1139.

S. Divine name+epithets
63. OB: 786, 794, 830(?), 840, 841, 849, 855, 881, 893, 904, 954, 962, 984, 1051(?).
64. OA: 1140, 1143.

III. Atypical seal inscriptions
T. Two personal names (PN+PN₂)
65. Sargonic: 478(?).
66. Ur III: 553.
67. OB: 794(?).

U. Daughter (PN+DUMU.MÍ PN₂ or PrN)
68. EOB: 715.
69. OB: 824(?).

V. Wife (PN+DAM PN₂)
70. Ur III: 565.
71. EOB: 701.

W. "Man" (PN+LÚ PN₂)
72. Sargonic: 414(?).
73. Ur III: 532(?).

X. Queen
74. (RN+royal titles+queen's name+PN+

DUB.SAR+PrN+ÌR.ZU): 429.

Y. Prayers
75. OB: 819, 1052(?), 1053.

Inscriptions[15]

112. Uncertain.

243. (1) *En-na-il*

The signs are read from left to right, as is often the case in seals and monuments of ED II and early ED III times; e.g. U.11825 = *UE* II, pls. 191, 198; Sollberger, *Corpus* sub Ur-Nanshe 1. The personal name is Old Akkadian, to be explained as "Mercy, oh God!" or the like; Gelb, *MAD* 3 (1957), p. 52. It occurs at Abū Ṣālābīkh as a scribal name (Biggs, *Orientalia* 36 [1967], p. 61), and at Nippur as a royal name (Goetze, *JCS* 15 [1961], pp. 107–09).

253. (1) UR.KISAL.

The signs are read from left to right, as in No. 243.

254. (1) SÁ.TU.

If correctly read, the signs face in the opposite direction from the figures. The name may be regarded as another way of writing the ED Sumerian name SA.UTU, for which cf. e.g. *RA* 20:3 (= Sollberger, *IRSA* sub IE3a, who however, considers a reading SÁ.TAM for ŠÀ.TAM, trustee); *BIN* 8, 347:13.

266. Uncertain.

269. The signs are TÙR (byre) and NIR (staff), but may function as parts of the design rather than as writing here.

297. (2) AB.LÁL

The Sumerian word for "window" is usually written AB.LAL or AB.LÀL (see *CAD* s.v. *aptu*) and not a likely candidate for a personal name. Perhaps the inscription can be read in "negative" as UR.ÈŠ and compared to personal names like UR.ÈS.LÍL.LÁ for which see Hallo, *Titles*, p. 38.

300. It is doubtful whether an inscription is intended. For possible congeners of the symbol involved, see I. Fuhr, *Ein Altorientalisches Symbol*.

303. (6) ÚR.NI
     DUB.SAR
"Urani, the scribe."

"Scribe" is the most common designation on cylinder seals from c. 2500–1500 B.C. Literally the term means tablet writer, and replaces earlier umbisag, "teller, recorder." It may be an honorific, alluding to the seal owner's social standing as graduate of the scribal

15. Numbers in parentheses refer to the types of seal inscriptions identified in the preceding typology.

curriculum, rather than a strictly professional designation. The traditional translation will, nevertheless, be employed throughout rather than e.g. "Dr. Urani."

The personal name is taken to stand for ÚR.RA.NI, "his lap," i.e. "the deity's lap is good" or the like, a common name type in Early Dynastic and Neo-Sumerian times; see e.g. Edzard, *Sumerische Rechtsurkunden des III. Jahrtausends*, p. 212 s.v.; Limet, *L'Anthroponymie sumérienne*, pp. 313f. respectively.

317. (2) SI.GÀR

Possibly to be interpreted as GÀR.(E).SI, "filling the pocket." For the name type, cf. Edzard, *ZA* 53 (1959), pp. 12–15.

351. Faint traces

398. (17) A-bu-DÙG.
DUMU LÚ-ᵈINANNA
DAM.GAR
"Abu-tâb, son of Lu-Inanna the merchant." The professional name applies to the patronymic rather than to the seal owner when, as here, it follows the latter. The professional designation of the seal owner himself regularly *precedes* the patronymic in Neo-Sumerian usage. A merchant named Lu-Inanna is attested for Umma in Oppenheim, *Eames*, No. *18 and Schneider, *An.Or.* 7, 374:51. See the lists of Ur III merchants compiled by Fish, *BJRL* 22 (1938), pp. 163f. and Leemans, *The Old-Babylonian Merchant*, p. 48.

399. (3) BÙ.BÙ
"Bubu."

The name recurs in this spelling in *BIN* 8, 177, a Sargonic text from Nippur (?). In Neo-Sumerian texts, it is written BU.BU. (Our inscription is listed by Edzard, "Die Inschriften der altakkadischen Rollsiegel," *AfO* 22 [1968–69], p. 12 as No. 10.6)

407. (7) UR.L[Ú-...]
DUB.SAR
"Ur-L[u-...] the scribe."

410. (17?) DUMU.I₇
UR.UR

If read from right to left, the personal name would mean "son of the river," an unusual name at best, and in place of the professional name we would have the word for single combat (Akk. *šitnû*) or some kind of weapon (ᴳᴵˢURBIGU; for the reading see Falkenstein, *OLZ* [1942], col. 398.). If read from left to right, we could render: "Ur-ur, son of A-engur." Edzard, *AfO* 22 (1968–69), p. 17 sub No. 6.5 reads i-x-x, UR.UR; cf. *ibid.*, p. 15 No. 15.42 for UR.UR as PN.

414. (72?) NI.ZA.NI
ÌR LÚ.NI.DA

Perhaps to be interpreted as:
ZA.NI.NI
LÚ ÌR.DA.NI,
"Zanini, man of Irdani ('his servant')."

For Zanini as an Early Dynastic III name at Lagash, see *RTC* 16, ii 6, iii 1. For this type of Old Akkadian seal inscription, see Edzard, *AfO* 22 (1968–69), p. 16 sub 23; Hallo, *HUCA* 33 (1962), p. 19 and n. 166.

415. Faint traces.

417. (19?) Šu-ì-li
Eš₄-dar-al-su
ÌR.ZU
"Su-ili, Ištar-alšu (is) your servant."

If line 3 is interpreted as Akkadian, it would mean "(is) his servant" (*warassu*). The patronymic means "Ištar (is) upon him" according to Gelb, *MAD* 3 (1957), pp. 36f. Listed by Edzard, *AfO* 22 (1968–69), p. 16 sub No. 24.30.

418. (7) ME.BA.ŠÀ(?).SÙ(?) DUB.S[AR]
"Meba-šasu the scribe."

For the name-type, cf. ME.BA.TUG of Adab in Luckenbill, *OIP* 14, p. 9 = Banks, *Bismaya*, 264. The sign DUB is clear on the original.

419. (24) [x]-ri-a
I-lí-il-la-at
AŠLAG (GEŠTÚ.KAR.RÁ)
ÌR.ZU
"[...]-ria, Ili-illat the fuller (is) your servant."

According to *CAD* A s.v. *ašlaku*, this writing of the professional name occurs only in pre-Sargonic texts, but it is still found in the so-called MU-ITI texts; cf. e.g. Nikolski, *Dokymenti* 2, p. 11.

420. Faint traces.

423. (26) (i) LÚ.DINGIR.RA.NA
SANGA IN ᵏⁱ
(ii) LÚ.DINGIR.RA
DUB.SAR ÌR/.[DA]/NI
"Lu-dingirana pontiff of In — Lu-dingira the scribe, his servant."

For other holders of this priestly office, see M. Lambert, "Le pontife de la cité d'In," *Ar. Or.* 35 (1967), 521–23; Edzard, *Sumerische Rechtsurkunden*, Nos. 84, 85 and 85a. For other Old Akkadian seal inscriptions of this type see Edzard, *AfO* 22 (1968–69), p. 17 sub 25. For the suggested equation of IN with Isin, see J. N. Postgate, *Sumer* 30 (1974), pp. 207–09.

424. (17) EN.LUL
DUMU IR.BU.BU DAM.GÀR(?)
"En-lul, son of Irbubu the merchant."

Reading uncertain. For the first name, cf. EN.NÍG.LUL.LA, *RTC* 881:14.

425. (43) LUGAL.ENGAR.DU₁₀
DUB.SAR
DUMU UR.ME.ME
UGULA.É
ᵈINANNA.KA

"Lugal-engardu the scribe, son or Ur-Meme the prefect of the temple of Inanna."

For full discussion of this seal inscription, see Hallo, *JNES* 31 (1972), p. 88 with note 6 and p. 95 (with text of the tablet NBC 10590).

427. (7) NUN.KA(?) DUB.SAR

"NUN.KA(?) the scribe."

428. (3) KU.DAG

429. (74) (i) ᵈŠar-kà-li/-šàr-ri
LUGAL
ba₁₁-u-la-ti
ᵈEN.LÍL
Tu-tá-šar-li-bi-iš
NIN
(ii) NIN
Iš-ku-un/-ᵈDa-[gan]
DUB.[SAR]
ŠABRA [Gu]/-ti-[umᵏⁱ??]
ÌR.[ZU]

"Šar-kali-šarri king of the subjects (or dominions) of Enlil (and) Tuta-šar-libbiš the queen — Iškun-Dagan the scribe, 'steward' of Gutium(?), your servant."

See Hallo, "Gutium," *RLA* 3 (1971), p. 710, for other references to Iškun-Dagan in connection with Gutium and for his and other seals dedicated to Šar-kali-šarri of Akkad and his queen.

430. (47) I-ti-a-bum
ŠABRA.É
DA.DA
DUB.SAR
ÌR.ZU

"Iddin-abum, temple steward — Dada the scribe, your servant."

For the office of ŠABRA-É, see Hallo, *JNES* 31 (1972), p. 91. The form of the sign TI in line 1 is characteristic of the period immediately preceding the Akkad dynasty; see Stephens in *BIN* 8, p. 7, Group 7. The same office was occupied by this or another Dada under Shar-kali-šarri; cf. Edzard, *AfO* 22 (1968–69), p. 16, No. 24:23.

431. (7) UR.LI
DUB.SAR

"Ur-LI the scribe."

441. (22) NAM.LUGAL(A).NI.[DU₁₀]
ÌR ᵈŠARA

"Namlugalani-du servant of Šara."

The personal name is restored from the tablet, which writes NAM.LUGAL.A.NI.DU₁₀ i.e. "His kingship is good." This form of seal inscription (servant of the deity) is not otherwise attested for the Old Akkadian period.

452. (23) BÀD-mu-pi₅
DUB.SAR
ÌR Ru-ba-tim

"Dūrum-mūpî the scribe, servant of Rubātum (or: of the princess)."

Durum-mupi also appears on the unpublished Sargonic text NBC 6847. For our inscription, see Edzard, *AfO* 22 (1968–69), p. 16 sub 23.la.

455. (3) Daq-qum.

457. (7) DU-DU
EN?:.KAS₄

"Dudu the courier(?)."

The professional name, if correctly read, recurs, apparently as a personal name, on Neo-Sumerian seal impressions, where it frequently varies with simple KAS₄ on the associated tablets; see Hallo, *HUCA* 29 (1958), p. 87 and note 27; below, No. 620.

465. (i) [x-b]i₅-um
[x]-AB.[TUM]?
(ii) ⌈NE.DI⌉??

466. (25) Na-ra-am-É-a
ENSÍ UNUG.KI-GA
I-šar-be-lí
NIMGIR ÌR.ZU

"Narâm-Ea governor of Uruk, Išar-bēli the herald, your servant."

472. (7) ŠEŠ.BÉ.MU.SI(?).GA
SAHAR

"Šešbe-musiga the equerry."

474. (7?) [ᵈ]U.DU IŠIB

"Dudu the incantation-priest."

Reading and restoration uncertain; cf. No. 587.

478. (65?) PA.LÍL.ME.HA.IL
Mu-ba-lí'-si-in

The inscription, entered on the seal in positive, rather than the usual negative sense, yields no satisfactory sense. *Muballissin* may be a personal name or an epithet, "the one who keeps them (fem.) alive."

491. (17) UR.GU
DUMU LUGAL-SAG.ZU?
UGULA TIBIRA

"Urgu, son of Lugal-x foreman of the metal-workers."

For tibira written DUB.NAGAR, rather than URUDU.NAGAR, see the Neo-Sumerian texts from Ur (Legrain, *UET* 3 s.v.) and Mari (Jestin, *RA* 46 [1952], nos. 9, 11, 12), and the discussion in *CAD* G s.v. *gurgurru;* cf. H. Limet, *Le travail du métal*, p. 119 et passim.

503. (10) AB.BA.KAL.LA
　　　　DUB.SAR
　　　　DUMU LÚ.ᵈNIN.GÍR.SU

"Abba-kalla the scribe, son of Lu-Ningirsu."

The same seal inscription appears on de Genouillac, *La trouvaille de Dréhem*, No. 89, edited by Sollberger, *TCS* 1 (1966), No. 320.

507. (10) AN.AB.KAL
　　　　DUB.SAR
　　　　DUMU GU.ZA.NA

"A. the scribe, son of Guzana."

The tablet reads i.a., KI GU.ZA.NA.TA AN.AB.KAL Ì.DA.GÁL.

511. (13) A LÚ.Ì.ZU
　　　　　DUMU UR.ÀM.MA

　　(13) B LÚ.ᵈŠARA
　　　　　DUMU UR.ÀM.MA

The tablet reads KI.KA.GUR₇.[TA] KIŠIB.AŠ.A (or: À[M]) LÚ.Ì.ZU, "from the granary-keeper, 'receipted as one,' (by) Lu-izu."

512. (18) *A-hu-ma*
　　　　DUMU DINGIR.A.MU
　　　　SIPA.UDU.NIGAₓ (ŠE)

"Ahumma, son of Dingir-amu the shepherd of the fatted sheep."

513. (13) UR-ᵈLAMMA
　　　　DUMU UR.GAR

"Ur-Lamma son of Urgar."

514. (41) UR.E₁₁.E DUB.SAR
　　　　DUMU UR.NIGÌN.⌈GAR⌉

"Ur-e'e the scribe, son of Ur-nigingar."

The scribal seals of the Ur III period have been catalogued by N. Schneider, *Or.* 15 (1946), pp. 64–88, but most of the examples of this inscription listed there (p. 77) arrange it in three lines and have a different design. On this Ur-e'e, see in detail Jones and Snyder, *Sumerian Economic Texts,* pp. 322ff.

515. (13) NÍG.MU
　　　　DUMU AB.BA

"Nigmu, son of Abba."

516. (41) A.KAL.[LA]
　　　　DUB.[SAR]
　　　　DUMU UR.N[IGÌN.GAR]

"Akalla the scribe, son of Ur-nigingar."

Inscription restored from YBC 1226. Other seals of the same individual add the title SAHAR in the third line (e.g. *YOS* 4, 156) or after the third line; see No. 640.

517. (11) EN.MÍ.ÚS.SÁ
　　　　GUDÚ E₁₁.[E]!
　　　　DUMU LU₅.Ú.LU₅

"En-miussa, the annointing priest of the E'e, son of Lu'lu."

The text says i.a., GEME SÁ.DU₁₁/E₁₁.E.ŠÈ/EN. MÍ.ÚS.SÁ Ì.DÍB, "slave-girl(s) as offerings for the E'e (which) En-miussa received."

518. (53) ᵈEN.KI
"Enki."

519. (13) [x].É.KU.BI
　　　　DUMU NÍG.DU₁₀.GA

". . . , son of Nig-duga."

Note that each line is in its own "case."

520. (18) URU.KI.BI
　　　　DUMU GU.MU
　　　　DAM.GÀR

"Uru-kibi, son of Gumu the merchant."

521. (8?) ŠA.x-[. . .]
　　　　SIPA. [. . .]

"Ša-. . . , shepherd of . . ."

522. (18) UR.ᵈA.ŠÁR
　　　　DUMU LUGAL.ITI.DA
　　　　NU.ᴳᴵˢ GIRI₁₁

"Ur-ašar, son of Lugal-itida the gardener."

Text has i.a., KIŠIB UR.ᵈA.SÁR DUMU LUGAL. ITI.DA. For the theophoric element see J. J. M. Roberts, *The Earliest Semitic Pantheon* (1972), pp. 16f. and 71f.

523. (13) DA.A.GA
　　　　DUMU Ù.MA.NI

"Da'aga, son of Umani."

524. (18) AD.DA
　　　　DUMU LUGAL.NUN.KI.ŠÈ
　　　　SÌLA.ŠU.DU₈ ᵈBA.Ú

"Adda, son of Lugal-Eriduše the cupbearer of Ba'u."

525. (8?) [EN.NAM].ŠITAₓ.GUB
　　　　[ENᵈX]-TUN. GÍR.DUL.LÍ.KI

Restoration of line 1 suggested by the priestly name discussed by Kang in *BIN* 3, pp. 7f.

526. (13) UR.ᵈINANNA
　　　　[DUMU] UR.É.AN.NA

"Ur-Inanna son of Ur-e'anna."

527. (4) ᵈINANNA.KA!

"Inannaka." The name is a variant of Inanna-kam, "she/he-is-Inanna's." For a high-born woman of this name (in both spellings) see Hallo, *JNES* 31 (1972), pp. 91f. with notes 29–34.

528. (13) LUGAL.EZEN
　　　　DUMU LUGAL.PA.[È]

"Lugal-ezen son of Lugal-pa'e."

529. (11) LUGAL.PA.È
LÚ.BAPPIR.MAH
DUMU UR.ᵈŠARA

"Lugal-pa'e the chief brewer, son of Ur-Šara."

530. UR.ᵈX
[IR]? LUGAL?.X

"Ur- . . . servant(?) of Lugal(?) . . ."

532. (73?) Na-dí-um
LÚ?NIN.DINGIR ŠEŠ

"Nadi'um, man(?) of the priestess of Š."

533. UR.ᵈBA.Ú
[SÌLA.ŠU.DU₈ᵈNIN]-[ ]
ÌR.[. . .]

"Ur-Ba'u cup-bearer of Nin-. . . , servant of . . . ."

The traces of the many impressions are very faint and the reading of the inscription is quite uncertain.

534. (43) NÍG.BA.E
DUB.SAR
DUMU LUGAL.GABA
ŠABRA

"N. the scribe, son of Lugal-gaba the prefect."

The same seal inscription recurs on other tablets (e.g. *UDU*, 42; *CTC*, 36; Nikolski, *Dokymenti*, 312) but the texts always give the owner's name as Gar-lagar-e. Cf. No. 584.

536. (18) UR-ᵈ[KA.TAR]
DUMU LUGAL. ⌜UR₅.ŠA₆.GA⌝(?)
UKU.UŠ ENSÍ

"Ur-K., son of Lugal-uršaga(?) the soldier of the governor."

Restored on basis of tablet, line 3: KIŠIB UR.ᵈKA.TAR.

538. (28) (i) GÙ.DÉ.A
ENSÍ
ŠIR.BUR.LA!KI
(ii) SIPA:ᵈNIN.GÍR.SÚ-KE₄.Ì.PÀ
RÁ.GABA ÌR.ZU

"Gudea, governor of Lagash, Sipa-Ningirsuke-ipa the rider, your servant."

Other seals dedicated to Gudea governor of Lagash are impressed on Lagash tablets dated to the reigns of Amar-Suen (*ITT* 2:839, 859) and Šu-Sin (*ITT* 5: 9827; 2:4216). A seal impression of Sipa-ningirsuke-ipa occurs on a Lagash tablet from the reign of Amar-Suen (*Figulla*, BM 12266).

For another "Gudea-seal," see Porada, *Andrews University Seminary Studies* 6 (1968), pp. 134–49, pls. 1–5 (cf. Hallo, *JNES* 31 [1972], p. 90).

540. (11) *A-da-làl*
DAM.GÀR
DUMU DINGIR-*ba-ni*

"Adallal the merchant, son of Ilum-bani."

The tablet is receipted by *A-da-làl ù A-la-tum* and dated ITI KIRₓ (SAL.SÍLA).SI.AK, an otherwise unknown month name.

541. (44) UR.[É.NINNU]
DUB.SAR
[DUMU] AL.LA.[MU] / ŠABRA

"Ur-eninnu the scribe, son of Allamu the prefect."

Inscription largely effaced; restored from text (unopened case). The same inscription, but with a different design, is impressed on *HSS* 4:157; *ITT* 2:979, 5:10041; Pinches, *Amherst*, p. 112.

544. (41) LÚ.GIRI\(KA).ZAL
DUB.SAR
DUMU DA.DU.MU

"Lu-girizal the scribe, son of Dadumu."

A similar but not identical seal inscription occurs in Nikolski, *Dokymenti* 2, p. 228.

547. (41) LUGAL.É.MAH.E
DUB.SAR
DUMU LUGAL.KÙ.GA.NI

"Lugal-emahe the scribe, son of Lugal-kugani."

For a recent edition of this seal inscription, see Sollberger, *TCS* 1 (1966), No. 34.

553. (66) ÚR.RA.DINGIR
Ì.DU.DU

"Urra-dingir, Idudu."

558. (41) DA.A.GA
DUB.SAR
DUMU UR.GIŠ.ŠÀ.GA

"Da'aga the scribe, son of Ur-giššaga."

The same seal inscription (but no design) is given by Fish, *CST*, 633.

559. (11) UR.DINGIR.RA SAHAR
DUMU A.GI

"Ur-dingira the equerry, son of Agi."

561. (13) SAG.ŠA₆
DUMU LUGAL.BI

"S., son of Lugalbi."
Cf. No. 683.

562. (28)(i) UR.ŠA₆.GA
GÌR.NITÁ
GIŠ.ÙH.KI
(ii) UR.ŠUL
ŠABRA
ÌR.ZU

"Ur-šaga commander of Umma, Ur-šul the prefect, your servant."

563. (43) UR.NIGÌN.GAR
DUB.SAR
DUMU UR.ŠA₆.GA
NU.BÀNDA KURUŠDA

"Ur-nigingar the scribe, son of Ur-šaga the oxherd (and) fattener." Cf. No. 590.

564. (13) UR.ᵈDUMU.ZI.DA
DUMU ŠEŠ.ŠA₆.G[A]

"Ur-Dumuzida son of Šeš-šaga."

565. (70) NIN.KAL.LA
DAM I.AZ??.TI.IL

"Nin-kalla wife of I."

567. (18) ᵈNIN.MAR.KI.KA
DUMU LA.LA
NU.ᴳᴵˢ GIRI₁₁

"Ninkimaraka, son of Lala the gardener."

568. Inscription largely effaced.

569. (i) LÚ.[. . .]
[. . . . .]
D[UB.SAR?]
(ii) [. . . . .]
[. . . . .]
A.RU.A

If correctly restored, this would be the seal of a person dedicated (A.RU.A) to a temple, which appears improbable. See Gelb, "The Arua institution," *RA* 66 (1972), pp. 1–32.

570. (41) LÚ.ᵈKAL.KAL
DUB.SAR
DUMU UR.ᵈLAMA

"L. the scribe, son of Ur-Lama."

Same seal impression on *UDT,* 14; same seal inscription: Mercer, *JSOR* 12:41 No. 28.

571. (41) LUGAL.BÁRA.GE.SI
DUB.SAR
DUMU UR.ᵈIG.ALIM

"Lugal-barage-si the scribe, son of Ur-Igalima."

For names of the type Lugal-barage-si, "the king fills (occupies) the throne," see Edzard, *ZA* 53 (1959), pp. 12–15.

572. (41) GU.Ú.GU.A
DUB.SAR
DUMU MA.AN.SÌ

"Gugua the scribe, son of Mansi."

For additional duplicates, see Schneider, *Or.* 15 (1946), p. 69.

573. (41) UR.ÀM.MA
DUB.SAR
DUMU LUGAL.É.MAH.E

"Ur-amma the scribe, son of Lugal-emahe."

The last sign of the inscription is written into the design.

574. (41) UR.GI₆.PÀR
DUB.SAR
DUMU A.A.KAL.LA

"Ur-gipar the scribe, son of A'a-kalla."

Same inscription: Nikolski, *Dokymenti* 2, p. 146.

575. (28) (i) UR.ᵈLI.SI₄
ENSÍ
GIŠ.ÙH.KI
(ii) LÚ.IGI.ŠA₆.ŠA₆
DUB.SAR
ÌR.ZU

"Ur-Lisina governor of Umma, Lu-igišaša the scribe, your servant."

Same impression presumably on YBC 1299 (*YOS* 4, 102). For the text of NBC 676, see Goetze, *JCS* 2 (1948), p. 187.

576. (18) *Šu-ma-ma*
DUMU UR.ᴳᴵˢGIGIR GUDÚ

"Šu-mama, son of Ur-gigir the anointing priest."

577. (20) UD.IŠ.NA.NI
ÌR *Nu-úr-Eš₄-dar*

"U. servant of Nur-Ištar."

The inscription is of a type introduced at various dates in the Early Old Babylonian period; see Hallo, *HUCA* 33 (1962), pp. 19f.

580. (18) (I) UR.ᵈNA.MUŠ.DA
DUMU LÚ.ŠA₆.MU / AŠGAB
(13) (II) LUGAL.LE.IGI.SUD
DUMU LUGAL.A.MA.RU

(I) "Ur-Namušda, son of Lušamu the leather-worker."

(II) "Lugale-igisud, son of Lugal-amaru."

The name of the deity of Kazallu is otherwise written ᵈNU.MUŠ.DA at this time.

581. (13) *Ig-mu-lum*
DUMU *I-ti-ti*

"Igmulum son of Ititi."

582. (20) UR.ᵈGIŠ.BÍL.GA.MEŠ
ÌR UR.GI₆.PÀR

"Ur-Gilgameš, servant of Ur-gipar."

See comment to No. 577.

584. (41) LUGAL.GAR.LAGAR.E
DUB.SAR
DUMU DA.DA

"Lugal-garlagare the scribe, son of Dada." Cf. No. 534.

586. (20) ᵈNANNA.MU.DAH
ÌR ᵈUTU.Ì.DU

"Nanna-mudah, servant of Utu-idu."

See comment to Nos. 577 and 582. The first name is well attested (Limet, *Anthroponymie*) and the fanciful suggestion of Langdon, *JRAS*(1932), p. 570 (cf. von Soden, *GGA* 198 [1936], p. 42) may be ignored.

587. (8) DU.DU
    IŠIB.MAH ᵈ⌈INANNA⌉?
    UNUG.INNIN.KI.KA

"Dudu, chief incantation priest of Inanna(?) of Zabalam."

For the reading of the place name, see Sjöberg, *TCS* 3 (1969), pp. 115f. Cf. also No. 474.

588. (13) INIM.ᵈINANNA
    DUMU LUGAL.ITI.DA

"Inim-Inanna son of Lugal-itida."

589. Faint traces.

590. (43) LÚ.ᵈEZIN
    DUB.SAR
    DUMU UR.ŠA₆.GA
    NU.BÀNDA ⌈KURUŠDA⌉

"Lu-Ezin the scribe, son of Ur-šaga the oxherd (and) fattener."

Cf. No. 563.

591. (18) UR.MES
    DUMU LÚ.ᵈ/NIN.GÍR.SÚ
    LÚ.BAPPIR

"Ur-mes, son of Lu-Ningirsu the brewer."

592. DA.DA.KAL.LA / PA. [UDU]?
    DUMU MIR.KI.ÁG(A)/⌈NA⌉-[GADA]?

"Dada-kalla the shepherd(?), son of Mir-kiaga the herdsman(?)."

593. Traces of old inscription.

595. (41) *Šu-i-lí*
    DUB.SAR
    DUMU UR.ᵈUTU

"Šu-ili the scribe, son of Ur-Utu."

596. (27?) (i) ᵈŠUL.GI
    da-núm
    LUGAL ŠEŠ./AB.KI
    (ii) *Nu-úr-i-li*
    x - y
    DUMU SI.A.A/GÌR.NITÁ

"Šulgi the great, king of Ur, Nur-ili the . . . , son of Sia'a the commander."

See in part already von Soden, *GGA* 198 (1936), p. 42.

597. (41) BÍ.DU₁₁.GA
    DUB.SAR
    DUMU LA.A.ŠA₆

"Biduga the scribe, son of La'aša."

The same inscription with a different design is found on YBC 1518 (*YOS* 4, 185). For other examples see Schneider, *Or.* 15 (1946), p. 68, No. 79; *Eames*, W 32. See also No. 667.

598. (41) KÙ.ᵈNIN.UR₄.RA
    DUB.SAR
    DUMU NA.[DI]

"Ku-Ninurra the scribe, son of Nadi."

Restored from *Eames*, W 95, a tablet with the same date and seal impression.

599. (41) UR.ᵈŠARA
    DUB.SAR
    DUMU LUGAL.USARₓ (LÁL×NIGÍN)

"Ur-Šara the scribe, son of Lugal-usar."

Cf. No. 618.

600. (44) LUGAL.KÙ.ZU
    DUB.SAR
    DUMU UR.NIGÌN.GAR SAHAR

"Lugal-kuzu the scribe, son of Ur-nigingar the equerry."

Other examples listed by Schneider, *Or.* 15 (1946), p. 74, No. 263. Note a similar design on the seal of his brother Ušmu, *Or.* 15, p. 68, No. 75.

601. (41) UR.LUGAL
    DUB.SAR
    DUMU DA.A.GI₄

"Ur-lugal the scribe, son of Da'agi."

Cf. *Or.* 15 (1946), p. 79. No. 443.

602. (45) MU.NI DUB.SAR
    DUMU A.A.KAL.LA
    GUDÚ ᵈNIN.UR₄.RA

"Muni the scribe, son of A'a-kalla the anointing priest of Ninurra."

For a different seal impression of the same(?) scribe see *CHEU* (1915), No. 21, dated Šu-Sin 9.

603. (46) (i) UR.GÁ ŠITIM.GAL
    ᵈEN.LÍL.LÁ
    LÚ ᵈNANNA
    (ii) DUB.SAR
    DUMU.NI

"Urga the masterbuilder of Enlil, Lu-Nanna the scribe (is) his son."

For other Ur III seal inscriptions of this form, see Schneider, *Or.* 5 (1936), pp. 118f. For the text of the letter-order bearing this impression, see Hallo, *Bi.Or.* 26 (1969), p. 174, No. 381.

604. (41) URU.KI.BI
    DUB.SAR
    DUMU LUGAL.EZEN

"Uru-kibi the scribe, son of Lugal-ezen."

605. Traces of worn inscription.

606. (27) (i) ᵈŠUL.GI
    NITA.KALA.GA
    LUGAL ŠEŠ.AB./KI.MA

(ii) LUGAL.EZEN
RÁ.GABA
ÌR.ZU

"Šulgi the great man, king of Ur, Lugal-ezen the rider (is) your servant."

See the publication of the text by Hackman, *BIN* 5 (1937), No. 345.

607. (13) *A-lí-a-hu-a*
DUMU *A-bu-um*-DINGIR

"Ali-ahua son of Abum-ilum."

608. (44) NÍG.Ú.RUM
DUB.SAR
DUMU KU.LI NU.BÀNDA

"Nig-urum the scribe, son of Kuli the oxherd."

609. (i) LUGAL.ENGAR/.DU₁₀
UGULA É ᵈINANNA

(ii) x-[. . .]
DUB.SAR? ¹ X-X

"Lugal-engardu prefect of the temple of Inanna, . . . the scribe [is your servant?]."

Partly restored on the basis of other seals of "The House of Ur-Meme," for which see Hallo, *JNES* 31 (1972), pp. 87–95.

611. (41) UR.ᵈDUMU.ZI.DA
DUB.SAR
DUMU ŠEŠ.KAL.LA

"Ur-Dumuzida the scribe, son of Šeš-kalla."

612. (18) UR.MES
DUMU NA.GA NAR

"Ur-mes, son of Naga the singer."

613. (41) UŠ.MU (or: NITA.MU)
DUB.SAR
DUMU LUGAL.ŠA₆. [GA]

"U. the scribe, son of Lugal-šaga."

Cf. Schneider, *Or.* 15 (1946), p. 79, Nos. 463f.

614. (41) LÚ.ᵈŠARA
DUB.SAR
DUMU UR.ŠA₆.GA

"Lu-Šara the scribe, son of Ur-šaga."

Cf. Schneider, *Or.* 15 (1946), p. 71, No. 187.

615. (28?) UR.ᵈŠUL.PA. ⌈È⌉
SUKKAL. ⌈MAH⌉
AMAR. [. . .]
ÌR [ZU]

"Ur-šulpa'e the grand-vizier, A. (is) your servant."

For other seals mentioning this high official, see Hallo, *AOS* 43 (1957), p. 114 with notes 4–7.

616. (41) ᵈŠARA.KAM
DUB.SAR
DUMU LUGAL.ᴳᴵˢ GIRI₁₁

"Šarakam the scribe, son of Lugal-giri."

No. 638 may be a later seal of the same person. Cf. also Schneider, *Or.* 15 (1946), p. 68, No. 91.

617. (41) ŠEŠ.KAL.LA
DUB.SAR
DUMU DA.DA

"Šeš-kalla the scribe, son of Dada."

618. (43) UR.ᵈŠARA
DUB.SAR
DUMU LUGAL.USARₓ (LÁLₓNIGÍN)
NU.BÀNDA.GU₄ ᵈŠARA

"Ur-Šara the scribe, son of Lugal-usar the oxherd of the oxen of Šara."

Cf. above, No. 599, and Schneider, *Or.* 15 (1946), p. 77, No. 400.

619. (45) LUGAL.EZEN DUB.SAR
DUMU LUGAL.É.MAH.[E]
ŠABRA

"Lugal-ezen the scribe, son of Lugal-emahe the prefect."

Cf. Schneider, *Or.* 15 (1946), p. 73, No. 243.

620. (41) EN.KAS₄
DUB.SAR
DUMU UR.ᵈKA.DI

"E. the scribe, son of Ur-Ištaran."

The seal owner's name appears on the tablet as KAS₄, a variation frequently noted: see No. 457.

621. (41) LÚ.ᵈUTU
DUB.SAR
DUMU BA.ZI

"Lu-Utu the scribe, son of Bazi."

622. (41) [UKKIN].NÉ
DUB.SAR
DUMU UR.ᴳᴵˢ GIGIR

"Ukkine the scribe, son of Ur-gigir."

The owner's name is restored from the text of the tablet; it recurs, e.g. in *Eames,* E 23 and W 32.

623. (18) LÚ.ᵈŠARA
DUMU AL.LA SUKKAL

"Lu-Šara, son of Alla the messenger."

For a similar seal inscription (without SUKKAL) see Schneider, *Or.* 47–49 (1930), p. 250.

624. (44) UR.É.MAŠ
DUB.SAR
DUMU UR.TAR SUKKAL

"U. the scribe, son of U. the messenger."

625. (31) UR.ᵈL[IX.SI₄]
ENSÍ GIŠ.[ÙH.KI]
MA.AN.SÌ

DUMU UR.[NIGÌN.GAR]
ÌR.ZU

"Ur-Lisina governor of Umma, Mansi son of Ur-nigingar (is) your servant."

626. (43) UR.ᵈNUN.GAL
DUB.SAR
DUMU UR.ᵈŠARA
ŠAₓ(GÁ).DUB.BA.KA

"Ur-Nungal the scribe, son of Ur-Šara the archivist."

Cf. Schneider, *Or.* 15 (1946), p. 77, No. 393 and Sjöberg, *AfO* 24 (1973), p. 26.

627. (50) (i) ᵈAMAR.ᵈEN.ZU
NITA.KALA.GA
LUGAL ŠEŠ.AB./KI.MA
LUGAL AN.UB/.DA LIMMÚ.BA
(ii) LUGAL.ITI.DA
DUB.SAR
DUMU UR.ᵈDUMU/.ZI.DA
ÌR.ZU

"Amar-Suena the strong man, king of Ur, king of the four heavenly quarters, Lugal-itida the scribe, son of Ur-Dumuzida (is) your servant."

Cf. Schneider, *Or.* 5 (1936), III.

628. (13) Da-mi-iq-DINGIR
DUMU I-ri-iš-Ag-ga

"Damiq-ili son of Iriš-Agga."

This reading assumes no loss at the ends of the lines. Otherwise, a restoration such as Damiq-ilišu son of Iris-Akšak or Iriš-Aggade might be suggested.

629. Traces of old inscription.

630. Traces of old inscription.

631. (13) HI.NI.
DUMU I.ti.la.nim?

"H. son of I."

632. (30) A-da-làl
AŠLAGₓ (LÚ.TÚG)
ÌR ᵈNANNA

"Adallal the fuller, servant of Nanna."

636. (50) (i) ᵈI-bí-ᵈEN.ZU
LUGAL.KALA.GA
LUGAL ŠEŠ.AB./KI.MA
LUGAL AN.UB/.DA LIMMÚ.BA
(ii) Ù.MA.NI
DUB.SAR
DUMU ŠEŠ.KAL.LA
ÌR.ZU

"Ibbi-Sin the great king, king of Ur, king of the four heavenly quarters, Umani the scribe, son of Šeš-kalla (is) your servant."

For other inscriptions of this type, see Schneider, *Or.* 5 (1936), pp. 113f.

637. (48) (i) Šu-ᵈEN.ZU
NITA.KALA.GA
LUGAL ŠEŠ.AB./KI.MA
LUGAL AN.UB/.DA LIMMÚ.BA
(ii) BA.BA.TI
DUB.SAR
ÌR.ZU

"Šu-Sin the great man, king of Ur, king of the four heavenly quarters, Babati the scribe (is) your servant."

For the use of the older title "great man" instead of "great king," see Hallo, *AOS* 43 (1957), p. 93 and note 4.

638. (41) ᵈŠARA.KAM
DUB.SAR
DUMU LUGAL.ᴳᴵˢGIRI₁₁

"Šarakam the scribe, son of Lugal-giri."

See No. 616.

639. (27) (i) ᵈŠUL.GI
NITA.KALA.GA
LUGAL ŠEŠ./AB.KI.MA
LUGAL AN.UB/.DA LIMMÚ.BA
(ii) LU.ᵈ/BA.Ú
RÁ.GABA
ÌR.ZU

"Šulgi the great man, king of Ur, king of the four heavenly quarters, Lu-Ba'u the rider (is) your servant."

640. (43) A.KAL.LA
DUB.SAR
DUMU UR.NIGÌN.GAR / SAHAR

"A-kalla the scribe, son of Ur-nigingar the equerry."

See Schneider, *Or.* 15 (1946), p. 67, No. 53, and No. 516 above.

641. (41) UŠ.MU (or: NITA.MU)
DUB.SAR
DUMU LUGAL.ŠA₆.GA

See No. 613.

642. (49) (i) ᵈŠUL.GI
NITA.KALA.GA
LUGAL ŠEŠ.AB./KI.MA
(ii) ᵈUTU.[GÍR.GAL]
DUB.S[AR]
ŠÀ.TAM Ì[R-ZU]

"Šulgi the great man, king of Ur, Utu-girgal the scribe (and) trustee (is) your servant."

Seal owner's name is restored from text of the envelope.

643. (27) (i) ᵈŠUL.GI
NITA.KALA.GA
LUGAL ŠEŠ.AB./KI.MA
(ii) NA.ŠA₆
KURUŠDA
ÌR.[ZU]

"Šulgi the great man, king of Ur, Naša the fattener (is) your servant."

As in the parallel text *TRU*, 122, Abba-šaga's receipt for animals is sealed with the seal of Naša, his predecessor as chief "receiving official" at Drehem; see Jones and Snyder, *Sumerian Economic Texts*, pp. 212–18. It is interesting that their Sumerian title was the fairly modest one of "fattener" (see *CAD* K s.v. *ša kuruštê*); this may be a clue to their primary function. The reading NA.BA.ŠA6 in *BRM* 3:31 is not borne out by inspection of the original, and may be doubted also in the case of *Trouvaille de Drehem*, 91 (= *Brussels*, 75); see the photograph, frontispiece.

644. (41) ŠEŠ.A.NI
DUB.SAR
DUMU DA.DA

"Šešani the scribe, son of Dada."

See Schneider, *Or.* 15 (1946), p. 75, No. 303.

645. (41) MES.É
DUB.SAR
DUMU DA.DA

"Mes-e the scribe, son of Dada."

646. (50) (i) ^{d}Šu-^{d}EN.ZU
LUGAL.KALA.GA
LUGAL ŠEŠ.AB./KI.MA
LUGAL AN.UB/.DA LIMMÚ.BA
(ii) UR.KÙ.NUN.NA
DUB.SAR
DUMU LÚ.^{d}NIN/.GÍR.SÚ KURUŠDA
ÌR.ZU

"Šu-Sin the great king, king of Ur, king of the four heavenly quarters, Ur-kununa the scribe, son of Lu-Ningirsu the fattener, (is) your servant."

The same inscription recurs, e.g. on *TCL* 2:5548 (= *Louvre A.*, 259), Langdon, *TAD*, 14 and (allegedly without the title kurušda) on *An.Or.* 7:45, 46 and 51 (see Schneider, *Or.* 15, p. 66, No. 19). Like Naša and Abba-šaga (see No. 643), Ur-kununa was a prominent link in the "basic organization of Drehem" (Jones and Snyder, *Sumerian Economic Texts*, pp. 218–21) and the title may here, exceptionally, refer to him rather than to his "father."

647. (50) (i) Šu-^{d}EN./ZU
LUGAL.KALA.GA
LUGAL ŠEŠ.AB./KI.MA
(ii) LUGAL.ME.LÁM
DUB.SAR
DUMU UR.^{d}LAMMA?
ÌR.ZU

"Šu-Sin the great king, king of Ur, Lugal-melam the scribe, son of Ur-Lamma, (is) your servant."

648. (27) (i) ^{d}ŠUL.GI
NITA.KALA.GA
LUGAL ŠEŠ.AB.KI.MA
(ii) *Na-ra-am/-i-lí*
SUKKAL Ì.DU8
ÌR.ZU

"Šulgi the great man, the king of Ur, Naram-ili the messenger (and) doorkeeper (is) your servant."

For other examples of this seal inscription, see Schneider, *Or.* 45–46 (1930), p. 22, No. 7. The professional name should perhaps be translated simply as doorkeeper; see *MSL* 12 (1969), p. 96 lines 92–95.

649. (50) (i) *I.bí/-*^{d}EN.ZU
LUGAL.KALA.GA
LUGAL ŠEŠ.AB./KI.MA
LUGAL AN.UB/.DA LIMMÚ-BA
(ii) UR.^{d}ŠU.MAH
DUB.SAR
DUMU UR.NIGÌN.GAR
ÌR.ZU

"Ibbi-Sin the great king, king of Ur, king of the four heavenly quarters, Ur-Šumaha the scribe, son of Ur-nigingar (is) your servant."

This seal is impressed on the otherwise uninscribed envelope (cf. No. 761) of the letter published by Sollberger, *TCS* I (1966), No. 125. Note that the final sign of the "unframed" last line of col. i is squeezed behind the elbow of the seated figure.

Other letters had envelopes sealed by the sender and otherwise inscribed only with the address (P. Michalowski, *JCS* 28 [1976], p. 165; M. Birot, *Syria* 50 [1973], pp. 8f.; *CT* 52:52, 187, 189, etc.), or with the message and a shortened form of the address (Hallo, *Bi.Or.* 26 [1969], p. 174:383). For a letter with an unsealed envelope inscribed only with the (divine) address, see Hallo, *JAOS* 88 (1968), p. 79, note 24. For a sealed envelope with an abbreviated text of the enclosed letter, see H. Lewy, *HUCA* 39 (1968), pp. 30-32 (cf. M. T. Larsen, *Mesopotamia*, 4 [1976], p. 135).

650. (50) ^{d}Šu-^{d}EN.ZU
LUGAL.KALA.GA
LUGAL ŠEŠ.AB.KI.MA
LUGAL AN.UB.DA LIMMÚ.BA
UR.^{d}ŠUL.PA.È
DUB.SAR
DUMU UR.^{d}HA.IÀ
ÌR.ZU

"Šu-Sin the great king, king of Ur, king of the four heavenly quarters, Ur-šulpa'e the scribe, son of Ur-Haia, (is) your servant."

Cf. Schneider, *Or.* 15 (1946), p. 66, No. 18.

651. (27) (i) ^d*Šu*-^dEN.ZU
        LUGAL.KALA.GA
        LUGAL ŠEŠ.AB./KI.MA
        LUGAL AN.UB/.DA LIMMÚ.BA
    (ii) A.A.KAL.LA
        ENSÍ
        GIŠ.ÙH.KI
        ÌR.ZU

"Šu-Sin the great king, king of Ur, king of the four heavenly quarters, A'a-kalla governor of Umma (is) your servant."

652. (27) Inscription equals 651, except that in col. 1, line 2 reads NITA.KALA.GA and, in col. ii, lines 2 and 3 are apparently written as one. For both seals see Pamela A. Parr, "Ayakala, governor of Umma," *JCS* (forthcoming).

653. (29) (i) ^d*I.bí*/-^dEN.ZU
        LUGAL.KALA.GA
        LUGAL ŠEŠ.AB./KI.MA.KE₄
    (ii) ^dNIN.[. . .]
        SUKKAL ŠÀ [
        AGA.[
        ÌR.DA.NI.[IR]
        IN.NA.[BA]

"Ibbi-Sin the great king, the king of Ur, presented (this seal) to Nin-[. . .] the messenger of [. . .], the . . . his servant."

For this type of seal inscription, see Schneider, *Or.* 5 (1936), pp. 119f.; Hallo, *HUCA* 33 (1962), pp. 39f.; Sollberger, *JCS* 19 (1965), pp. 29f. There is some temptation to restore the first two lines of col. ii as ^dNIN.LÍL.AMA.MU/SUKKAL.MAH as in *UET* 1:97 (=3:45; cf. Sollberger, *JCS* 19 [1965], n. 23), or as ^dNIN.LÍL.AMA.MU/SUKKAL ŠÀ É.A.KA (for this profession see *MSL* 12:95f., lines 90f.) as in *UE* 10:418a (cf. *IRSA*, p. 160), but these restorations remain conjectural.

654. (29) (i) [^d*Šu*]-^dEN.ZU
        [LUGAL] KALA.GA
        [LUGAL ŠE]Š.AB/[KI].MA
        [LUGAL A]N.UB/.DA LIMMÚ.[BA].KE₄
        [B]A.BA.TI
        ŠA_x(GÁ).DUB.BA
        ŠÀ.TAM LUGAL
        GÌR.NITÁ
        [*maš*]-*kán-šar-um*/^{KI}-MA
        [E]NSÍ
    (ii) A-[. . .]
        x-[. . .]
        KÙ.[. . .]
        MA.D[A. . .]
        [. . .]
        [^d*Be-la-at-šuh-nir*]
        Ù ^d[*Be-la-at*]-*te-r*[*a-ba-an*]
        ŠEŠ *A-b*[*í-/sí*]-*im-*[*ti*]
        AMA KI-Á[G-GÁ-NA]
        ÌR.DA.NI.[IR]
        IN.NA.[BA]

"Šu-Sin the great king, king of Ur, king of the four heavenly quarters, has presented (this seal) to Babati the archivist, the royal trustee, the commander of Maškan-šarrum, the governor of A-. . ., . . ., Ku-. . ., the land of . . ., . . . of Belat-šuhnir and Belat-teraban, brother of Abi-simti his (Šu-Sin's) beloved mother, his servant."

Babati (also written Wa-wa-ti and Mà-mà-ti) was an important official under Šu-Sin and figures in the literary letters of that king as well as the contemporary archives. See now R. M. Whiting, *JCS* 28 (1976), p. 178 for the restorations in lines 16–19.

655. (18) ÙR.RE.BA.AB.⌈DU₇⌉
        DUMU A.TU AŠGAB

"Ure-babdu, son of Atu the leather-worker."

For an Atu receiving leather at Lagaš in Šu-Sin 3, see *ITT* 5:6913.

656. (43) UR.NIGÌN.GAR
        DUB.SAR
        DUMU *Şíl-lí*-x
        ŠABRA NIN

"Ur-nigingar the scribe, son of Şilli-x the queen's (?) prefect."

Although the text of the (unopened) envelope refers to the "seal of KA₅.A.MU, son of the prefect of the house," the seal inscription clearly belongs to Ur-nigingar (against copy), apparently his brother. For this type of "stellvertretende Siegelung der Vertragsurkunden der Ur III-Zeit," see Schneider, *Or.* 16 (1947), p. 419.

657. (41) UR.NIGÌN.[GAR]
        DUB.SAR
        DUMU UR.^dBA.Ú

"Ur-nigingar the scribe, son of Ur-Ba'u."

658. (41) LÚ.ŠA₆.GA
        DUB.SAR
        DUMU LUGAL.NU.DU₁₁.[GA]?

"Lu-šaga the scribe, son of Lugal-nuduga."

659. (13) ÌR
        DUMU KA₅.A

"Ir son of Ka'a."

660. (51) (i) ^dŠUL.GI
        NITA.KALA.GA
        LUGAL ŠEŠ.AB./KI.MA
        ^[d]ŠARA.KAM
    (ii) DUB.SAR
        DUMU INIM.^dŠARA
        SA₁₂.SUG₅.LUGAL(A)/.KA
        ÌR.ZU

"Šulgi the great man, the king of Ur, Šarakam the scribe, son of Inim-Šara the royal surveyor, (is) your servant."

Another bulla from Drehem impressed with the same seal and dated Amar-Sin 3 was published in *BRM* 3:72 (MLC 2351).

661. (30?) LUGAL.NIR.GÁL
⌜x y⌝
ÌR ᵈŠARA

"Lugal-nirgal . . . , servant of Šara."

The personal name is restored from the tablet which reads i.a., GÌR LUGAL.NIR.GÁL.

663. (41) UR.ᵈŠUL.PA.È
DUB.SAR
DUMU LUGAL.KÙ.GA.NI

"Ur-šulpa'e the scribe, son of Lugal-kugani."

For additional examples of this impression, see Schneider, *Or.* 15 (1946), p. 78 No. 409 and *BRM* 3:140.

665. (13) UR.ᵈBÍL.GA.MES
DUMU DU.RU.A.BI

"Ur-Gilgameš, son of D."

666. The seal inscription is illegible, but the tablet has, i.a., KIŠIB NAM.<ŠÀ>.TAM UR.ᵈNISABA, which implies that Ur-Nisaba sealed the text; see Schneider, *Or.* 16 (1947), p. 420. For the omission of ŠÀ in the phrase, cf. Kang, *SACT* 2 (1973), No. 77 (refs. courtesy M. Gallery).

667. (41) Same text as No. 597. This is the third seal design of the same scribe.

668. Traces of old inscription.

669. (18) DA.AR(?)
DUMU MA.MA NAR

"Dar, son of Mama the musician."

670. (13) AN.NÉ.ZU
DUMU LUGAL.EZEN

"Annezu, son of Lugal-ezen."

671. (41) UR.ᵈEN.ZU
DUB.SAR
DUMU NA.DI

"Ur-Sin the scribe, son of Nadi."

672. (41) LUGAL.DUB.LÁ
DUB.SAR
DUMU UR-ᵈGIŠ.BAR.È

"Lugal-dubla the scribe, son of Ur-Gišbare."

For the deity Gišbare at Lagash, see Falkenstein, *An.Or.* 30 (1966), pp. 74f. But as a theophoric element, it occurs also in names from Drehem; see Limet, *L'anthroponymie*, s.v. LÚ.ᵈGIŠ.BAR.È.

673. (41) (A) ⌜UR⌝.ᵈBA.Ú
[DUB].SAR
[DUMU X.Š]A₆.GA

(B) UR.ᵈN[ANŠE]
DUB.[SAR]
DUMU UR.ᵈI[G.ALIM]

(A) "Ur-Ba'u the scribe, son of x-šaga."

(B) "Ur-Nanše the scribe, son of Ur-Igalim."

674. (13) LUGAL.DINGIR ŠITAₓ?.GAL?
DUMU LUGAL.KI?.BÀD

"Lugal-dingir the . . . , son of L."

675. (8) Ša-lim-ni-aš
GEMÉ.NIN

"Šalim-niaš, maidservant of the queen."

For the name (and title), see *Eames*, G 34 iv 9 and parallels cited there. For the reading, see Gelb, *MAD* 2² (1961), p. 131 (13).

677. (13) PÚZUR.LÚ
DUMU ZU.ZU.A

"Puzur-lu, son of Zuzua."

678. (13) UR.ᵈEN.[ZU]
DUMU UR.É/GIŠ?.[. . .]

"Ur-Sin, son of U."

Tablet reads: KIŠIB UR.ᵈEN.ZU

679. (48) (i) Ṣe-lu-uš-/ᵈDa-gan
ENSÍ
SI.MU.RU.UM/ᴷᴵ.MA
(ii) Ì-bí-ᵈ/IŠKUR
DUB.SAR
ÌR.ZU

"Šelluš-Dagan, governor of Simurrum, Ibbi-Adad the scribe (is) your servant."

See Hallo, "Simurrum and the Hurrian frontier," RAI 24 (1978), pp. 77f.

680. (18) A.A.KAL.LA
DUMU AB.BA.MU AŠGAB

"A'a-kalla, son of Abbamu the leather worker."

For A'a-kalla the leather worker receiving tanning materials, see *TCL* 5:5680 iv 5–9, 6037 viii.

681. (40) (i) ᵈAMAR.ᵈEN.ZU
LUGAL AN.UB/.DA LIMMÚ.BA
KI.ÁG ᵈINANNA
LUGAL.ENGAR.DU₁₀
UGULA.É. ᵈINANNA
(ii) NU.ÈŠ ᵈEN.LÍL.LÁ
DUMU ᵈEN.LÍL/.Á.MAH
UGULA.É. ᵈINANNA
NU.ÈŠ ᵈEN/.LÍL.LÁ ÌR.ZU

"Oh Amar-Sin, king of the four heavenly corners, beloved of Inanna — Lugal-engardu, prefect of the temple of Inanna (and) priest of Enlil, son of Enlil-amaha, prefect of the temple of Inanna (and) priest of Enlil is your servant."

See Hallo, *JNES* 31 (1972), pp. 87ff.

683. (20) *Šu-Ìr-ra*
ÌR SAG.SA

"Šu-Irra, servant of Sagsa"

For the second name, cf. No. 561: SAG.ŠA₆. Or restore SAG.⌈É⌉?

688. (4) BA.LI (or ŠA or TA?)LU.UM

Reading uncertain, possibly Bal-ilum.

692. (41) Ù.MA.NI
DUB.SAR
DUMU UR.ᴳᴵˢGIGIR

"Umani the scribe, son of Ur-gigir."

695. (54) ᵈEN.ZU

"Sin."

701. (71) NIN.PÀ
DAM UR.MES

"Nin-pa wife of Ur-mes."

For the name, cf. NIN.ŠÀ.TA.PÀ.DA, daughter of Sin-kašid of Uruk (Hallo, "Royal correspondence of Larsa," forthcoming.)

709. (14) *Na-bi-ì-lí-šu*
DUMU *Nu-úr-ì-lí-šu*

"Nabi-ilišu, son of Nur-ilišu."

712. (57) ᵈUTU ⌈ᵈA-A⌉

"Šamaš (and) Aia."

Only traces of inscription preserved.

714. ᵈX-ME

Doubtful.

715. Traces.

716. (68) *Tu-li-id-ša-[maš]*
DUMU.MÍ *Bur-*ᵈIŠKUR [. . .]

"Tulid-Šamaš, daughter of Bur-Adad."

The reading of the name is uncertain; ṢI.IL.LU.BI-[. . .] is also possible.

719. (54) ᵈA.A

"Aia."

739. (14) NE.NA.A
DUMU I.BA.ŠE.ME

"N. son of I."

741. (58) ᵈUTU
ᵈA.A

"Šamaš, Aia."

Old Babylonian seal inscriptions frequently consist simply of the name of a deity and his or her consort and, among these, the divine pair Šamaš and Aia are perhaps encountered most of all. For additional examples see 57f. in typology above, and the early compilation by J. Krauss, *Die Götternamen in den babylonischen Siegelzylinderlegenden*, p. 38.

742. (58) Inscription as on No. 741.

743. (59) ᵈNIN.KAR.RA.AK
ᵈPA.BIL.SAG

"Nin-karrak, Pabilsag."

For Nin-karrak as a form of Nin-isina and Pabilsag as the consort of Nin-isina, see F. R. Kraus, *JCS* 3 (1949), pp. 69 and 75–80.

744. (58) Inscription as on No. 741

745. (5) A.ZI.IA

"Azia."

This personal name is not common, but it recurs, e.g. in *UET* 5:62:8 and 91:23.

746. (22) *A-bu-wa-qar*
ÌR ᵈMAR.TU

"Abu-waqar, servant of Amurru."

Seal inscriptions of the form "PN servant of DN" occur as early as Sargonic times (No. 441) and in Ur III times. In the Old Babylonian period, they are replaced generally by the type of No. 753.

749. (58) ᵈA.A
ᵈUTU

"Aia, Utu."

Cf. No. 741.

751. (42) ᵈDA.MU.GAL.ZU
DUB.SAR
DUMU ⌈NÍG⌉.GA.ᵈEN.ZU

"Damu-galzu the scribe, son of N."

The tablet is edited by Walters, *YNER* 4 (1970), p. 111, No. 81.

The same seal impression occurs on NBC 6292, *YNER* 4, No. 80; copy pl. XIII no. 34.

752. (20) [traces]
ÌR ᵈIŠKUR.DINGIR-*šu*

". . . , servant of Adad-ilšu."

The seal inscription may belong to a different seal from the design; note it is only 22mm in height. For a possible restoration of the seal owner, see Walters, *YNER* 4 (1970), p. 113, No. 83.

753. (32) *Nu-úr-* ᵈEN.ZU
DUMU *At-ta-ma-nu-um*
ÌR *Su-mu-*DINGIR

"Nur-Sin, son of Atta-mannum, servant of Sumu-el."

For other seals of servants of Sumu-el see *BIN* 7:116; *UET* 5:766f., 784 (Hallo, *Bi.Or.* 18 [1961], p. 8 sub Sumu-il 5f.).

756. (54) ᵈA.A

"Aia."

Text published as *YOS* 14:28.

758. [traces]
    DUMU [traces]

"... son of ...."

There are five other seal inscriptions on the text, one of them by a "servant of Nur-Adad." The text is dated MU BÀD.GAL UD.UNUG.KI BA.DÙ, a fairly rare form of Sin-iqišam 3 (Gungunum 21 being excluded by the aforementioned seal). Note reverse line 1: KIŠIB ŠÀ.TAM.E.NE, "seals of the trustees."

759. (54) [ᵈUTU]
    ᵈA.A

Cf. No. 741. (The seal inscription is no longer visible.) The text was published by A. Goetze, *JCS* 4 (1950), p. 112.

760. (30a) ᵈNANNA.MA.AN.SÌ
    MÁŠ.ŠU.GÍD.GÍD
    ÌR ᵈNANNA
    [ù] *Nu-úr-*ᵈIŠKUR

"Nanna-mansi, the diviner, servant of Nanna [and] Nur-Adad."

761. (32) ᵈUTU-*na-ṣe-*[*er*]
    DUMU *Šu-mi-a-hi-*ʳia¹
    ÌR ᵈEN.ZU-*i-d*[*in-nam*]

"Šamaš-naṣir son of Šumi-ahia, servant of Sin-iddinam."

The uninscribed sealed envelope (cf. No. 649) encloses a letter from Šamaš-naṣir to Awil-ili, and one to Sin-malik. The same patronymic recurs on the seal of Sin-iddinam (not the king); see Goetze, *JCS* 4 (1950), p. 115 top.

769. (32) *Ì-lí-i-din-nam*
    DUMU *Ma-a-nu-um*
    ÌR AN.ÀM

"Ili-iddinam son of M., servant of Anam."

This is the first recorded example of a seal acknowledging Anam of Uruk.

779. (59?) ᵈIŠKUR
    ᵈŠA.LA
    MI

"Adad, Šala, protection (?)."

This divine couple is well attested in seal inscriptions; see Krauss, *Die Götternamen* ..., pp. 45f. The interpretation of the third line is uncertain. Cf. No. 838.

784. (59) ᵈEN.[KI]
    ᵈDAM.GAL.NUN.[NA]

"Enki, Damgalnunna."
Seal inscription extremely faint.

785. (59) Inscription as on No. 784.

786. (63) ᵈNIN.ŠUBUR
    SUKKAL.ZI
    GIDRI.KÙ ŠU.DU₇

"Nin-šubur the good 'angel' who holds the holy scepter."

For similar seal inscriptions, see Krauss, *Die Götternamen* ..., pp. 61–63. Cf. also No. 962.

787. (32) *Ša-lim-*IN
    DUMU NI.IP.PI
    ÌR ᵈ*Ri-im* ᵈEN.ZU

"Š. son of N., servant of Rim-Sin."

The first name recurs in *TIM* 2:3, pp. 11 and 20 (reference courtesy M. Stol). A reading ŠAŠIN may be possible; both names would then be foreign.

788. Text published by [F. W. Geers in] H. H. von der Osten, *OIP* 22 (1934), p. 165, No. 661.

791. (32) (First seal)
    ʳx¹-[*y*]
    DUMU [KU].UN.BA?.RI?.ʳx¹
    [SANGA] ᵈZA.MÀ.[MÀ.]
    [ù] ᵈ[...]
    ÌR ʳ*Ha-am-mu*¹-[*ra-pi*]

"... son of ..., priest of Zamama [and ...], servant of Hammurabi."

    (37) (Second seal)
    E-li-e-ri-iz-[*za*]
    DUMU.MÍ DINGIR-*šu-*[*ib*]-*ni-*[*šu*]
    GEMÉ ᵈZA.MÀ.[MÀ]
    Ù ᵈBA.ʳÚ¹

"Eli-eressa daughter of Ilšu-ibnišu, maidservant of Zamama and Ba'u."

Two other seals are impressed on the envelope, one of a servant of Zamama and N[in-...], one of a servant of Lugal-Gudua.

793. (14) *Nu-úr-*ᵈUTU
    DUMU *Tam-li-ku-um*

"Nur-Šamaš son of Tamlikum."

The signs are disposed in the free spaces left by the design.

794. (67?) ᵈ*La-qí*ʲ*-pu-um*
    ᵈ*A-hu-ú-a*

"La-qipum, Ahua."

The signs are placed within the design. Both names are used here as divine names, not personal names. For the first, see A. Deimel, *Pantheon Babylonicum* (1914), p. 161, Nos. 1807f.; the second occurs in theophoric personal names, especially at Larsa (cf. *UCP* 9:342 No. 18:7, *YOS* 8, p. 26 s.v., and *BIN* 7:163). Both together occur in the form ᵈ*A-hu-ù-a* / ù ᵈ*La!-qì-ip* on a seal (*Louvre A.*, 493) impressed on the Larsa tablet *TCL* 10:18.

The tablet has a second seal inscribed with the same text as Nos. 841 and 855, but with a different design.

799. (12) *Nu-úr-*ᵈMAR.TU
DAM.GÀR
DUMU *En-nam-í-lí*

"Nur-Amurru the merchant, son of Ennam-ili."

The text is published by Simmons, *YOS* 14, No. 42 and the seal impression, *YOS* 14, No. 9*. (For the other seal inscriptions see *YOS* 14, No. 10*–14*.)

802. (32) ᵈEN.ZU-*mu-uš-ta-al*
DUMU ᵈEN.ZU-*ma-*⸢*gir*⸣
ÌR ᵈ*Ri-im-*ᵈEN.ZU

"Sin-muštal son of Sin-magir, servant of Rim-Sin."

The king in line 3 may be Rim-Sin II, if Sin-muštal is the governor (*šāpiru*) of Larsa known from that reign; see M. Stol, *Studies in Old Babylonian History*, pp. 51f. For a seal of the same(?) Sin-muštal son of Sin-magir dedicated to Samsu-iluna see *YOS* 12:113 and 167 (dated Samsu-iluna 4 and 6 respectively).

804. (33) MU.ZU.ŠÈ
DUMU *An-*KA-ᵈ*Eš₄-dar*
ÌR ᵈNIN.ŠUBUR

"Muzuše son of An-pi-Ištar, servant of Nin-šubur."

806. Seal inscriptions published in *YOS* 12, catalogue of seal impressions, sub *A-ak-ka-lu-um*, *A-hu-um-wa-qar*, *Ap-lu-ša*, *Ba-li-lum*, *Mu-ha-du-um* and *Ri-iš-*ᵈUTU.

807. (33) *Ib-ni-*[ᵈIR-RA]
DUMU *E-tel-*[*pi₄-šu*]
[ÌR] ᵈLUGAL-[. . .]

"Ibni-Irra son of Etel-pišu, servant of Lugal-. . . ."

809. (57) Inscription as on No. 741 (in single line).

811. (33) *Ì-lí-e-ri-*[*ba*]
DUMU DINGIR-*šu-mu-*[. . .]
ÌR ᵈPA.[. . .]

"Ili-eriba son of Ilšu-mu . . . , servant of . . . ."

The divine name can perhaps be restored as Nusku (ᵈPA.UDU) or Hendursag (ᵈPA.SAG).

813. (22) ᵈEN.ZU-*na-ap-še-ra*
[ÌR] ᵈNIN-SI₄-AN-NA

"Sin-napšera [servant] of Ninsianna."

The omission of the patronymic is rather unusual.

814. (33?) KU.DU.Ú
DUMU *I-bi-*ᵈNIN.ŠUBUR
ÌR ᵈ[. . .]

"K. son of Ibbi-Ilabrat, servant of . . . ."

815. Inscription illegible.

816. (54) ᵈUTU
"Šamaš"

For the two other seal inscriptions see *YOS* 12, catalogue of seal impressions, sub *Ap-*[. . .] and *I-din-*ᵈ*Na-na-a*.

818. See the publication of the inscription in *OIP* 22 (1934), p. 163, No. 264, but read the patronymic as *Šal-li-lu-mur*, "Šalli-lumur" (with *CAD* A, 2:9a).

819. (75) *ri-me-ni*
⸢ᵈ⸣*É-a*
mu-bal-lí-iṭ
⸢*kur*⸣-*ba-a-šu*

"Take pity on me, Ea, who preserves alive (him who says) 'bless him'!" The inscription is of a type otherwise confined to Kassite seals. See Limet, *Les légendes des sceaux cassites*, pp. 78f.

820. (14) [*U*]⸢?-*bi-*⸣*ì*⸢*l*⸣⸢?⸣
⸢DUMU⸣ *I-bi-*[. . .]

"U. son of Ibbi-. . ."

821. (33) *Mu-na-wi-rum*
DUMU ᵈ[. . .]-*im-gur-ra-an-ni*
ÌR ᵈNUSKU

"Munawwirum son of . . .-imguranni, servant of Nusku."

822. (33) ᵈUTU-*ki-ma-ì-lí-ia*
DUMU ᵈNIN-URTA-MU-IGI./RU-
DA-NI-KI-ÁG
ÌR ᵈNIN-ŠUBUR

"Šamaš-kima-ilia son of Ninurta-mupadani-kiag, servant of Nin-šubur."

823. Text published in *OIP* 22, p. 163, No. 235.

824. (69?) *Sa-bi-tum*
DUMU.MÌ *Ṣíl-lí-*ᵈAM[AR.UD?]
traces

"Sabitum daughter of Ṣilli-Marduk? . . ."

Von Soden, *GGA* 198 (1936), p. 42 read line 3 as *hīrat* (i.e. MÍ.UŠ.DAM) and regarded line 4 as blank.

825. Text edited by Limet, *Les légendes des sceaux cassites* (1971), p. 103, No. 8.3.

826. (33) ÌR-ᵈ*Ab-nu-um*
DUMU *Ma-ṣi-a-am-i-lí*
ÌR ᵈLUGAL.GÚ.DU₈.A

"Warad-Abnum son of Maṣiam-ili, servant of Lugal-Gudua."

The expected form of the seal owner's name is ÌR-*Ab-nim*, as in Falkenstein, *Baghdader Mitteilungen* 2 (1963), p. 72, l. 7. or A. Shaffer, '*Atiqot* 9–10 (1971), p. 198 (reference courtesy M. Stol); cf. Shaffer, note 3 for additional references to the divine name or epithet Abnum, "the Rock." This is the first occurrence with the divine determinative.

827. (33) ᵈNÈ.IRI₁₁.GAL-*e-mu-qá*-[*šu*ˀ]
DUMU *Ị-a-ṣị*-DINGIR
ÌR ᵈAN.MAR.TU

"Nergal-emuqašu son of Ịaṣi-el, servant of Il-Amurrim."

828. (40a) ᵈNANNA.ITI_x (U₄.ᵈNANNA).Ì.ZALAG
[GUDÚ-ABZU] ᵈNIN-GÌR-SÚ
[DUMU] LUGAL-NE.AŠ.ŠA
ÌR ᵈŠE.TIR

"Nanna-iti-izalag (or: Nanna-itini-zalag) *gud-apsû*-priest of Nin-Girsu, son of L. servant of Ašnan (or: Ezinu)."

829. Text published in *OIP*, 22, p. 163 No. 263.

830. (63?) ᵈIŠKUR EN.[GAL]

"Iškur, great lord, . . ."

The second and third lines of the inscription were left blank.

831. (33) *U-bar*-ᵈUTU
DUMU *Nu-úr*-ᵈ*Kab*ˈ-*ta*
ÌR ᵈEN.KI

"Ubar-Šamaš son of Nur-Kabta, servant of Enki."

832. Traces of worn inscription.

833. (33) *A-pil-i-lí-šu*
DUMU *A-pil*-ᵈEN.ZU
ÌR ᵈLUGAL.BÀN.DA

"Apil-ilišu son of Apil-Sin, servant of Lugal-banda."

834. (33) *Ì-lí-tu-ra-am*
DUMU *Ì-lí-ia-tum*
ÌR ᵈNIN.ŠUBUR

"Ili-turram son of Iliatum, servant of Nin-šubur."

835. Traces of worn inscription.

836. Text published in *OIP* 22, p. 163, No. 237.

837. Faint traces of inscription.

838. (59) ᵈIŠKUR
ᵈŠA.LA

"Adad, Šala."

Cf. No. 779.

839. Text published in *OIP* 22, p. 163, No. 239. Note that the temple built by Hammurabi in Babylon for Adad, here called "lord of abundance" (en-nam-hé), was called "house of abundance" (é-nam-hé); see *RLA* s.v.

840. (63) ᵈAN.MAR.TU
DUMU.AN.NA
ŠU.SAG.SÌ.HUL.GI₄

"Il-Amurrim son of Heaven (An), who avenges (or: averts?) destructive defeat."

For other seals inscribed to Amurrum or Il-Amurrim, see Kupper, *Amurru*, pp. 56–68.

841. (63) ᵈ*Na-bi-um*
DUB.SAR SAG.ÍL
KI-ÁGˈ ᵈAMAR.UD

"Nabium scribe of Esagila, beloved of Marduk."

The same inscription occurs on Nos. 794, 855, and on *De Clercq*, 224 for which see Krauss, *Götternamen*, p. 96.

843. Text published in *OIP* 22, p. 163, No. 240.

844. Text published in *OIP* 22, p. 163, No. 242. See also Kupper, *Amurru*, p. 65.

846. Text published in *OIP* 22, p. 163, No. 247, but read in line 1: *E*ˈ-*ri-iš-ti*-ᵈ*A-a*, "Erišti-Aia."

848. (33) *Bu-ri-i*[*a*]
DUMU ᵈIŠKUR-*na*-[. . .]
ÌR *ša* ᵈ[. . .]

"Buria son of Adad-na-. . . , servant of . . . ."

849. (63) ᵈSAK.KUD
PA₄.GAL AN.KI.A
NÍ.ME.LÁM GÚ.È.A

"Sakkud, foremost in heaven and earth, wrapped in divine splendor." For PA₄.GAL = *ašaridu* see Sjöberg, *Heidelberger Studien*, p. 216, n. 24; for NÍ.ME.LÁM = *puluhtu (u) melammu* see Cassin, *La Splendeur Divine*.

855. (63) Inscription as on No. 841.

857. (54) ᵈMAR.TU

"Martu."

This god is paired with a wide variety of male and female deities in other seal inscriptions; see Kupper, *Amurru*, pp. 57–60. Only rarely — as here — does he appear alone; *Amurru*, p. 59, n. 1.

858. (59) ᵈNÈ.IRI₁₁.GAL
ᵈ*Ma-mi-tum*

"Nergal, Mamitum."

The same inscription occurs on Goucher College Seal No. 2, published by I.M. Price, *AJSL* 26 (1910), p. 170f.; see Krauss, *Götternamen*, p. 70f. with note 2.

859. Faint traces.

860. (33) ᵈ*Na-bi-um*-MA.AN.SÌˀ
DUMU *Li-pí-it-Eš₄-dar*ˀˈ
ÌR ᵈNUSKU

"Nabium-iddinam son of Lipit-Ištar, servant of Nusku."

861. Traces of worn inscription.

862. Text published in *OIP* 22, p. 163, No. 234.

870. (59) ᵈEN.ZU
ᵈNIN.GAL

"Sin, Ningal."

873. (59) Inscription as on No. 784.

876. (37) *Il-ta-ni*
DUMU.MÍ DINGIR-*im-gur-an-ni*
GEMÉ ᵈIŠKUR
Ù ᵈNIN-É?ᶦAN.NA

"Iltani daughter of Ili-imguranni, maid-servant of Iškur and Nin-eanna."
Line 4 emended from ᵈNIN.SI₄?.AN.NA in view of Limet, *Les légendes . . .* , pp. 58f., Nos. 2.9 and 2.13.

881. (63) ᵈAN.MAR.TU
DUMU.AN.NA

"Il-Amurrim son of Heaven (An)."
The identical inscription occurs, e.g. in *BN*, No. 257; see Kupper, *Amurru*, pl. vii No. 39, and p. 65.

885. (59) ᵈNIN.URTA
ᵈNIN.EN.LÍL. <KI>

"Ninurta, Nin-Nibrua."
These were the chief god and goddess, re-spectively, of the local pantheon at Nippur.

892. (9) *Ṭab-qì-bi-tum*
GEMÉ ᵈIŠKUR
Ù ᵈŠA.LA

"Tab-qibitum, maidservant of Iškur and Šala."

893. (63) ᵈIŠKUR
DUMU.AN.NA

"Iškur son of Heaven (An)."

896. (Traces)
(Traces)
⌈ÌR ᵈAN.MAR.TU⌉

". . . , servant of Il-Amurrim."

898. Text published in *OIP* 22, p. 162, No. 207.

899. (32) *Ig-mil-* ᵈEN.ZU
DUMU *Ra-ma-nu*
ÌR *Ṣíl-lí.* ᵈEN.ZU

"Igmil-Sin son of R., servant of Ṣilli-Sin."
Given the form of the inscription, Ṣilli-Sin must be a petty dynast of the Old Babylonian period.

900. (60) ᵈKAL.KAL
ᵈ(blank)

904. (63) Inscription as on No. 893.

910. (36) *Hi-iš!-ša-tum*
DUMU ᵈEN.ZU-[. . .]-*ul*
GEMÉ ᵈNÈ.IRI₁₁.GAL

"Hiššatum daughter (!) of Sin-ludlul (?), maidservant of Nergal."

911. (60) ᵈNIN.SI₄.AN.NA
ᵈKAB.TA

"Ninsianna, Kabta."
For identical or similar inscriptions see Krauss, *Die Götternamen . . .* , pp. 86f.

913. Traces of worn inscription.

918. Inscription as on No. 898.

919. (36) *A-ha-tum*
DUMU.MÍ *Nu-úr-ša-x-y*
GEMÉ ᵈNÈ.IRI₁₁.GAL

"Ahatum daughter of Nurša-. . . , maidser-vant of Nergal."

921. Faint traces.

923. (33) ᵈEN.ZU-*mu-di*
DUMU ᵈEN.ZU-*ga-mi-il*
ÌR ᵈAN.MAR.TU

"Sin-mudi son of Sin-gamil, servant of Il-Amurrîm."

932. (22) *Im-gur-*ᵈEN.ZU
ÌR ᵈNIN.SI₄.AN.NA

"Imgur-Sin servant of Ninsianna."

934. Text published in *OIP* 22, p. 162, No. 218.

940. (58) Inscription as on No. 741.

942. (55) ᵈIŠKUR
Ù ᵈNA.U.MAŠ-U.MAŠ

"Iškur and Namašmaš (?)."
In YBC 2401 (ed. Litke, MS), ᵈNA.MAŠ.MAŠ appears as one of three daughters of Iškur (An = *Anum* III 251); cf. *KAV* 48, ii 2.

943. (60) ᵈŠE.TIR
ᵈNISABA

"Ašnan (Ezinu), Nisaba."
The same text occurs on Musée Guimet No. 71; see Krauss, *Die Götternamen . . .* , p. 75.

952. (33) ᵈUTU-*ma-gir*
[DUMU] [*E*]-*tel-*KA-ᵈ[ ]
ÌR ᵈUTU

"Šamaš-magir [son] of Etel-pi-. . ., servant of Utu."

954. (63) ᵈMAR.TU
DUMU.AN.NA
DINGIR ŠU.LUH.BI SIKIL

"Amurru son of Heaven (An), deity whose lustration is pure (cleansing)." The lines are placed within the design.

956. (54) Inscription as on No. 816.

959. ᵈUTU??-X-NA

960. (33) (A) *A-bu-wa-qar*
DUMU *I-ku-pi₄-*⌈*Eš₄+dar*⌉
ÌR ᵈ⌈MA⌉?.MA

(B) ⌜*Tu-um-ru-um*⌝
DUMU *Ú-qá-a-*⌜*a*⌝
ÌR ᵈNÈ.IRI₁₁.⌜ GAL⌝

"Abu-waqar son of Iku(n)-pi-Ištar, servant of Mama."

"Tumrum, son of Uqa, servant of Nergal."

It is assumed that the second inscription goes with design B, but it is not certain.

961. (5?) ⌜ᵈ⌝EN.ZU-*i.*[*qí*]ʔ-[   ]

"Sin-iqišam (?)."

962. (63) ᵈNIN.ŠUBUR
SUKKAL.ZI.AN.⌜NA⌝

"Nin-šubur the good 'angel' of Heaven (An)."

The same text occurs below, No. 1140 and on De Clercq, Nos. 161 and 206. Cf. also No. 786.

980. (58) Inscription as on No. 741.

983. (33) *Ri-iš-*ᵈ[x]
DUMU ᵈEN.ZU-*ga-*[x]
ÌR ᵈNIN-[x]

"Riš-x son of Sin-gamil (?), servant of Nin-x."

984. (63) ᵈNIN.[ŠUBUR]
SUKKAL.ZI.A[N.NA]
GIDRI (PA).KÙ Š[U.DU₇]

"Nin-šubur the good 'angel' of Heaven (An) who holds the holy scepter."

Cf. Nos. 786 and 962.

986. (33?) ᵈAMAR.UD-*zu-uq-qí-i*[*p*]
DUMU *A-hu-um-*[*wa-qar*]
ÌR ᵈ*Sa-*[*am-su-i-lu-na*]

"Marduk-zuqqip son of Ahum-waqar, servant of Samsu-iluna (or Samana?)."

Personal names restored from texts of *YOS* 12:401 and 380 (which has the same seal). But note that 401 writes (in text): ᵈAMAR.UD-*zu-un-qí-ip.*

991. (35) (A) SIG-ᵈA.A
DUMU ᵈUTU-TAB.BA-*šu*
ÌR É.UD.RA

(35) (C) UR-ᵈ[. . .]
DUMU [. . .]-ŠU?
ÌR É.UD.UD.RA

(33) (D) DINGIR-*šu-ib-ni-*[*šu*]
DUMU DUMU-*er-ṣe*[*tim*]
ÌR ᵈ[. . .]

(A) "Ipiq-Aia son of Šamaš-tappašu, servant of Ebabbara."

(C) "Ur-[. . .] son of [. . .]-šu, servant of Ebabbara."

(D) Ilšu-ibnišu son of Mar-erṣetim, servant of . . . ."

For other seal inscriptions on this tablet, see *YOS* 12:536.

993. Inscription virtually illegible.

996. (14) *I-din-*ᵈN[*a-bi-um*]
DUMU UR.[. . .]

"Iddin-Nabium son of Ur-. . . ."

Text published *YOS* 13:278, but without this or several other seal inscriptions.

998. (34) Šuʔ-[. . .]
DUMU X-[. . .]
ÌR ᵈ[. . .]
Ù ᵈ[. . .]

"Šu-[. . .] son of . . . , servant of . . . and . . . ."

Text published *YOS* 13:402, but without this and other several other seal inscriptions.

1003. (34) *An-*KA-[. . .]
DUMU ÌR-ᵈ[. . .]
ÌR ᵈ[. . .]
Ù ᵈNINʔ-[. . .]

"An-pi-[. . .] son of Warad-[. . .], servant of . . . and Nin-[. . .]."

1005. (33) (A) DINGIR-*šu-ib-ni*
DUMU ᵈAMAR.UD-*na-ṣe-ir*
ÌR ᵈ[. . .]

(B) ᵈEN.ZU-*i-ri-*[*ba-am*]
DUMU *Ib-ni-*ᵈ[MAR.TU]
ÌR ᵈMAR.[TU]

(A) "Ilšu-ibni son of Marduk-naṣer, servant of . . ."

(B) "Sin-eribam son of Ibni-Amurru, servant of Amurru."

For copies of these inscriptions, see Finkelstein, *YOS* 13:89. For discussion, see *Ash C*, p. 228, No. 551 and M. Stol, *Bi.Or.* 33 (1976), p. 148 and n. 5.

1008. Seal inscription published by Finkelstein, *YOS* 13, p. 89:314A.

1021. (52) ᵈEN.ZU-*iš-me-*[*a-an-ni*]
DUB.[SAR]
DUMU ᵈAMAR.[UD-*mu-ba-lí-it*]
ÌR ᵈ[. . .]

"Sin-išmeanni the scribe, son of Marduk-muballiṭ, servant of . . . ."
See *YOS* 13:262.

1023. Seal inscriptions published by Finkelstein, *YOS* 13, p. 93:521D (A-B) and p. 93:521A (C).

1036. (54) ᵈAN.[MAR.TU]

"Il-Amurrim (?)."

1042. (A) [. . .]-ME DUBʔ.S[AR]?
(B) Ú.NI.HU.RU[M]?

1043. (22) AP-X
ÌR ᵈMAR.TU

"Ap-. . ., servant of Amurru."

The reading of the divine name is assured by the iconography. For other examples of two opposed crooks over the back of a gazelle see Kupper, *Amurru*, p. 44, note 1.

1045. (33) ᵈEN.ZU-*ri-me-ni*
    DUMU UR.MES.UKKIN.NA
    ÌR ᵈ*Na-bi-um*

"Sin-rimeni son of Ur-mesukkina, servant of Nabium."

For the patronymic, cf. *UET* 5, p. 63 s.v. UR.DUB.PISÁN.NA.

1046. Traces of worn inscription.

1047. (33) *Pír-hu-um*
    DUMU ᵈEN.ZU-*ra-bi*
    ⌜ÌR⌝ ᵈIŠKUR

"Pirhum son of Sin-rabi, servant of Adad."

1048. (33) [*Be*]-*la-nu-um*
    DUMU *A-wi-il*-ᵈINANNA
    ÌR ᵈNÈ-IRI₁₁!.GAL

"Belanum son of Awil-Ištar, servant of Nergal."

For a similar seal inscription, cf. *YOS* 13:285, 291, and 440.

1049. (33) *Ú-qa*-SA.MA.AN
    DUMU *Ì-lí*-AR.TA.x.A
    ÌR ᵈ*Na-bi-um*

"Uqa-S. son of Ili-a., servant of Nabium."

1050. Inscription published in *OIP* 22, p. 163, No. 233.

1051. (63?) ᵈUTU ŠU.
    E.ŠU
    a-šib er-ṣe-tim
    URU.MAŠ.GÁN
    NÁG.ŠAM.URU

"Šamaš ... who dwells on earth, city and country, city and country."
Reading and translation highly uncertain.

1052. (75?) ᵈAMAR.UD
    ᵈINANNA-TI
    ka-ri-ba-ZU

"Oh Marduk, I. is your worshipper."

Reading and translation uncertain.

1053. (75) ᵈIŠKUR
    DUMU AN.NA
    GÚ.GAL AN.KI
    [SA]?.AR.DINGIR
    [ÌR].ZU HÉ.[TI]

"Oh Iškur son of Heaven (An), canal inspector of heaven and earth, Sar-il(?) (is)your servant: may he live"!

For the second divine epithet, commonly found with Iškur (Adad), see *CAD* G s.v. *gugallu*.

1054. Text published in *OIP* 22, p. 163, No. 258.

1056. (34) *Ib-ni*-ᵈ*Uraš*
    DUMU *Ku-úr-ku-du*?!-*a-bi*
    ÌR ᵈEN.ZU
    Ù ᵈMAR.TU

"Ibni-Uraš son of Kurkudu-abi, servant of Sin and Amurru."

1057. Text published in *OIP* 22, p. 162, No. 231.

1058. (33) HU.PI
    DUMU Ú.TU.NA
    ÌR ᵈIŠKUR

"Hupi son of U., servant of Adad."

1059. Text published in *OIP* 22, p. 164, No. 271. Cf. No. 840.

1060. Text published in *OIP* 22, p. 162, No. 223.

1061. (59) ᵈEN.LÍL
    ᵈNIN.LÍL

"Enlil (and) Ninlil."

For the same inscription see e.g. Krauss, *Die Götternamen...*, p. 23.

1062. Text published in *OIP* 22, p. 164, No. 269.

1063. Text published in *OIP* 22, p. 164, No. 267.

1064. Traces of worn inscription.

1065. (5) *A-lí-a-hi*

"Ali-ahi."

1067. (22) ᵈEN.ZU-*e-mu-qí*
    ÌR ᵈNIN.ŠUBUR

"Sin-emuqi, servant of Ninšubur."

1068. (60) Inscription as on No. 911.

1092. (39) *Ša-at*-ᵈMAR?!.TU?
    DUMU *Ṭà-ab-ba*?-*la*?-*zu*
    GEMÉ?ᵈURAŠ? *hi-Iír*?-*tim*?

"Šat-Amurru child of Ṭab-balassu, maidservant of Uraš the spouse (of An)."

Readings conjectural.

1093. (15?) *Šu*-ᵈNIN.ŠUBUR
    DUMU *Šu-ì-lí* SU

"Šu-Ilabrat son of Šu-ili the ....."

1093A. (28?) *Si-li-bi*
    NU?!.BÀNDA
    A.DA.PA.ŠUB?
    ŠU.I ÌR

"Šelibi the lieutenant (?), A. the barber (is your) servant."

The first name may conceivably be compared with Šelibi (Šelibum), associated with Sabum and Anšan in a variety of spellings in Ur III texts; see *MAD* 3, p. 258.

1095. Reading uncertain.

1096. (38) *Ha-ab-lu*
DUMU *Ap-li*
ÌR *šà* ᵈNÈ.IRIGAL ₓ (IRI₁₁)

"Hablu son of Apli servant of Nergal."

Readings uncertain.

1097. (61?) ᵈLAMMA (?)
ᵈALÀD (?)

The readings are little more than conjectures. See most recently von Soden, "Die Schutzgenien Lamassu und Schedu . . . ," *Baghdader Mitteilungen* 3 (1964), p. 148–56.

1098. (38) *El¹-me-šum*
DUMU Ù.A.KU (or ENGUR?)
ÌR ᵈU₄.TA.ULU

"Elmešum son of U., servant of Uta'ulu(?)."

1099. (38) *É-a-i-qí´-ša*
DUMU *Šu-nu-ma*-DINGIR
ÌR É.A

"Ea-iqišă son of Šunuma-El, servant of Ea."

1136. (21?) *Da-di-e-ba-al*
ÌR *Pu-ul-sú-na*-/ᵈIŠKUR

"Dadi-ebal servant of Pulsuna-Adad."

1139. (62) Inscription as on Nos. 911 and 1068.

1140. (64) Inscription as on No. 962.

1141. (56) ᵈDUMU.[ZI]
ù ᵈ[AN.MA]R.TU

"Dumuzi and Il-Amurrim."

1143. (64) Inscription as on No. 893.

1146. (16) (B) *La-qí-pu-um*
DUMU *I-za-li-a*

"La-qipum son of Izalia."

The inscription was carved in positive fashion, so that the impression appears as a negative, and line 2 precedes line 1. This is a common practice with Old Assyrian seals, though not always recognized.

1149. (58) Inscription as on No. 741.

This is a typical Old Babylonian inscription; see above for the characterization of the design as Old Babylonian.

1150. (16) (C) X-ŠA.UD?.MAS?
[DU]MU? E?/KU?.AN/MU-X

Reading uncertain.

1153. ⌜uncertain signs⌝
DUMU KÀ.RI.IM X
GA.A.KU.ŠA.KU.LI

In line 2, read perhaps Mar-Karim and compare the personal name Mar-Garia for which see Stephens, *Personal Names of Cappadocia* (= *YOR* 13/1, 1928) p. 57. Inscription carved in positive fashion.

1159. (16) *A-šir!*-PA. [UDU]
DUMU *Púzur-Eš₄-dar*

"Aššur-re'um son of Puzur-Ištar."

Same seal impression on *TCL* 21:247B (seal no. 45). Inscription carved in positive fashion.

1165. (16) *A-šir-ba-ni*
DUMU *En-na-su-in*

"Aššur-bani son of Enna-Sin."

Same seal impression in *TCL* 21, pl. CCXXXIII (seal no. 46) = de Genouillac, *Céramique Cappadocienne* 1, pl. A, no. 6. Carved in positive fashion.

1197. Text published in *OIP* 22, p. 162, No. 222.

1203. The legible hieroglyphics include, according to my colleague W. K. Simpson, the Djed sign and the Nefer sign. These and the other signs are amulaic in character and not intended to constitute a coherent inscription.

1204. See the discussion of the seal by von der Osten, *OIP* 22, pp. 49f., No. 319.

1283. NA₄-KIŠIB
LUKUR ŠA.AM.BI
MUNUS URU ??? HA.AM./BA.AN

"Stone seal of the priestess Š., woman of the city (?) Hamban."

Reading and translation conjectural. For Hamban see most recently Salonen, *Bi.Or.* 25 (1968), pp. 101f. and *Die Fussbekleidung der alten Mesopotamier*, pp. 82–85.

Indices by Brian Lewis

PERSONAL NAMES

Adallal 540, 632
A.DA.PA.ŠUB? 1093A
ADDA 524
A.ENGUR(?) 410; cf. 1098
A.GA[. . ./- . . . I]M 654
AGI 559
A-ha-ba-nu-um 1054
Ahatum 919
Ahumma 512, 1062
Ahum-waqar 806, 986
Ahu-waqar 788
A.KALLA 516, 640
Ali-ahi 1065
Ali-ahua 607
ALLA 623
ALLAMU 541
AMAR.SUENA 627, 681
AMAR.[   ] 615
AN.AB.KAL 507
ANAM 769
ANNEZU 670
An-pi-Ištar 804
An-pi-[. . .] 1003
Apil-ilišu 833
Apil-Sin 833
Apli 1096
Apluša 806
Ap-. . . 1043
Aššur-bani 1165
Aššur-re'um 1159
Atta-mannum 753
ATU 655
Awil-Ištar 1048
Awil-Marduk 823
AZIA 745

BABATI 637ii, 654
Bal-ilum (?) 688, 806
BAZI 621
Belanum 1048, 1050
BIDUGA 597, 667
BUBU 399
Bur-Adad 716
Buria . . . 848

DA'AGA 523, 558
DA'AGI 601
DADA 430, 584, 617, 644, 645
DADA.KALLA 592
DADUMU 544
Dadi-ebal 1136
Damiq-ili 628
DAMU.GALZU 751
Daqqum 455, 934
DAR 669
DINGIR.AMU 512
DUDU 457, 474, 587
DUMU.I 410
DU.RU.A.BI 665
Durum-mupi 452

Ea-iqiša 1099
E.?/KU?.AN/MU-x 1150
Ea-. . . 1023 (521)
Eli-eressa 791
Elmešum 1098
EN.KAS₄ 620
ENLIL.AMAHA 681
EN.LUL 424
EN.MIUSSA 517
Enna-il 243
Ennam-ili 799
[EN.NAM].ŠITAₓ.GUB 525
Enna-Sin 1165
Erišti-Aia 846
Etel-pišu 807
Etel-pi. . . 952

GUDEA 538
GUGUA 572
GUMU 520
GUZANA 507

HA.BA.AN.NA 862
Hablu 1096
Hammurabi 791
HI.NI 631
Hiššatum 910
HUPI 1058
Huzalum 818

Iaṣi-el 827
I.AZ?.TI.IL 565
I.BA.ŠE.ME 739
Ibbi-Adad 679
Ibbi-Ilabrat 814
Ibbi-Sin 636, 649, 653
Ibbi-. . . 820
Ibni-Amurru 1005
Ibni-Irra 807
Ibni-Uraš 1056
Iddin-abum 430
Iddin-Ea 823
Iddin-Nabium 996
IDUDU 553
Igmil-Sin 899
Igmulum 581
Iku(n)-pi-Ištar 960
Ili-AR.TA.x.A? 1049
Iliatum 834
Ili-eriba 811
Ili-iddinam 769
Ili-illat 419
Ili-imguranni 876
Ili-turram 834
Ilšu-ibni 1005
Ilšu-ibnišu 791, 991
Ilšu-mu-. . . 811
Iltani 876
Ilum-bani 540
Imgur-Sin 932
INANNAKA 527

^dINANNA.TI 1052
INIM.INANNA 588
INIM.ŠARA 660
Ipiq-Aia 991
Ipiq-erṣetim 825
IR 659
IRBUBU 424
IRDANI 414
Iriš-Agga 628
Irra-ellatsu 836
Išar-beli 466
Iškun-Dagan 429
Ištar-alšu 417
Itebšunu 1057
I-ti-la-nim? 631
Ititi 581
Izalia 1146B

KA'A 659
KU.DAG 428
KU.DU.Ú 814
KULI 608
⌈KU⌉.UN.BA?.RI?-⌈x⌉ 791
KU.NINURRA 598
Kurkudu-abi 1056

LA'AŠA 597, 667
LALA 567
La-qipum, 1146
Lipit-Ištar 860
LU.BA'U 639
LU.DINGIRA 423
LU.DINGIRANA 423
LU.EZIN 590
LUGAL.AMARU 580
LUGAL.BARAGE.SI 571
LUGALBI 561
LUGAL.DINGIR 674
LUGAL.DUBLA 672
LUGALE.IGISUD 580
LUGAL.EMAHE 547, 573, 619
LUGAL.ENGARDU 425, 609, 681
LUGAL.ERIDUŠE 524
LUGAL.EZEN 528, 604, 606, 619, 670
LUGAL.GABA 534
LUGAL.GARLAGARE 584
LUGAL.GIRI 616, 638
LUGAL.IBILA 836
LUGAL.ITIDA 522, 588, 627
LUGAL.KI?.BAD 674
LUGAL.KUGANI 547, 663
LUGAL.KUZU 600
LUGAL.MELAM 647
LUGAL.NE.AŠ.ŠA 828
LUGAL.NIRGAL 661
LUGAL.NUDUGA 658
LUGAL.PA'E 528, 529
LUGAL.SAG.ZU? 491
LUGAL.ŠAGA 613, 641
LUGAL.URŠAGA 536

LUGAL.USAR 599, 618
LUGAL-. . . 530, 807
LU.GIRIZAL 544
LU.IGIŠAŠA 575
LU.INANNA 398
LU.IZU 511
LÚ-^dKAL.KAL 570
LU'LU 517
LU.NANNA 603i
LU.NINGIRSU 503, 591, 646
LU.ŠAGA 658
LUŠAMU 580
LU-ŠARA 511, 614, 623
LU.UTU 621
LÚ-[ ] 569, 1023 (521)

Ma-a-nu-um 769
MAMA 669
MANSI 572, 625
Marduk-muballiṭ 1021
Marduk-naṣer 1005
Marduk-zuqqip 986
Mar-erṣetim 991
Mar-Ištar 843
Mar-Karim 1153
Maṣiam-ili 826
MEBA.ŠASU 418
MES.E 645
Muballissin 478
Muhaddum 806
Munawwirum 821
MUNI 602
Mu?-ra?-gi-mu 1062
Mutanum 1057
MUZUŠE 804

Nabi-ilišu 709
Nabi-Sin 829
Nabium 841, 849
Nabium-iddinam 860
NADI 598, 671
NAGA 612
NAMLUGALANI.DU 441
NANNA.ITI.IZALAG (or NANNA.ITINI.ZALAG) 828
Nanna-mansi 760
NANNA.MUDAH 586
Naram-Ea 466
Naram-ili 648
NAŠA 643
Nati'um 532
NE.NA.A 739
Nergal-abzu 1197
Nergal-emuqa 827
NÍG.BA.E 534
NIG.DUGA 519
⌈NÍG⌉.GA.^dEN.ZU 751
NIGMU 515
NIG.URUM 608
NIN.INIMZIDA 1197
NIN.KALLA 565

NINKIMARAKA 567
NINPA 701
NINURTA.MUPADANI.KIAG 822
NIN-[. . .] 653, 983, 1003
NI.IP.PI 787
NIR.KIAGA 592
NITA.MU (or UŠ.MU) 613, 641
NÍ.TUK 1008
NUN.KA(?) 427
Nur-Adad 760
Nur-Amurru 799
Nur-Ištar 577
Nur-ili 596
Nur-ilišu 709, 788
Nur-Kabta 831
Nur-Sin 753
Nur-Šamaš 793
Nurša-. . . 919

PA.LÍL.ME.HA.IL 478
Pirhum 1047
Pulsuna-Adad 1136
Puzur-Ištar 1159
PUZUR.LU 677

Ra-ma-nu 899
Rim-Sin 787, 788, 802
Riš-Šamaš 806
Riš-x 983
Rubatum 452

Sabitum 824
SAGSA 683
SAG.ŠA$_6$ 561
Sakkud-ta'ar 1050
Samsu-ditana 1023 (521)
Samsu-iluna 986
Samum 843
SAR.IL(?) 1053
Sa-ru-um 1060
SÁ.TU 254
SIA'A 596
SI.GÀR 317
Sin-emuqi 1067
Sin-eribam 1005
Sin-gamil 923, 983(?)
Sin-iddinam 761
Sin-iqišam(?) 961
Sin-išmeanni 1021
Sin-ludlul 910
Sin-magir 802
Sin-muballiṭ 1050
Sin-mudi 923
Sin-muštal 802
Sin-napšera 813
Sin-rabi 1047
Sin-rimeni 1045
ᵈ*Sin-tappe* 934
SIPA.NINGIRSUKE.IPA 538

Sumu-el 753
Ṣilli-Marduk 824
Ṣilli-Sin 899
Ṣilli-x 656
Ṣelluš-Dagan 679
ŠA.AM.BI 1283
ŠA.LIM-IN 787
Šalim-niaš 675
Šalli-lumur 818
Šamaš-andul 862
Šamaš-kima-ilia 822
Šamaš-magir 952
Šamaš-naṣir 761
Šamaš-tappašu 991
ŠARAKAM 616, 638, 660
Šar-kali-šarri 429
Šat-Amurru 1092
Ša-x-[. . .] 521
Šelibi 1093A
ŠEŠANI 644
ŠEŠBE.MUSIGA 472
ŠEŠ.KALLA 611, 617, 636
ŠEŠ.ŠAGA 564
Šu-Ilabrat 1093
Šu-ili 417, 595, 1093
Šu-Irra 683
ŠULGI 596, 606, 639, 642, 643, 648, 660
Šu-mama 576
Šumi-ahia 761
Šunuma-El 1099
Šu-Sin 637, 646, 647, 650, 651, 652, 654
ŠU-[. . .] 998

Tamlikum 793
Taribu 1008
Tuta-šar-libbiš 429
Tulid-Šamaš 716
Tumrum 960
Ṭab-balassu 1092
Ṭab-qibitum 899

Ù.A.KU (or ENGUR?) 1098; cf. 410?
Ubar-Šamaš 831
[*U?*]-*bi-ḫIⁱ?* 820
UD.IŠ.NA.NI 577
UKKINE 622
UMANI 523, 636, 692
Ú.NI.HU.RU[M] 1042
Uqa 960 (2)
Uqa-SA.MA.AN 1049
UR.AMMA 511, 573
URANI 303
UR.AŠAR 522
UR.BA'U 533, 657, 673
UR.DINGIRA 559
UR.DUMUZIDA 564, 611, 627
UR.E'ANNA 526
URE.BABDU 655
UR.E'E 514
UR.É.MAŠ 624
UR.ENINNU 541

UR.ÈŠ (or AB.LÁL) 297
UR.É/GIŠ.[. . .] 678
URGA 603
URGAR 513
UR.GIGIR 576, 622, 692
UR.GILGAMEŠ 582, 665
UR.GIPAR 574, 582
UR.GIŠBARE 672
UR.GIŠŠAGE 558
URGU 491
UR.HAIA 650
UR.IGALIMA 571, 673
UR.INANNA 526
UR.IŠTARAN 620
UR-ᵈ[KA.TAR] 536
UR.KISAL 253
UR.KUNUNA 646
UR.LAMA 513, 570, 647?
UR.LI 431
UR.LISINA 575, 625
UR.LUGAL 601
UR.L[U. . .] 407
UR.MEME 425
UR.MES 591, 612, 701
UR.MESUKKINA 1045
UR.NAMUŠDA 580
UR.NANŠE·673
UR.NIGINGAR 514, 516, 563, 600, 625, 640, 649,
    656, 657
UR.NISABA 666
UR.NUNGAL 626
URRA.DINGIR 553
UR-SIN 671, 678
UR.ŠAGA 562, 563, 590, 614
UR.ŠARA 529, 599, 618, 626
UR.ŠUL 562
UR.ŠULPA'E 615, 650, 663
UR.ŠUMAHA 649
UR.TAR 624
URU.KIBI 520, 604
UR.UR 410
UR.UTU 595
UR-. . . 996
UR-ᵈ[. . .] 530, 991
UŠ.MU (or NITA.MU) 613, 641
UTU.GIRGAL 642
UTU.IDU 586
Ú.TU.NA 1058
ᵈUTU?-X-NA 959

Warad-ᵈAb-nu-um 826
Warad-[. . .] 1003

ZANINI 414
ZUZUA 677
[. . .]-ME 1042
[. . .]-RIA 419
[. . .]-ŠU 991
[x]-É-KU.BI 519
X-ŠAGA 673
X-ŠA-UD!-MAŠ? 1150
ᵈ[. . .]-*imguranni* 821

EPITHETS

A. Degree

DUB.SAR 303 et passim

B. Role

AŠGAB 580A, 655, 680
AŠLAG (GEŠTÚ.KAR.RÁ) 419
ASLAG$_X$ (LÚ.TÚG) 632
DAM-GÀR 398, 424, 520, 540, 799
EN 525
EN.KAS$_4$ 456
ENSÍ 466, 536, 538, 575, 625, 651, 652, 654, 679
GÌR.NITÁ 562, 596, 654
gudapsû 828
GUDÚ 517, 576, 602, 829
I.DU$_8$ 648
IŠIB 474
IŠIB.MAH 587
KURUŠDA 563, 590, 643, 646
LÚ.BAPPIR 591
LÚ.BAPPIR.MAH 529
LUGAL 429, 596, 606, 627, 636, 637, 639, 642,
    643, 646, 647, 648, 649, 650, 651, 652, 653,
    654, 660, 681
LUKUR 1283
MÁŠ.ŠU.GÍD.GÍD 760
NA.[GADA]? 592
NAR 612, 669
NIMGIR 466, 1023, (521)
NIN 429, 656, 675
NIN.DINGIR 532
NU.BÀNDA 563, 590, 608, 618, 1093A
NU.ÈŠ 681
NU.^{GIŠ}GIRI$_{11}$ 522, 567
RÁ.GABA 538, 606, 639
SAHAR 472, 559, 600, 640
SANGA 423, 791
SA$_{12}$.SUG$_5$.LUGAL(A)/.KA 660
SÌLA.ŠU.DU$_8$ 524, 533
SIPA 512, 521, 592(?)
SUKKAL 623, 624, 648, 653
SUKKAL.MAH 615
ŠABRA 429, 534, 541, 562, 619, 656
ŠABRA.É 430
ŠA$_X$(GÁ).DUB.BA 626, 654
ŠÀ.TAM 254(?), 642
ŠÀ.TAM LUGAL 654
ŠITA$_X$?.GAL? 674
ŠITIM.GAL 603
ŠU.I 1093A
TIBIRA 491
UGULA 491, 609, 681
UGUAL.É 425
UKU.UŠ 536

C. Status

DAM 565, 701
DUMU 398 et passim
DUMU.MÍ 716, 824, 876, 919

D. Rank

GEMÉ DN 791, 846, 862, 876, 892, 910, 919,
    1054, 1092
GEMÉ ON 675
ÌR DN 441, 632, 661, 746, 760, 804, 807, 811,
    813, 814(?), 818, 821, 822, 823, 826, 827, 828,
    829, 831, 833, 834, 836, 843, 848, 860, 896,
    923, 932, 934, 952, 960(1), 960(2), 983, 986,
    991(D), 998, 1003, 1005, 1021, 1023(521A),
    1043, 1045, 1047, 1048, 1049, 1056, 1057,
    1058, 1062, 1067, 1096, 1099
ÌR ON 452(?)
ÌR PN 452(?), 530(?), 533(?), 577, 582, 586, 683,
    752, 753, 761, 769, 787, 1008, 1023 (521D),
    1098, 1136
ÌR RN 787, 788, 791, 802, 899
ÌR TN 991
ÌR.ZU 417, 419, 429, 430, 466, 538, 562, 575,
    606, 615, 625, 627, 636, 637, 639, 642, 643,
    646, 647, 648, 649, 650, 651, 652, 660, 679,
    681, 825, 1053, 1093A
ÌR.DA.NI 414, 423, 653, 654
LÚ 414(?)
LÚ ON 532
MÍ GN? 1283

DIVINE NAMES

Adad 794, 779, 830, 838, 839, 843, 876, 892,
    893, 904, 942, 1047, 1053, 1058, 1143
Aia 712, 719, 741, 742, 744, 749, 756, 759,
    809, 846, 940, 980, 1149
ᵈALÀD(?) 1097
Amurru 746, 844, 857, 898, 918, 954, 1005,
    1043, 1056, 1057, 1062
AŠNAN (or: EZINU) 828, 943
BA'U 524, 791
Belat-šuhnir 654
Belat-teraban 654
DAMGALNUNNA 784, 785, 873
DUMUZI 1141
Ea 819, 829, 1099
ENKI 518, 784, 785, 823, 831, 873
ENLIL 429, 603, 681, 1061
Il-Amurrim 827, 840, 881, 896, 923, 934, 1036,
    1054, 1056, 1059, 1141
INANNA 425, 587, 681
IŠKUR—see Adad
Ištar 829
KABTA 911, 1068, 1139
ᵈKAL.KAL 900
ᵈLAMMA(?) 1097
Laqipum 794
LUGALBANDA 833
ᵈLUGAL-GUDUA 826
ᵈLUGAL-. . . 807
MAMA 960
Mamitum 858
Marduk 794, 841, 849, 855, 1052
Nabium 794, 841, 855, 1045, 1049
NAMAŠMAŠ 942
NANNA 632, 760, 825

NERGAL 836, 858, 910, 919, 960, 1048, 1062,
    1063, 1096
NIN-EANNA 876
NIN-EGAL 862
NINGAL 870
NIN-GIRSU 828
NIN.KARRAK 743
NINLIL 1061
NIN.NIBRUA 885
NINSIANNA 813, 911, 932, 1068, 1139
NIN.ŠUBUR 786, 804, 822, 834, 962, 984, 1067,
    1140
NINURRA 602
NINURTA 885
NIN- 533
NISABA 943
NUSKU 821, 860
PABILSAG 743
ᵈPA.[ ] 811
SAKKUD 848, 1023 (521), 1050
Sin 818, 870, 1056
ᵈSUMUQAN? 1008
ŠALA 779, 838, 892
Šamaš 712, 741, 742, 744, 749, 759, 809, 816,
    846, 940, 952, 956, 980, 1051, 1149
ŠARA 441, 618, 661
URAŠ 818, 1092
UTA'ULU 1098
ZAMAMA 791
ᵈX-ME 714
ᵈX-TUN.GÍR.DUL.LÍ.KI 525

DIVINE EPITHETS

DINGIR ŠÀ.LÁ.SÙ . . . TI.LA.A.NI 825
DINGIR ŠU.LUH.BI SIKIL 954
DUMU.AN.NA 840, 844, 881, 893, 898, 904, 918,
    954, 1053, 1059, 1063, 1143
EN.GAL 830
EN.NAM.HÉ 839
GIDRI.KÙ ŠU.DU₇ 786, 844, 984
GÚ.GAL AN.KI 1053
KALAM.E ZI SÌ.MU 839
mu-bal-li-iṭ ⸢kur⸣-ba-a-šu 819
NÍ.ME.LÁM GÚ.È.A 848
PA₄.GAL AN.KI.A 848
SUKKAL.ZI 786
SUKKAL.ZI.AN.NA 962, 984, 1140
ŠU E.ŠU a-šib er-ṣe-tim URU.MAŠ.GÁN . . . 1051
ŠU.SAG.SÌ.HUL.GI₄ 840

GEOGRAPHICAL NAMES

A- . . . 654
EBABBARA 991
É.ᵈINANNA 425, 609, 681
ESAGILA 841, 849
GUTIUM 429
HAMBAN 1283
IN 423
LAGAŠ 538

Maškan-šarrum 654
SIMURRUM 679
ŠEŠ 532
UMMA 562, 575, 625, 651, 652

UR 596, 606, 627, 636, 637, 639, 642, 643, 646, 647, 648, 649, 650, 651, 652, 653, 654, 660
URUK 466
ZABALAM 587

CONCORDANCE OF MUSEUM NUMBERS

Buchanan	MLC	MLC	Buchanan
424*†	1946	113*	764
626*†	2658	202*	983
643*†	2338	203*	983
654*†	1822	210*	1019
666*†	1902	222*	996
754*	1218	223*	1019
755*	1688	425*	1002
764*	113	446*	1012xx
791*†	1220	455*	1019x
817*	1581	555*	1039
952*	959	606*	1005
	967	610*	983
	945	644*	1023
961*†	1307	807*	1016
971*	no no.	811*	1018
978*	1682	828*	1011
983*†	202	836*	1034
	610	897*	1042
	203	945*	952
983x*	1618	959*	952
995*	1287	967*	952
996*†	222	1206*	1033
999x*	1524	1214*	1000x
1000x*	1214	1218*	754
1000xx*	1392	1220*	791
1002*	425	1287*	995
1005*†	606	1307*	961
1006*	1388	1331*	1021
1008*†	1394	1334*	1016x
1009xx*	1690	1388*	1006
1011*	828	1392*	1000xx
1012xx*	446	1394*	1008
1014x*	1564	1515*	1029
1016*	807	1524*	999x
1016x*	1334	1564*	1014x
1017*	2228	1570*	1021x
1018*	811	1581*	817
1019*	223	1604*	1025
	210	1618*	983x
1019x*	455	1628*	1022x
1020*	2212	1654*	1027
1021*†	1331	1656*	1024
1021x*	1570	1682*	978
1022*	1742	1688*	755
1022x*	1628	1690*	1009xx
1022xx*	2559	1742*	1022
1023*†	644	1822*	654
1024*	1656	1902*	666
1025*	1604	1946*	424
1027*	1654	2212*	1020
1029*	1515	2228*	1017
1033*	1206	2338*	643
626		2658*	626
1034*	836	no no.*	971
1039*	555		
1042*†	897		

*impression on clay object
†inscription

Buchanan	Newell (NCBS)	Buchanan	Newell (NCBS)
5	(873)	223	(833)
10	370	227	650
50	367	238	(819)
63	366	240	681
86	(874)	246	80
90	9	249	78
92	8	251	(745)
93	1	252	81
96	6	256	86
97	5	257	79
98	4	258	(867)
99	2	260	77
100	7	263	76
103	3	267	72
106	11	271	(772)
107	10	272	(801)
108	371	273	647
115	20	274	49
118	12	275	(830)
119	13	277	65
120	15	278	(823)
121	14	279x	(719)
122	17	279xx	(812)
123	16	281	44
125	19	282	50
126	18	283	51
127	(875)	284	670
132	21	289	113
133	690	290	(863)
135	669	293	75
137	61	294	(779)
138	22	297†	73
139	695	299	38
146	29	302	85
148	30	307	74
153	31	308	83
159	(853)	313	87
163	27	314	88
164	28	315	678
166	24	316	(785)
167	25	321	(720)
171	(791)	322	(783)
172	26	323	(753)
174	57	325	34
180	62	328	40
186	(814)	329	39
187	64	330	43
188	63	336	(792)
189	(842)	337	(816)
190	(856)	339	37
197	(869)	340	46
199	69	342	42
201	66	343	41
207	68	345	47
208	70	347	48
217	32	348	(864)
221	(714)	349	35

*impression on clay object
†inscription

Buchanan	Newell (NCBS)	Buchanan	Newell (NCBS)
350	36	481	671
352	(742)	483	52
353	(748)	487	55
354	67	488	54
357	58	489	53
358	60	490	45
359	59	491†	185
363	(697)	501	(744)
366	(858)	505	(700)
368	295	512*†	(2248)
372	(699)	513†	93
373	82	521†	108
374	(698)	523*†	(2247)
377	(862)	524†	104
378	(724)	526†	(800)
379	(757)	527†	107
380	(764)	530†	(829)
381	(850)	531	109
382	111	532†	105
383	110	535	158
386	112	541*†	(2251)
388	(765)	542	170
389	(778)	543	(841)
390	106	545	(848)
393	91	546	186
394	90	548	116
395	(793)	549	138
396	89	552	(827)
399†	677	553†	674
401	101	554	122
403	679	556	114
404	(857)	561†	118
405	102	565†	124
408	(773)	566	121
409	103	567†	140
410†	100	568†	117
411	(852)	569†	128
414†	99	571*†	(2244)
416	98	573x	(855)
417†	95	578	119
420†	92	579	120
422	673	581†	131
423†	96	583	(810)
426	94	586†	126
428†	97	590*†	(2250)
431*†	(2281)	592*†	(2252)
436	154	594	172
438	153	596†	135
439	151	599*†	(2241)
445	(859)	605†	129
447	167	607†	(838)
449	648	610	132
453	(805)	617xx*	(2234)
457†	680	628†	(849)
464	683	632†	136
472†	668	633	134
476	115	639*†	(2249)

*impression on clay object
†inscription

Buchanan	Newell (NCBS)	Buchanan	Newell (NCBS)
648x*	(2307)	833†	265
657*†	(2243)	835†	232
658*†	(2253)	836†	237
659†	(820)	839†	239
662	197	841†	238
663*†	(2268)	843†	240
664	141	844†	242
665†	143	845	212
670†	127	846†	247
672*†	(2263)	847†	246
674†	142	848†	(746)
676	(806)	852	184
680*	(701)	854	(777)
682	(739)	856	651
682x	159	857†	229
683†	160	859†	228
690	253	861†	(735)
691	187	862†	234
693	(715)	865	(771)
696	123	866	(797)
697	125	867	163
698	139	870†	(759)
703	175	871	219
705	181	873†	190
706	(780)	874	(775)
707	(741)	875	188
708	(776)	877	(717)
711	211	878	(769)
712x	145	882	244
714†	(718)	822x	243
715†	(768)	883	248
717	201	883x	251
720	(824)	886	256
721	(721)	887	(782)
722	144	888	257
727	208	889	259
729	148	891	255
731	150	894†	(828)
734	261	897	(770)
735	162	898†	207
736	147	904†	249
737	146	905	220
741†	174	906	157
743†	178	907	213
744†	173	908	252
747	179	909	155
750	177	913†	241
788†	661	914	254
818†	264	915	203
820†	(726)	917	245
822†	268	918†	191
823†	235	919†	266
824†	230	920	217
825†	273	921†	221
827†	262	922	(756)
829†	263	923†	224
831†	260	925	189

*impression on clay object
†inscription

Buchanan	Newell (NCBS)	Buchanan	Newell (NCBS)
926	(837)	1120	(870)
927	192	1127	183
928	(811)	1132	200
929	182	1133	193
931	215	1138	202
932†	214	1140†	227
933	216	1141†	236
934†	218	1144	226
937	225	1145	(704)
938	205	1166	(752)
939	194	1168	56
940†	198	1169	287
942†	206	1174	279
948	250	1175	(702)
949	196	1180	312
953	(705)	1181	164
956†	180	1189	324
967	84	1190	327
968	166	1191	339
973	(766)	1192	315
975	161	1192x	(731)
975x	(732)	1196	152
977	(808)	1197†	222
981	(750)	1198	165
982	(787)	1199	656
1044	336	1201	305
1050†	233	1204†	319
1054†	258	1205	309
1057†	231	1207	304
1059†	271	1208	306
1060†	223	1212	303
1062†	269	1213	314
1063†	267	1216	300
1066	210	1221	298
1068†	(798)	1223	299
1070	652	1224	332
1071	204	1226	316
1072	(738)	1227	338
1073	(762)	1229	330
1074	(836)	1230	317
1080	521	1231	308
1081	171	1232	307
1088	23	1234	313
1089	(876)	1235	333
1098	209	1237	340
1101	280	1243	320
1105	156	1245	322
1108	(743)	1246	325
1109	(788)	1248	311
1110	149	1249	452
1111	169	1251	347
1112	(703)	1252	349
1113	285	1253	342
1116	283	1254	346
1117	286	1255	344
1118	282	1256	348
1119	284	1258	(707)

*impression on clay object
†inscription

Buchanan	Newell		Newell	Buchanan
1259	318		40	328
1263	345		41	343
1265	334		42	342
1267	331		43	330
1270	321		44	281
1272	(706)		45	490
1273	329		46	340
1274	335		47	345
1275	310		48	347
1276	337		49	274
1277	302		50	282
1278	301		51	283
1279	297		52	483
1281	294		53	489
1284	343		54	488
1286	341		55	487
			56	1168
			57	174
			58	357
Newell	**Buchanan**		59	359
1	93		60	358
2	99		61	137
3	103		62	180
4	98		63	188
5	97		64	187
6	96		65	277
7	100		66	201
8	92		67	354
9	90		68	207
10	107		69	199
11	106		70	208
12	118		72	267
13	119		73	297
14	121		74	307
15	120		75	293
16	123		76	263
17	122		77	260
18	126		78	249
19	125		79	257
20	115		80	246
21	132		81	252
22	138		82	373
23	1088		83	308
24	166		84	967
25	167		85	302
26	172		86	256
27	163		87	313
28	164		88	314
29	146		89	396
30	148		90	394
31	153		91	393
32	217		92	420
34	325		93	513
35	349		94	426
36	350		95	417
37	339		96	423
38	299		97	428
39	329		98	416

*impression on clay object
†inscription

Newell	Buchanan	Newell	Buchanan
99	414	160	683
100	410	161	975
101	401	162	735
102	405	163	867
103	409	164	1181
104	524	165	1198
105	532	166	968
106	390	167	447
107	527	169	1111
108	521	170	542
109	531	171	1081
110	383	172	594
111	382	173	744
112	386	174	741
113	289	175	703
114	556	177	750
115	476	178	743
116	548	179	747
117	568	180	956
118	561	181	705
119	578	182	929
120	579	183	1127
121	566	184	852
122	554	185	491
123	696	186	546
124	565	187	691
125	697	188	875
126	586	189	925
127	670	190	873
128	569	191	918
129	605	192	927
131	581	193	1133
132	610	194	939
134	633	196	949
135	596	197	662
136	632	198	940
138	549	200	1132
139	698	201	717
140	567	202	1138
141	664	203	915
142	674	204	1071
143	665	205	938
144	722	206	942
145	712x	207	898
146	737	208	727
147	736	209	1098
148	729	210	1066
149	1110	211	711
150	731	212	845
151	439	213	907
152	1196	214	932
153	438	215	931
154	436	216	933
155	909	217	920
156	1105	218	934
157	906	219	871
158	535	220	905
159	682x	221	921

*impression on clay object
†inscription

Newell	Buchanan	Newell	Buchanan
222	1197	287	1169
223	1060	294	1281
224	923	295	368
225	937	297	1279
226	1144	298	1221
227	1140	299	1223
228	859	300	1216
229	857	301	1278
230	824	302	1277
231	1057	303	1212
232	835	304	1207
233	1050	305	1201
234	862	306	1208
235	823	307	1232
236	1141	308	1231
237	836	309	1205
238	841	310	1275
239	839	311	1248
240	843	312	1180
241	913	313	1234
242	844	314	1213
243	882x	315	1192
244	882	316	1226
245	917	317	1230
246	847	318	1259
247	846	319	1204
248	883	320	1243
249	904	321	1270
250	948	322	1245
251	883x	324	1189
252	908	325	1246
253	690	327	1190
254	914	329	1273
255	891	330	1229
256	886	331	1267
257	888	332	1224
258	1054	333	1235
259	889	334	1265
260	831	335	1274
261	734	336	1044
262	827	337	1276
263	829	338	1227
264	818	339	1191
265	833	340	1237
266	919	341	1286
267	1063	342	1253
268	822	343	1284
269	1062	344	1255
271	1059	345	1263
273	825	346	1254
279	1174	347	1251
280	1101	348	1256
282	1118	349	1252
283	1116	366	63
284	1119	367	50
285	1113	370	10
286	1117	371	108

*impression on clay object
†inscription

Newell	Buchanan	(NCBS)	Buchanan
452	1249	(748)	353
521	1080	(750)	981
647	273	(752)	1166
648	449	(753)	323
650	227	(756)	922
651	856	(757)	379
652	1070	(759)	870
656	1199	(762)	1073
661	788	(764)	380
668	472	(765)	388
669	135	(766)	973
670	284	(768)	715
671	481	(769)	878
673	422	(770)	897
674	553	(771)	865
677	399	(772)	271
678	315	(773)	408
679	403	(775)	874
680	456	(776)	708
681	240	(777)	854
683	463	(778)	389
690	133	(779)	294
695	139	(780)	706
		(782)	887
(NCBS)		(783)	322
		(785)	316
(697)	363	(787)	982
(698)	374	(788)	1109
(699)	372	(791)	171
(700)	505	(792)	336
(701)	680	(793)	395
(702)	1175	(797)	866
(703)	1112	(798)	1068
(704)	1145	(800)	526
(705)	953	(801)	272
(706)	1272	(805)	453
(707)	1258	(806)	676
(714)	221	(808)	977
(715)	693	(810)	583
(717)	877	(811)	928
(718)	714	(812)	279xx
(719)	279x	(814)	186
(720)	321	(816)	337
(721)	721	(819)	238
(724)	378	(820)	659
(726)	820	(823)	278
(731)	1192x	(824)	720
(732)	975x	(827)	552
(735)	861	(828)	894
(738)	1072	(829)	530
(739)	682	(830)	275
(741)	707	(833)	223
(742)	352	(836)	1074
(743)	1108	(837)	926
(744)	501	(838)	607
(745)	251	(841)	543
(746)	848	(842)	189

*impression on clay object
†inscription

(NCBS)	Buchanan	Buchanan	NBC
(848)	545	21	10979
(849)	628	22	10968
(850)	381	23	10973
(852)	411	24	10974
(853)	159	25	10966
(855)	573x	26	10971
(856)	190	27	10970
(857)	404	28	10975
(858)	366	29	10969
(859)	445	30	12034
(862)	377	31	12030
(863)	290	32	12019
(864)	348	33	9338
(867)	258	34	11009
(869)	197	35	12031
(870)	1120	36	12052
(873)	5	37	12056
(874)	86	38	12039
(875)	127	39	10964
(876)	1089	40	10965
		41	11023
(NCBT)		42	12016
		43	12015
(2234)*	617xx	44	6630
(2241)*	599	45	10999
(2243)*	657	46	10997
(2244)*	571	47	11001
(2247)*	523	48	10996
(2248)*	512	49	9378
(2249)*	639	51	10998
(2250)*	590	52	12033
(2251)*	541	53	12020
(2252)*	592	54	11003
(2253)*	658	55	9379
(2263)*	672	56	12044
(2268)*	663	58	11020
(2281)*	431	59	12029
(2307)*	648x	60	12063
		62	12068
Buchanan	NBC	64	11000
		65	11002
1	12067	66	11021
2	9376	67	11004
3	9377	68	12037
4	12027	69	11022
7	12023	71	10967
8	12024	72	11007
9	12047	73	12058
12	12017	75	11005
13	11019	77	11006
14	12042	78	12021
15	12045	79	12048
16	12059	80	12046
17	10976	81	12051
18	10977	83	11008
19	10978	85	12064
20	10972	87	12041

*impression on clay object
†inscription

Buchanan	NBC	Buchanan	NBC
88	12060	229	12009
89	11024	230	12014
91	9337	231	9346
101	5985	232	10963
104	9380	233	12007
105	5984	236	11034
109	12061	239	11053
110	12032	247	6008
111	12062	253†	9125
113	11018	255	9101
116	5986	261	9349
117	2550	262	9366
124	6520	266†	11049
128	2547	268	9102
129	9360	269†	9350
130	9339	270	5997
134	2579	276	11048
141	9143	279	5940
143	9357	280	6000
144	9100	286	9344
147	11044	291	11047
151	9328	296	9359
152	10982	298	2585
155	9132	303†	3216
157	3968	304*	5823
158	9128	305	3291
161	9141	306	9358
165	2577	309	2588
168	2591	310	6004
169	5989	311	5931
170	2580	324	6007
173	2587	326	11081
175	3165	327	5987
176	9329	332	1200
177	5988	333	5972
178	6005	335	12006
183	9330	338	2589
185	3286	344	11052
191	3983	346	9119
195	9134	355	11043
198	9251	360	10983
200	8145	361	11061
202	12011	362	9247
203	12008	364	2590
204	12002	365	9244
205	12003	369	10984
206	11045	371	9103
210	9133	375	9364
211	9130	376	9097
215	12010	384	3214
216	11073	385	11046
218	12066	391	6678
219	11075	397	9111
220	10951	400	2581
222	11091	406	3965
224	9362		
225	11074		

*impression on clay object
†inscription

Buchanan	NBC		Buchanan	NBC
412	6018		534*†	3262
413	6006			3247
419†	9361		537	9383
421	11033		539*	7768
425*†	10590		540*†	7804
427†	3795		541x*	23
429†	4142		547*†	8094
433	7918		551	9117
434	4953		555	5974
435	5994		557	2593
437	3210		558x*	3282
442	9116		558xx*	351
443	1517		560	2600
450	9241		562†	6010
452*†	5812		563*†	28
	5859		564*†	3344
	6861		570*†	2
	5908		571xx*	1838
454	3212		573*†	3409
456	5990		574*†	645
458	8956		575*†	4335
459	7917		576	6015
461	6017		580†	5953
462	6012		582†	9126
463	5991		585	11042
465†	11086		587*†	320
466†	9123		589†	6022
469	6011		591*†	6
470	9127		593†	9099
471	5992		597*†	3505
473	3170		598*†	577
474†	3285		600*†	690
475	6016		601*†	2783
477	5993		602*†	2815
479	11071		603*†	9268
480	5958		604†	9254
484	9139		608*†	8
485	9121		609*†	11314
486	5963		612*†	4261
492	1493		614*†	4331
494	9345		616*†	3615
497	9351		617*†	26
500	9138		617x*	14
503*†	2200		621*†	5592
506	9112		622*†	4290
508	6675		625*†	486
509	5970		630†	9106
510	5959		634	9110
514*	2356		640*†	2023
516†	3249			3401
517*†	3641		644*†	3271
518†	4952		646*†	638
519†	2594			167
520†	6009		649*†	6645
522†	318		650*†	4405
525*†	9265			2688
525x*	18		652*†	4288

*impression on clay object
†inscription

Buchanan	NBC	Buchanan	NBC
653*†	5607	837†	11038
655†	6003	838†	6677
656*†	27	849†	6516
661*†	4393	853	5981
663*†	4277	855†	3289
669†	11013	858†	2595
671*†	264	864	11039
675†	6023	869	5982
677*†	9223	876†	10992
678*†	1007	880	11036
679*†	5613	890	5933
681*†	11330	896†	11035
684	9135	899†	9118
685	9353	903	5960
687	11037	911†	2597
689	9120	912	3294
691x*	2296	916	5941
691xx*	10	924	9255
692*†	1857	930	5932
694	5961	935	2583
695†	7927	941	2584
701†	3016	943†	7923
704	5957	944	7681
710	5979	945	7920
718	6021	947	3292
724	9104	950	7921
726	5937	951	8927
730*	5382	954†	3218
730x*	8596	965*	8535
732	11087	966*	9266
740	2601	966x*	8013
742†	2578	972	6517
745†	3288	972xx*	8236
748	9149	976	5980
751*†	5500	978x*	6187
752*†	5410	979	9113
758*†	9267	980†	3293
761xx*	6747	984*†	8570
762*	7309	985*	8885
765*	5347	988*	9264
766*	9762	1003*†	1273
767*	8604	1009*	5575
768*	6751	1012x*	5456
	8603	1013*	5355
769†	1199	1031*	6811
782*	9263	1038*	11431
785*†	8937	1045†	6019
787*†	9039	1046†	5999
789*	7687	1047†	6001
790*	8898	1051†	8926
807x*	8556	1052†	11028
807xx*	8693	1053†	2582
811*†	6799	1055	8928
821*†	8672	1056†	8925
826†	9107	1058†	5950
830†	5998	1064†	5934
832†	2596	1067†	9242

*impression on clay object
†inscription

Buchanan	NBC	Buchanan	NBC
1078x	4011	1158x*	3994
1091	9256	1158xx*	3995
1093†	6002	1158xxx*	3997
1093A†	11094	1159*†	4013
1094	5964	1160*	4014
1097†	11010	1161*	4015
1099†	11093	1162*	4018
1100	7821	1162x*	4033
1102	8916	1163*	4034
1103	8142	1163x*	6569
1106	11030	1164*	6572
1121	8918	1165*	6599
1122	7819	1167	11064
1123	7827	1170	12065
1125	6020	1171	10986
1126	8391	1172	10952
1128	10985	1173	8319
1131	11041	1176	10991
1134	12013	1177	9381
1135	8408	1179	7812
1136†	8915	1182	7824
1139	3164	1184	7818
1143†	5935	1186	7530
1146*	1845	1187	7820
1147*	1846	1188	7928
1147x*	1883	1193	11051
1148*	1884	1194	10955
1149*†	1892	1195	7826
1150*†	1902	1200	8316
1151*	1905	1202	8929
1152*	1906	1203†	7680
1153*†	1907	1209	7816
1153x*	3796	1210	7810
1153xx*	3824	1211	11089
1154*	3843	1214	8409
1155*	3847	1217	7813
	3938	1218	9249
	1880	1219	8315
	1882	1225	7811
	3711	1228	10990
	3748	1233	7825
	3887	1236	10956
	3890	1240	5955
	3933	1241	7814
	3936	1242	7926
	3992	1244	9368
1156*	3845	1260	9373
1156x*	3893	1261	9375
1157x*	3895	1262	7924
1157xx*	3896	1266	10989
1157xxx*	3898	1271	8930
1157xxxx*	3900	1280	2598
1157xxxxx*	3981	1282	11050
1157xxxxxx*	3990	1283†	8322
1158*	3993	1285	8931

*impression on clay object
†inscription

NBC	Buchanan	NBC	Buchanan
2*	570	2588	309
6*	591	2589	338
8*	608	2590	364
10*	691xx	2591	168
14*	617x	2593	557
18*	525x	2594	519
23*	541x	2595	858
26*	617	2596	832
27*	656	2597	911
28*	563	2598	1280
167*	646	2600	560
264*	671	2601	740
318*	522	2688*	650
320*	587	2783*	601
351*	558xx	2815*	602
486*	625	3016	701
577*	598	3164	1139
638*	646	3165	175
645*	574	3170	473
690*	600	3210	437
1007*	678	3212	454
1199*	769	3214	384
1200	332	3216	303
1273*	1003	3218	954
1493	492	3247*	534
1517	443	3249*	516
1838*	571xx	3262*	534
1845*	1146	3271*	644
1846*	1147	3282*	558x
1857*	692	3285	474
1880*	1155	3286	185
1882*	1155	3288	745
1883*	1147x	3289	855
1884*	1148	3291	305
1892*	1149	3292	947
1902*	1150	3293	980
1905*	1151	3294	912
1906*	1152	3344*	564
1907*	1153	3401*	640
2023*	640	3409*	573
2200*	503	3505*	597
2296*	691x	3615*	616
2356*	514	3641*	517
2547	128	3711*	1155
2550	117	3748*	1155
2577	165	3795*	424
2578	742	3796*	1153x
2579	134	3824*	1153xx
2580	170	3843*	1154
2581	400	3845*	1156
2582	1053	3847*	1155
2583	935	3887*	1155
2584	941	3890*	1155
2585	298	3893*	1156x
2587	173	3894*	1157

*impression on clay object
†inscription

NBC	Buchanan	NBC	Buchanan
3895*	1157x	5950	1058
3896*	1157xx	5953	580
3898*	1157xxx	5955	1240
3900*	1157xxxx	5957	704
3933*	1155	5958	480
3936*	1155	5959	510
3938*	1155	5960	903
3965	406	5961	694
3968	157	5963	486
3981*	1157xxxxx	5964	1094
3983*	191	5970	509
3990*	1157xxxxxx	5972	333
3992*	1155	5974	555
3993*	1158	5979	710
3994*	1158x	5980	976
3995*	1158xx	5981	853
3997*	1158xxx	5982	869
4011	1078x	5984	105
4013*	1159	5985	101
4014*	1160	5986	116
4015*	1161	5987	327
4018*	1162	5988	177
4033*	1162x	5989	169
4034*	1163	5990	456
4142*	429	5991	463
4261*.	612	5992	471
4277*	663	5993	477
4288*	652	5994	435
4290*	622	5997	270
4331*	614	5998	830
4335*	575	5999	1046
4393*	661	6000	280
4405*	650	6001	1047
4952	518	6002	1093
4953	434	6003	655
5347*	765	6004	310
5355*	1013	6005	178
5382*	730	6006	413
5410*	752	6007	324
5456*	1012x	6008	247
5500*	751	6009	520
5575*	1009x	6010	562
5592*	621	6011	469
5607*	653	6012	462
5613*	679	6015	576
5812*	452	6016	475
5823*	304	6017	461
5859*	452	6018	412
5908*	452	6019	1045
5931	311	6020	1125
5932	930	6021	718
5933	890	6022	589
5934	1064	6023	675
5935	1143	6187*	978x
5937	726	6516	849
5940	279	6517	972
5941	916	6520	124

*impression on clay object
†inscription

NBC	Buchanan	NBC	Buchanan
6569*	1163x	8570*	984
6572*	1164	8596*	730x
6599*	1165	8603*	768
6630	44	8604*	767
6645*	649	8672*	821
6675	508	8693*	807xx
6677	838	8885*	985
6678	391	8898*	790
6747*	761xx	8915	1136
6751*	768	8916	1102
6799*	811	8918	1121
6811*	1031	8925	1050
6861*	452	8926	1051
7309*	762	8927	951
7530	1186	8928	1055
7680	1203	8929	1202
7681	944	8930	1271
7687*	789	8931	1285
7768*	539	8937*	785
7804*	540	8956	458
7810	1210	9039*	787
7811	1225	9087	376
7812	1179	9099	593
7813	1217	9100	144
7814	1241	9101	255
7816	1209	9102	268
7818	1184	9103	371
7819	1122	9104	724
7820	1187	9106	630
7821	1100	9107	826
7824	1182	9110	634
7825	1233	9111	397
7826	1195	9112	506
7827	1123	9113	979
7917	459	9116	442
7918	433	9117	551
7920	945	9118	899
7921	950	9119	346
7923	943	9120	689
7924	1262	9121	485
7926	1242	9123	466
7927	695	9125	253
7928	1188	9126	582
8013*	966x	9127	470
8094*	547	9128	158
8142	1103	9130	211
8145	200	9132	155
8236*	972xx	9133	210
8315	1219	9134	195
8316	1200	9135	684
8319	1173	9138	500
8322	1283	9139	484
8391	1126	9141	161
8408	1135	9143	141
8409	1214	9149	748
8535*	965	9223*	677
8556*	807x	9241	450

*impression on clay object
†inscription

NBC	Buchanan	NBC	Buchanan
9242	1067	10969	29
9244	365	10970	27
9247	362	10971	26
9249	1218	10972	20
9251	198	10973	23
9254	604	10974	24
9255	924	10975	28
9256	1091	10976	17
9263*	782	10977	18
9264*	988	10978	19
9265*	525	10979	21
9266*	966	10982	152
9267*	758	10983	360
9268*	603	10984	369
9328	151	10985	1128
9329	176	10986	1171
9330	183	10989	1266
9337	91	10990	1228
9338	33	10991	1176
9339	130	10992	876
9344	286	10996	48
9345	494	10997	46
9346	231	10998	51
9349	261	10999	45
9350	269	11000	64
9351	497	11001	47
9353	685	11002	65
9357	143	11003	54
9358	306	11004	67
9359	296	11005	75
9360	129	11006	77
9361	419	11007	72
9362	224	11008	83
9364	375	11009	34
9366	262	11010	1097
9368	1244	11013	669
9373	1260	11018	113
9375	1261	11019	13
9376	2	11020	58
9377	3	11021	66
9378	49	11022	69
9379	55	11023	41
9380	104	11024	89
9381	1177	11028	1052
9383	537	11030	1106
9762*	766	11033	421
10590*	425	11034	236
10951	220	11035	896
10952	1172	11036	880
10955	1194	11037	687
10956	1236	11038	837
10963	232	11039	864
10964	39	11041	1131
10965	40	11042	585
10966	25	11043	355
10967	71	11044	147
10968	22	11045	206

*impression on clay object
†inscription

NBC	Buchanan	NBC	Buchanan
11046	385	12048	79
11047	291	12051	81
11048	276	12052	36
11049	266	12056	37
11050	1282	12058	73
11051	1193	12059	16
11052	344	12060	88
11053	239	12061	109
11061	361	12062	111
11064	1167	12063	60
11071	479	12064	85
11073	216	12065	1170
11074	225	12066	218
11075	219	12067	1
11081	326	12068	62
11086	465		
11087	732		
11089	1211		
11091	222		
11093	1099	Buchanan	YBC
11094	1093		
11314*	609	6	9722
11330*	681	11	13054
1·1431*	1038	57	9977
12002	204	61	13051
12003	205	70	12758
12006	335	74	13034
12007	233	76	12661
12008	203	82	13055
12009	229	84	9995
12010	215	94	13066
12011	202	95	8423
12013	1134	102	9715
12014	230	112	12759
12015	43	114	12757
12016	42	131	12598
12017	12	140	12742
12019	32	142	13060
12020	53	145	12508
12021	78	149	12504
12023	7	150	12596
12024	8	154	12832
12027	4	156	9683
12029	59	160	12624
12030	31	162	12762
12031	35	179	12767
12032	110	181	6958
12033	52	182	12750
12034	30	184	12501
12037	68	192	12587
12039	38	193	13061
12041	87	194	12590
12042	14	196	12826
12044	56	209	12658
12045	15	212	12599
12046	80	213	12582
12047	9	214	12786

*impression on clay object
†inscription

Buchanan	YBC	Buchanan	YBC
226	12496	502	12583
228	12648	504	12614
234	12627	507*†	13483
235	12760	511*†	1203
237	12507	515†	12637
241	13062	522x*	13219
242	12653	528*†	13112
243†	6962	529*†	1759
244	12825	533*†	1668
245	13048	534*†	897
248	9686	536*†	14697
250	9677	538†	9685
254†	9990	544*†	11244
259	12623	547*†	919
264	12631	550	13063
287*	13070	558*†	1636
288*	13069	559*†	1559
292	12642	572*†	1704
300†	13053	577†	12604
301	12633	584*†	7087
312	8940	588*†	11243
317†	9991	595†	12605
318	13040	606*†	4758
319	12616	611*†	1498
320	12626	613*†	9816
331	13047	613x*	571
334	8941	615*†	1302
341	9717	618*†	1067
351†	12761		9807
356	12634	619*†	6765
367	13076	620*†	1296
370	12603	623*†	579
387	9669	624*†	1652
392	8942	626x*	1367
398†	11232	627*†	3653
402	13115		3675
407†	12510	629†	9673
415†	9718	631†	9665
418†	12622	635*	11198
432	12763	636*†	13286
440	12837	637*†	294
441*†	10978	638*†	1170
444	9682	641*†	1261
446	9999	642*†	3905
448	12586	645*†	1374
451	12769	647*†	3918
455	16396	648*†	3648
460	12764	651*†	14698
467	12816	660*†	3647
468	9676	667*†	1341
478†	9707	673*†	13463
482	12643	686	13042
493*	10534	688†	12784
495	12630	699	13052
496	12628	700*	11164
498	12745	702	9674
499	12579	709†	9721

*impression on clay object
†inscription

Buchanan	YBC	Buchanan	YBC
712†	13044	806*†	6232
713	12626	806x*	4209
716†	12822	807*†	4313
719†	9699	807xxx*	12261
723	12629	808*	6039
725	9684	809*	4246
728	12612	810*	5910
733	9671	810*	7966
738	9679	812*	7160
739†	9998	813*†	6083
746†	9689	814*†	6174
749†	9720	815*†	5998
753*†	13113	816*†	4214
756*†	11169	816x*	4303
756*	11173	828†	9664
757*	11158	834†	9711
759*†	4485	840†	9712
760*†	4970	842	9672
760*	5205	850	12632
760*	3268	851	12797
761*†	5472	860†	9985
761x*	5170	863	9993
763*	5698	868	9992
770*	5616	872	12635
771*	4483	879	9987
772*	5852	881†	9719
773*	6217	884	9680
774*	8705	885†	12813
775*	5668	892†	12818
776*	5729	893†	9688
777*	5377	895	12820
778*	12141	900†	12824
779*†	4217	901	12800
779*	4219	902	12812
780*	4484	910†	12766
781*	5463	936	13075
781x*	5749	946	9678
783*	4323	951x	9709
784*†	8441	955*	13216
786*†	4378	957*	12984
792*	7153	958*	13103-
793*†	10486		13107
794*†	4348	959*†	8615
795*	7758	960*†	13110
796*	4435	962*†	8114
796*	5654	963*	3017
797*	7150		3008
798*	4474	966xx*	12248
799*†	11151	969	12748
800*	11159	970*	6836
801*	7676	972x	7700
802*†	4234	974	9681
803*	6972	986*†	7743
804*†	6744	987*	7665
804x*	8679	989*	4407
804xx*	7972	990*	5956
805*	4424	991*†	4981

*impression on clay object
†inscription

Buchanan	YBC		Buchanan	YBC
992*	5665		1137	9670
992x*	11926		1142	12777
993*†	5939		1178	12594
994*	11990		1185	12506
996x*	6790		1201x*	5128
997*	12983		1206	12618
998*†	5477		1215	12580
999*	5920		1220	9695
1000*	12259		1222	12798
1001*	5501		1238	12779
1004*	4771		1239	12806
1006x*	12034		1247	12775
1007*	4329		1250	9690
1009*	6769		1257	9705
1010*	9118		1264	8189
1010x*	11927		1268	12602
1012*	5987		1269	12774
1014*	4962			
1015*	7813			
1025x*	10624		YBC	Buchanan
1026*	3285		294*	637
1028*	8308		571*	613x
1030*	6518		579*	623
1030x*	6785		897*	534
1032*	8017		919*	547
1035*	8499		928*	1037
1036*†	5295		1067*	618
1037*	928		1170*	638
1040*	13215		1203*	511
1041*	13109		1261*	641
1043†	12638		1296*	620
1048†	9687		1302*	615
1049†	12610		1341*	667
1061†	12584		1367*	626x
1065†	12823		1374*	645
1069	9702		1498*	611
1075	12591		1559*	559
1076	12619		1636*	558
1077	12589		1652*	624
1078	9723		1668*	533
1079	12588		1704*	572
1082	9710		1759*	529
1083	12497		3008*	963
1084	12772		3017*	963
1085	12600		3268*	760
1090*	5447		3285*	1026
1092†	12834		3647*	660
1095†	12611		3648*	648
1096†	12771		3653*	627
1104	12770		3675*	627
1107	8943		3905*	642
1114	9697		3918*	647
1115	12831		4209*	806x
1117x	12815		4214*	816
1124	12494		4217*	779
1129	9704		4219*	779
1130	9667		4234*	802

*impression on clay object
†inscription

YBC	Buchanan	YBC	Buchanan
4246*	809	6972*	803
4271	1004	7087*	584
4303*	816x	7150*	797
4313*	807	7153*	792
4323*	783	7160*	812
4329*	1007	7665*	987
4348*	794	7676*	801
4378*	786	7700*	972x
4407*	989	7743*	986
4424*	805	7758*	795
4435*	796	7813*	1015
4474*	798	7966*	810
4483*	771	7972*	804xx
4484*	780	8017*	1032
4485*	759	8114*	962
4758*	606	8189	1264
4962*	1014	8308*	1028
4970*	760	8423	95
4981*	991	8441*	784
5128*	1201x	8499*	1035
5170*	761x	8615*	959
5205*	760	8679*	804x
5295*	1036	8705*	774
5377*	777	8940	312
5447*	1090	8941	334
5463*	781	8942	392
5472*	761	8943	1107
5477*	998	9118*	1010
5501*	1001	9664	828
5616*	770	9665	631
5654*	796	9667	1130
5665*	992	9669	387
5668*	775	9670	1137
5698*	763	9671	733
5729*	776	9672	842
5749*	781x	9673	629
5852*	772	9674	702
5910*	810	9676	468
5920*	999	9677	250
5939*	993	9678	946
5986*	990	9679	738
5987*	1012	9680	884
5998*	815	9681	974
6039*	808	9682	444
6083*	813	9683	156
6174*	814	9684	725
6217*	773	9685	538
6232*	806	9686	248
6518*	1030	9687	1048
6744*	804	9688	893
6765*	619	9689	746
6769*	1009	9690	1250
6785*	1030x	9695	1220
6790*	996x	9697	1114
6836*	970	9699	719
6958	181	9702	1069
6962	243	9704	1129

*impression on clay object
†inscription

YBC	Buchanan	YBC	Buchanan
9705	1257	12579	499
9707	478	12580	1215
9709	951x	12582	213
9710	1082	12583	502
9711	834	12584	1061
9712	840	12586	448
9715	102	12587	192
9717	341	12588	1079
9718	415	12589	1077
9719	881	12590	194
9720	749	12591	1075
9721	709	12594	1178
9722	6	12596	150
9723	1078	12598	131
9807*	618	12599	212
9816*	613	12600	1085
9977	57	12602	1268
9981	879	12603	370
9985	860	12604	577
9990	254	12605	595
9991	317	12610	1049
9992	868	12611	1095
9993	863	12612	728
9995	84	12614	504
9998	739	12616	319
9999	446	12618	1206
10486*	793	12619	1076
10534*	493	12622	418
10624*	1025x	12623	259
10978*	441	12624	160
11151*	799	12625	320
11158*	757	12626	713
11159*	800	12627	234
11164*	700	12628	496
11169*	756	12629	723
11173*	756	12630	495
11198*	635	12631	264
11232	398	12632	850
11243*	588	12633	301
11244*	544	12634	356
11926*	992x	12635	872
11927*	1010x	12637	515
11990*	994	12638	1043
12034*	1006x	12642	292
12141*	778	12643	482
12248*	966xx	12648	228
12259*	1000	12653	242
12261*	807xxx	12658	209
12494	1124	12661	76
12496	226	12742	140
12497	1083	12745	498
12501	184	12748	969
12504	149	12750	182
12506	1185	12757	114
12507	237	12758	70
12508	145	12759	112
12510	407	12760	235

*impression on clay object
†inscription

YBC	Buchanan		YBC	Buchanan
12761	351		13103*	958
12762	162		13107*	958
12763	432		13108*	958
12764	460		13109*	1041
12766	910		13110*	960
12767	179		13112*	528
12769	451		13113*	753
12770	1104		13115*	402
12771	1096		13215*	1040
12772	1084		13216*	955
12774	1269		13219*	522x
12775	1247		13286*	636
12777	1142		13463*	673
12779	1238		13483*	507
12784	688		14697*	536
12786	214		14698*	651
12797	851		16396	455
12798	1222			
12800	901			
12806	1239		Buchanan	Goucher
12812	902		136*	869
12813	885		430*†	883
12815	1117x		647x*	884
12816	467		964*	835
12818	892			
12820	895		Goucher	Buchanan
12822	716		835*	964
12823	1065		869*	136
12824	900		883*	430
12825	244		884*	647x
12826	196			
12831	1115		Buchanan	Gimbel Collection
12832	154		265	1
12834	1092		285	3
12837	440		295	2
12983*	997		668†	4
12984*	957		1183	5
13034	74			
13040	318		Gimbel	Buchanan
13042	686		1	265
13044	712		2	295
13047	331		3	285
13048	245		4	668
13051	61		5	1183
13052	699			
13053	300		Buchanan	Yale Art Gallery
13054	11			[Pier Collection]
13055	82		1086	36.34
13060	142		1087	36.33
13061	193			
13062	241		Buchanan	American Oriental Society
13063	550		819†	March (no no.)
13066	94			
13069*	288			
13070*	287			
13075	936			
13076	367			

*impression on clay object
†inscription

BIBLIOGRAPHY

Alp, S., *Zylinder- und Stempelsiegel aus Karahüyük bei Konya.* Ankara, 1968.

American Journal of Archaeology, The. [*AJA*]

American Journal of Semitic Languages and Literatures, The. [*AJSL*]

American Oriental Series. [*AOS*]

Amiet, P., *Elam.* Auvers-sur-Oise, 1966. [*Elam*]

——*La glyptique mésopotamienne archaïque.* Paris, 1961. [*Amiet*]

Anadolu Arastirmalari (= Jahrbuch für kleinasiatische Forschung). [*Anadolu*]

Analecta Orientalia. [*An.Or.*]

Anatolia. Revue annuelle de l'Institut d'Archéologie de l'Université d'Ankara.

Andrews University Seminary Studies.

Annals of Archaeology and Anthropology. University of Liverpool. [*AAA*]

Annual of the American Schools of Oriental Research. [*AASOR*]

Archäologische Mitteilungen aus Iran. Berlin. [*AMI*]

Archaeology.

Archiv für Orientforschung. Berlin, Graz. [*AfO*]

Archiv Orientální. Prague. [*Ar.Or.*]

Art Bulletin.

Artibus Asiae.

Assyriological Studies. University of Chicago. [*AS*]

'Atiqot. Journal of the Israel Department of Antiquities

Babylonian Expedition of the University of Pennsylvania, Series A: Cuneiform Texts. [*BE*]

Babylonian Inscriptions in the Collection of J. B. Nies. New Haven: Yale University Press. [*BIN*]

Babylonian Records in the Library of J. Pierpont Morgan. New Haven: Yale University Press, 1912-.[*BRM*]

Baghdader Mitteilungen.

Banks, E. J., *Bismaya.* New York and London, 1912.

Basmadschi, F., *Landschaftliche Elemente in der mesopotamischen Kunst des IV. und III. Jahrtausends.* Basel, 1943. [*Basmadschi*]

Bass, G.F. et al., *Cape Gelidonya: A Bronze Age Shipwreck* (= TAPhS 57, 1967).

Berliner Jahrbuch für Vorgeschichte. [*BJV*]

Bibliotheca Orientalis. [*Bi.Or.*]

Bibby, G., *Looking for Dilmun.* New York, 1969.

Bittel, K. et al., eds., *Moortgat Festschrift.* Berlin, 1964.

Boehmer, R. M., *Die Entwicklung der Glyptik während der Akkad-Zeit.* (= Untersuchungen zur Assyriologie und vorderasiatischen Archäologie 4). Berlin, 1965. [*Boehmer*]

Braidwood, R. J. and L. S. Braidwood, *Excavations in the Plain of Antioch 1* (= OIP 61).

Chicago: University of Chicago Press, 1960. [*OIP* 61]

British Museum Quarterly. London. [*BMQ*]

Buchanan, B., *Catalogue of Ancient Near Eastern Seals in the Ashmolean Museum, Cylinder Seals.* Oxford: Clarendon Press, 1966. [*Ash C*]

Bulletin du Musée d'Art et d'Histoire de Genève. [*Genève*]

Bulletin of the American Schools of Oriental Research. Jerusalem and Baghdad. [*BASOR*]

Bulletin of the John Rylands Library. [*BJRL*]

Bulletin of the School of Oriental and African Studies. [*BSOAS*]

Cahiers de la Délégation Archéoloque Française en Iran. Paris. [*DAFI*]

Carnegie, Lady H. M., ed., *Catalogue of the Collection of Antique Gems Formed by James, Ninth Earl of Southesk, K. T.* London, 1908. [*Southesk*]

Cassin, E., *La splendeur divine.* Paris, The Hague, 1968.

Chicago Assyrian Dictionary. [*CAD*]

Conteneau, G., *Contribution a l'histoire économique d'Umma.* Paris, 1915. [*CHEU*]

—— *La magie chez les assyriens et les babyloniens.* (Bibliothèque historique). Paris, 1947. [*La magie*]

—— *Umma sous la dynastie d'Ur.* Paris, 1916. [*UDU*]

Conteneau, G. and R. Ghirshman, *Fouilles du Tépé Giyan . . . 1931, 1932.* Paris, 1935. [*Giyan*]

Cuneiform Texts from Babylonian Tablets . . . in the British Museum. London: British Museum, 1896-. [*CT*]

de Clercq, L., *Collection de Clercq 1, Cylindres orienteaux.* Paris, 1888. [*De Clercq*]

Deimel, A., ed., *Pantheon Babylonicum.* Rome, 1914.

Delaporte, L. J., *Catalogue des cylindres, cachets et pierres gravées de style oriental, Musée du Louvre, 1: Fouilles et missions.* Paris, 1920. *2: Acquisitions.* Paris, 1923. [*Louvre*]

—— *Catalogue des cylindres orienteaux de la Bibliothèque Nationale.* Paris, 1919. [*BN*]

Delougaz, P., H. D. Hill, and S. Lloyd, *Private Houses and Graves in the Diyala Region* (= OIP 88). Chicago: University of Chicago Press, 1967. [*OIP* 88]

Dunand, M., *Fouilles de Byblos 1, 2.* Paris, 1937, 1950.

Ebeling, E. et al., *Reallexikon der Assyriologie.* Berlin: de Gruyter, 1932–. [*RLA*]

Edzard, D. O., *Die "zweite Zwischenzeit" Babyloniens.* Wiesbaden, 1957. [*ZZw*]

—— *Sumerische Rechsurkunden des III. Jahr-*

tausends aus der Zeit vor der III. Dynastie von Ur. Munich, 1968. [Edzard *SR*]

Ehrich, R. W., ed., *Chronologies in Old World Archaeology.* Chicago, 1965. [*Ehrich*]

Eisen, G. A., *Ancient Oriental Cylinder and Other Seals. Collection of Mrs. William H. Moore* (= OIP 47). Chicago: University of Chicago Press, 1940. [*Moore*]

Falkenstein, A., *Archaische Texte aus Uruk.* Berlin, 1936.

Figulla, H. H., *Catalogue of the Babylonian Tablets in the British Museum.* London, 1961. [*Figulla*]

Fish, T., *Catalogue of Sumerian Tablets in the John Rylands Library.* Manchester: Manchester University Press, 1932. [*CST*]

Frankfort, H., *Cylinder Seals.* London, 1939. [*Frankfort*]

———— *More Sculpture from the Diyala Region* (= OIP 60). Chicago: University of Chicago Press, 1943. [*OIP* 60]

———— *Stratified Cylinder Seals from the Diyala Region* (= OIP 72). Chicago: University of Chicago Press, 1955. [*OIP* 72]

Fuhr, I., *Ein altorientalisches Symbol: Bemerkungen zum sogenannten "Omegaformigen Symbol" und zur Brillenspirale.* Wiesbaden, 1967.

Garelli, P., ed., *Gilgameš et sa légende* (= Groupe François-Thureau-Dangin. Cahier, 1). Paris, 1960.

Gelb, I. J., *Hurrians and Subarians* (= Studies in Ancient Oriental Civilization, 22). Chicago: University of Chicago Press, 1944.

———— *Materials for the Assyrian Dictionary.* Chicago: University of Chicago Press, 1952–. [*MAD*]

Genouillac, H. de, *Céramique cappadocienne* 1, 2. Paris, 1926.

———— *Fouilles de Telloh. Mission archéologique du Musée du Louvre et du Ministère de l'Instruction Publique* 1, 2. Paris, 1934, 1936. [*Telloh*]

———— *La trouvaille de Drehem; étude avec un choix de textes de Constantinople et Bruxelles.* Paris, 1911.

Gibson, M. and R. D. Biggs, eds., *Seals and Sealings in Ancient Mesopotamia* (= Bibliotheca Mesopotamica 6, 1977).

Göttingische gelehrte Anzeigen, unter der Aufsicht der königlichen Gesellschaft der Wissenschaften. [*GGA*]

Goff, B. L., *Symbols of Prehistoric Mesopotamia.* New Haven and London, 1963.

Goldman, H., *Excavations at Gözlü Küle, Tarsus* 2. Princeton, 1956. [*Tarsus 2*]

Güterbock, H. G. and T. Jacobsen, *Studies in Honor of Professor Benno Landsberger on his Seventy-Fifth Birthday.* Chicago: University of Chicago Press, 1965. [*Studies Landsberger*]

Hallo, W. W., *Early Mesopotamian Royal Titles; a philologic and historical analysis* (= AOS 43). New Haven, 1957. [Hallo *Titles*]

Hallo, W. W. and W. K. Simpson, *The Ancient Near East: a History.* New York, 1971.

Hebrew Union College Annual. [*HUCA*]

Heidelberger Studien zum alten Orient. Wiesbaden, 1967.

Heinrich, E., *Fara. Ergebnisse der Ausgrabungen der deutschen Orientgesellschaft in Fara und Abu Hatab, 1902–03.* Berlin, 1931. [*Fara*]

Hogarth, D., *Hittite Seals.* Oxford, 1920. [*Hogarth*]

Hrozny, B., *Inscriptions cunéiformes du Kultépé* 1, 2. Praha, 1952, 1962. [*Inscriptions Kultépé*]

Hussey, M. I., *Sumerian Tablets in the Harvard Semitic Museum* 1, 2. (= Harvard Semitic Series, 3, 4). Cambridge, Mass., 1912, 1915. [*HSS*]

Illustrated London News. [*ILN*]

Inventaire des tablettes de Tello conservées au Musée Impérial Ottoman. Paris. [*ITT*]

Iran. Journal of the British Institute of Persian Studies.

Iraq. London: British School of Archaeology in Iraq.

Jacobsen, T., *Cuneiform Texts in the National Museum, Copenhagen.* Copenhagen, 1939. [*CTC*]

Jones, T. B. and J. W. Snyder, *Sumerian Economic Texts from the Third Ur Dynasty; a catalogue and discussion of documents from various collections.* University of Minnesota Press, 1961.

Journal Asiatique.

Journal of Cuneiform Studies. [*JCS*]

Journal of Near Eastern Studies. [*JNES*]

Journal of the American Oriental Society. [*JAOS*]

Journal of the Royal Asiatic Society. [*JRAS*]

Journal of the Society for Oriental Research. [*JSOR*]

Kang, S. T., *Sumerian Economic Texts from the Drehem Archive* (= Sumerian and Akkadian Cuneiform Texts in the Collection of the World Heritage Museum of the University of Illinois 1, 2.) University of Illinois Press, 1972. [*SACT*]

Kang, S. T., see Keiser

Keiser, C. E., *Neo-Sumerian Account Texts from Drehem* (= BIN 3, 1971).

Kienast, B., *Die altassyrischen Texte des orientalischen Seminars der Universität Heidelberg und der Sammlung Erlenmeyer, Basel* (= Untersuchungen zur Assyriologie und vorderasiatischen Archäologie 1). Berlin, 1060. [*Altassyrische Texte*]

Kinnier Wilson, J. V., *Indo-Sumerian.* Oxford, 1974.

Kraus, F. R., *Vom Mesopotamischen Menschen.* Amsterdam and London, 1973.

Krauss, J., *Die Götternamen in den babylonischen Siegelcylinderlegenden.* Leipzig, 1911.

Kupper, J.-R., *L'Iconographie du Dieu Amurru dans la glyptique de la 1e dynastie babylonienne*

(= Académie royale de Belgique. Classe des lettres et des sciences morales et politiques. Mémoires). Brussels, 1961. [*Amurru*]

Landsberger, B. et al., *Materialen zum sumerischen Lexikon.* Rome: Pontifical Biblical Institute, 1937–. [*MSL*]

Langdon, S. H., *Tablets from the Archives of Drehem.* Paris, 1911. [*TAD*]

Langsdorf, A. and D. E. McCown, *Tall-I-Bakun A, Season of 1932* (= OIP 59). Chicago: University of Chicago Press, 1942. [*OIP 59*]

Larsen, M. T., *The Old Assyrian City-State and its Colonies* (= Mesopotamia, 4). Copenhagen, 1976.

Leemans, W. F., *The Old-Babylonian Merchant, his Business and his Social Position* (= Studia et documenta ad iura Orientis antiqui pertinentia, 3). Leiden, 1950.

Legrain, L., *Le temps des rois d'Ur.* Paris, 1912. [*TRU*]

————— *The Culture of the Babylonians* (= University of Pennsylvania. The University Museum. Publications of the Babylonian Section, 14). Philadelphia, 1925. [*Philadelphia*]

Lewy, J., ed., *Die Keilschrifttexte aus Kleinasien.* (= Texte und Materialen der Frau Professor Hilprecht Sammlung von babylonischen Antiquitäten im Eigentum der Universität Jena, 1). Leipzig, 1932. [*TMH 1*]

Limet, H., *L'Anthroponymie sumérienne dans les documents de la 3ᵉ dynastie d'Ur.* Paris, 1968.

————— *Les legendes des sceaux cassites.* Brussels, 1971.

————— *Le travail du métal au pays de Sumer, au temps de la 3ᵉ dynastie d'Ur.* Paris, 1960.

Mackay, E., *A Sumerian Palace and the "A" Cemetery at Kish.* Chicago, 1929. [*Mackay*]

Marshall, Sir J. H., ed., *Mohenjo Daro and the Indus Valley Civilization.* London, 1931. [*Mohenjo Daro*]

McCown, D. E. and R. C. Haines, *Nippur 1. Temple of Enlil, Scribal Quarter, and Soundings* (= OIP 78). Chicago: University of Chicago Press, 1967. [*OIP 78*]

Mission archéologique en Iran. Mémoires. Paris, 1900–. [*MMAI*]

Mitteilungen des deutschen archäologischen Instituts Athen und Kairo. [*MDAI*]

Moortgat, A., *Vorderasiatische Rollsiegel. Ein Beitrag zur Geschichte der Steinschneidekunst.* Berlin, 1940. [*Berlin*]

Museum Journal, The. University of Pennsylvania, The University Museum.

Nagel, W., *Der mesopotamische Streitwagen und seine Entwicklung im ostmediterranen Bereich* (= Berliner Beiträge zur Vor- und Frühgeschichte 10). Berlin, 1966. [*BBV 10*]

Nies, J. B., *Ur Dynasty Tablets, Texts Chiefly from Tello and Drehem Written During the Reigns of Dungi, Bur-Sin, Gimil-Sin, and Ibn-Sin.* Leipzig, 1920. [*UDT*]

Nikolski, M. V., *Dokymenti khozjaistvennoj otcetnosti Drevnejsej epokhi khaldej iz.* Petrograd, 1908. [Nikolski, *Dokymenti*]

Nougayrol, J., *Le palais royal d'Ugarit, 3, Textes accadiens et hourrites des archives est, ouest et centrales.* Paris, 1955–56. [*PRU 3*]

Özgüç, N., *Seals and Seal Impressions of Level Ib from Karum Kanish.* Ankara, 1968. [*Seals*]

————— *The Anatolian Group of Cylinder Seal Impressions from Kültepe.* Ankara, 1965. [*Anatolian*]

Özgüç, T. and N. Özgüç, *Kültepe Kazisi Raporu 1949; Ausgrabungen in Kültepe; Bericht über die im Aufträge der türkischen historischen Gesellschaft 1949 durchgeführten Ausgrabungen.* Ankara, 1953. [*Kültepe 1949*]

Opificius, R., *Das altbabylonische Terrakottarelief* (= Untersuchungen zur Assyriologie und vorderasiatischen Archäologie, 2). Berlin, 1961. [*Opificius*]

Oppenheim, A. L., *Catalogue of the cuneiform tablets of the Wilberforce Eames Babylonian Collection in the New York Public Library.* (= AOS, 32). New Haven, 1948. [*Eames*]

Oppenheim, A. L., ed., *Texts from Cuneiform Sources.* Locust Valley, N. Y., n. d. [*TCS*]

Orientalia. [*Or.*]

Orientalistische Literaturzeitung. [*OLZ*]

Osten, H. H. von der, *Altorientalische Siegelsteine der Sammlung Hans Silvius von Aulock* (= Studia Ethnographica Upsaliensia, 13). Uppsala, 1957. [*Aulock*]

————— *Ancient Oriental Seals in the Collection of Mrs. Agnes Baldwin Brett* (= OIP 37). Chicago: University of Chicago Press, 1936. [*Brett*]

————— *Ancient Oriental Seals in the Collection of Mrs. Edward T. Newell* (= OIP 22). Chicago: University of Chicago Press, 1934. [*Newell* or *OIP* 22]

————— *Researches in Anatolia, 7, The Alishar Hüyük, Seasons of 1930–32 1* (= OIP 28). Chicago: U. of Chicago P., 1937. [*OIP 28*]

————— *Researches in Anatolia, 8, The Alishar Hüyük, Seasons of 1930–32 2* (= OIP 29). Chicago: U. of Chicago P., 1937. [*OIP 29*]

Parrot, A., *Glyptique mésopotamienne fouille de Lagash (Tello) et de Larsa 1931–33.* Paris, 1954. [*Parrot*]

————— *Mari. Documentation photographique de la Mission archéologique de Mari.* Paris, 1953. [*Mari*]

————— *Mission archéologique de Mari, 1. Le temple d'Ishtar.* Paris, 1956. [*MAM 1*]

————— *Mission archéologique de Mari, 2. Le palais.* Paris, 1958–59. [*MAM 2*]

Persica.

Petrie, F., *Buttons and Design Scarabs.* London, 1925. [*Buttons*]

————— *Scarabs and Cylinders with Names.* London, 1917. [*Scarabs*]

Pier, G. C., *Egyptian Antiquities in the Pier Collection.* Chicago, 1906. [*Pier Collection*]

Pinches, T. G., ed., *The Amherst Tablets.* London, 1908. [*Amherst*]

Piotrovskii, B., *The Kingdom of Urartu.* London, 1967. [*Urartu*]

Porada, E., *The Art of Ancient Iran.* New York, 1965. [*Ancient Iran*]

————— *The Collection of the Pierpont Morgan Library* (= Corpus of the Ancient Near Eastern Seals in North American Collections, 1). New York, 1948. [*CANES*]

————— "Seal Impressions of Nuzi," *AASOR* 24, New Haven, 1947.

Ravn, O. E., *A Catalogue of Oriental Cylinder Seals and Seal Impressions in the Danish National Museum.* Copenhagen, 1960. [*Copenhagen*]

Rencontre assyriologique internationale. [*RAI*]

Revue Archéologique.

Revue d'Assyriologie et d'Archéologie Orientale. Paris. [*RA*]

Roberts, J. J. M., *The Earliest Semitic Pantheon* (= The Johns Hopkins University Near Eastern Studies 2, 1972).

Salonen, A., *Die Fussbekleidung der alten Mesopotamier* (= AASF B 157). Helsinki, 1969.

Schroeder, O., *Keilschrifttexte aus Assur verschiedener Inhalts.* Leipzig, 1920. [*KAV*]

Sollberger, E., *Corpus des inscriptions "royales" presargoniques de Lagaš.* Geneva, 1956. [*Corpus*]

Sollberger, E. and J.-R. Kupper, *Inscriptions royales sumériennes et akkadiennes.* Paris, 1971. [*IRSA*]

Speelers, L., *Catalogue des intailles et empreintes orientales des Musées Royaux du Cinquantenaire.* Brussels, 1917. [*Brussels*]

————— *Catalogue des intailles et empreintes orientales des Musées Royaux d'Art et d'Histoire. Supplément.* Brussels, 1943. [*Brussels Suppl.*]

Speiser, E. A., *Excavations at Tepe Gawra 1.* Philadelphia, 1935. [*Gawra 1*]

Stol, M., *Studies in Old Babylonian History.* Leiden, 1976.

Sumer. Journal of Archaeology and History in the Arab World.

Symbolae Biblicae et Mesopotamicae F.M.T. de Liagre Böhl Dedicatae. Leiden, 1973.

Syria, Revue d'art oriental et d'archéologie.

Textes cunéiformes du Louvre. Paris: Geuthner, 1910–.

Texts in the Iraq Museum. [*TIM*]

Thureau-Dangin, F., *Recueil de tablettes chaldéennes.* Paris, 1903. [*RTC*]

Tobler, A. J., *Excavations at Tepe Gawra 2.* Philadelphia, 1950. [*Gawra 2*]

Transactions of the American Philosophical Society. [*TAPhS*]

Troy. Princeton University.

Unger, R., *Der Beginn der altmesopotamischen Siegelbildforschung.* Vienna, 1966. [*Beginn*]

University of California Publications in Semitic Philology. [*UCP*]

Van Buren, E. D., *Clay Figurines of Babylonia and Assyria* (= YOR 16) New Haven, 1930. [*Clay Figurines*]

————— *The Fauna of Ancient Mesopotamia as Represented in Art* (= An.Or. 18). Rome, 1939. [*Fauna*]

Vorläufiger Bericht über die von dem deutschen Archäologischen Institut und der Deutschen Orientgesellschaft unternommenen Ausgrabungen in Uruk-Warka. Berlin. [*UVB*]

Ward, W. H., *The Seal Cylinders of Western Asia.* Washington, D.C., 1910. [*Ward*]

Weber, O., *Altorientalische Siegelbilder* (= Der alte Orient 17–18.) Leipzig, 1920. [*Weber*]

Wiseman, D. J., *Cylinder Seals of Western Asia.* London, n. d. [*Wiseman*]

Wissenschaftliche Veröffentlichung der deutschen Orient-Gesellschaft. [*WVDOG*]

Woolley, C. L., *Carchemish. Report on the Excavations at Jerablus on behalf of the British Museum 2.* London: British Museum, 1921. [*Carchemish*]

Woolley, C. L. and H. R. Hall, *Joint expedition of the British Museum and the Museum of the University of Pennsylvania to Mesopotamia. Ur Excavations.* London, [*UE*]

Yale Library Gazette. New Haven.

Yale Near Eastern Researches. [*YNER*]

Yale Oriental Series. Babylonian Texts. [*YOS*]

Yale Oriental Series. Researches. [*YOR*]

Zeitschrift für Assyriologie. [*ZA*]